Market Devices

A selection of previous *Sociological Review* Monographs

The Laws of the Markets*
ed. Michel Callon
Actor Network Theory and After*
eds John Law and John Hassard
Whose Europe? The Turn Towards Democracy*
eds Dennis Smith and Sue Wright
Renewing Class Analysis*
eds Rosemary Cromptom, Fiona Devine, Mike Savage and John Scott
Reading Bourdieu on Society and Culture*
eds Bridget Fowler
The Consumption of Mass*
eds Nick Lee and Rolland Munro
The Age of Anxiety: Conspiracy Theory and the Human Sciences*
eds Jane Parish and Martin Parker
Utopia and Organization*
ed. Martin Parker
Emotions and Sociology*
ed. Jack Barbalet
Masculinity and Men's Lifestyle Magazines*
ed. Bethan Benwell
Nature Performed: Environment, Culture and Performance*
eds Bronislaw Szerszynski, Wallace Heim and Claire Waterton
After Habermas: New Perspectives on the Public Sphere*
eds Nick Crossley and John Michael Roberts
Feminism After Bourdieu*
eds Lisa Adkins and Beverley Skeggs
Contemporary Organization Theory*
eds Campbell Jones and Rolland Munro
A New Sociology of Work*
eds Lynne Pettinger, Jane Parry, Rebecca Taylor and Miriam Glucksmann
Against Automobility*
eds Steffen Böhm, Campbell Jones, Cris Land and Matthew Paterson
Sports Mega-Events: Social Scientific Analyses of a Global Phenomenon*
eds John Horne and Wolfram Manzenreiter
Embodying Sociology: Retrospect, Progress and Prospects*
ed. Chris Shilling

*Available from Marston Book Services, PO Box 270, Abingdon, Oxon OX14 4YW

Most earlier monographs are still available from: Caroline Baggaley, The Sociological Review, Keele University, Keele, Staffs ST5 5BG; e-mail srb01@keele.ac.uk

The Sociological Review Monographs

Since 1958 *The Sociological Review* has established a tradition of publishing Monographs on issues of general sociological interest. The Monograph is an edited book length collection of research papers which is published and distributed in association with Blackwell Publishing. We are keen to receive innovative collections of work in sociology and related disciplines with a particular emphasis on exploring empirical materials and theoretical frameworks which are currently under-developed. If you wish to discuss ideas for a Monograph then please contact the Monographs Editor, Rolland Munro, at *The Sociological Review*, Keele University, Newcastle-under-Lyme, North Staffordshire, ST5 5BG.

Market Devices

Edited by Michel Callon, Yuval Millo and Fabian Muniesa

Blackwell Publishing/The Sociological Review

Editorial organisation © 2007 The Editorial Board of the Sociological Review
Chapters © 2007 by the chapter author

BLACKWELL PUBLISHING
350 Main Street, Malden, MA 02148–5020, USA
9600 Garsington Road, Oxford OX4 2DQ, UK
550 Swanston Street, Carlton, Victoria 3053, Australia

All rights reserved. No part of this publication may be reproduced, stored in a retrieval system, or transmitted, in any form or by any means, electronic, mechanical, photocopying, recording or otherwise, except as permitted by the UK Copyright, Designs, and Patents Act 1988, without the prior permission of the publisher.

Every effort has been made to trace copyright holders. The authors apologise for any errors or omissions and would be grateful to be notified of any corrections that should be incorporated in the next edition or reprint of this volume.

First published 2007 by Blackwell Publishing Ltd

2   2008

Library of Congress Cataloging-in-Publication Data

Market devices / edited by Michel Callon, Yuval Millo and Fabian Muniesa.
   p. cm. – (Sociological review monographs)
   Includes bibliographical references and index.
   ISBN 978-1-4051-7028-4
   1. Marketing–Sociological aspects.   2. Economics–Sociological aspects
 I. Callon, Michel   II. Millo, Yuval, 1969–   III. Muniesa, Fabian, 1972–
   HF5414.M385 2007
   306.3–dc22

2007029399

A catalogue record for this title is available from the British Library

Set by SNP Best-set Typesetter Ltd., Hong Kong

Printed and bound in Singapore by Fabulous Printers Pte Ltd

The publisher's policy is to use permanent paper from mills that operate a sustainable forestry policy, and which has been manufactured from pulp processed using acid-free and elementary chlorine-free practices. Furthermore, the publisher ensures that the text paper and cover board used have met acceptable environmental accreditation standards.

For further information on Blackwell Publishing, visit our website:
http://www.blackwellpublishing.com

Contents

An introduction to market devices 1
Fabian Muniesa, Yuval Millo and Michel Callon

Calculators, lemmings or frame-makers? The intermediary role of securities analysts 13
Daniel Beunza and Raghu Garud

Where do analysts come from? The case of financial chartism 40
Alex Preda

The death of a salesman? Reconfiguring economic exchange in Swedish post-war food distribution 65
Hans Kjellberg

Struggling to be displayed at the point of purchase: the emergence of merchandising in French supermarkets 92
Sandrine Barrey

A sociology of market-things: on tending the garden of choices in mass retailing 109
Franck Cochoy

A market of opinions: the political epistemology of focus groups 130
Javier Lezaun

Performance testing: dissection of a consumerist experiment 152
Alexandre Mallard

Framing fish, making markets: the construction of Individual Transferable Quotas (ITQs) 173
Petter Holm and Kåre Nolde Nielsen

Making things deliverable: the origins of index-based derivatives 196
Yuval Millo

The Q(u)ALYfying hand: health economics and medicine in the shaping of Swedish markets for subsidized pharmaceuticals 215
Ebba Sjögren and Claes-Fredrik Helgesson

Price as a market device: cotton trading in Izmir Mercantile Exchange   241
Koray Caliskan

Parasitic formulae: the case of capital guarantee products   261
Vincent-Antonin Lépinay

Scorecards as devices for consumer credit: the case of Fair, Isaac & Company Incorporated   284
Martha Poon

Notes on contributors   307

Index   312

An introduction to market devices

Fabian Muniesa, Yuval Millo and Michel Callon

The social sciences have been providing fertile ground for programmatic calls in recent decades, and this seems particularly true within contemporary economic sociology. Explorations moving in new directions have emerged in this field, often out of epistemic discomfort or as a result of problematic positioning vis-à-vis mainstream economics. Of particular relevance has been the development of a 'pragmatic turn' in the study of markets and economic activities in general. Some aspects of this pragmatic turn might be identified in a number of recent contributions that have considered multiple regimes of worth or multiple conventions of valuation (eg, Beunza and Stark, 2004; Boltanski and Thévenot, 2006; Favereau, Biencourt and Eymard-Duvernay, 2002; Stark, 1999; Thévenot, 2000, 2001), that have examined practical operations of testing, critique and verification (Bessy and Chateauraynaud, 1995; Chateauraynaud, 2004; Hennion, 2004; Maurer, 2005; Millo and Lezaun, 2006; Power, 1997; Teil and Muniesa, 2006), that have explored how economic things become calculable through particular metrics and languages (Desrosières, 1998; Espeland and Stevens, 1998; Hopwood and Miller, 1994; Miller and Rose, 1990; Power, 1996), that have studied the performative capacities of economic knowledge (Callon, 1998; MacKenzie, 2003, 2004, 2006; MacKenzie, Muniesa and Siu, 2007; Fourcade, 2007; Kjellberg and Helgesson, 2006), that have analysed networks of economic innovation (Callon, 1991; Garud and Karnøe, 2001, 2003), that have revealed the agency of documents and instruments in organizations (Cooren, 2000, 2004; Czarniawska and Hernes, 2005), or that have emphasized the materiality of economic settings and devices (Appadurai, 1986; Beunza, Hardie and MacKenzie, 2006; Callon and Muniesa, 2005; Cochoy, 2004; du Gay and Pryke, 2002; Keane, 2003; Miller, 2005; Muniesa, 2007).

The works offered in this volume further contribute to these types of concerns, bringing to them new analytical perspectives and empirical materials. They are pragmatic in a number of ways. They tend, for instance, to avoid ex-ante explicative principles and they adopt an anti-essentialist position that is particularly suited to the study of situations of uncertainty. They also focus on actors' capacities to operate across multiple spaces and are attentive to the empirical intricacies of agency. They pay particular attention to the trials in which actors test the resistance that defines the reality of the world surrounding them.

We believe that the notion of 'market device' – a simple way of referring to the material and discursive assemblages that intervene in the construction of markets – can be useful in addressing these concerns. After all, can a market exist without a set of market devices? From analytical techniques to pricing models, from purchase settings to merchandising tools, from trading protocols to aggregate indicators, the topic of market devices includes a wide array of objects. As crucial as market devices are in practice, they have often been overlooked by social scientists. The authors participating in this volume are working at the intersection of economic sociology and science and technology studies, an intersection that has proved particularly fruitful in considering market devices as objects of sociological inquiry.

A set of introductory precautions may be necessary in order to approach market devices from a sociological or anthropological perspective. The notion of 'device' is useful. With this notion, objects can be brought inside sociological analysis (see Beuscart and Peerbaye, 2006). Moreover, these objects can be considered as objects with agency: whether they might just help (in a minimalist, instrumental version) or force (in a maximalist, determinist version), devices do things. They articulate actions; they act or they make others act. But the notion of 'device' can also suggest a bifurcation of agency: the person on one side and the machine on the other, the trader on one side and the trading screen on the other, Bourdieu's *dispositions* on one side and Foucault's *dispositifs* on the other. In our view, this bifurcation needs to be avoided or, at least, handled with caution. Instead of considering distributed agency as the encounter of (already 'agenced') persons and devices, it is always possible to consider it as the very result of these compound *agencements* (and this applies to economic action in particular).

The notion of agencement is particularly helpful in tackling this issue (Callon, 2007; Hardie and MacKenzie, 2007). Close to notions of ordinary language that foster a similar intuition (display, assemblage, arrangement), the notion of agencement is also a philosophical concept whose proponents, Gilles Deleuze and Félix Guattari, can be considered as part of a French pragmatist tradition (Deleuze and Guattari, 1980). In his discussion of Foucault's notion of 'device' (*dispositif* in French), Deleuze (1989) develops an account that is closer to the idea of agencement. For Deleuze, the subject is not external to the device. In other words, subjectivity is enacted in a device – an aspect, we think, that is better rendered through the notion of agencement. In Deleuze's phrasing, a device 'is a tangle, a multi-linear ensemble. It is composed of different sorts of lines. And these lines do not frame systems that would be homogeneous as such (eg, the object, the subject, the language). Instead, they follow directions, they trace processes that are always at disequilibrium, sometimes coming close to each other and sometimes getting distant from each other. Each line is broken, is subjected to *variations in direction*, bifurcating and splitting, subjected to *derivations*' (Deleuze, 1989: p. 185, our translation, emphasis in original). In actor-network theory, a perspective always attentive to the distributed character of action, the notion of 'socio-technical device' (*dispositif socio-technique* in

French) is also close to this idea of agencement, an idea that emphasizes the distribution of agency and with which materiality comes to the forefront. An agencement is constituted by fixtures and furnishings, by elements that allow tracing lines and constituting a territory. It is only when devices are understood as agencements that the evolving intricacies of agency can be tackled by the sociologist or the anthropologist (otherwise she may need to conform to the great agency divides that so often characterize the sociological tradition).

What is for a device to be a 'market device' or for an agencement to be an 'economic agencement'? We can imagine that there are several kinds of agencements that do not need to be economic in nature, but they can turn economic through some aspect. A sexual relation, for instance, can be considered in certain circumstances as a biological agencement (an encounter between cells) or as an affective agencement (an encounter between affected bodies). But it can also be qualified as an economic agencement (an encounter between exchange counterparties), as in the cases analysed by Zelizer (2005). A nuclear reactor can be considered as a molecular agencement (an encounter between atomic particles), but can be also 'economized', as shown by Hecht (1998) in her analysis of French nuclear power econometrics. A shopping cart is a material device for sure. But it is also enacted, in particular, as a 'market' device because it reconfigures what shopping is (and what shoppers are and can do), as shown by Grandclément and Cochoy (2006). The same happens to the stock ticker analysed by Preda (2006): it is a telecommunication device that reconfigures what trading is (and what traders are) in financial markets. The pricing equation studied by MacKenzie (2006) can be considered, as such, as a mathematical device, but it is definitely an economic one too, because it contributes to the construction of markets widely considered as genuinely economic ones.

An economic agencement is, in a broadest sense, one that renders things, behaviours and processes economic. Emphasis is put here on the 'rendering', not on any substantive definition of what should 'economic' mean. The meaning of what it is to be 'economic' is precisely the outcome of a process of 'economization', a process that is historical, contingent and disputable. It seems undeniable that, in so-called advanced liberal societies, 'economic' often refers to the establishing of valuation networks, that is, to pricing and to the construction of circuits of commerce that render things economically commensurable and exchangeable; but 'economic' can also be said of a particular configuration that aims at 'economizing' in the sense of saving or rationing. The fact that an institution, an action, an actor or an object can be considered as being economic is precisely the result of this process of economization. And the historical contingency of this process does not call its reality into question. The reality of this process is as hard as the trials it imposes and the resistance that it triggers. Local and durable irreversibilities of economization are possible that stabilize the forms and meanings of what is to be considered as economic in a particular site and at a particular time.

The multiplicity of possible (and sometimes contradictory) definitions of what may be 'economic' about an agencement should not be regarded as a sign of arbitrariness. This ambivalence is the result of a history, a history of agencements. 'Being economic' is a path-dependent feature, which implies that the economy is always an issue whose formulation partly depends on (but is not fully determined by) previous events and trajectories. In addition, 'being economic' is not a qualification that comes from outside the agencement: this qualification is included in the agencement, for instance through the presence of instruments for the calculation of prices, of rules that organize competition, or of accounting methods that identify and allocate profit. The presence of economics (its categories and vocabulary, its tools and methods, its theories and models) inside an agencement is another prominent indicator of the fact that an economization process might be going on.

Market agencements are one kind of economic agencements. Like any other socio-technical agencements involved in a process of economization, markets contain devices that aim at rendering things more 'economic' or, more precisely, at enacting particular versions of what it is to be 'economic'. Emphasis is put on the conception, production and circulation of goods, their valuation, the construction and subsequent transfer of property rights through monetary mediation, exchange mechanisms and systems of prices. Market agencements detach things from other things and attach them to other things. The same is done to persons (physical or moral), to their reciprocal duties and to their relations to things. Although attachment and detachment – or entanglement and disentanglement (Callon, 1998) – are phenomena that can be identified in many realms, we observe that in market agencements these movements are particularly effervescent and purposeful. Markets are one form of economic agencement that is marked typically by circulation, pricing and exchange. Without devices such as the ones analysed in this book, these movements that animate markets would be virtually impossible.

Market devices can also help us with abstraction, a difficult topic for economic sociology. Abstraction has been at the centre of many analyses of monetary mediations, mercantile enterprises and capitalistic forms (Maurer, 2006). One common way of phrasing what economic agencements do is indeed to say that they 'disembed', ie, they 'abstract'. Not exactly 'from society' – because abstraction is in itself a social operation – but from other agencements which were probably less economic. But then, what does abstraction mean? From our point of view, abstraction needs to be considered an action (performed by an agencement) rather that an adjective (that qualifies an entity). Abstraction, or rather 'to abstract', is an action, an action of transformation and displacement, close to 'to extract' or 'to draw away', as suggested by its etymology: *'abs'* (away) *'trahere'* (tract).

To a large extent, 'to abstract' is to transport into a formal, calculative space (Callon and Muniesa, 2005). Market socio-technical agencements are cluttered with a variety of abstractive calculative devices: pricing techniques, accounting methods, monitoring instruments, trading protocols and benchmarking procedures are abstractors that enter into the construction of economic agencements. Economists too are abstractive agencies: they calculate aggregates; they produce formal models or metric configurations that can be, almost by definition, parts of economic agencements.

Several aspects of market devices are addressed by each contribution to this volume, based on original empirical material. Of general concern is the part played by market devices in configuring economic calculative capacities and in qualifying market objects. Calculation is neither a universally homogeneous attribute of humankind, nor an anthropological fiction. It is the concrete result of social and technical arrangements. Likewise, the qualities of goods and services are the output of complex operations of qualification, of framing and reframing, of attachment and detachment. The ways in which market devices are tinkered with, adjusted and calibrated affect the ways in which persons and things are translated into calculative and calculable beings.

Financial products and their abstractive properties provide good examples of this process; they appear in several of the chapters in this book. Other paramount illustrations of contemporary market devices that are present in these chapters show also how these devices enact economic properties, how they provoke economic behaviours, and how they render economic qualities explicit, in a variety of (frequently disputable) manners. This is true not only for openly instrumental or operational devices but also for devices that are meant to work on a more analytical or observational level (like a financial chart, a focus group or a health-economics indicator such as 'quality-adjusted life years').

The analyses of market devices provided in this book are also characterized by close attention to the different types of knowledge required to produce and stabilize these devices, which points to the issue of performativity. In markets, representation and intervention are intertwined. Markets are both the objects and the products of research. From financial engineering to marketing research, the sciences of the market are in themselves a part of markets. Experimental practices (or testing practices at large) play a crucial role in these kinds of research. It is therefore important to clarify how these forms of knowledge perform their objects, that is, how they enact or help rendering them explicit.

The book opens with a contribution by Daniel Beunza and Raghu Garud, who explore one of the many interfaces that mediates decisions in financial markets: the analyst's report. How do securities analysts value companies in contexts where information is unclear and subject to multiple interpretations? How do their analyses operate so as to provide guidance in investment assessments? Beunza and Garud study the reports written on Amazon.com by securities analyst Henry Blodget and by rival analysts during the years 1998–2000. The authors show that analysts' reports are structured by internally consistent associations. They refer to these associations as 'calculative frames', and propose that analysts function as 'frame-makers'. Their contribution helps put controversial issues such as analysts' accuracy and independence in new light. In addition, it provides important clues about how to study the cognitive prostheses that populate contemporary financial markets.

In the following chapter, Alex Preda presents a sociological inquiry into the practice of financial analysis with an exploration of its historical origins. The market device Preda focuses on is the financial chart. He studies the emergence of technical analysis (or chartism) and how it gained legitimacy in a period where the chart's explanatory frame was at odds both with academic economics and with standard notions of value. Preda shows how chartism was legitimated by a 'double loop' between groups of producers and users of technical charts, highlighting the ways in which an interest in using charts as a forecasting instrument was generated. He explains how financial chartism emerged when a group of users switched to the production of an expert knowledge, which they monopolized. Financial chartism was constituted not only as an interpretation of the market but also as a tool used in market actions. This case provides useful insights for the study of performativity: the theory of the market (here, technical analysis) describes its domain of reference but, at the same time, forms an intrinsic part of this domain.

In the third contribution, Hans Kjellberg studies the economic encounter between wholesalers and retailers in Swedish food distribution in the late 1940s. The case focuses on Hakonbolaget, the largest privately owned wholesale company in Sweden, and on its attempt to reorganize the established economic order of that time. Of particular interest is how Hakonbolaget developed the purchasing centre, a market device explicitly aimed at 'economizing' the market. Kjellberg analyses the way in which a new calculative space was carefully adjusted so as to bring buyers and sellers together through an order form, thereby rendering the human intermediary (the salesperson) disposable. Did this innovation intend to 'remove the market' or rather to 'produce more market'? The author goes beyond this question by focusing on the proliferation of devices that aim at organizing economic communications and transactions. Actors in charge of economizing the wholesale exchange needed to concentrate in the procedures and protocols that allowed transactions to be carried out between wholesaler and retailers.

The next contribution also inquires into the different techniques that aim at producing purchasing connections in a specific market setting. Sandrine Barrey analyses the birth and development of merchandising techniques in the French agro-food retail industry. Merchandising is a crucial management instrument that helps construct the encounter of supply and demand through a controlled arrangement of products at the point of purchase. The author analyses how retailers progressively gained control over merchandising techniques, and the concomitant shift in the balance of power with producers. Barrey documents the formation of these types of techniques in France using archival material and interviews with merchandising practitioners. She also presents a case study on the merchandising techniques put forward by a producer in the frozen agro-food sector. Through her emphasis on the materiality of supermarket display, Barrey provides crucial insights on how market devices contribute to product attachment and, ultimately, to purchase by consumers.

For Franck Cochoy too the analysis of material devices is crucial for a sociological understanding of how different market scenes are framed. Cochoy pursues this research goal with an ethnographic study of choice in supermarkets. Supermarket settings work as 'capturing devices' that aim at orchestrating the deployment of choice. In supermarkets, Cochoy observes, interactions with objects are more frequent than face-to-face social interactions – thus it is necessary to modify the ethnographic gaze in order to capture the richness and complexity of these 'things' as market participants. The sociologist who aims at analysing the encounter between supply and demand is forced to take a detour (in this case, equipped with a camera), passing along the shelves in search of market gestures and signs that, although completely familiar to us as supermarket users, often go unnoticed in sociological analysis.

Market devices do not only intervene at the point of purchase: market professionals make extensive use of research instruments that intervene upstream. One particularly pervasive device of market research is the focus group. Provoking a conversation among a small group of people assembled in a room has become a popular way of generating useful knowledge. Javier Lezaun analyses some features of this device, which has become a pervasive technology of social investigation, a versatile experimental setting where a multitude of ostensibly heterogeneous issues, from politics to economics, are productively addressed. It is perhaps in the marketing sciences, and through its utility in producing forecasts of economic behaviour, that the focus group has acquired its most visible and widespread form. Lezaun draws attention to some of the strategies used by focus group moderators to extract 'tradable opinions' (statements representing authentic and genuine viewpoints) out of experimentally generated conversations. His goal is to regain a sociological appreciation of the extent to which opinions about the market, or about any other issue under experimental investigation, evolve as problematic objects in focus groups, and the ways in which expert actors, the professional focus group moderators, interpret, reconfigure and represent these opinions.

Focus groups are just one example of the variety of testing devices that take part in the construction of markets. Alexandre Mallard focuses on other kinds of market experiments: consumer tests. Consumer press and consumer organizations are key player in today's markets. On the one hand, they help to shape demand through recommendations and advice given to the public on products and services. On the other hand, they tend to impact on supply, through a series of operations targeted at firms or public authorities. The visibility of these operations in the public sphere helps to generate decisions with economic consequences: denunciation of dishonest manufacturers, alerts concerning dangerous products and even court cases to trigger changes in legal decisions on consumption. Mallard investigates the performative features of consumerist tests. He studies the construction of comparative tests with a deliberate focus on the work of the professionals involved in comparative testing. This including the practical operations they bring into play and the difficulties they encounter. The author shows that this activity, apart from being relatively rich and fairly original, aims at defining a very particular position for the consumer.

Markets are sites for economic innovations that can proliferate in many directions. But one mainstream axis seems to inform a great portion of such innovations in today's economies: commoditisation, in the neo-liberal (or neo-classical) sense. Petter Holm and Kåre Nolde Nielsen focus on the emergence of a market for quotas in Norwegian fisheries. Twenty years ago, there was open access to fish. Today, fish has become private property and fishermen have become quota owners and property managers. The authors examine the trajectory that has turned fish from common to private property. What kind of framing is capable of producing fish quotas as tradable objects? What constitutes the fish quota? What ingredients – besides the fish – go into the stew that makes up property rights? More specifically, the authors analyse the historical sequence of events that has led to the particular kind of quota that emerges now. They explain the actual form of quotas in detail (reference to vessel size, group identity and county residency) and ask if a slight hitch in the historical sequence might not have turned the quota into a completely different entity. Individual Transferable Quotas (ITQs) play here the role of the market device whose meanders happen to shape the life of fish and fishermen as it is.

Increasingly sophisticated devices allow for the proliferation of increasingly complex markets. Yuval Millo's contribution draws attention to what is arguably one of the most salient market innovations in recent decades: financial derivatives. A fundamental aspect in the evolution of markets is the dynamic process through which items acquire certain qualities that make them tradable, that is to say, the qualification of products. Millo analyses the qualification process of financial derivative contracts, focusing on the historical process leading to one of today's most popular financial products: index-based derivative contracts. He focuses on the various controversies and qualification processes that the underlying product for such derivative contracts underwent. He draws attention to the fact that the birth and development of genuinely 'financial' derivatives (ie, derivative contracts not based on agricultural commodities) was controversial, demanding an intensive efforts in order to prevent these products from being regarded as gambling, and to exempt them from the obligation of delivering the underlying product. These difficulties in the qualification process were also present, in a peculiar manner, in the framing of index-based derivatives in the 1980s. The author shows the shifting nature of the qualification of financial products: the qualities that the markets assigned to index-based contracts were remarkably different from the ones that were assigned to the products initially.

In their study of Swedish markets for subsidized pharmaceuticals, Ebba Sjögren and Claes-Fredrik Helgesson also explore the economic qualification of products, with an emphasis on the crucial role played by classification schemes. Settling the qualities of an exchanged good and determining who should pay what for it are central activities in markets. It is well understood by now that not only sellers and buyers are engaged in such activities. They also involve entities such as classification tools, standardization bodies, consumer organizations, advertising agencies, etc. Sjögren and Helgesson examine a Swedish governmental agency whose task is to characterize pharmaceuticals as equivalents or non-equivalents for the purpose of deciding what pharmaceuticals are to be reimbursable. The authors focus on the agency's work to determine the qualities of pharmaceuticals and particularly on how this work draws on and mediates between several pre-existing classifications systems (ie, clinical effect, chemical groups, etc.), a process that ends up with the pre-eminence of properly economic qualification. As the authors show, establishing metrics for the description and the assessment of products is a crucial ingredient of the performative processes that shape markets.

The next chapter explores further the different processes that lead to the performance of markets. Here, attention is drawn on pricing. Koray Caliskan proposes an ethnographic account of the production of cotton's global price. Suggesting that practices of pricing are always articulated in particular geographies, the author focus on one local instance of the pricing chains of cotton markets: the Izmir Mercantile Exchange, in Turkey. Caliskan studies the exchange relationships and the market technologies deployed by regional and local traders in Izmir. He analyses several kinds of prices that play important roles in the composition of global pricing chains: not only actual prices that engage traders in economic exchange but also 'prosthetic' prices that are used in order to explore or anticipate pricing possibilities, and 'rehearsal' prices that help framing trading activity as a performance, in an almost theatrical sense.

Vincent-Antonin Lépinay's contribution turns attention back to derivative contracts: not to the standardized products, such as options and futures, that are traded in exchanges but to rather more complex, 'over the counter' financial products. Lépinay analyses the characteristics and behaviours of a 'parasitic' derivative contract: a capital guarantee product. The author explores the work of the financial engineers in charge of designing, pricing, and selling this complex, sometimes cumbersome product. How do they manage to 'derive' value? In what sort of drift do they embark? The product is a parasite, in Michel Serres' sense, as it is based on the manipulation of already available underlying goods, subverting their initial project. The author observes how this particular kind of product challenges the calculative practices of the financial engineering team, but also the overall 'industrial' routines of the investment bank. His account allows for an understanding of the materiality of these 'abstractive' derivative devices.

In the last chapter of this book, Martha Poon focuses on consumer credit scoring as a market device. Consumer credit is an interesting product because its production poses particular risks to its 'maker'. Of specific concern is the possibility that the credit that has been extended may not be repaid. In a consumer credit market, then, the point of account origination involves important managerial decision making to control which people should be included as consumers in the market. Since the end of the 1950s, these decisions have increasingly been delegated to statistical tools designed by engineers, statisticians and operations researchers. This chapter traces the innovation of one of these tools, known as a 'scorecard' from its humble roots as a table of points on a printed sheet of cardboard, to its gradual dissolution, in the USA, into a distributed calculative apparatus that produces a system of commercially circulating, brand-name, individual consumer credit scores (FICO® credit bureau scores).

Examining the scorecard at three moments in its development (custom application scorecards, application pre-screening, credit bureau scores), the chapter demonstrates how the same calculative apparatus, from the point of view of math and statistics, has had diverse ways of constituting risk. The technology, Poon argues, has therefore had different effects on extending consumer credit markets, depending on the conditions under which it has been implemented.

We believe that all these chapters contribute to a 'pragmatic turn' in economic sociology that is deeply inspired by science and technology studies. The notion of device, re-adjusted through the concept of agencement, serves this approach or set of approaches well. It is of great help in tackling materiality and in pointing to the distributed nature of economic actions and skills. It helps also to overcome a major danger: that of reverting to an idea of pure instrument. Pure instruments in the hand of pure agents reproduce the idea of pure objects in the hands of pure subjects. With such a divide, the analysis of economizing processes is in trouble. The idea of agencements, on the contrary, allows overcoming it without falling either into essentialism (considering that some behaviours or institutions are intrinsically economic) or into relativism (considering economic qualification as a mere convention).

Finally, market devices – thus characterized as economic agencements – do allow for a reformulation of the problem of economic agency and to the opening of newer paths for sociological research. We think that all the contributions to this book, although stemming from a variety of research concerns, present analytical innovations that permit progressing in such direction. They highlight several features of what we have called here 'market devices': the importance of display and material composition in the achievement of purchase or transactions, the highly consequential investments in economic knowledge and analytical techniques, the emphasis on experimental methods for the elicitation of economic properties, and the establishment of pricing or valuation networks.

Acknowledgements

Earlier versions of the works presented in this edited volume were discussed at the 4S & EASST Conference (joint meeting of the Society for Social Studies of Science and the European Association for the Study of Science and Technology) held at the Ecole des Mines de Paris (France), 25–28 August, 2004. Three interrelated panels on 'the performativities of economics' (organized by Donald MacKenzie, Fabian Muniesa and Lucia Siu, also as a separate workshop), on 'social and consumer sciences shaping market(-ing) practices' (organized by Catherine Grandclément, Claes-Fredrik Helgesson and Hans Kjellberg) and on 'economic experiments' (organized by Fabian Muniesa, Yuval Millo and Javier Lezaun) hosted the discussions. We would like to thank all participants for their contributions to the debate. We thank in particular Donald MacKenzie, whose initiative was crucial in motivating this book project, along with its 'companion' project *Do Economists Make Markets?* (Princeton University Press, 2007).

We also thank Martha Poon, whose collaboration with the editorial tasks proved invaluable, and Onuralp Topal, who kindly provided the picture (taken at the Istambul Stock Exchange) that illustrates the front cover of this book.

References

Appadurai, A. (ed.) (1986) *The social life of things: commodities in cultural perspective*, Cambridge: Cambridge University Press.
Bessy, C. and Chateauraynaud, F. (1995) *Experts et faussaires: pour une sociologie de la perception*, Paris: Métailié.
Beunza, D., Hardie, I. and MacKenzie, D. (2006) 'A price is a social thing: towards a material sociology of arbitrage', *Organization Studies* 27(5): 721–745.
Beunza, D. and Stark, D. (2004) 'Tools of the trade: the socio-technology of arbitrage in a Wall Street trading room', *Industrial and Corporate Change* 13(2): 369–400.
Beuscart, J.-S. and Peerbaye, A. (2006) 'Histoires de dispositifs', *Terrains & Travaux* (11): 3–15.
Boltanski, L. and Thévenot, L. (2006) *On justification: economies of worth*, Princeton: Princeton University Press.
Callon, M. (1991) 'Techno-economic networks and irreversibility', in J. Law (ed.) *A sociology of monsters: essays on power, technology and domination*. London: Routledge.
Callon, M. (1998) 'Introduction: the embeddedness of economic markets in economics', in M. Callon (ed.) *The laws of the markets*, Oxford: Blackwell.
Callon, M. (2007) 'What does it mean to say that economics is performative?' in D. MacKenzie, F. Muniesa and L. Siu (eds) *Do economists make markets? On the performativity of economics*, Princeton: Princeton University Press.
Callon, M. and Muniesa, F. (2005) 'Economic markets as calculative collective devices', *Organization Studies* 26(8): 1229–1250.
Chateauraynaud, F. (2004) 'L'épreuve du tangible: expériences de l'enquête et surgissement de la preuve', in B. Karsenti and L. Quéré (eds) *La croyance et l'enquête: aux sources du pragmatisme*, Paris: Editions de l'EHESS.
Cochoy, F. (ed.) (2004) *La captation des publics: c'est pour mieux te séduire, mon client...* Toulouse: Presses Universitaires du Mirail.
Cooren, F. (2000) *The organizing property of communication*, Amsterdam: John Benjamins.
Cooren, F. (2004) 'Textual agency: how texts do things in organizational settings', *Organization* 11(3): 373–393.
Czarniawska, B. and Hernes, T. (eds) (2005) *Actor-network theory and organizing*, Malmö: Liber & Copenhagen Business School Press.
Deleuze, G. (1989) 'Qu'est-ce qu'un dispositif?' in *Michel Foucault philosophe: rencontre internationale Paris 9, 10, 11, janvier 1988*, Paris: Seuil.
Deleuze, G. and Guattari, F. (1980) *Mille plateaux (capitalisme et schizophrénie 2)*, Paris: Editions de Minuit.
Desrosières, A. (1998) *The politics of large numbers: a history of statistical reasoning*, Cambridge (Massachusetts): Harvard University Press.
du Gay, P. and Pryke, M. (eds) (2002) *Cultural economy: cultural analysis and commercial life*, London: Sage.
Espeland, W. N. and Stevens, M. L. (1998) 'Commensuration as a social process', *Annual Review of Sociology* 24: 313–343.
Favereau, O., Biencourt, O. and Eymard-Duvernay, F. (2002) 'Where do markets come from? From (quality) conventions!' in O. Favereau and E. Lazega (eds) *Conventions and structures in economic organization: markets, hierarchies and networks*, Cheltenham: Edward Elgar.
Fourcade, M. (2007) 'Theories of markets and theories of society', *American Behavioral Scientist* 50(8): 1015–1034.

Garud, R. and Karnøe, P. (eds) (2001) *Path dependence and creation*, Mahwah (New Jersey): Lawrence Erlbaum Associates.
Garud, R. and Karnøe, P. (2003) 'Bricolage versus breakthrough: distributed and embedded agency in technology entrepreneurship', *Research Policy* 32(2): 277–300.
Grandclément, C. and Cochoy, F. (2006) 'Histoires du chariot de supermarché: ou comment emboîter le pas de la consommation de masse', *Vingtième Siècle* (91): 77–93.
Hardie, I. and MacKenzie, D. (2007) 'Assembling and economic actor: the *agencement* of a hedge fund', *Sociological Review*, 55(1): 57–80.
Hecht, G. (1998) *The radiance of France: nuclear power and national identity after World War II*, Cambridge (Massachusetts): MIT Press.
Hennion, A. (2004) 'Pragmatics of taste', in M. Jacobs and N. Hanrahan (eds) *The Blackwell companion to the sociology of culture*, Oxford: Blackwell.
Hopwood, A. G. and Miller, P. (eds) (1994) *Accounting as social and institutional practice*, Cambridge: Cambridge University Press.
Keane, W. (2003) 'Semiotics and the social analysis of material things', *Language and Communication* 23(3–4): 409–425.
Kjellberg, H. and Helgesson, C.-F. (2006) 'Multiple versions of markets: multiplicity and performativity in market practice', *Industrial Marketing Management* 35(7): 839–855.
MacKenzie, D. (2003) 'An equation and its worlds: bricolage, exemplars, disunity and performativity in financial economics', *Social Studies of Science* 33(6): 831–868.
MacKenzie, D. (2004) 'The big, bad wolf and the rational market: portfolio insurance, the 1987 crash and the performativity of economics', *Economy and Society* 33(3): 303–334.
MacKenzie, D. (2006) *An engine, not a camera: how financial models shape markets*, Cambridge (Massachusetts): MIT Press.
MacKenzie, D., Muniesa, F. and Siu, L. (eds) (2007) *Do economists make markets? On the performativity of economics*, Princeton: Princeton University Press.
Maurer, B. (2005) *Mutual Life, Limited: Islamic banking, alternative currencies, lateral reason*, Princeton: Princeton University Press.
Maurer, B. (2006) 'The anthropology of money', *Annual Review of Anthropology* 35: 15–36.
Miller, D. (ed) (2005) *Materiality*, Durham (North Carolina): Duke University Press.
Miller, P. and Rose, N. (1990) 'Governing economic life', *Economy and Society* 19(1): 2–31.
Millo, Y. and Lezaun, J. (2006) 'Regulatory experiments: genetically modified crops and financial derivatives on trial', *Science and Public Policy* 33(3): 179–190.
Muniesa, F. (2007) 'Market technologies and the pragmatics of prices', *Economy and Society* 36(3): 377–395.
Power, M. (ed) (1996) *Accounting and science: natural inquiry and commercial reason*, Cambridge: Cambridge University Press.
Power, M. (1997) *The audit society: rituals of verification*, Oxford: Oxford University Press.
Preda, A. (2006) 'Socio-technical agency in financial markets: the case of the stock ticker', *Social Studies of Science* 36(5): 753–782.
Stark, D. (1999) 'Heterarchy: distributing authority and organizing diversity', in J. H. Clippinger (ed.) *The biology of business: decoding the natural laws of enterprise*, San Francisco: Jossey-Bass.
Teil, G. and Muniesa, F. (2006) 'Donner un prix: observations à partir d'un dispositif d'économie expérimentale', *Terrains & Travaux* (11): 222–244.
Thévenot, L. (2000) 'Pragmatic regimes governing the engagement with the world', in T. R. Schatzki, K. Knorr Cetina and E. Von Savigny (eds) *The practice turn in contemporary theory*, London: Routledge.
Thévenot, L. (2001) 'Organized complexity: conventions of coordination and the composition of economic arrangements', *European Journal of Social Theory* 4(4): 405–425.
Zelizer, V. A. (2005) *The purchase of intimacy*, Princeton: Princeton University Press.

Calculators, lemmings or frame-makers? The intermediary role of securities analysts

Daniel Beunza and Raghu Garud

Introduction

As Wall Street specialists in valuation, sell-side securities analysts constitute a particularly important class of market actor.[1] Analysts produce the reports, recommendations and price targets that professional investors utilize to inform their buy and sell decisions, which means that understanding analysts' work can provide crucial insights on the determinants of value in the capital markets.

Yet our knowledge of analysts is limited by insufficient attention to Knightian uncertainty. Analysts estimate the value of stocks by calculating their net present value or by folding the future back into the present. In so doing, they are faced with the fundamental challenge identified by Frank Knight, that is, with the difficulty of making decisions that entail a future that is unknown. These decisions, as Knight wrote, are characterized by 'neither entire ignorance nor complete . . . information, but partial knowledge' of the world (Knight, [1921] 1971: 199).

The finance literature has not examined the Knightian challenge faced by analysts. Indeed, existing treatments circumvent the problem by adopting one of two extreme positions. In the first, put forward by orthodox economists, it is assumed that Knightian uncertainty is non-existent and that calculative decision-making is straightforward. Analysts are presented as mere calculators in a probabilistic world of risk (Cowles, 1933; Lin and McNichols, 1998; Lim, 2001). In the second, put forward by neo-institutional sociologists and behavioural finance scholars, analysts face too much uncertainty to engage in individual calculation. Analysts confront this uncertainty by resorting to a lemming-like imitation of their colleagues' opinions (see respectively Rao, Greve and Davis, 2001; Scharfstein and Stein, 1990; Hong, Kubik and Solomon, 2000). None of these views, however, examines the Knightian challenge that analysts confront, namely, the imperative to decide with a significant but limited knowledge of the world.

In recent years, an emerging sociological literature has begun to redress this neglect of Knightian uncertainty by viewing analysts as critics. According to the analysts-as-critics approach, the function performed by these professionals is to assess the value of securities whose value is uncertain (cf. Zuckerman, 1999, 2004; Zuckerman and Rao, 2004). Like film reviewers, food experts or wine connoisseurs, analysts bring a social dimension back into decision-making. They do so, even if buyer and seller do not have an ongoing social relation, because they tend to reproduce the prevailing social order in their critiques (Hirsh, 1972, 1975; Rao, 1998; Benjamin and Podolny, 1999). For instance, Zuckerman (1999) argues that analysts reinforce existing industry categories by engaging in selective company coverage. Analysts exclude companies that lie outside established industry categories, depressing their value and creating a 'categorical discount.' In this manner, the analysts-as-critics approach restores Knightian uncertainty to the centre of our understanding of securities analysts.

While notably advancing our knowledge of analysts, the critics approach leaves several questions unanswered. First, if security analysts do little more than classify stocks into categories, it is unclear how their work could offer added value to the users of the reports, the portfolio managers. Portfolio managers, as any other participant in a speculative market, are less interested in accurate valuations than in finding profit opportunities. Second, passive classification cannot explain the rise of new categories, yet new categories have presided over almost all major valuation episodes within the post-war decades: to name a few, the 'tronics bubble, the emergent markets bubble, the biotech bubble or the Internet bubble (Malkiel, 1973). Finally, the critics approach does not explain how unknown analysts can rise to star positions. In short, the view of analysts as critics does not fully explain how these professionals add value, innovate, rise to fame, or fall into oblivion.

Seeking a detailed understanding of the activity performed by analysts, we ask: What is the meaning of analysis under Knightian uncertainty? We address this question with a grounded-theory, qualitative content analysis of selected analyst reports. These documents have the unique advantage of providing a window into the cognitive processes followed by analysts in real time, a window not obscured by retrospective reconstruction. In developing our grounded theory methodology, we rely on the constant comparative method advocated by Glaser and Strauss (1967). We centre on the financially volatile period of the Internet 'bubble' of 1998–2000 because it best captures the problem of analysis under extreme uncertainty. We further focus on a single well-known company, Amazon.com, and compare the reports written about it by the top Amazon analyst at the time, Henry Blodget, against those of maximally different rival analysts.

Our findings point to an insight that has been underdeveloped in economic sociology. Underlying the assessments made by securities analysts, we find internally consistent associations between categorizations, analogies and key metrics. We label these 'calculative frames'. For example, one particular calculative frame for Amazon categorized the company as an Internet company, presented it as analogous to Dell Computers, and appraised its prospects in terms of revenue growth. Analysts who used this frame typically had a buy recommendation for the firm. A contrasting frame viewed Amazon as a book retailer, analogous to Barnes & Noble, and valued it on the basis of its profits at the time. Analysts who espoused this alternative frame tended to have a more pessimistic 'sell' or 'hold' recommendation for Amazon. We find, moreover, that these frames were robust over time, leading to sustained controversies among analysts over the value of Amazon. We suggest that there is utility in viewing analysts as frame-makers, that is, as specialized intermediaries that help investors value stocks in contexts of extreme uncertainty.

The chapter is structured as follows. After reviewing the academic literature on analysts, we outline the guiding principles of our grounded theory research design. Next, we examine three episodes in the financial controversy over Amazon, located in December 1998, May 1999 and June 2000. Each of these moments yields rich theoretical insights that build up to a rounded perspective on analysts as frame-makers. We conclude by examining the implications of this perspective for an understanding of analysts as market intermediaries and of the social determinants of value in the capital markets.

Perspectives on analysts

Despite the extensive academic attention bestowed upon analysts, existing treatments provide a limited account of their intermediary role. Extant work is best understood as three broad streams. One approach, rooted in the finance and accounting literatures, views analysts as information processors and stresses their activeness in searching, assembling and communicating information. Another approach, based on neo-institutional sociology and behavioural finance, documents the tendency of analysts to mimic each other. We refer to this as the imitation perspective. Finally, a more recent sociological approach has started to outline the role of analysts as critics.

Analysts as information processors

The information-processing literature on analysts rests on a remarkable finding: securities analysts, long regarded as valuation experts, are unable to provide accurate forecasts of stock prices. Beginning with Cowles' (1933) seminal piece, titled 'Can Stock Market Forecasters Forecast?' numerous finance and accounting theorists have documented the failure of analysts' recommendations to produce abnormal returns and accurate forecasts of earnings and price targets (Lin and McNichols, 1998; Hong and Kubick, 2002; Michaely and Womack, 1999; Lim, 2001; Boni and Womack, 2002; Schack, 2001).

Two complementary explanations have been put forward to account for this failure. One view, based on the efficient market hypothesis (EMH), argues that accurate financial forecasting is simply impossible in an efficient capital market (Samuelson, 1965; Malkiel, 1973). According to the EMH, stock prices in a competitive capital market capture all of the relevant information about the value of a security, following a random walk. There are no mispricings, no possibilities for any actor to find extraordinary profit opportunities, and indeed, no scope for financial intermediaries to help their clients to do so (Fama, 1965, 1991; Samuelson, 1965; Malkiel, 1973). The bleak implication for analysts is that accurate forecasting and lucrative advice giving are impossible.

An additional explanation for analysts' inaccuracies, based on agency theory, is that the fiduciary relationship between analyst and investor is distorted by a variety of conflicts of interest, producing dysfunctional biases in their forecasts and recommendations. These distortions include investment banking ties (Lin and McNichols, 1998; Hong and Kubick, 2002; Michaely and Womack, 1999), access to company information (Lim, 2001), brokerage interests of the bank employing the analyst (Boni and Womack, 2002), investment interests of the clients of the bank (Sargent, 2000), or the investment interests of the analysts themselves (Schack, 2001). In short, in this literature analysts come across as conflict-ridden intermediaries.

The aforementioned conflicts have become particularly prominent following the Wall Street scandals of 2000–2001. During these years, top-ranked Internet analysts (including Henry Blodget) resisted downgrading their recommendations even as prices fell from record highs to zero (Boni and Womack, 2002). Other analysts were recorded privately criticizing companies that they publicly recommended (Gasparino, 2005). Such was the public uproar against analysts, that the Securities and Exchange Commission issued explicit guidelines that advised investors to use analyst reports with caution (Securities and Exchange Commission, 2002).

Whether in the form of market efficiency or conflicts of interest, the two approaches to analysts presented so far share a common premise: both assume that the core intermediary function performed by security analysts is to forecast the future and to provide recommendations. Analysts are accordingly presented as engaged in the search, assembly and diffusion of information. To highlight this common focus on information, we refer to this literature as the 'information processing approach'.

Analysts as imitators

The information processing literature outlined above has been challenged by work in behavioural finance. In an important attack on the neoclassic emphasis on processing, assembling and calculating data, behavioural theorists have documented the tendency of analysts to imitate each other or to herd (Scharfstein and Stein, 1990; Banerjee, 1992; Trueman, 1994; Prendergast and Stole, 1996; Hong, Kubick and Solomon, 2000). According to the seminal work of Scharfstein and Stein (1990), overly comparative compensation schemes such as firing and promoting analysts based on their performance relative to one another; pressure them to herd, that is, to copy each other to the extreme of ignoring their own private information when the latter is inconsistent with the view of the majority. The concept has received important empirical support. For instance, Hong, Kubick and Solomon (2000) found that the career paths of securities analysts make imitation a worthwhile strategy. 'Analysts,' the authors conclude, 'are more likely to be terminated and less likely to be promoted when they make relatively bold forecasts,' which suggests that the pressures for herding are indeed present (Hong, Kubick and Solomon, 2000: 123).

In a related challenge to information processing, the literature in neo-institutional sociology argues that the search for legitimacy among analysts promotes imitation and conformity (Phillips and Zuckerman, 2001; Rao, Greve and David, 2001). For instance, Rao, Greve and Davis (2001) argue that the work of analysts is characterized by imitation, and that one reason they do so is that their work conforms to a well-studied decision-making pattern known as 'informational cascades.' An informational cascade arises when economic actors face a decision in a context of risk. Decisions are made in a sequential pattern, and the last actors to decide see the decisions that were made by the first. In these circumstances, the emerging consensus among the first decision-makers creates pressure for subsequent actors to swing in their favour, thereby adding to the consensus and reinforcing this pressure for the following ones. As a result, the last actors to decide invariably end up agreeing with the consensus, even if their private information should make them disagree (Bikchandani, Hirshleifer and Welch, 1992). Rao, Greve and Davis argue that this cascading dynamic characterizes the coverage decisions made by analysts.

Where is the analysis?

The information processing and imitation perspectives provide complementary perspectives on the shortcomings of the analyst profession. Our overall assessment of this literature, however, remains mixed: while purporting to examine the intermediary role played by analysts, existing treatments have glossed over the content of the analytic work itself, that is, over the arguments, tables, charts and figures that make up analysts' reports. As a result, these treatments overlook the social, cognitive and material processes that make forecasting possible. In this section we present empirical and theoretical arguments suggesting that a proper understanding of analysis needs to address the content of the reports.

Analysis is more than forecasting

One important reason why we reject equating analysis with forecasting is that the latter is not critically important for institutional investors, the actual users of analysts' reports. This surfaces clearly from the 'All-American' rankings complied by *Institutional Investor* magazine, the most widely-used source of data about the impact of analysts' work. For instance, in the 2003 *Institutional Investor* rankings, the magazine asked its readers to rank in importance eight different dimensions of analyst merit: industry knowledge, written reports, special services, servicing, stock selection, earnings estimates, market making and quality of sales force. Among these, investment recommendations and earnings estimates were ranked sixth and seventh out of a total of eight criteria. The top two criteria, in contrast, were 'written reports' and 'industry knowledge.' This suggests that analysts' arguments and ideas are far more helpful to investors than the brief numbers that the analysts attach to the reports in the form of recommendations and price targets.

Our reading of investors' responses is supported by anecdotal evidence from analysts. For instance, the analyst profession has never accepted the idea that their core intermediary function is forecasting prices or recommending stocks: as far back as 1933, analyst Robert Rhea replied to the charge that analysts provided unprofitable recommendations (first formulated by Cowles, 1933) by countering that research reports were intended 'as educational pieces, not as investment advice' (Bernstein, 1992: 35). More recently, a top-ranked securities analyst argued in the *Wall Street Journal* that 'the analysts' clients (. . .) could not care less if you say "buy, hold or sell." They just want to know why' (Kessler, 2001: A18). In a similar vein, a prominent analyst at investment bank Brown Brothers Harriman stated that,

> One reason institutional investors continue to value the work of an analyst whose recommendations have been off-base is that they pay less attention to analysts' recommendations than you might think (. . .) the institutional clients make their own buy or sell decisions. They want the analyst to add value to their decision-making (Brenner, 1991: 24)

Forecasts and recommendations, then, do not seem to be the key to analysts' work. According to this analyst, investors want diversity in opinions: 'an articulate case from both the bull and the bear' (Brenner, 1991: 25, cited in Nanda and Groysberg, 2004).

We conclude from this review of investor data that forecasting and investment advice are probably not the most important functions that analysts perform. We are led to inquire about the analyst functions that investors do value. Turning again to the survey results of *Institutional Investor*, we ask, what do the top-ranked survey responses, 'written reports' and 'industry knowledge,' actually mean? In particular, how do the 'written reports' produced by analysts help investors? What is the nature of the 'industry knowledge' that analysts convey?

Limited treatment of uncertainty

While the information processing literature assumes that the future is readily calculable, the imitation approach assumes that imitation replaces calculation. In both cases, the difficulties associated with calculating when the future is unknown are overlooked. Similarly, the final numbers provided by analysts are the only output that appears to matter in both approaches: both overlook the question of how those price targets were developed in the first place, how analysts decided between opposing scenarios, and where those scenarios came from. In the paragraphs below, we argue that this inattention to Knightian uncertainty leads to an unrealistic and unbalanced view of analysts.

An under-calculative view of analysts

As mentioned above, the imitation literature on analysts is characterized by a lack of interest in the ways in which analysts calculate value. Rao, Greve and Davis (2001), for example, view imitation as an economical alternative to calculation. According to the authors, analysts imitate their peers in contexts of uncertainty, just as a driver might imitate other drivers in deciding 'how fast to drive on a certain stretch of highway' (Rao, Greve and Davis, 2001: 504).

Our position, by contrast, is that imitation does not fully account for the intermediary activity performed by analysts. Whereas imitation emphasizes similarity, we observe a great deal of heterogeneity among them: for instance, none of the Internet analysts ranking within the top five in 1998 retained their status by 2001 (*Institutional Investor*, 1998, 1999; Sargent and Kenney 2000a, 2000b, 2000c; Justin 2001; Abramowitz, Bloomenthal, Burke and D'Ambrosio, 2000). Another way in which analysts depart from Rao *et al.*'s imitators is that these professionals are Wall Street's valuation specialists: unlike the occasional driver venturing in an unfamiliar highway, assessing companies is the core job of an analyst. Analysts are generously paid to do this and the positions they adopt can have career-altering consequences for them. Instead of taking shortcuts to avoid the costly work of calculating value, it seems more plausible to expect that they would devote most of their time and energy to valuation.

Indeed, several prominent economic sociologists have recently emphasized the importance of understanding calculation rather than simply denying it exists (Callon, 1998; Stark, 2000; MacKenzie and Millo, 2003; Granovetter, 2004). As noted by Callon (1998), the assumption that actors never calculate (as some sociological treatments make) is as unrealistic as the contrasting neoclassic position that market actors always do so. Instead, Callon argues for granting the possibility that actors might calculate, and asks how this might be accomplished. In response he offers an 'anthropology of calculation' – that is, a detailed attention to 'the material reality of calculation, involving figures, writing mediums and inscriptions' (Callon, 1998: 5). In other words, far from overlooking the social determinants of value, a proper sociological understanding of markets should expand the theoretical scope of 'the social' to encompass how collectively constructed calculative technology shapes the encounter between information and prices (Stark, 2000; Granovetter, 2004). From this vantage point, the neo-institutional work on analysts comes across as an under-calculative rendering of their activity.

An over-calculative view of analysts

While the imitation literature assumes that calculation is rarely feasible, the information processing perspective is hampered by the contrasting assumption that calculation is straightforward and unproblematic. As customary in the rational choice paradigm, Knightian uncertainty is assumed away with recourse to Savage's (1954) theory of Bayesian decision-making. According to Savage's model, rational decision-makers develop probability estimates by updating their subjective prior beliefs as incoming news arrive. Rational updating entails following the rules of Bayesian inference. Accordingly, two Bayesian decision-makers facing the same news with different priors will update their estimates in the same direction, even if not necessarily by the same magnitude. Thus, for example, the arrival of good news about a company should make *all* rational decision-makers value the company more, not less, although by different degrees. As additional information arrives and updating continues, actors will converge in their estimates and their final position will be solely shaped by incoming information.

While Bayesian convergence is a useful stylized portrayal of decision-making in numerous contexts, a detailed analysis of the cognitive mechanism it involves suggests that it can easily break down under Knightian uncertainty. If the range of future possible outcomes and probabilities is unknown (Knight, [1921] 1971), unforeseen contingencies prevent Bayesian updating. This blind spot of Bayesian models has been recognized even in contemporary economic literature, and is referred to as a 'zero-probability event' (Barberis, Shleifer and Vishny, 1998; Brandenburger, 2002). The related concept of ambiguity offers an additional reason. Savage's model assumes that all rational decision-makers classify news in the same manner, whether as positive or negative. But in contexts of ambiguity, that is, of confusion over how a piece of news should be classified (March, 1987), different actors may update in different directions, barring convergence from taking place.

In sum, in a world of Knightian uncertainty, economic calculation requires far more conditions than those considered in Bayesian models. Information-processing theories that build on Bayesian treatments do not address how market actors incorporate information into their estimates when this information is incomplete, ambiguous, divergent or contradictory. In particular, they do not attend to the social and cognitive mechanisms employed in representing, manifesting, and settling differences. For this reason, we refer to the processing approach as over-calculative.

Bringing uncertainty back into analysis

A more realistic theory of analysts would address how analysts combine mental models and social cues in their calculations to overcome the challenge of Knightian uncertainty. Empirically, this treatment would explain how the different estimates made by analysts arise, diffuse and evolve among them. Indeed, an emerging stream of literature, centred on the analysts-as-critics' literature, has begun to address the significance of Knightian uncertainty for analysts.

Analysts as critics

A recent stream literature led by Ezra Zuckerman argues that analysts should be understood as critics (Zuckerman, 1999, 2004; Zuckerman and Rao, 2004). Building on the sociological work on critics developed by Hirsh and Podolny

(Hirsh, 1972, 1975; Podolny, 1993, 1994; Benjamin and Podolny, 1999; Hsu and Podolny, 2005), Zuckerman argues that analysts function as specialists in conveying the worth of a stock when its value is uncertain. As critics, the activity that analysts perform is fundamentally based on classification: given the difficulty of simply plugging disputed or incomplete information into a valuation formula, analysts assess the value of a company by comparison with other companies in the same category.

According to Zuckerman (1999), however, the comparative valuation undertaken by analysts takes place in a passive manner, leading to dysfunctional consequences for the companies being valued. Analysts strive to maintain legitimacy in the face of investors. This leads to a rigid insistence on fitting companies into existing slots (as opposed to creating new ones when required), which in turn makes investors screen out of their coverage those companies that do not belong to any pre-existing category, depressing their market value as a result. Consequently, analysts are said to create an 'illegitimacy discount' for hybrid organizations that perpetuates existing industry structure and stifles innovation.

The critics approach to analysts sets the stage for several interesting and unanswered questions. For instance, how can the notion of categorical discount be reconciled with the observation that new analytical categories do emerge? Turning again to the years 1998–2000, we find a new industry category, 'Internet and New Media' (*Institutional Investor*, 1999: 107; Justin 2001: 179; Abramowitz *et al.*, 2000: 136). Instead of being penalized with a discount, companies in this category – the so-called 'dot-coms' – actually traded at a rather generous valuation premium. One implication is that analysts may be drawing on a richer calculative tool-kit than calculation-by-category, giving them the possibility of valuing a company while arguing that it belongs to a new category.

In addition, we observe that those Internet analysts who first granted higher valuations to Internet firms (as Blodget did), went on to enjoy very high rankings in *Institutional Investor*, suggesting that the creation of new categories plays an significant role in the value that investors accord to a security analyst. This suggests that legitimacy may not be the only pressure that analysts face, an assumption which begs the question of what parallel forces might also be in play.

Pending questions

To sum up, the literature on analysts is best seen in terms of three overriding streams: analysts as information processors, as imitators and as critics. Each perspective offers some insight into the roles played by analysts. At the same time, each raises further questions: How do analysts' reports and industry knowledge help investors? How do new industry categories emerge? Why do some analysts become stars, while others remain unknown? These add up to a single central question: In real time, how do analysts value securities under conditions of extreme uncertainty? It is to this question that we turn our attention in the rest of this chapter.

Methods

Our study examines the work of securities analysts with a grounded-theory, qualitative content analysis of selected analyst reports on Amazon.com during 1998 to 2000. We favour grounded theory for its potential to break out of the existing theoretical paradigm (Glaser and Strauss, 1967). Our aim, in other words, is not to verify hypotheses from the literature but is to develop new ones. In the following paragraphs we describe the different steps that we undertook to build theory, including our choice of theoretical sampling, constant comparison, theoretical saturation and the use of data slices.

Research design and sample selection

In operationalizing grounded theory, we chose a qualitative content analysis design. Qualitative content analysis is of particular value because virtually all previous treatments of analysts have focused on quantitative indicators such as price target accuracy or recommendation profitability, ignoring the actual text of the reports. To select our reports, we undertook a theoretical sampling procedure, choosing our reports on the basis of theoretical purpose rather than representativeness. Thus, for instance, to address the theoretical issue of how analysts confront Knightian uncertainty, we looked for a company whose future could not be easily extrapolated from the past. We centred on the emergence of the Internet during the so-called technological 'bubble' of 1998–2000, a technological discontinuity that induced Knightian uncertainty to the actors involved (Tushman and Anderson, 1986; Garud and Rappa, 1994; Christensen, 1997). Of the several candidate Internet companies to be analysed, the size and visibility of Amazon.com made it particularly appropriate. Our choice of focal analyst was equally guided by the principle of theoretical relevance. We focused on Henry Blodget, the analyst whose work was, according to *Institutional Investor*, most valuable to investors.

Inference of hypotheses

To develop our theoretical categories we followed the constant comparative method advocated by Glaser and Strauss (1967). We contrasted Blodget's reports with those of rival analysts with maximally different messages along three different points in time. Our first comparison sought to understand the mechanisms of valuation used by analysts; for that purpose, we selected two analysts that valued Amazon very differently. On December 1998, securities analyst Henry Blodget famously valued Amazon at $400, while Jonathan Cohen valued it at $50. A comparison of the two reports suggested a new theoretical category, which we denote 'calculative frame.'

Our second sampling decision sought to understand how frames mediated value. For that purpose, we chose the reports by Blodget and *Barron's* journalist Abel Abelson. Both actors espoused drastically different frames, and responded very differently to news of losses in May 1999. This disparity gave us the opportunity to see how analysts used their frames and led to a new construct, 'framing controversies.'

Having established how analysts value companies and how their methods matter, we turned to the limits of calculative frames. The third episode in our comparison centers on a debate between Blodget and analyst Ravi Suria that took place in June 2000. Suria challenged Blodget's perspective with a pessimistic report on Amazon. Blodget countered Suria's attack with another report, but fellow analysts and investors abandoned Blodget's frame. The episode gave us the opportunity to develop a new theoretical category that seeks to explain how calculative frames are abandoned. We refer to this category as 'asynchronous confrontation.'

Data and sources

Our primary sources of data were the analyst reports contained in the *Investext* database and the analyst rankings of *Institutional Investor* magazine. We obtained full-text Adobe PDF files of reports of these analysts from *Investext*, a database that stores the research reports written by analysts from investment banks and other financial research institutions. The rankings of securities analysts during the years 1998–2000 were obtained from *Institutional Investor*.

Additional considerations

Finally, we highlight two important characteristics of our grounded research design. First, the empirical validity of our findings is not based on the size of our sample; instead, our process of constant comparison aims at generating new hypotheses (Glaser and Strauss, 1967). The findings reported here, however, have yet to be explored in other settings. The second observation pertains to the involvement of our focal analyst, Blodget, in the analyst scandals of 2001. On November 2001, Blodget abandoned his job at Merrill Lynch as part of a judicial settlement with the Attorney General of New York, Eliot Spitzer. The settlement followed an investigation of Blodget's internal communications with his colleagues at Merrill Lynch, revealing internal e-mails in which Blodget criticized some of the companies that he was officially recommending. The abrupt end of Blodget's career as a security analyst might be interpreted as evidence that Blodget was not helping investors but simply deceiving them, rendering his reports an inadequate data source to learn about the mental models used by analysts.

On this issue, we note that the episodes of conflict took place after the time period that we examine, and for companies different from Amazon (we elaborate this point in the next section below; see also Gasparino, 2005). More interesting though, is the question: How it is that analysts such as Blodget were able to convince investors and rise to the top of the rankings despite the potential for conflict of interest? Our chapter addresses this question by suggesting that what analysts do is create and provide a compelling frame that is persuasive.

The financial controversy over Amazon.com

Barely one year after Amazon's debut on Wall Street, a sharp controversy over its value erupted among Wall Street analysts. The company had opened up for business on the Web in 1995, and had placed itself under the eye of investors with its initial public offering in 1997. Within a year, the stock price had risen to unprecedented heights. As one of so many business cases put it, 'never in the history of financial markets had a company reached such market capitalization ... without a single dollar in profits' (González, 2000: 11). Accordingly, a widespread debate ensued about the merits of the company, as well as about the Internet and electronic commerce in general. The controversy continued until the end of the year 2000, when the company's mounting losses settled the case against the optimists. In this section we examine three episodes of this controversy and their lessons for the work of securities analysts.

First episode: Blodget vs. Cohen

On December 16th 1998, investors were faced with a blunt dispute over the value of Amazon. Blodget, an Internet analyst at Canadian bank CIBC Oppenheimer, raised his price target from $150 to $400 following the company's stellar Thanksgiving sales. Such brusque change in the analyst's recommendation was exceptional enough to be featured on the *Wall Street Journal*. On that same day, however, Jonathan Cohen of Merrill Lynch advanced a very different perspective: in a research note on the company issued only hours after Blodget's report, Cohen rated Amazon a 'sell' and valued it at $50, arguing that it would never be able to reach the profits that Blodget predicted. The resulting controversy among investors was such that trading volume in Amazon stocks surpassed $100 million, more than ten times its average. The episode finally resolved itself in Blodget's favour. The stock exceeded the $400 price target in three weeks, and Blodget entered *Institutional Investor*'s All-Star team.

The uncertainty, tension and drama of December 1998 are hardly consistent with the literature on analysts. The information-processing approach presents analysts as aiming to have forecasting accuracy but the disparity between the two analysts seems too wide to be attributed to inaccuracy or measurement error. Similarly, the neo-institutional literature presents analysts as averse to deviating from the consensus and as unwilling to upset the companies they follow, but we find Blodget and Cohen clashing directly with each other, ignoring the consensus and, in the case of Cohen, bitterly criticizing Amazon. What, then, accounts for the sharp divergence among the analysts?

Behind the numbers: formulae and estimates

A broader survey of the work produced by Blodget and Cohen, including their September and October reports, offers additional clues about the origins of their disparity. Between September and December 1998, Blodget and Cohen wrote a total of five documents each. These reveal the nuts and bolts of their calculative technique. Our examination of these early reports revealed that the key to their difference lies in the analysts' choice of estimates. Cohen's revenue estimate for the year ending in December 2000 was $0.8 billion (Cohen and Pankopf, 1998a:10), whereas Blodget's was three times higher, totalling $2.5 billion (Blodget and Erdmann, 1998: 10). Similarly, Cohen's operating margin estimate stood at a conservative 10 per cent (Cohen and Pankopf, 1998a: 6), versus a more generous margin estimate by Blodget of 12 per cent (Blodget and Erdmann, 1998: 13). Compounded in their respective formulae, these differences produced the valuation gap of $400 versus $50. Examining the justifications that both analysts give to their respective estimates, we observe a striking regularity: both analysts draw from categories, analogies and key metrics. Below, we examine how these three elements allowed the two analysts to estimate Amazon's future operating margin and revenue.

1. Margin estimate. Blodget estimated an aggressive 2003 operating margin of twelve per cent. In explaining his figure, Blodget first rejected the use of Amazon's *current* profits to predict the *future* operating margin of the company. Blodget argued that as a young start-up company, Amazon was still in its initial money-losing phase. The proper proxy for Amazon's long-term margin was instead the margin of a similar company. Blodget went on to consider four possible, similar companies, from book retailers to Internet portals. He wrote:

> Most investors appear to come to one of four conclusions regarding the future profitability of Amazon.com's business model: (1) It will never make any money; (2) It will have a 1%–2% net margin, like other retailers; (3) It will have an 8% net margin, like 'direct' manufacturer Dell, or (4) It will have a 15% net margin, like a Dell-Yahoo hybrid (Blodget and Erdmann, 1998: 13).

Of these, Blodget opted for Dell Computers and its 'direct' sales model. Both companies sold directly to customers, and both had the same gross margin. Thus, Blodget concluded, 'a mature Amazon.com will be able to generate Dell-like profitability.' (Blodget and Erdmann, 1998: 13).

Cohen's margin estimate, on the other hand, was a more modest ten per cent margin. He justified this lower figure by categorizing Amazon as a bookstore and adding that bookstores are characterized by low operating margins. He noted:

> Bookselling is an inherently competitive and low-margin business. Because the intellectual property value contained in published works typically represents only a small portion of the price to end-users, we do not expect that moving that business to an online environment will meaningfully change those characteristics (Cohen and Pankopf, 1998a: 1).

In short, Cohen emphasized Amazon's book selling core, ignoring the company's potential to leverage its e-commerce capabilities into other products.

To this categorization-based argument, Cohen added an analogy: Amazon, Cohen argued, was like Barnes & Noble. Indeed, Cohen went as far as to argue that Amazon was even inferior to the latter in several ways, because, as he noted:

> Amazon's current market capitalization of $4.0 billion is roughly equivalent to more than twice the capitalization of Barnes & Noble, a highly profitable company with more than 1,000 retail outlets and a vastly larger revenue base (Cohen and Pankopf, 1998a:3).

2. Revenue estimate. Blodget estimated Amazon's revenue for the year 2000 at a very aggressive $2.5 billion, whereas Cohen estimated far more conservative revenues of less than $1 billion. Blodget justified his estimate by proposing that Amazon belonged to an entirely new industry category, 'the Internet Company.' He argued:

> We see [Amazon] as an electronic customer-services company in the business of helping its customers figure out what they want to buy (. . .) and then delivering it to them at a good price with minimum hassle (Blodget and Erdmann, 1998: 1).
> We see no reason, therefore, why Amazon will stop with books, music, and videos. Over the next few years, we wouldn't be surprised were it to add software, toys, credit cards, auctions, foods or whatever product offering makes sense (Blodget and Erdmann, 1998: 20).

Thus, we see that Blodget estimated without concern for the number of books or CDs sold that the figure implied. His categorization was crucial in allowing him to develop his estimate.

Cohen also relied on categories to justify his choice of margin estimate. He categorized Amazon as a bookseller, which implied a more limited revenue growth, since book retailing as a whole 'is an inherently competitive and low-margin business' (Cohen and Pankopf, 1998a: 1).

Calculative frames

The regularities described so far suggest that the combined use of categories, analogies and metrics in analysts' reports makes up a whole with an entity on its own. To underscore this point and to highlight its theoretical relevance, we denote by *calculative frame* the internally consistent network of associations, including (among others) categories, metrics and analogies, that yield the necessary estimates which go into the valuation of a company. (See Figure 1 for a representation of these frames).

Calculative frames are not just an abstract entity, but also have a tangible presence that takes the obvious form of text, tables and numbers in the reports of analysts, as well as of Excel spreadsheet files. We found anecdotal evidence of this materiality in an interview with a portfolio manager at a large Wall Street mutual fund. Having said that he 'rarely' used the price targets and recommendations produced by securities analysts, the portfolio manager added: 'what I do is, I call up the analyst and say "hey, can you send me your model?" Then he sends me the spreadsheet and I can find out exactly which are the assump-

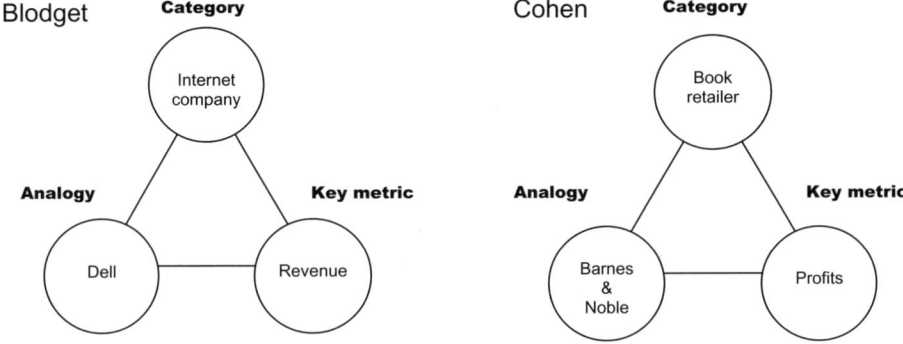

Figure 1: *Blodget and Cohen's calculative frames for Amazon.com*
Blodget's calculative frame included a choice of category, an analogy and a key metric with which to value Amazon.com. Cohen's frame included the same elements, but with different contents. Source: Blodget and Erdmann (1998) and Cohen and Pankopf (1998).

tions that go in.' One sign that the circulation of Excel files is prevalent on Wall Street is that the first page of analyst reports always cite the direct phone number and email address of the analyst, one for each analyst if the report is co-authored.

Securities analysts as frame-makers

The notion of calculative frame suggests a new perspective on the intermediary function performed by analysts. The rise of Blodget from obscurity to celebrity following his December call indicates that providing new frames is an important part of analysts' work. Doing so helps investors by equipping them with the tools that are needed to measure company value. Accordingly, we denote by *frame-making* the activity of creating, providing, and promoting calculative frames such as we see being done in the work of Blodget and Cohen.

Second episode: Blodget vs. Barron's

The notion of frame-making put forward above gives rise to an additional question: How do these frames shape the way analysts use information? A subsequent episode in the controversy over Amazon speaks to this issue. In April 1999, Amazon announced larger end-year losses than it initially anticipated. One month later, a highly critical article in *Barron's* written by journalist Abel Abelson interpreted Amazon's statement as proof that the company was severely over-valued. Shortly afterwards, Blodget challenged Abelson's arguments in a special research report, titled 'Amazon.Bomb? Negative Barron's Article.' Again, we see two disparate reactions to the same piece of information, namely, Amazon's expected 1999 performance. In this section we explore this disparity to understand how frames mediate the incorporation of new information into existing valuations.

Consider first Abelson's article. The journalist criticized Amazon's strategy on several grounds: margins in book retailing, he claimed, were low. Amazon's model of a virtual bookstore did not help, for the company was spending too much in acquiring customers. Amazon's expansion into CDs 'only (. . .) proved so far (. . .) that it can lose money selling books and lose still more money selling CDs' (Abelson, 1999: 5). Compared with Barnes & Noble, Abelson concluded, Amazon was overvalued. The journalist proposed a total value for Amazon between $10 and $25, a paltry one seventh of the company's market price at the time.

Blodget's reply to Abelson used the information mobilized by the journalist, but interpreted it differently. Blodget began his report by acknowledging Abelson's criticisms, but went on to address each of the points raised by the journalist and concluded that most of them were not reasons for concern and in some cases, were in fact reasons to buy the stock. Consider, for example, Blodget's treatment of Amazon's lack of profitability. As noted above, Abelson had emphasized Amazon's losses. In reply to this, Blodget wrote,

> As any smart investor understands, there is a big difference between 'losing' money and 'investing' money. Amazon.com is investing money, not losing it, so near-term profitability is not a good measure of future worth. Put another way, if Amazon.com were to cut back on its investments in order to post a near-term profit, we believe it would be worth considerably less in three to five years than it will be if its current investments pay off. (Blodget and Anning, 1999: 6).

In presented Amazon's losses as investments, Blodget performed a judo-like manoeuvre that reinterpreted his opponent's information in a way that not only altered but actually *reversed* its implications (Figure 2).

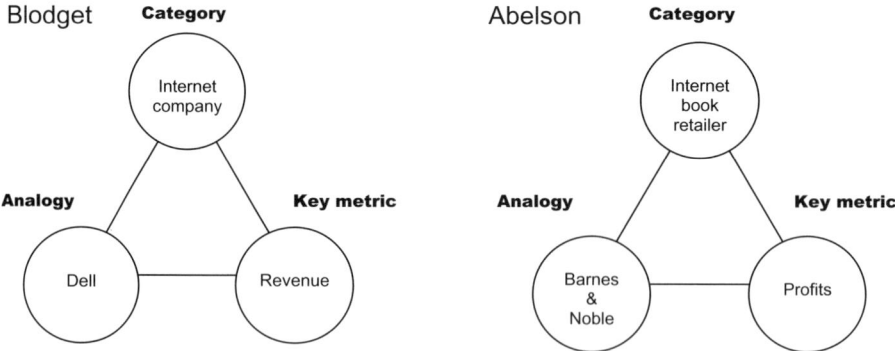

Figure 2: *Blodget and Abelson's calculative frames for Amazon.com*
Both frames included a choice of category, an analogy and a key metric with which to value Amazon.com, but with different contents. Blodget (1999) and Abelson (1999).

Interpretation vs. Bayesian updating

The disparity among the two analysts' assessments challenges the Bayesian model that inspires the information processing literature. According to Bayes' model, all rational analysts should update their probability assessments in the same direction; instead, we observe that Blodget and Abelson did so in opposite ways. Furthermore, these differences can be explained by the frames used by the analysts. Abelson categorized Amazon as a traditional retailer, saw it as being analogous to Barnes & Noble, and chose to focus on its lack of current profitability. As a result, greater losses were for him an additional sign that Amazon's business model was not working. Blodget, on the other hand, did not see 1999 losses as a relevant measure of future value. This prompted him to focus instead on how the company's investments could increase its future revenue. The theoretical lesson here is that in contexts of ambiguity, when different and inconsistent bodies of meaning are available to explain the same set of news, analysts accord meaning to it with recourse to their existing frame. The implication is that calculative frames mediate how analysts accord meaning to information.

Framing controversies

An additional lesson from the episode is that debate about and discrepancies between frames persist over time. Comparing Blodget's December frame with the one in May, we see that news of greater losses did not make Blodget modify his December 1998 frame; instead, it prompted him to redefine the news as positive. We conclude that analysts tend to persist in their positions due to perseverance in their frames, and refer to these continued disparities as *framing controversies*: sustained differences in valuation that arise from a disparity in calculative frames.

Third episode: Blodget versus Suria

The two previous episodes present the work of security analysts as ongoing controversies over how to calculate value. But seeing analysis in terms of divergence rather than consensus leads to an important question: if a frame can coexist with its opposite for a sustained period of time, does that mean it can survive forever? In other words, are framing controversies ever closed? And if so, how? To address these questions, we set out to examine the mechanisms of frame-adoption and frame-abandonment used by analysts and investors. We centre on a third and final episode which presents a striking change in the fortunes of Henry Blodget.

On June 3rd 2000, analyst Ravi Suria of Lehman Brothers wrote a scathing report on Amazon. Suria, a convertible bond analyst, proposed a broad revision of prevailing thinking about the company: Amazon, he argued, was a traditional retailer. When measuring the company as such, its performance appeared rather mediocre. Furthermore, Suria argued, the company could well run out of money within a year. The analyst rated Amazon a 'sell,' prompting intense trading activity during that day as well as several articles in the financial press (eg, *The Economist*, 2000: 65).

One month later, on June 29th, Blodget countered Suria's attack with an optimistic report on Amazon. The report emphasized the company's similarities with America Online, an Internet company that overcame difficulties and produced outstanding returns to investors. This time, however, Blodget's arguments failed to persuade investors. The price of Amazon began a long decline. The analyst gradually fell out of favour with portfolio managers in the *Institutional Investor* rankings, and Suria's contrarian success turned him into a star analyst (Vickers, 2000: 25).

Blodget's reversal invites the question of what led investors and fellow analysts to believe him in December 1998 and change course two years later. The reports themselves do not answer this, for both Suria's attack and Blodget's defence of Amazon relied on a solid, three-pronged calculative frame based on categorizations, analogies and key metrics. Thus, for instance, Suria categorized Amazon as having the operational and cash flow characteristics of a retailer, while Blodget insisted that its low stock price was due to poor sentiment surrounding the e-commerce sector. In terms of analogies, Suria related the company to online and traditional firms such as Best Buy, Musicland, Barnes & Noble, Borders and Books A Million; whereas Blodget focussed his report on an analogy to AOL. And in terms of metrics, Suria focussed on retailer variables such as working capital and cash flow, whereas Blodget insisted on more ethereal, Internet-like, variables such as sales growth, stock market undervaluation or the quality of its management. Both analysts, in short provided a tight, internally consistent explanation. Why did investors choose one over the other? (See Figure 3 for a graphical representation). In search of an explanation, we enlarged our lens to include the economic and social context surrounding the analysts at the time.

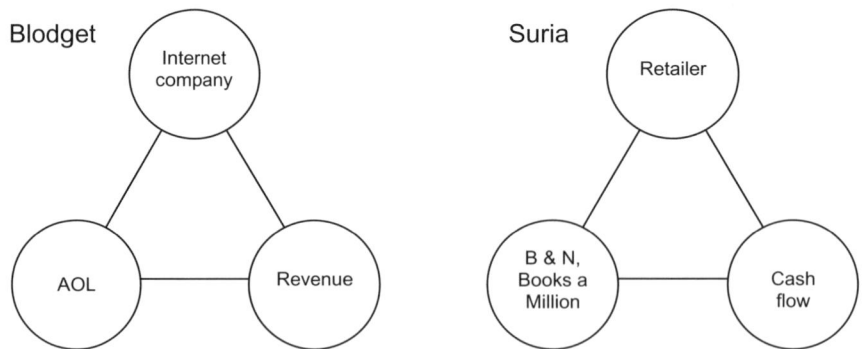

Figure 3: *Blodget and Suria's calculative frames for Amazon.com*
Source: Suria and Oh (2000), Blodget (2000a).

Perhaps the most crucial background event in June 1999 was the continued lack of profitability of Amazon.com. Back in 1998, Blodget had asked investors to wait for three years before demanding profits. He recommended the stock for 'strong-stomached, long-term investors,' and wrote that he 'expected the company's accumulated deficit to balloon to more than $300 million before it finally starts reporting profits in the spring of 2001' (Blodget and Erdmann, 1998: 25). Two years later, however, that profitability seemed more distant than ever. By October 1999 Amazon announced that it would pursue diversification rather than higher profits. Blodget reacted to this by claiming to be 'simply exhausted by the endless postponement of financial gratification' (Veverka, 1999: 64). On July 26th 2000, Amazon even failed to reach the revenue figure that Blodget predicted, making the analyst appear hopelessly out of touch. On the following day, six analysts simultaneously downgraded their recommendations for the company's stock.

Determinants of frame adoption and abandonment

The central issue examined in this episode relates to the dynamics of frame abandonment. How do market actors abandon a frame that they previously espoused? The events presented so far suggest that frames are abandoned through a confluence of forces (Mohr, 1982) that include elements of information processing and the social context. Analysts and investors reacted to information about Amazon, but the manner in which they did so – the timing, the process and the reasons – was defined by their social context.

We observe that news investors and analysts sold Amazon and lowered their ratings immediately after Suria's report of June 22nd and Amazon's earnings announcement of July 27th. The question is, why? After all, they did not lower their ratings when Barron's Ableson had attacked Amazon's performance and Blodget's framing just over a year ago. So, what had changed?

The episode underscores the central importance of the social context in shaping the reactions by the actors to data that is generated and whether they consider such data as meaningful information or not. Specifically, we want to draw attention to the notion of time that is built into analyst's frames as a critical element that determines how data that is generated in real time will be treated by market actors. As with other initiatives where entrepreneurs build milestones into projections (Garud and Karnoe, 2001), Blodget too, in his initial 1998 report, had built time into his frame by suggesting that investors would have to wait till 2001 to observe positive performance on the part of Amazon. Consequently, a key difference between the Ableson and Suria episodes was the proximity of June 2000 to the January 2001 milestone for profitability that Blodget had established. In contrast with May 1999, when Blodget simply reframed news of losses as positive, in June 2000 Blodget was unable to persuade market actors to come around to his view.

Another way in which the social context shaped interpretation was through the general discrediting of the 'Internet' industry. The calculative frames espoused by Amazon analysts and investors appeared to be nested in a broader 'New Economy' frame that became suspect, dragging Blodget's frame along with it. The social movement's literature defines two frames as nested when one is the conceptual subset of the other (Turner and Turner, 1986). Nested frames, in other words, are arranged within one another 'like Chinese boxes' (Lindquist, 2001: 13). Changes in the credibility of the larger frame impact those frames nested within it. In the case of Amazon, Blodget's frame relied heavily for his generous revenue growth estimates on the categorization of the company as an Internet firm (Blodget and Erdmann, 1998: 10). When the dot-com crash undermined the credibility of the New Economy frame in April 2000, Blodget's frame became vulnerable. In this manner, the decision of investors and analysts to abandon Blodget's frame appears to have been based in part of the decisions made by other market actors, namely, disenchanted investors in New Economy stocks.

Once Blodget's frame became vulnerable, an opportunity opened up for Suria. The bond analyst marshalled several pieces of evidence – Amazon's losses, its large size or low inventory turnover – into a compelling narrative that displaced Blodget's. From this, we observe that investors and analysts were led by Suria, adopting the categories, analogies and metrics proposed by the analyst. Indeed, we see a massive and sudden abandonment of Blodget's frame on July 27th. This simultaneous move was in fact prompted by Blodget's and his public (and failed) forecast of Amazon's sales two days before. By forecasting sales of $579 million, Blodget defined as disappointing any sales figure below it. This presence of prominent actors acting as a coordinating force underscores once again the importance of the social context in frame abandonment.

In sum, the episode suggests an abandonment process that combines the information available to the actors and the broader social context. This stands in contrast to the existing literature. Whereas the information-processing approach views information as the sole determinant of abandonment and the imitation approach barely considers changes in frames, the lesson that emerges from this third episode is that frames are abandoned on the basis of concrete information (lack of profits, low sales growth, etc.), interpreted on the basis of the social context. Such context includes the actions taken by market actors with regards to other companies in the form of nested frames; the initiatives of emerging frame-breakers, and the milestones created by the frame-makers themselves.

Discussion

Our comparison of the different reports in the previous section led to three core theoretical concepts that address the meaning of analysis under uncertainty: calculative frames, frame-making and framing controversies. These build up to a comprehensive theory of analysis under uncertainty, detailing the elements of a calculative frame: how it appears, how it functions and when it is abandoned. In the following paragraphs we revisit the three Amazon episodes. In doing so, we consider how our theory relates to alternative accounts of securities analysis.

How do analysts confront Knightian uncertainty?

The first incident in the controversy over Amazon provides suggestive information on the nature of analysis under uncertainty. Our examination of the reports by Blodget and Cohen suggests that analysts overcome Knightian uncertainty by developing calculative frames, that is, analogies, categorizations and choices of metrics that allow them to value companies even their future is unknown. We denote this activity by frame-making.

The notion of frame-making challenges the lemming view of securities analysts that characterizes neo-institutional sociology and behavioural finance. The concept explains how and why analysts deviate from the consensus of their peers. As noted above, the analyst profession is structured around the rankings assembled by *Institutional Investor*. As with any other ranking, visibility breeds recognition and vice-versa, leading to a potentially closed loop in which newcomers would be excluded from the top. One way in which unknown analysts can break into high-ranking positions is by offering investors a dramatic profit opportunity. In an information-rich context such as Wall Street, the quickest route is by providing an original interpretation, namely, a new calculative frame. The case of Blodget illustrates this mechanism: Blodget rose from obscurity to top Internet analyst in 2000 precisely because of the original frame he developed in December 1998. In short, the notion of frame-making emphasizes the strong incentives that exist for analysts to produce original work.

Our perspective contributes to economic sociology by building on its central claim that markets are social. Markets are social, we contend, because calculation is social. The concept of calculative frame highlights the cognitive and material infrastructure that underlies economic calculations of value. Securities analysts make possible the world of calculation hypothesized by orthodox economics. In this manner, our perspective contrasts with the orthodox view that calculation is innate, abstract and individual. Instead, we view calculation as framed, material and social, in other words, as performed. Frame-making is thus consistent with the emerging performativity literature in economic sociology and its central claim that economic theories and artefacts format the economy by shaping the way in which value is calculated (Callon, 1998; Beunza and Stark, 2004; MacKenzie and Millo, 2003; Preda, 2006; Callon and Muniesa, 2005; MacKenzie, 2006).

Our view also contrasts with the literatures in behavioural finance and neo-institutional sociology. These portray decision-making as purely imitative and non-calculative. In contrast, the concept of frame-makers reconciles the concept of imitation with that of calculation. Market actors adopt the calculative frames employed by successful peers, but this does not mean that they abandon calculation altogether. Again, our view in this manner is consistent with Callon (1998) and the performativity literature.

Finally, the notion of frame-making qualifies and extends the analysts-as-critics' literature by identifying the devices that critics mobilize to perform assessments. The notion of frame-making builds on the basic claim of the critics' literature, namely, that Knightian uncertainty is the central problem that analysts and other intermediaries confront. We contend, however, that critique is not a purely mental activity but a material one as well. Analysts are active builders of frames, rather than passive classifiers of stocks into categories. In doing so, frame-making adds again to the recent literature in the social studies of finance and its attention to the 'metrological' instruments used within the capital markets (Callon, 1998; Beunza and Stark, 2004). In addition, our perspective departs from the critics approach and its claim that analysts exert a conservative influence on the market. We document the tendency of successful analysts to disrupt, rather than perpetuate, existing industry categorical schemes.

How do calculative frames operate?

The second episode in the Amazon controversy provides a compelling illustration of calculative frames at work. Frames persist in the face of disconfirming evidence, and sustained differences in frames lead to prolonged divergences in valuation. We refer to these divergences as framing controversies. The notion of framing controversies departs from the neoclassic view of Bayesian information processing. According to the latter, there is a single correct way to assemble existing information on company value. Over time, disagreements about valuation will disappear, because rational analysts eventually converge. By contrast, the notion of frame-making takes issue with this idea, arguing that divergence is persistent within the capital markets.

Framing controversies also depart from the behavioural tenet that failed predictions bring irrationality to the capital markets. The behavioural finance literature presents analyst inaccuracy as 'biases' that is, as mistakes that hamper the efficient functioning of the market. By contrast, the notion of framing controversies suggests that divergent predictions in fact contribute to market efficiency. Frames guide investors in interpreting incoming information, stabilizing the meaning of news across the investor community and over time. In addition, controversies underscore legitimate differences in perspectives, allowing investors to better locate their own position in ongoing debates (eg, what Brenner [1991: 24] referred to as 'an articulate case from both the bull and the bear'). Furthermore, the coherence of the categories, analogies and key metrics chosen by the analysts suggests that their positions are individually rational, at least in the sense provided by Savage (1954), that is, internally consistent.

The notion of framing controversy builds on the concept of scientific controversies developed in the social studies of science and technology literature. The latter are defined as 'alternative accounts of the natural world' whose persistence in the face of experimental data suggests that they 'are not directly given by nature, but . . . as products of social processes and negotiations' (Martin and

Richards, 1995:510; see also Bloor, 1976; Nelkin, 1979; Latour, 1987). Framing controversies extend the notion of scientific controversies to the capital markets, contributing to the emerging literature in the social studies of finance and its focus on the content of economic transactions, as opposed to social networks that underlie them (Lépinay and Rousseau, 2000; MacKenzie and Millo, 2003; Knorr Cetina and Bruegger, 2003; Beunza and Stark, 2004; Preda, 2005; Callon and Muniesa, 2005; MacKenzie, 2006).

How are frames abandoned?

Our analysis of the first two Amazon episodes established that valuation is a joint outcome of the information and the frame previously espoused by the actor. How, then, do actors decide to adopt or abandon a frame? The controversy over Amazon of June 2000 suggests why a certain frame might be abandoned. The focal event this time was the critical report that bond analyst Ravi Suria wrote on Amazon on June 2000. Despite Blodget's best efforts, analysts and investors abandoned Blodget's frame and adopted Suria's instead. This change resulted from a confluence of events: the dot-com crash, vulnerabilities that emerged in Blodget's frame, and Suria's report. All these combined to shape a new interpretation of Amazon's performance.

The episode suggests that changes in frames arise from the combined effect of information and the social context. Specifically, it suggests that market actors respond to information, but interpret this information within a social context of controversy. This controversy plays out as rivalry in frames, nested frames and self-imposed milestones. Such view contrasts with the information-processing approach, which contends that news of economic events are the sole determinant of change in opinion. It also departs from the imitation approach, which contends that market actors are fundamentally responsive to each other rather than to incoming news. In our view, then, economic actors are attuned to both ongoing events and the social context in which these occur.

Conclusion

Our objective in this chapter was to clarify the economic function performed by security analysts in contexts of Knightian uncertainty. The core finding emerging from our study is that securities analysts function as frame-makers. In the presence of Knightian uncertainty, analysts make up for their partial knowledge of the world by becoming active builders of interpretive devices that bracket, give meaning and make it possible to develop quantitative point estimates of value. We refer to these interpretive devices as calculative frames. These frames include categorizations, analogies and the selection of key dimensions of merit. In contexts of extreme uncertainty, we propose that the primary activity undertaken by securities analysts is not to forecast prices or to give investment advice, but to develop calculative frames.

Note

1 Beunza's work has been supported by grant SEJ2005-08391 from the Spanish Dirección General de Investigación Científica y Técnica and Garud's by summer research support grants from the Stern School of Business, New York University. The authors wish to thank Adam Brandenburger, Michel Callon, Emilio Castilla, Gary Dushnistsky, James Evans, Isabel Fernandez-Mateo Fabrizio Ferraro, Mauro Guillen, Witold Henisz, Robin Hogarth, Donald MacKenzie, Fabian Muniesa, Sarah Kaplan, Peter Karnoe, Javier Lezaun, Yuval Millo, Kamal Munir, Mikolaj Piskorski, Peter Roberts, Naomi Rothman, Graham Sewell, David Stark, Mary O'Sullivan, Mark Zbaracki, Ezra Zuckerman and other participants at the 2003 EGOS 'Markets-in-the-making' colloquium, 2003 Barcelona Gestió seminar, 2004 Performativity Workshop in Paris, EOI Seminar at Wharton and Strategy Research Forum in Athens for their inputs on earlier drafts of this paper.

References

Abelson, A. (1999) 'Up & down Wall Street: the answer to everything'. *Barron's*, May 3: 5–6.
Abolafia, M. Y. (1996) *Making Markets: Opportunism and Restraint on Wall Street*. Cambridge, MA: Harvard University Press.
Abramowitz, P., A. Bloomenthal, J. Burke, and M. D'Ambrosio. (2000) 'The 2000 All-American Research Team – the best analysts of the year: Technology & the Internet.' *Institutional Investor*, Oct. 34, 25(10): 136.
Banerjee, A. (1992) 'A simple model of herd behaviour'. *Quarterly Journal of Economics*, 107(3): 797–817.
Barber, B., R. Lehavy, M. McNichols and B. Trueman. (2001) 'Can investors profit from the prophets? Consensus analyst recommendations and stock returns'. *Journal of Finance*, 56(2): 531–563.
Barberis N., A. Shleifer and R. Vishny. (1998) 'A model of investor sentiment'. *Journal of Financial Economics*, 49(3): 307–343.
Benjamin, B. A. and J. Podolny. (1999) 'Status, quality, and social order in the California wine industry'. *Administrative Science Quarterly*, 44(3): 563–589.
Bernstein, P. (1992) *Capital Ideas: The Improbable Origins of Modern Wall Street*. New York: The Free Press.
Beunza, D. and D. Stark. (2004) 'Tools of the trade: the socio-technology of arbitrage in a Wall Street trading room'. *Industrial and Corporate Change*, 13(2): 369–400.
Bikhchandani, S., D. Hirshleifer and I. Welch. (1992) 'A theory of fads, fashion, custom, and cultural change as informational cascades,' *Journal of Political Economy*, 100(5): 992–1026.
Bidwell C. M. III. (1977) 'How good is institutional brokerage research?'. *Journal of Portfolio Management*, 3: 26–31.
Blodget, H. M. and N. Erdmann. (1998) 'Amazon.com. Initiating with Buy; Analyzing Competition, Profitability and Valuation'. Equity Research Report, CIBC Oppenheimer, October 13.
Blodget, H. M. and E. Anning. (1998) 'Amazon.com. Raising Price Target to $400'. Equity Research Report, CIBC Oppenheimer, December 16th.
Blodget, H. M. and E. Anning. (1999) 'Amazon.Bomb?' Equity Research Report, Merrill Lynch, June 1.
Blodget, H. M. and D. Good. (2000) 'Is AMZN now AOL in 1996', Equity Research Report, Merrill Lynch. June 29.
Bloor, D. (1976) *Knowledge and Social Imagery*. London: Routledge.
Boni, L. and K. Womack. (2002) 'Wall-Street's credibility problem: misaligned incentives and dubious fixes?' Brookings-Wharton Papers on Financial Services: 93-130.
Brandenburger, A. (2002) 'The power of paradox: some recent developments in interactive epistemology'. Manuscript, Stern School of Business.

Brenner, L. (1991) 'The Bull and the Bear.' *United States Banker*, January 101(1): 25–27.
Callon, M. (1998) 'Introduction: the embeddedness of economic markets in economics'. In M. Callon (ed.), *The Laws of the Markets*. Oxford: Blackwell.
Callon, M. and F. Muniesa. (2005) 'Economic markets as calculative collective devices.' *Organization Studies*, 26(8): 1229–1250.
Christensen, C. (1997) *The Innovator's Dilemma: When New Technologies Cause Great Firms to Fail*. Boston: Harvard Business School Press.
Cohen, J. and T. Pankopf. (1998a) 'Amazon.com Inc. The World's Leading Internet Commerce Company Is Too Expensive'. Equity Research Report, Merrill Lynch, September 1: 1–11.
Cohen, J. and T. Pankopf. (1998b) 'Research Note on Amazon'. Equity Research Report, Merrill Lynch, September 1: 1.
Cowles, A. (1933) 'Can stock market forecasters forecast?' *Econometrica*, 1(3): 309–325.
Damodaran, A. (2000) 'The dark side of valuation: firms with no earnings, no history and no comparables – Can Amazon.com be valued? Manuscript. Stern School of Business.
Dini, J. (2001) 'The 2001 All-America Research Team: The best analysts of the year – Internet Portals & Commerce,' *Institutional Investor*, 26(10): 1.
Fama, E. (1965) 'The behavior of stock-market prices'. *Journal of Business*, 38(1): 34–105.
Fama, E. (1970) 'Efficient capital markets: a review of theory and empirical work'. *Journal of Finance*, 25(2): 283–306.
Fama, E. (1991) 'Efficient capital markets II'. *Journal of Finance*, 46(5): 1575–1617.
Fiol, M. (1989) 'A Semiotic analysis of corporate language: organizational boundaries and joint venturing'. *Administrative Science Quarterly* 34(2): 277–304.
Fligstein, N. (2001) *The Architecture of Markets: An Economic Sociology of Twenty-First-Century Capitalist Societies*. Princeton, NJ: Princeton University Press.
Garud, R and P. Karnoe. (2001) 'Path creation as a process of mindful deviation'. In R. Garud and P. Karnoe (eds), *Path Dependence and Creation*. Mahwah, NJ: Lawrence Earlbaum Associates.
Garud, R. and M. Rappa. (1994) 'A socio-cognitive model of technology evolution'. *Organization Science*, 5(3): 344–362.
Gasparino, C. (2005) *Blood on the Street: The Sensational Inside Story of How Wall Street Analysts Duped a Generation of Investors*. New York: The Free Press.
Glaser, B. and A. Strauss. (1967) *The Discovery of Grounded Theory: Strategies for Qualitative Research*. New York: Aldine De Gruyter.
Gonzalez, R. (2001) 'Amazon.com'. Universitat Pompeu Fabra Business Case No. 12: 1–13.
Granovetter, M. (1985) 'Economic action and social structure: the problem of embeddedness'. *American Journal of Sociology*, 19(3): 481–510.
Granovetter, M. (2004) 'Polanyi Symposium: a conversation on embeddedness'. *Socio-Economic Review*, 2(1): 113–117.
Hirsch, P. (1972) 'Processing fads and fashions: an organization-set analysis of cultural industry systems. *American Journal of Sociology*, 77(4): 639–659.
Hirsch, P. (1975) 'Organizational effectiveness and the institutional environment'. *Administrative Science Quarterly*, 20(3): 327–344.
Hong, H., J. Kubik and A. Solomon. (2000) 'Securities analysts' career concerns and the herding of earnings forecasts'. *RAND Journal of Economics*, 31(1): 121–144.
Hong, H. and J. Kubik. (2002) 'Analyzing the analysts: career concerns and biased earnings forecasts'. *The Journal of Finance*, 58(1): 313–351.
Hsu, G. and J. Podolny. (2005) 'Critiquing the critics: an approach for the comparative evaluation of critical schemas'. *Social Science Research*, 34(1): 189–214.
Institutional Investor. (1998) 'The 1998 All-America Research team. The Best Analysts of the Year – The Internet & New Media,' *Institutional Investor*, 23(10): 91. Anonymous.
Institutional Investor (1999) 'The 1999 All-America research team. The best analysts of the year – The Internet & New Media,' *Institutional Investor*, 24(10): 103. Anonymous.
Kessler, A. (2001) 'Manager's Journal: We're All Analysts Now'. *The Wall Street Journal*, July 30, p. A.18.
Knight, F. (1971) *Risk, Uncertainty and Profit*. Chicago: University of Chicago Press.

Knorr Cetina, K. D. and U. Bruegger. (2002) 'Global microstructures: the virtual societies of financial markets', *American Journal of Sociology*, 107(4): 905–950.
Latour, B. (1987) *Science in Action: How to Follow Scientists and Engineers through Society*. Cambridge, MA: Harvard University Press.
Lépinay, V.-A. and F. Rousseau. (2000) 'Les trolls sont-ils incompétents? Enquête sur les financiers amateurs.' *Politix*, 13(52): 73–97.
Lim, T. (2001) 'Rationality and analysts' forecast bias'. *Journal of Finance*, 56(1): 369–385.
Lin, H. and M. McNichols. (1998) 'Underwriting relationships, analysts' forecasts and investment recommendations'. *Journal of Accounting and Economics*, 25(1): 101–127.
Lindquist, G. (2001) 'Elusive play and its relations to power'. *Focaal – European Journal of Anthropology*, 37: 13–23.
MacKenzie, D. and Y. Millo. (2003) 'Constructing a market, performing theory: the historical sociology of a financial derivatives exchange'. *American Journal of Sociology*, 109(1): 107–145.
MacKenzie, D. (2006) *An Engine, Not a Camera: How Financial Models Shape Markets*. Cambridge, MA: MIT Press.
March, J. (1987) 'Ambiguity and accounting: the elusive link between information and decision making'. *Accounting, Organizations, and Society*, 12(2): 153–168.
Malkiel, B. (1973) *A Random Walk Down Wall Street*, New York: W. W. Norton & Co.
Martin, B. and E. Richards. (1995) 'Scientific knowledge, controversy and public decision making'. In S. Jasanoff, G. Markle, J. Petersen and T. Pinch (eds), *Handbook of Science and Technology Studies*. Thousand Oaks, CA: Sage.
Michaely, R. and K. Womack. (1999) 'Conflict of interest and the credibility of underwriter analyst recommendations'. *Review of Financial Studies*, 12(4): 653–686.
Mohr, L. B. (1982) *Explaining Organizational Behavior*. San Francisco: Jossey-Bass.
Nanda, A. and B. Groysberg. (2004) 'Can they take it with them? The portability of star knowledge workers' performance: myth or reality.' Harvard Business School Working Paper Series, No. 05-029.
Nelkin, D. (1979) *Controversy: Politics of Technical Decisions*. London: Sage.
Phillips, D., and E. Zuckerman. (2001) 'Middle-status conformity: theoretical restatement and empirical demonstration in two markets'. *American Journal of Sociology*, 107(2): 379–420.
Prendergast, C. and L. Stole. (1996) 'Impetuous youngsters and jaded old-timers: acquiring a reputation for learning', *Journal of Political Economy*, 104(6): 1105–1134.
Podolny, J. M. (1993) 'A status-based model of market competition', *American Journal of Sociology*, 98(4): 829–872.
Podolny, J. M. (1994) 'Market uncertainty and the social character of economic exchange'. *Administrative Science Quarterly*, 39(3): 458–483.
Preda, A. (2006) 'Socio-technical agency in financial markets: the case of the stock ticker'. *Social Studies of Science*, 36(5): 753–782.
Rao, H. (1998) 'Caveat emptor: the construction of non-profit consumer watchdog organizations'. *American Journal of Sociology*, 103(4): 912–961.
Rao, H., H. Greve and G. Davis. (2001) 'Fool's gold: social proof in the initiation and abandonment of coverage by Wall Street analysts', *Administrative Science Quarterly*, 46(3): 502–526.
Samuelson, P. (1965) 'Proof that properly anticipated prices fluctuate randomly', *Industrial Management Review*, 6(2): 41–49.
Sargent, C. (2000) 'The All-American Research Team'. *Institutional Investor*, 25(10): 57–79.
Sargent, C. and B. K. Jane (2000) 'The 2000 All-America research team. The best analysts of the year – Convertibles.' *Institutional Investor*, 25(10): 1.
Sargent, C. and B. K. Jane (2000b) 'The 2000 All-America research team. The best analysts of the year – New Media.' *Institutional Investor*, 25(10): 1.
Sargent, C. and B. K. Jane (2000c) 'The 2000 All-America Research Team: The best analysts of the year – Technology.' *Institutional Investor*, 25(10): 1.
Savage, L. (1954) *The Foundations of Statistics*. Wiley: New York.
Schack, J. (2001) 'Should Analysts Own Stock in Companies They Cover?' *Institutional Investor*, 26(5): 60–71.

Scharfstein, D. and J. Stein, (1990) 'Herd behaviour and investment,' *American Economic Review*, 80(3): 465–479.
Securities and Exchange Commission. (2002) 'Investor Alert: "Analyzing Analyst Recommendations".' http://www.sec.gov/investor/pubs/analysts.htm
The Economist. (2000) 'E-commerce: Too few pennies from heaven.' July 1: 65. Anonymous.
Trueman, B. (1994) 'Analyst forecasts and herding behavior'. *Review of Financial Studies*, 7(1): 97–124.
Turner, V. and E. Turner. (1986) 'Performing ethnography.' In V. Turner and E. Turner (eds), *The Anthropology of Performance*. New York: PAJ Publications.
Tushman, M. and P. Anderson. (1986) 'Technological discontinuities and organizational environments'. *Administrative Science Quarterly*, 31(3): 439–465.
Veverka, M. (1999) 'Plugged in: Amazon's biggest bull is irked with the e-tailer for failing to move toward profitability'. *Barron's*. Nov 1, p. 64.
Vickers, M. (2000) 'Unconventional Wisdom from Lehman.' *Businessweek*, December 11, p. 65.
Zuckerman, E. W. (1999) 'The categorical imperative: securities analysts and the illegitimacy discount', *American Journal of Sociology*, 104(5): 1398–1438.
Zuckerman, E. W. (2004) 'Structural incoherence and stock market activity'. *American Sociological Review*, 69(3): 405–432.
Zuckerman, E. and H. Rao. (2004) 'Shrewd, crude or simply deluded? Comovement and the internet stock phenomenon'. *Industrial and Corporate Change*, 13(1): 171–212.

Where do analysts come from? The case of financial chartism

Alex Preda

Introduction

Financial analysts have received increased sociological attention in recent years, partly due to their prominence in global financial markets and partly because their market position and activities illustrate more general questions, related to forms of economic expertise, to the role of intermediary groups, and to the relationship between economic theories and market activities (eg, Swedberg, 2005; Bruce, 2002; Fogarty and Rogers, 2005; and also Beunza and Garud in this volume).[1] In contrast, the status of the analysts themselves and, in particular, their status as experts, has received relatively little attention.

At least two independent sets of theoretical arguments are being made with respect to financial analysts. The first set, coming from economic sociology, states that information intermediaries confer legitimacy upon financial securities by classifying these according to categories accepted by market actors (eg, Zuckerman, 1999). The second, more general argument, initiated in the sociology of scientific knowledge, claims that economic theories are not mere representations, but tools of active intervention (eg, Barry and Slater, 2002; Callon, 1998, 2004; MacKenzie and Millo, 2003). While the first argument is a structural-functionalist one, the second argument emphasizes the agential role of economic technologies. A central aspect of this agential role is that economic technologies (which include not only theories and classifications but also trading software) allow market actors to project paths of future action and thus to process transaction-relevant uncertainties. Against this general background, Beunza and Garud, for instance, argue in this volume that financial analysts coordinate classifications, analogies and metrics which, taken together, make value calculable. This argument expands on Ezra Zuckerman's position according to which analysts classify securities, conferring legitimacy upon them.

Both positions imply that financial analysis is a legitimate form of economic expertise, accepted as such by market actors. It is indirectly assumed that the relationship between academic economics and financial analysis is a non-problematic one. Fogarty and Rogers (2005, pp. 333–334) point at the constitution of financial analysts as a quasi-professional group, marked by internal differentiation, and sharing with academic economic theory a set of core assumptions about economic value. It is also indirectly assumed that financial analysts emerge because of a functional need of market participants, namely the need to classify, order, and process information with the aim of reducing uncertainties about value. In addition, a premise is made that (fundamental) value constitutes the most important piece of information with respect to market decisions. Only by making value calculable can market actors compare (fundamental) value with the price, and decide whether securities are over- or undervalued.

Nevertheless, can we find a branch of financial analysis[2] which does not fit this bill? What happens when there is apparently no need for classification and category-building as prerequisites for calculating value? Indeed, what happens when (fundamental) value isn't even taken into account? And what happens when this particular form of financial expertise does not share any set of core assumptions with academic financial theory but, on the contrary, they are at odds?

In contemporary financial markets, we encounter a group of information intermediaries who apparently do not classify securities as a means of evaluating their intrinsic value and who do not regard value as an explanatory variable. This group employs theory-like premises[3] that clash with the main assumptions of academic financial economics, namely the random walk hypothesis. It is the group of financial chartists, or technical analysts. Their presence, persistence, and success do not fit a structural-functionalist explanation. How then can we account for their emergence?

I examine here the case of technical analysts as a particular form of economic expertise, emphasizing the relationships between theory producers and users. In a first step, I outline the theoretical frame supporting the empirical analysis. This frame highlights the double bind between producing and using economic expertise. The production of expertise actively influences the users' agendas. According to this perspective, the success of technical analysis depends less on its capacity to calculate value, than on its capacity to shape cognitive agendas. At the same time, expert knowledge is not only a description of the domain of reference but also a tool used in interventions upon that domain. Second, I specify the methods used here. Third, I examine the emergence of technical analysis as a successful form of financial expertise, in spite of being at odds with academic theories and having little concern regarding the issue of value.

The empirical data used here consists of memoirs, articles, and manuals written by the founding fathers of financial chartism. These were a group of brokers-turned-analysts who were active between 1900 and 1930 on the East Coast of the USA. I focus on how brokers-turned-analysts formed a group of knowledge intermediaries and forged ties with the brokerage community in New York City, successfully selling their theory as a decision-making instrument, and as a privileged form of knowledge. The data has been obtained through research in several financial archives, which have been revisited and repeatedly combed for new data.[4] During these examinations, I could not identify any other, earlier group of financial chartists active on the East Coast of the USA and tied to New York City brokers. I am not aware of any other earlier group practicing financial chartism on a different major stock exchange of the time (ie, circa. 1900 or earlier), like London or Paris. In a historical perspective, therefore, I suggest that financial chartism was the product of the group I describe here.

Financial chartism as expert knowledge

Financial chartism (aka technical analysis) is defined as a 'method of forecasting the prices of stocks, futures contracts, indexes, or any kind of financial instrument' (New York Institute of Finance, 1989, p. xiii)[5]. It is one of the major methods for analysing financial securities, the other one being fundamental analysis. While fundamental analysts attempt 'to discern cause-and-effect relationships between a security and its price [. . .] technical analysts do not attempt to explain why prices move as they do. [. . .] They attempt to detect patterns in market action that they can identify as having happened often enough in the past to be reliable as an indicator of future price levels' (New York Institute of Finance, 1989, p. 2). Technical analysts claim that they are able to forecast the prices of financial securities without postulating a causal relationship between prices and fundamental economic data, such as profits and losses, balance of payments, or interest rates. This claim is grounded in the thesis that there are regularities of price movements and that future movements can be inferred by studying past regularities. The main analytical instruments are financial charts, or minute diagrams of variations in price and volume. In addition to diagrams of individual prices and volumes, financial chartists also use diagrams of price indexes, which aggregate securities by economic sectors and industries.

Chartism uses a special vocabulary in order to designate patterns of price movements: for example, analysts talk of breaking gaps, flat bottoms, sauce bottoms, falling flags, head and shoulders, or symmetrical coils, among others[6]. They geometrically process charts in order to highlight patterns of price movements; for instance, chartists draw channel lines in order to identify deviations in these movements, or trend lines in order to identify general market trends (New York Institute of Finance, 1989; DeMark, 1994).

The tenets of financial chartism run counter to academic financial economics, which maintains that price movements are random; therefore future movements cannot be inferred from past ones. They also run counter to the economic tenet that there must be a relationship between the prices of financial securities, on the one hand, and fundamental economic data, on the other. In spite of being considered 'unscientific,' chartism has made a very good career in financial markets. There are professional associations at the local and national level in North and South America, Europe, Asia, Africa, and Australia. More than 30 national associations are members of the International Federation of Technical Analysts. The US Market Technicians Association, for instance, has a membership of 430 full members and 1841 affiliates[7]. Major financial institutions employ technical analysts. Professional bodies at the national and international level are responsible for certifying technical analysts; they organize their schooling, conduct examinations, publish books and periodicals; they have annual meetings and seminars, and aggregate job market information. Technical chartists are then organized as a professional body at national and international levels. If we take into account that their practice is at odds with academic economics, this success becomes even more remarkable.

In the USA, for instance, the first professional association of technical analysts was founded in 1970 in San Francisco (http://www.tsaasf.org, downloaded on 09/07/04). Technical analysts, however, were active as a group several decades before formal organization occurred. It would be sensible, then, to examine that period as well, if we want to know more about the social processes through which it emerged. This argument is supported by the observation that the existence of a professional group does not necessarily imply its formal professional organization from the start. Andrew Abbott (1988, p. 79) argues that the social organization of a profession has three major aspects: groups, controls, and worksites. Before formal professional organization takes place, a group can establish jurisdiction over the expert knowledge it produces. Before establishing jurisdiction, however, expert knowledge has to be generated and defined as such.

We are confronted here with a successful body of expert knowledge, the adherents of which grew into a professional body and established themselves as theory intermediaries in financial markets. It should be stressed here again that technical analysis is not merely a recent fad: as expert knowledge, it has been successful for almost one hundred years. Neither can technical analysis be seen as collective illusion; this would imply that its practitioners, market actors, the broader public, and a considerable number of financial institutions have been under an irrational spell for a very long time. Nor can it be reduced to a self-fulfilling prophecy, since (a) it does not imply a simple belief, but structured body of knowledge which (b) is regarded as valid by producers and users.

Financial expertise and information intermediaries

A sociological analysis of information intermediaries in financial markets is confronted with the problems of extension (Collins and Evans, 2002) and multiplication. That is, how to analyse claims of authority that extend to forms of economic knowledge which are quasi-professionalized but do not enjoy the same epistemic status with academic economics? Moreover, how do claims of authority multiply in the economic field, to the effect that we might encounter forms of expertise which collide with each other, but retain their claims? In this perspective, the expertise of financial analysis is thus situated on a continuum that stretches from academic economics to lay economic knowledge; they claim special authority for a particular domain, an authority which is neither entirely derived from economic theories, nor matched by lay economic knowledge. Stephen P. Turner (2003, pp. 49–50) suggests that the authority of such expertise is motivated by persuasion devices and by the ability of a knowledge-producing group to achieve closure over a specific domain. What counts, then, is the group's successful, legitimate monopolization of a domain of knowledge rather than it responding to a pre-existing functional need for that domain. This monopolization requires not only control over access to knowledge production but also the successful persuasion of users that they need a special form of knowledge in their activities.

Expert knowledge has implicit, as well as explicit aspects. The former are given by the practitioners' skills and abilities[8] to tinker with and interpret (financial) data. The explicit aspects consist, among others, of rationalizing discourses offering a more or less coherent, systematic view of the domain over which experts claim epistemic authority. For instance, forms of economic expertise imply not only the ability to select, read, and interpret economic data, but also discourses about economic phenomena, which provides users with systematic explanations, rationalizations, and justifications of these phenomena. While not always subjected to (or able to withstand) empirical validity tests, these explanations have the capacity of absorbing empirical data.

Discourses of expertise have not only representational but also instrumental features. Their representational side designates the ability to reference a state of the world; their instrumental features, by contrast, are enacted when such a discourse is mobilized by a social group according to its own interests, as serving a particular agenda. What counts here is not the truth value of the underlying theory but the discourse's capacity to contribute to achieving the state desired by the group. A special situation can arise when the state to be achieved is the same as for the state of the world referenced by the discourse. For example, an economic or psychologic theory describes a state x'. At the same time, the theory is mobilized by certain social groups directly interested to effect a change in its state x. In this case, the theory helps achieve a change the state from the state x to the state x', which it claims to describe. It is not constative, but performative.

Cases where forms of expertise are mobilized by social groups according to their interests, thus changing the state of the world they describe, have been studied by, among others, Ian Hacking (1995), Donald MacKenzie and Yuval Millo (2003) and Michel Callon (1998). Ian Hacking, for instance, has shown how psychiatric theories of multiple personality disorder have been embraced by patient groups and therapists with specific agendas, thus creating the psychological reality they claimed to describe. While strongly contested initially in the psychiatric community, these theories became the norm after therapists systematically signalled cases of multiple personality disorder, confirmed by the patients themselves. Donald MacKenzie and Yuval Millo described how the Merton-Scholes-Black formula for computing the price of financial derivatives has been adopted by traders on the Chicago Board of Trade because it served their particular interests in the competition with the New York Stock Exchange. Once put to use in financial transactions, the formula generated the kind of price data needed to confirm its validity. Michel Callon, who must be credited with the introduction of the performativity concept in economic sociology, has reopened an earlier case studied by Marie-France Garcia (1986), where the organization of a producer market was re-shaped by the market manager according to the precepts of rational actorhood he had learned in an economics course.[9]

The argument, then, is that forms of expertise can have an instrumental character, determined by, among other factors, the interests of the group which adopts the theory in order to further its own agenda. Once the expert knowledge is adopted, this group adapts the referent to expert epistemic claims (ie, patient groups embrace multiple personalities, use of formulas generates adequate price data, and so forth).

Therefore, a first aspect is that expert knowledge can achieve closure over a domain by being adopted (and adapted) by user groups. This adoption makes the referential aspects of expert discourse interlock with instrumental features: the discourse describes a state x′, which it has helped create. A form of economic expertise which fits (or enhances) the users' agenda and shapes its domain of reference at the same time achieves closure: it is exclusively adopted by users and can withstand contestations.

There is, however, a further aspect. Expert knowledge is first adopted by practitioners because of their specific agendas; after adoption, expert knowledge modifies its own referent. The primary role here is played by the users' interests, which are taken as given. Groups of producers and users organize themselves around common, socially constituted interests and activities (Weber, 1978 [1921], pp. 302–303; Bourdieu, 1977; Swedberg, 2005). Expert knowledge can play an important role in this process: producer and user groups may become mutually susceptible to each other (MacKenzie, 2004) and shape each other's agenda (eg, Pinch, 2003). An example which comes to mind is that of some groups of Apple users, who are status groups (creative, unconventional, upper income) and have entered a relationship of mutual susceptibility with the producers of Apple software. Instead of withdrawing from the stage, producers act as intermediaries between user groups, actively influencing the constitution of the users' agendas and interests.

Therefore, we must examine the extent to which production and use of expert knowledge are mutually susceptible to each other, and how expert knowledge shapes its uses. An additional aspect here is that expert knowledge can include its own definition. Expert financial knowledge, for instance, can describe transactions relevant to its domain; these descriptions, however, can assume that a particular knowledge (ie, the expert knowledge itself) is appropriate to support transactions. Descriptions of financial transactions would include expert knowledge as its own referent. Under the conditions of closure achieved by an expert group, this circularity would almost automatically occur. More generally put, we can encounter situations where a theory describes the reference x. At the same time, the uses for this theory are part of x. In this case, the theory appears both as a description (or interpretation) of the users' actions and an intrinsic feature of these actions.

According to this argument, the relationship between producers and users of expert knowledge is constituted at two interdependent levels. At the first level, expert knowledge would shape the agenda of user groups, either by enhancing existing elements/ interests, or by introducing new ones. At a second level, users are already pre-configured by the expert knowledge (Woolgar, 1991, pp. 39, 42) they adopt. Users adopt then certain representations of themselves which, when put to work in practical actions, become intrinsic to the users' self-understanding and to their actions. The double bind of expert knowledge, essential in achieving stability and monopolistic closure, designates the loop between theory production and theory use at two levels: (1) that of group activities; (2) that of the status of the expertise as an interpretation and an integral part of the users' actions.

At this point, one question arises: isn't this similar to the notion of self-fulfilling prophecy (Merton, 1973, pp. 533–534)? I argue that it is not. Merton's concept of self-fulfilling prophecy is that of a set of beliefs that come true because they are enacted by their holders. These beliefs do not (necessarily) concern a body of knowledge. The double bind between producers and users focuses on the social mechanisms through which a body of expert knowledge adapts a referent to its own description of this referent. With respect to the notion of performativity of economic theories (and, more generally, of expert economic knowledge) advanced by Michel Callon and Donald MacKenzie, I suggest that the notion of double bind can help us better understand how expert knowledge achieves its performative character. The performativity of expert knowledge cannot be reduced to its adoption by users because it helps advance these users' agenda. The users' belief in expert knowledge, their attachment to it, and the ability of knowledge producers to achieve lasting monopolistic closure over their domain need to be accounted for too. These elements become even more important in cases where expert knowledge is not endowed with the prestige of academic theories (or even clash with these theories). In such cases, we have to explain how knowledge achieves authority and is regarded as valid by users, without being sanctioned by scientific authorities.

With respect to the sociological analysis of information intermediaries, this notion can help us better understand the following aspects: (1) how experts like chartists position themselves and are accepted as intermediaries between different user groups; (2) how expert knowledge becomes established in fields of economic practice, without necessarily being invested with academic authority.

In the following sections, I will examine the emergence of chartism along the lines defined above. Three aspects are in the foreground: the emergence of chartists as a status group and their ties to the community of stock brokers; the users' and producers' agendas; the authority of chartist theories in the community of practitioners and of theorists. I start here with a specification of the methods I use, followed by a short overview of what financial chartism is.

Methods

My argument has been that we cannot explain the emergence of financial experts (and expertise) like financial analysts only with respect to a functional need they cover; there are cases (such as technical analysts) which do not fit this model. Rather, we need to take into account (1) the relationship between production and use of expertise, together with (2) the ways in which users are pre-configured in the body of expert knowledge they employ. The main thrust of the argument is that a double bind locks in users to expert knowledge. Examining the relationship between production and use of expertise requires the investigation of the social processes through which expert groups of analysts emerged in financial markets and entered into relationships with practitioners. Then we should be able to investigate the link between production and use of charts analysis, and establish the mechanisms through which expert knowledge is adopted. This requires an investigation of the strategies through which producers distribute their expert knowledge and persuade users to adopt it. Since this knowledge is embodied in texts, visual tools (like charts), and statistics, we can highlight how users are pre-configured by expert knowledge. In a further step, these configurations can be related to the persuasion devices and strategies used by knowledge producers, in order to show how this body of knowledge locks in a domain of financial action.

An investigation of these processes, centered on a major financial market (the New York Stock Exchange) requires a focused case study. According to the above arguments, such a case study should identify and analyse a concrete group of analysts that forged a specific relationship with users – that is, with stock brokers and investors. Indeed, the empirical evidence shows that such a group existed, emerging some decades before fundamental analysts came on stage as a quasi-professional group. How, then, did this group of experts emerge?

Expert knowledge and the social organization of financial marketplaces in New York City

As mentioned above, the main tenet of technical analysis is that future price movements can be inferred from past ones. The key analytical instrument in this respect is the financial chart, which serves as a visual record of changes in price and volume data as they happen. In other words, the requirements for data are that they should be (1) minute, (2) accurate, (3) fresh, and (4) standardized. Price and volume data must be minute, because otherwise important trends might get lost. They must be accurate and standardized, because otherwise they could not truly reflect market processes. They must be fresh, because otherwise they could not be relevant.

The conditions (1)–(4) require a standardized process through which price data are continuously and accurately recorded as they are generated in transactions. Price records can be then processed in a chart form and used as the empirical basis for forecasting market movements. Such a standardized recording process should be an intrinsic part of financial transactions (data are recorded as they are generated) and an important element of the financial marketplace.

Price lists had existed since the 18th century, but the recording process was not standardized. In fact, until the 1870s, price data was recorded through a complicated social arrangement consisting of brokers on the trading floor, courier boys, and paper slips. Data were neither fresh, standardized, accurate, minute, nor continuous. The New York Stock Exchange consisted in an official, discontinuous market and a parallel, unofficial, yet continuous one. The first was known as the Regular Board, and the second as the Open Board (Preda, 2006). In addition, several official and unofficial stock exchanges were present in New York City. These parallel markets, together with a non-standardized system for recording price data, made the latter unreliable. In December 1867, the stock ticker was introduced to Wall Street brokerage offices and on the floor of the New York Stock Exchange. In 1872, it made its appearance on the London Stock Exchange. During the 1870s, after some technical difficulties were fixed, it was adopted on a larger scale by brokerage offices in New York City and in the USA. The stock ticker allowed recording price data in near real time, as this data were generated in financial transactions. Since the same type of instrument was used to record all price data from all transactions on the floor, it standardized price data to a considerable degree.

The diffusion of the stock ticker was accompanied by conflicts among several groups of actors interested in having control over this data:

(1) The telegraph companies, which fought for monopoly as data providers. In the late 1860s, there were several companies using different types of ticker to provide price data from the floor of the NYSE. By the mid-1870s, the Western Telegraph Company had achieved a monopoly and used a single type of ticker machine.
(2) The official stock brokers of the New York Stock Exchange were organized as a status group based on wealth and exclusive access to the intermediation of financial transactions. They tried to control the spread of stock tickers and prevent other stock exchanges (eg, the Consolidated Petroleum Exchange) from using these machines for data recording purposes. They also fought to drive tickers out of bucket shops and prevent these latter from having access to price data.[10] These efforts resulted in tickers on the floors of the NYSE and of the Chicago Stock Exchange being destroyed or removed, respectively, at least twice, in the 1880s and the 1890s, in order to prevent the uncontrolled spread of price data. The New York Stock Exchange reached an agreement with the Western Telegraph Company that stock tickers could be installed only in approved brokerage offices.
(3) The brokers on the London Stock Exchange and those on the NYSE clashed over the use of arbitrage-relevant price information. London brokers tried to restrict and control price data generated in London in order to keep an informational edge in arbitrage activities.
(4) The owners of bucket shops, not necessarily small scale operators, in some cases had enough financial clout to fight off NYSE attempts to cut them off from ticker services.

The 1880s and the 1890s were marked by continuous fights among at least these four groups over control of price data.

The introduction of the stock ticker enabled price data to be recorded in near real time. This minute recording led to a considerable increase in the available volume of data. The organization of the trading floor took this into account by introducing trading posts, each equipped with its own ticker and specializing in a certain class of financial securities (railways, mines, and the like). In the brokerage office, the increased data volume, together with the physical constraints of the stock ticker led to the introduction of a new profession: the tape reader, a clerk who stood by the ticker, following the tape, and selected and classified the price data according to security names or classes. Continuous price data required thus continuous attention, professional specialization, and differentiation in the tasks performed by the brokerage office.

The constitution of a group of experts

Against the background of these conflicts and organizational transformations, some brokers began shifting away from trading and reoriented themselves toward data interpretation.

The archival data I have identified show that many of the first technical analysts had engineering or statistical training. They noticed the errors and unreliable character of the statistics supplied by brokerage houses and began to produce their own statistics. An example in this sense is Richard Demille Wyckoff, who started by studying statistics in the 1880s (Wyckoff, 1930, p. 27). Another example is Roger Ward Babson, who studied engineering and business at MIT in the 1890s, graduated, worked for a brokerage house in Boston, and founded afterwards the Babson Statistical Organization (Babson, 1935, pp. 53, 76). Wyckoff worked around 1900 as a stock broker for the firm of Price, McCormick & Co., where he was also in charge of gathering information on stocks and writing a newsletter for customers (1930, p. 95). After this initiative failed, he left and founded his own brokerage firm in 1903; four years later, he shifted entirely to publishing investment advice literature. In October 1907, he published *The Ticker*, where the first technical analyses appeared. In 1910, Richard Wyckoff (under the pseudonym Rollo Tape) published what is probably the first book of technical analysis, called *Studies in Tape Reading* (Tape, 1910). The first issues of *The Ticker* were a mixture of gossip about famous speculators, investment advice, and technical analyses (primitive compared with the ones we encounter today) (Wyckoff, 1930, p. 159). In the beginning, *The Ticker* was a one-man show, with Wyckoff writing all the gossip articles and compiling all the statistics. By 1917, however, Wyckoff had managed to enroll other chartists as contributors, as well as known speculators, who could confirm chartism as the best method available (Wyckoff, 1930, p. 219).

One of the chartists who published articles in *The Ticker* was Roger Ward Babson, who had founded the Babson Statistical Organization in Boston in

1904. Initially, Babson's firm indexed the circulars of bond offerings and sold this information monthly to brokerage houses. He won Boston's brokerage houses, as well as houses from New York, Chicago, Cleveland, Detroit, and Saint Louis, as his customers. (Babson met Wyckoff on an advertising trip to New York.) He then sold this information service to Arthur B. Elliott, the founder of the National Quotation Bureau (Babson, 1935, p. 138). The National Quotation Bureau (NQB), founded in 1911, compiled price and volume data from various brokerage offices active in the over the counter market (known as the Pink Sheets). In other words, the NQB service circumvented the monopoly of the Western Telegraph and of NYSE on price data and bundled together price data coming from smaller exchanges and offices which were not members of the NYSE.

After selling the bond information newsletter, Babson started another information service, collecting and compiling data on stock earnings. This information was sold to banks and brokerage offices alike. Shortly thereafter, Babson added evaluations to this newsletter, but met with adversity from banks and brokers whenever he issued critical evaluations of stock (Babson, 1935, p. 139). Since the income on this service fluctuated according to how stocks were evaluated, Babson abandoned it. In 1907, he bought the Moody Manual Company from his friend John Moody. The Moody Manual Company compiled information on the earnings and stock prices of listed stock companies. In addition to this service, Babson started in 1907 the *Babson Reports*, which consisted of two features:

> (1) They show *when* to buy and *when* to sell; and (2) *what* to buy and *what* to sell. It is the first of this features for which the Babsonchart is used. [. . .] There was nothing new about charting the ups and downs of the production or the price of individual commodities or securities. Everyone was doing this. A few of us had begun to combine different commodities or securities into a composite chart, although I was the first to use this name. Really upon this composite idea the organization was founded. *Our contribution to the analysis and forecasting of business conditions was in connection with the study of the* areas *above and below this Normal Line.* Other systems of forecasting considered only the *high* and *low* of the charts, while our system considered the *areas* of the charts (Babson, 1935, p. 147; italics in original).

The 'Normal Line,' Babson's invention, was concocted in discussions with Professor George E. Swain, the head of the civil engineering course at MIT. Today, the 'normal line' is known among technical analysts as the 'trend line.' The *Babson Reports*, therefore, used charts for forecasting market movements. In the above quote, Babson states clearly that he was not the only one doing this around 1907. Richard D. Wyckoff, discussed above, is another case in point.

Relevant here is the fact that these former brokers and information providers knew each other and acted as a group: Babson published articles in a magazine edited by Wyckoff. John Moody was a friend of Babson and sold him the Moody Manual Company. In the 1920s, Wyckoff's associate editor at the *The Ticker*, George Selden, published books promoting technical analysis as the true method of forecasting the market (Selden, 1922). Another acquaintance of Wyckoff, Samuel Armstrong Nelson, republished in 1902 Charles Dow's articles from the *Wall Street Journal* (Nelson, 1902, ch. 7–20). (Dow was the editor of the *Wall Street Journal*. He had died in 1902 without publishing anything beyond these articles.) Wyckoff republished the articles in 1920 in *The Magazine of Wall Street* (heir to *The Ticker*), with a preface by Selden, under the title *Scientific Stock Speculation*. In his articles and memoirs, Wyckoff systematically promoted Charles Dow as the man on whose ideas technical analysis is based.[11]

This group compiled, published, and sold data on bonds, stocks, and company earnings. Its members founded companies of technical analysis. Babson did this with his Babson Statistical Company, co-owned with his wife. Wyckoff followed him in 1920 with the Richard D. Wyckoff Analytical Staff, Inc. Subscription to its services cost $1,000 per year. The company provided a Trend Trading Service, an Analytical Staff Service, and an Investors' Advisory Board (Wyckoff, 1930, p. 249). While Wyckoff sold both to brokerage houses and the investing public, Babson sold exclusively to brokerage houses and banks. Wyckoff, for example, had in 1911 an exclusive contract for technical analysis with the brokerage house Thompson, Towle &Co, but he also sold *The Ticker* to the general public (1930, p. 188). The group also actively sought contact with brokerage houses. Wyckoff was frustrated that, as a broker, he was not allowed to advertise on a large scale (eg, by sending circulars). Initially, Babson sold his newsletter door-to-door to brokerage houses. At least some of its members had brokerage experience: Wyckoff and Babson were former brokers, and John Moody worked for a brokerage house in New York. Wyckoff systematically enrolled known speculators (with whom he had contracts) as contributors to his magazine, for confirming, from the viewpoint of practice, the adequacy of technical analysis.

In the 1930s, technical analysis became firmly established, with several organizations selling it as a product to brokerage houses, and several publications (books, magazines) promoting it to investors. The use of the typewriter and of the mimeograph made it easier to publish and distribute chartist books on a larger scale.[12] At least the following books were published in the 1930s as mimeographs: Orline Norman Foster's *Ticker Technique* (New York, 1935); D.W. McGeorge's *Tacking in the Stock Market* (Oakmont, PA, 1934); Meyer H. Weinstein's *The Real Boom in the Stock Market Is Here* (New York, 1936). In addition to them, there were at least the printed books of Wyckoff (*Studies in Tape Reading*, 1910), Babson (*The Future Method of Investing Money. Economic Facts for Corporations and Investors,* Boston, 1914), and William D. Gann (*Truth of the Stock Tape*, New York, 1923; *Wall Street Stock Selector*, New York, 1930). Authors like Weinstein and Gann worked for firms named the Financial Information Company (Weinstein) and the Financial Guardian (Gann). In view of the above, it can be argued that in the 1930s there was already a body of chartist literature available to investors and brokerage firms, and this literature was at least in part published by firms specialized in the collection and interpretation of financial price data.[13]

The producers' and users' agendas

From the reminiscences of the first chartists, it appears that there were several grounds for them leaving brokerage houses: (1) tight controls and restrictions exercised by brokers and (2) low status within the brokerage firms. Among the restrictions set in place by brokerage houses, the ban on advertising played a prominent role. On the brokers' part, this ban was set in place in order to avoid falling under federal regulation. The New York Stock Exchange was organized as a private association and therefore not susceptible to any regulation at the federal level. Mounting criticism of financial speculation, however, had repeatedly called for regulatory measures. One way for regulating stock exchange transactions was provided by the interstate commerce laws; advertising could be easily construed as (interstate) commerce by mail, therefore bringing transactions within easy regulatory reach. The ban on advertising was one of the most severely enforced by the board of the New York Stock Exchange, and cases were known where brokers had been expelled for this. Nevertheless, people like Richard Wyckoff wanted to circulate their statistics and use them both as a distinct commodity and as a means of attracting new clients. Some bucket shops, for instance, regularly distributed statistics as a marketing strategy. (But they were neither regarded as proper businesses nor members of the New York Stock Exchange.)

A second kind of control was control over the opinion expressed by statisticians and data compilers. Roger Babson mentioned that he clashed with his employers over negative recommendations he had made, and that this motivated him to leave his job. Banks and brokerage houses were interested in selling securities to clients, not to have the quality of their product questioned from within.

A further aspect was the low status enjoyed by data compilers and statisticians within brokerage houses. They were often asked to do menial jobs and their work was not acknowledged as important. Compiling statistics ranked low within brokerage houses, in financial, as well as in prestige terms. Both Babson and Wyckoff noticed that this was a feature of their situation at the career start, and that they wanted acknowledgment for skilled, difficult work. On the producers' side there were good reasons to want to become autonomous, to escape tight controls, and gain recognition. One of the ways to achieve this would have been to part company with brokerage houses and create a new, autonomous commodity (the chart), not subjected to constraints or to governmental regulation.

On the side of the potential users, there was perhaps a motive ranking above all: control over price information. Brokerages could not formally prevent people like Wyckoff or Selden from leaving and starting their own business. Brokers could not prevent such people from taking their skills with them. Moreover, if data interpretation was to become separated from brokerage, it could be used for attracting new clients without fear of regulatory consequences. A business alliance between brokers and data interpreters was rather favoured by pre-existing ties too. Another element influencing the brokers' agenda was imitation: once a few prominent speculators started endorsing Chartism, others followed. (As I will show below, the first chartist took care to get such endorsements.) Thus, while the producers and the users had different agendas, these were not incompatible and allowed for a producer-customer relationship. Such a relationship, however, would have required the transformation of analysis into an autonomous product, with its own standing and tradition.

Inventing a tradition

Financial chartists created their own figure of a founding father in the person of Charles Dow. Dow, who had died in 1902, did not produce a systematic theory; rather, his aim was to outline the general lines of reasoning which should be followed when observing the market. According to Dow: (1) surface appearances are deceptive; (2) one should cut losses short and let profits run; (3) correctly discounting the future is the road to wealth. The market has three kinds of overlapping movements: (a) day-to-day; (b) the short swing, running from two weeks to one month; (c) long time movements of four years or more (Nelson, 1902, pp. 36, 39). Applying the general lines of reasoning to these three movements (which should be studied with specific methods) will ensure financial success. Moreover, according to the way in which the general principles are applied to market movements, several methods of trading and types of traders can be distinguished, with different consequences (Nelson, 1902, pp. 58, 65). Richard Wyckoff, George Selden, and Samuel Armstrong Nelson republished Dow's articles and claimed that chartism was following Dow's principles.

Concomitantly, chartists sought to 'rediscover' publications as a support for their principles and methods. Babson (1935, p. 146) was influenced by *Benner's Prophecies of Futures Ups and Downs in Prices* (Benner, 1876) and *How Money Is Made in Security Investments* (Hall, 1908). Benner, who signed as 'an Ohio farmer,' considered that future prices of commodities could be predicted, although not on the grounds of agricultural statistics, which were unreliable (Benner, 1876, p. 23). Instead of statistics, price prophecies should be founded on the following ideas: (1) prices are exponents of 'accumulated wisdom'; (2) ups and downs of prices are repeated in cycles, and (3) extreme ups and downs alternate:

> An up and down or down and up in average prices, is in this book denominated a cycle.... And inside this rule, like a wheel within a wheel, is to be found our 'Cast iron rule,' which is that *one extreme invariably follows another*, as can be witnessed in all the operations of nature, in all the business affairs of man, and in all the ramifications of trade and industry; and in every cycle of average prices it is shown to what extent these extremes run (Benner, 1876, p. 27).

Benner, who did not purport to provide the reader with any explanation of why cycles occur, stated that 'we will risk our reputation as a prophet, and our chances for success in business upon our 11 year cycle in corn and hogs; in our 27 year cycle in pig and iron, and in our 54 year cycle in general trade, upon which we have operated with success in the past' (Benner, 1876, p. 122).

Benner's notion of cycles, similar to those of 'the law of action and reaction' and of 'market swings' expressed what intuition and experience had shown most traders and investors: prices go up and down.[14] Yet, this seemingly trivial notion of ups and downs was formulated as a law-like repeatability, one which cannot be revealed from the study of unreliable production statistics. The distrust towards what could be called 'fundamental' data was corroborated with the chartists' own observations about the low prestige of statistical work in brokerage firms.

Chartists also managed to enlist the support of well known speculators for their theories. People like J.W. Harriman, Frank A. Vanderlip, or Theodore E. Burton published articles in *The Ticker*, supporting the theories promoted by Wyckoff as an editor (Wyckoff, 1930, p. 219). Academic support was mobilized too. Roger Babson mentions in his memoirs that he discovered the 'Babson line' (aka the trend line) together with Prof. George E. Swain from the MIT. This discovery was presented as grounded in Newton's 'Law of Action and Reaction,' which 'may apply to economics as it does to physics, chemistry, astronomy, and other fields' (Babson, 1935, p. 147). Chartist theories did not come from nowhere, but had a founding father and were supported by the principles of natural science. This rhetoric of tradition combined three distinct kinds of voices, with different authorities: that of practical experience and commonsense (the 'Ohio farmer'), that of natural science (the MIT professor), and that of the financial establishment (Charles Dow). Yet, chartists were still facing the major task of persuading the public and, above all, the potential users in brokerage offices, that this sort of knowledge required special abilities.

The US economics literature of the 1910s and the 1920s did not treat financial markets as an object of systematic theoretical inquiry. In some cases, academic economists stressed the importance of the stock ticker as a means of getting fresh data (eg, Huebner, 1934 [1922], pp. 217–221), thus confirming the importance attributed to this machine by financial chartists. The situation, however, changed in the 1930s, when economists and statisticians started questioning the predictive claims of technical analysis. In 1933, Alfred Cowles 3rd published a paper based on a talk he had given at the American Statistical Association Meeting the previous year (Cowles, 1933), in which he examined the forecasts of financial services, publications, and insurance companies, concluding that there was no true predictive power in these forecasts. Criticisms continued in the 1950s and the 1960s; papers published in major economics journals claimed that chartist patterns were nothing more than statistical artefacts (Roberts, 1959) and that chart reading is 'perhaps an interesting pastime' (Fama, 1965, p. 34). In spite of these contestations, technical analysis managed to maintain its authority within financial markets, to continue its professionalization, and to expand its circle of practitioners.

One aspect which helps explain its endurance is that technical analysis had a manifold status. It was (1) an explanation of financial markets; (2) a technique of forecasting the market – that is, of generating interpretations of future price movements; (3) a set of instruments with the help of which these interpretations were produced; (4) a commodity sold by the members of the group to brokerage houses and, to a certain extent, to the investing public; (5) a product around which data producing enterprises/organizations emerged (like Babson's Statistical Organization or Wyckoff's Analytical Staff, Inc.); (6) a media discourse imbricated with other narratives of financial markets (eg, with speculators' accounts). These aspects cannot be separated from each other: the development of the theory and of the associated forecasting instruments was closely intertwined with the media discourse and the organizations of enterprises selling the theory to brokerage houses and banks.

The configuration of users

The ties among these analysts, together with their common preoccupation for gathering and processing financial data makes them into a group which, with respect to brokers and investors, tried to establish a monopoly over a set of knowledge activities relevant for these latter. Through its relationship with brokerage houses and known speculators, the expert group contributed to creating an interest in using the charts and the interpretive methods they promoted. Users were represented as depending upon the cognitive tools promoted by this group. Some of the persuasion strategies employed here are described by Richard Wyckoff in his memoirs:

> I had a friend who had been a member of the Exchange and who was well up on the technique of the market from the standpoint of the floor trader. We often discussed the difference between reading the tape simply to follow price changes (as most clients did) and reading the tape to judge the probable action of stocks in the immediate future. [. . .] This ideal tape operator should have no hopes or fears. He must play the game without a sign of nerves or mental strain; look upon profits or losses with equal equanimity. He must develop the kind of intuition that becomes a sixth sense in trading. Such an operator, we agreed, was generally evolved from a series of failures over many months or years; his education could be completed only through a long series of transactions, spread over long periods, which would perfect his operating personality into one that could play the game cold. He must have persistence to carry him through adverse times without discouragement, until his expertness and self-confidence match that of the surgeon who performs many operations, losing some patients but never losing his nerve. Such a man, with such a character and with that experience, should be a success at reading the tape (Wyckoff, 1930, pp. 168, 170).

True forecasting requires character; concomitantly, only experienced men, 'operating personalities' can become successful tape readers. Technical analysis is presented as appealing not only to the intellect, but to the entire personality of the trader.

The ticker and the chart played an essential role in connecting producers of expert knowledge with users. Both tools were indispensable instruments for brokers but, because they required permanent attention, they made necessary an early division of labour. Data compilers (the tape readers) appeared, and indeed became distinct from data users (brokers and investors). These data compilers were different from statistics compilers, who investigated archives and read past price lists, trying to reconstruct previous price movements. Compiling price data meant near real time compiling. It required attention, concentration, and time, which stock brokers could simply not afford to devote to this task.

The great quantity of continuously generated price data also required new modes of interpretation. The division of labour between compiling and using price data was thus tied to the need of interpreting price data in a way adequate to its continuous and massive character. According to the technical analysts, a new mode of interpretation should account for the sheer mass of price data now available and take this mass into account when explaining the market. Market judgment was re-conceptualized as distinct from (yet tied to) market action. Those involved in decision-making and market action had neither the time nor the attention and concentration necessary for judging the market. In the words of Richard Wyckoff:

> A broker's time is so occupied with the routine of the business that he is rarely able to devote sufficient time to the study and analysis of the stock market. Few people – stock brokers or others – are mentally equipped for the difficult work of forecasting price movements on the Stock Exchange and selecting the stocks that will yield more profits than losses to those who make commitments. Almost anyone with some years of experience in Wall Street can be correct in his judgment from time to time; but the problem is to be correct *most* of the time (Wyckoff, 1930, p. 116, italics in original).

In his memoirs, Wyckoff says that he decided to abandon brokerage and switch to analysis because as a broker he could not find time for the study of the market (p. 117). In Roger Babson's account, what inspired him to switch to data compiling and analysis was a lecture given by Booker T. Washington about his social experiments at Tuskegee.[15] Babson took over Washington's emphasis on the division of labour and combined it with the insight that in banks and brokerage houses data compilation had a shaky status. In some cases, brokers tried to do the compiling themselves. In some other cases, specialized data compilers were treated no better than office boys. Babson decided then to get out of brokerage and specialize in data compiling and analysis as a separate line of business (Babson, 1935, pp. 133–134). In both accounts, there is a stress put on the special status of financial knowledge: theory requires contemplation, not action (Wyckoff) and is not given due respect by brokers (Babson). Therefore, the production of theory has to be separated from its use, yet remain related to it.

The users were configured as depending upon a body of specialized knowledge, which they cannot obtain by themselves and therefore need experts in the interpretation of price movements. At the same time, the technological apparatus on which this knowledge depends (stock ticker, charts) is represented as requiring special skills and powers of interpretation, which brokers, being too busy, have not fully developed. In other words, this expert discourse claims an epistemic monopoly over the apparatus on which financial transactions depended to a large extent. Purchasing expert knowledge from its producers is seen as conferring authority and legitimacy upon brokers. Experts represented their relationship with brokers as a necessary symbiosis for sound decision-making.

Technical analysis as a successful theory of the market

In the previous sections, I have examined the processes through which technical analysis emerged and was adopted by brokers as a necessary body of expert knowledge. My argument has been that technical analysis was not only a theory but also a set of forecasting instruments, a discourse, and a commodity. Brokers were locked into using this expert knowledge, not only by their interest in accessing price interpretations, but also by the norms of 'good judgment' and 'good financial behaviour' produced by this discourse. Increased volumes of price data and new requirements for data interpretation were accompanied by a differentiation which restructured the activities of data compilers: the statistics compiler could not meet the new technology-related requirements. The low prestige associated with data compiling in brokerage firms was counteracted when analysts established a monopoly on data interpretation. They constituted themselves as a status group centered upon the production of a market theory, based in the interpretation of price data. They established authority for their theory by enrolling a founding father, the authority of the natural sciences, and of known speculators. The group of theory producers created an interest for their commodity on the part of brokers, by persuading the latter that their product enhanced the brokers' personality and their acumen. At the same time, theory producers addressed the investing public as a group of users distinct from that of brokers. The theory became a commodity, sought after by brokerage firms, and a general discourse about financial markets.

These social processes may help explain how technical analysis was accepted, yet we still lack here a full account of its epistemic monopoly. Technical analysis did not emerge against an empty background. During the last four decades of the 19th century, we can identify several attempts at assembling a theoretical perspective on financial markets:

(1) There were attempts at causal explanations formulated in the popular literature addressing investors, attempts which tied price movements to political and economic events.
(2) There were attempts at non-causal explanations, grounded in a biologistic interpretation of financial markets rather than a physicalist one (eg, Lefevre, 1870). These attempts, developed mainly in France, stressed the analogy between society and the human body; they ascribed the stock exchange a central place (ie, the heart), and argued that a causal explanation was irrelevant. What counted was a functionalist explanation of the social and economic functions of the stock exchange. Any attempts at searching for the causes of price movements were bound to fail.

(3) There were attempts at probabilistic explanations of the price movements, which also took an anti-causal stance. This line of reasoning, developed mostly in France (eg, Regnault, 1863; Bachelier, 1900; Jovanovic and Le Gall, 2001; Jovanovic, 2000) maintained that one can only compute the probability of the securities prices attaining a certain level. One could not discover the cause of price movements, because there were too many factors at play here.
(4) There were attempts at explaining investors' behaviour as opposed to attempts at explaining price behaviour. One of Louis Bachelier's key contributions in this respect was that it switched the perspective from investor behaviour to price behaviour.

Abstract, probabilistic models of price movements were developed preponderantly in France, which – and this is a significant element – did not have a price recording technology comparable to the ticker. (In fact, it had none at least until the 1930s.) In France, abstract models of price variations emerged partly as a sign of distrust in the accuracy of price recordings,[16] and partly as a more general distrust in statistics, which was seen as inferior to modeling (Desrosières, 1998, p. 282; Ménard, 1980, p. 534). Attempts to combine theoretical and statistical analysis of price movements, like that of Marcel Lenoir in 1913, were completely ignored in France (Desrosières, 1998, p. 283). Non-standardized, parallel price data, combined with a distrust of statistical data and a professional division between formal economic analysis (done in France mainly by engineers and actuaries, prone to modeling) and informal political economy (the domain of legally-trained French economists – see Breton, 1992, p. 32) contributed to the predominant position of formal modeling in France.

In New York, however, technical analysis did not encounter initial serious competition from an incompatible explanatory model like Regnault's and Bachelier's probabilistic explanations.[17] Chartists, too, distrusted statistics provided by companies and saw ticker price data as more reliable. In addition to this, however, they relied not on analytical principles borrowed from physics and/ or biology (although they paid lip service to the natural sciences), but rather on a tradition of 'prophecy', which mixed up practical experience with some statistical observations (see the place given to Benner's 'prophecies'). It could be conjectured here that this peculiar combination between technology and 'prophecy' (absent in France, where engineers and actuaries tried to compensate inaccurate data by abstract analysis) played a role in the emergence of chartism in a specific context.

As stated above, the aim of technical analysis is to forecast price movements on the grounds of detailed price charts, starting from the principles that (1) patterns of price variations are repeatable and (2) these patterns occur in repeatable situations:

> A lot of people say that charts are of no value in determining the future; that they simply represent past history. That is correct; they are records of the past, but the future is nothing but a repetition of the past. Every business man goes on the past

record of business in determining how to buy goods for the future. He can only judge by comparison with past records. We look up the record of a man, and if his past record has been good, we judge that his future will be good (Gann, 1923, p. 51).

This statement echoes the notion of prophesizing the past, one which relies on recognizing objects and events not as singular, but as types (Schutz, 2003 [1945], p. 257). Claims of forecasting price movements had been made before in the popular investment literature. These claims, however, were mostly tied to idiosyncratic knowledge of the 'market conditions' – that is, of the specific coalitions of speculators at work i n the market at a given time, of their ties with politics, of their interests, and the like. By contrast, technical analysis does not rely on knowledge of specific, historically contingent coalitions of interests, but claims that there are repeatable patterns of such forces, and repeatable reactions to them. These reactions are psychosocial in nature and follow general psychological rules. Regular patterns are fully reflected in patterns of price movements. On the one hand, then, prices are held fully to process and reflect the information available in the market; otherwise, the repeatability postulate would not hold:

> The tape tells the news minutes, hours and days before the news tickers, or newspapers, and before it can become current gossip. Everything from a foreign war to the passing of a dividend; from a Supreme Court decision to the ravages of the boll-weevil is reflected primarily on the tape (Tape, 1910, p. 11).

And:

> Stocks are no different than human beings – they have their peculiar habits and moves. It is just as easy to tell what a stock will do by getting acquainted with it and watching its moves over a long period of time, as it is to tell what a human being will do under certain conditions after you have known him for many years (Gann, 1923, pp. 59–60).

On the other hand, technical analysis admits fear, panic, ebullience, correlating price patterns to behaviour, which acts as an explanandum. In this respect, technical analysis appears as a vernacular sociology of financial markets. As Wyckoff put it, 'the market is mental':

> The market is made by the minds of many men. The state of these minds is reflected in the prices of securities in which their owners operate. Let us examine some of the individuals, as well as the influences behind certain stocks and groups of stocks in their various relationships. This will, in a sense, enable us to measure their respective power to affect the whole list or the specific issue in which we decide to operate (Tape, 1910, p. 38).

Authors like Babson concurred to this view: there are three kinds of stock market movements and each corresponds to a class of investors. Daily fluctuations cannot be foretold in any way and have no relations to the intrinsic value of the securities traded. The class of gamblers corresponds to this movement. The second kind is given by 'broad breaks and rallies of from five to ten points, extending over a few weeks.' These are due to the 'impatience and avariciousness' of professional traders. Finally, there are the 'long swings extending over one or more years.' To these corresponds the class of 'those with money and the courage of their convictions' (Babson, 1914, pp. 13–18).

Other authors, like William Gann (1923, pp. 55–57) distinguished seven zones of activity in the market, each corresponding to a stage of activity. The 'Normal Zone' corresponds to 'something near actual intrinsic value, as far as human judgment can be depended upon and as far as the ticker tape can analyze it from supply and demand.' Then there is the 'First Zone above Normal,' corresponding to periods of quite advancing prices. The 'Second Zone above Normal' corresponds to active pools of speculators which try to get the public interested in the market. The 'Third Zone or highest above Normal' corresponds to the public buying madly and will end in rapid and violent fluctuations, followed by a fall to the zones below normal. The 'First Zone below Normal' is the one where people who have missed the third stage above normal sell out. The 'Second Zone below Normal' is the one where conservative investors become active. Finally, the 'Third Zone below Normal' is marked by panic, 'great excitement throughout the country and reports of poor business.' While the 'Normal Zone' is something rather abstract, all the others are dominated by a certain class of market actors. In this perspective, there is little difference between Babson types of market movements and Gann's zones of the market.

This vernacular sociology of the market is grounded in knowledge about classes of market actors: it includes a typology, knowledge about what these classes do in certain situations, and how they react to events. At the same time, the knowledge crystallized in this theory is also the knowledge used by market actors in their actions. Knowledge about panic in the 'Third Zone below Normal' is also knowledge used when panics happen in this zone. Seen from this perspective, forecasting market movements, as technical analysis claims to do, is grounded in knowledge intrinsic to these market movements. To put in the terms of Harold Garfinkel (2002), technical analysis is not only a gloss on the market (ie, an interpretation of this latter), but also a formulation of the social order of the market. As such, it is intrinsic to market action. In this sense, its forecasting capacity consists in its account of the market as an orderly social phenomenon. In the form of technical charts, this account is integrated in the market action itself. What appears as dizzying price movements can be translated at any time into the language of classes of actors, of strategy patterns, and of emotions – that is, it can be made intelligible as an orderly social phenomenon. It is this intelligibility which is captured by the expert language of technical analysis.

Conclusion

My argument has been that technical analysis is characterized by a double bind between production and use of expert knowledge. At a first level, the agendas of producers and users shape the reciprocal positioning of these groups.

Analysts wanted more prestige and less control, while brokers, interested in access to price interpretation, wanted both a legitimating tool and an orderly, objectified account of the market. At a second level, expert knowledge appears both as a description of the users' actions and as an intrinsic feature of these actions. It describes what market actors do, but its categories are the categories through which the actors themselves make sense of their actions and reciprocal positions in the market.

Technical analysis does not include a formula for computing theoretical prices, towards which real prices will converge as a result of the use of this formula. In this rigorous sense, the question about its forecasting power can be answered in the negative. There is, however, a second sort of forecasting: prophesizing the past, a mode which is based on the assumption that events belong to knowable types and categories. Alfred Schutz saw Teiresias, the blind prophet of ancient Athens as paradigmatic for this kind of forecasting, relying on categories-based 'anticipations of everyday life [which] will be [all] realized *modo potentiali*, as chances' (Schutz, 2003 [1945], p. 260). Such anticipations are grounded in the assumption of the orderliness of social phenomena, subsumable to known types and categories. This form of prophecy (or performativity, if one wants to call it so) contributes to creating orderly phenomena, by legitimating and reproducing operational categories of order. In this perspective, technical analysis did something other forms of financial expertise could not do: it provided market actors with an account of 'the market' as an orderly, totalizing phenomenon (in Durkheim's sense), one which could not be derived from isolated, individual experiences (Durkheim, 1965 [1915], p. 489). This account, based on observing and processing mechanically generated price data, did not come from outside the market, from ethnographers observing transactions (which could not even be observed in their totality) but from within, from market practitioners turned observers. It became intrinsic to the phenomenon of 'the market', indispensable for traders and investors acting from the observation of abstract numbers. (It is relevant here that contemporary online traders, who derive their information almost exclusively from on-screen observation, rely heavily on technical analysis.) Technical analysis created social categories (both actor and action types) which could be identified on price charts. These categories represent markets to users as orderly, intelligible entities, without the users being able (or need) directly to access the totality of financial transactions supposed to constitute the market.

Technical analysis endowed a group (the analysts) with powers of representation, contributing to the social closure of stock exchanges, yet reproducing the notion (if not illusion) of wider accessibility. Once this power of representation became autonomous, it allowed for internal differentiations according to principles, methods, schools, and styles of analysis, for a variety of competing groups gathering around different forms of expertise, yet mutually supporting each other in this competition. We witness today many styles of market prophecy, as well as their growing influence, related, among others, to the spread of online trading. Teiresias' gift of 'seeing' seems to be anything but vanished.

Alex Preda

Notes

1 Initial versions of this chapter have been presented at the workshop 'Perfomativities of Economics,' Ecole des Mines de Paris, 2004, at the Annual Meetings of the American Sociological Association in Philadelphia, 2005, and of the Society for Social Studies of Science, Vancouver, 2006. The chapter has greatly benefited from the comments of Michel Callon, Donald MacKenzie, Fabian Muniesa, and Yuval Millo, as well as from conversations with Lucia Siu and Philip Roscoe.
2 I should stress here that financial analysis cannot be reduced to the dichotomy fundamental/technical analysis. There are forms of financial analysis related to credit worthiness, for instance, which I will not examine in this context (but see, for instance, Cohen 1999).
3 Rigorously seen, technical analysis has a deductive-nomological structure, but does not calculate or predict exact price values. Throughout this chapter, I employ the term theory in relationship to technical analysis.
4 The archives used were the New York Public Library, the New York Historical Society, the Library Company of Philadelphia, the Guildhall Library and the British Library.
5 Research in financial economics suggests that stock prices are influenced by analysts' recommendations; investors look at these recommendations for information returns. The costs for searching for information are reflected in commissions for trading, and therefore appear as an indirect product of financial analysis (eg, Womack, 1996, pp. 138, 164).
6 A breaking gap, for example, is a gap in the price chart which indicates the start of a new level of action in the market. A bottom is an event where the price reaches a low and remains there, or a low, then another lower low, then another higher low. A saucer is a gradual change in the trend line. A falling flag is a bearish continuation chart pattern which lasts less than three weeks and slopes against the prevailing trend. A symmetrical coil is made by two trend lines which intersect in rising and declining, respectively. (A more comprehensive overview of technical terms is provided by numerous publications, as well as by websites such as stockcharts.com, for instance.)
7 See http://www.mta.org/eweb/DynamicPage.aspx?Site=MTA&WebKey=9263a439-9ca6-46a8-aa49-a0d3e6b5d139, downloaded on 04/11/05.
8 These skills and abilities can include special forms of hand-eye coordination, motoric perception, the ability to 'see' things, etc.
9 See Garcia-Parpet (2007) for an English translation of Marie-France Garcia's article.
10 Bucket shops were brokerage houses of varying financial power and reputation, which were not members of (stock) exchanges, such as the NYSE.
11 Dow's articles were non-technical, non-analytic, and he did not employ charts. In his Wall Street Journal articles, he rather enunciated general principles of reasoning when observing the market. The articles relied on a notion of economic cycles enunciated in the 1870s by an author writing under the name of 'Benner.' Dow's 'theory of cycles' is still popular today with some observers of financial markets (see, for instance, Mahar, 2004).
12 The mimeograph was a printing machine that could be operated individually, by a non-professional and used typically for small runs (only tens or hundreds of copies).
13 I should add here that during six years of archival research I never encountered books which were more used up, annotated, and underlined than the copies of financial chartist literature I have examined.
14 Henry Hall took over Benner's notion of cycles and re-worked it as cycles of prosperity and depression, distinguishing between five, ten, and twenty year cycles. He considered that the prices of stocks and bonds are related to 'the prevalence of good or bad times' (Hall, 1908, p. 55).
15 Booker T. Washington was the first principal of the Tuskegee Normal and Industrial Institute (1881), where he created a curriculum combining practical skills with academic education, and emphasizing economic independence as a means of emancipating African Americans.
16 Multiple price lists continued to exist on the Paris Bourse well into the 20th century, among others because the French state tolerated (if not encouraged) an unofficial securities market (the

coulisse), while giving substantial privileges to the official stock brokers. These markets were adjacent and each had its own price lists. Attempts made by official brokers to dismantle the unofficial market were not supported by the state and short-lived.

17 Regnault's relevance has only recently been brought to light by Franck Jovanovic, while Bachelier's impact on financial economics was mainly from the 1950s on.

References

Abbott, A. (1988) *The System of the Professions: An Essay on the Division of Expert Labor*, Chicago: The University of Chicago Press.
Babson, R. W. (1914) *The Future Method of Investing Money: Economic Facts for Corporations and Investors*, Boston: Babson's Statistical Organization.
Babson, R. W. (1935) *Actions and Reactions: An Autobiography of Roger W. Babson*. New York: Harper & Brothers.
Bachelier, L. (1900) *Théorie de la spéculation*. Paris: Annales scientifiques de l'ENS.
Barry, A. and D. Slater (2002) 'Technology, Politics, and the Market: An Interview with Michel Callon.' *Economy and Society* 31(2): 285–306.
Benner, S. (1876) *Benner's Prophecies of Future Ups and Downs in Prices*. Cincinnati, the author.
Bourdieu, P. (1977) *La Distinction*. Paris: Minuit.
Breton, Y. (1992) 'L'économie politique et les mathématiques en France 1800–1940.' *Histoire & Mesure* 7(1–2): 25–52.
Bruce, B. (2002) 'Stock Analysts: Experts on Whose Behalf?' *The Journal of Psychology and Financial Markets* 3(4): 198–201.
Callon, M. (1998) 'Introduction: the Embeddedness of Economic Markets in Economics', in M. Callon (ed.), *The Laws of the Markets*. Oxford: Blackwell.
Callon, M. (2004) 'Europe Wrestling with Technology.' *Economy and Society* 33(1): 121–134.
Cohen, B. (1999) 'Marketing Trust: Credit Reporting and Credit Rating in the 19th Century United States. ASA conference paper.
Collins, H. M. and R. Evans (2002) 'The Third Wave of Science Studies: Studies of Expertise and Experience.' *Social Studies of Science* 32(2): 235–296.
Cowles, A. III (1933) 'Can Stock Market Forecasters Forecast?' *Econometrica* 1(3): 309–324.
DeMark, T. (1994) *The New Science of Technical Analysis*. New York: John Wiley & Sons.
Desrosières, A. (1998) *The Politics of Large Numbers: A History of Statistical Reasoning*. Cambridge (Massachusetts): Harvard University Press.
Durkheim, E. (1965 [1915]) *The Elementary Forms of the Religious Life*. New York: Free Press.
Fama, E. F. (1965) 'The Behavior of Stock Market Prices.' *Journal of Business* 38(1): 34–105.
Fogarty, T. J. and R. K. Rogers (2005) 'Financial Analysts' Reports: An Extended Institutional Theory Evaluation.' *Accounting, Organizations and Society* 30(4): 331–356.
Gann, W. D. (1923) *Truth of the Stock Tape*. New York: Financial Guardian Publishing Co.
Garcia, M.-F. (1986) 'La construction sociale d'un marché parfait: le marché au cadran de Fontaines-en-Sologne.' *Actes de la Recherche en Sciences Sociales* 65: 2–13.
Garcia-Parpet, M.-F. (2007) 'The Social Construction of a Perfect Market: The Strawberry Auction at Fontaines-en-Sologne', in D. MacKenzie, F. Muniesa and L. Siu (eds), *Do Economists Make Markets? On the Performativity of Economics*. Princeton (New Jersey): Princeton University Press.
Garfinkel, H. (2002) *Ethnomethodology's Program*. Lanham (Maryland): Rowman and Littlefield.
Hacking, I. (1995) *Rewriting the Soul: Multiple Personality and the Sciences of Memory*. Princeton (New Jersey): Princeton University Press.
Hall, H. (1908) *How Money is Made in Security Investments*. New York: DeVinne Press.
Huebner, S. S. (1934 [1922]) *The Stock Market*, revised ed. New York: D. Appleton-Century.
Jovanovic, F. and P. Le Gall (2001) 'Does God Practice a Random Walk? The 'Financial Physics' of a Nineteenth Century Forerunner, Jules Regnault.' *European Journal of the History of Economic Thought* 8(3): 332–362.

Jovanovic, F. (2000) 'The Origin of Financial Theory: A Reevaluation of the Contribution of Louis Bachelier.' *Revue d'Economie Politique* 110(3): 396–418.
Lefevre, H. (1870) *Traité des valeurs mobilières et des opérations de Bourse, placement et spéculation.* Paris: E. Lachaud.
MacKenzie, D. and Y. Millo (2003) 'Constructing a Market, Performing a Theory: The Historical Sociology of Financial Derivatives.' *American Journal of Sociology* 109(1): 107–145.
MacKenzie, D. (2004) 'Social Connectivities in Global Financial Markets.' *Environment and Planning D: Society and Space* 22(1): 83–101.
Mahar, M. (2004) *Bull: A History of the Boom and Bust 1982–2004.* New York: Collins.
Ménard, C. (1980) 'Three Forms of Resistance to Statistics: Say, Cournot, Walras.' *History of Political Economy* 12(4): 524–541.
Merton, R. K. (1973) *Social Theory and Social Structure.* New York: Free Press.
Nelson, S. A. (1902) *The ABC of Stock Speculation.* New York: S.A. Nelson.
New York Institute of Finance (1989) *Technical Analysis: A Personal Seminar.* New York: New York Institute of Finance.
Pinch, T. (2003) 'Giving Birth to New Users: How the Minimoog Was Sold to Rock and Roll', in N. Oudshoorn and T. Pinch (eds), *How Users Matter: The Co-Construction of Users and Technologies.* Cambridge (Massachusetts): The MIT Press.
Preda, A. (2006) 'Socio-technical Agency in Financial Markets: The Case of the Stock Ticker.' *Social Studies of Science* 26(5): 753–782.
Regnault, J. (1863) *Calcul des chances et philosophie de la Bourse.* Paris: Mallet-Bachelier.
Roberts, H. V. (1959) 'Stock Market 'Patterns' and Financial Analysis: Methodological Suggestions.' *Journal of Finance* 14(1): 1–10.
Schutz, A. (2003 [1945]) 'Teiresias oder unser Wissen von zukünftigen Ereignissen [Teiresias, or our Knowledge of Future Events]', in M. Endreß and I. Srubar (eds), *Theorie der Lebenswelt: Die pragmatische Schichtung der Lebenswelt.* Konstanz: UVK.
Selden, G. C. (1922) *Scientific Investing and Trading.* New York and Philadelphia: W.H. McKenna & Co.
Swedberg, R. (2005) 'Investors and the Conflicts of Interest in the US Brokerage Industry', in K. Knorr Cetina and A. Preda (eds), *The Sociology of Financial Markets.* Oxford: Oxford University Press.
Tape, Rollo aka R. D. Wyckoff (1910) *Studies in Tape Reading.* New York: The Ticker Publishing Company.
Turner, S. P. (2003) *Liberal Democracy 3.0.* London: Sage.
Weber, M. (1978 [1921]) *Economy and Society: An Outline of Interpretive Sociology.* Berkeley (California): University of California Press.
Womack, K. L. (1996) 'Do Brokerage Analysts' Recommendations Have Investment Value?' *The Journal of Finance* 51(1): 137–167.
Woolgar, S. (1991) 'The Turn to Technology in Social Studies of Science' *Science, Technology & Human Values* 16(1): 20–50.
Wyckoff, R. D. (1930) *Wall Street Ventures and Adventures through Forty Years.* New York: Harper & Brothers.
Zuckerman, E. (1999) 'The Categorical Imperative: Securities Analysts and the Illegitimacy Discount.' *American Journal of Sociology* 104(5): 1398–1438.

The death of a salesman? Reconfiguring economic exchange in Swedish post-war food distribution

Hans Kjellberg

Introduction

How are economic orders established?[1] Is there any point in singling out market exchange from other forms of exchange, or indeed, from social interaction at large? And if so, what is specific about markets? Is it the calculations that forego the transactions, or the type of transactions performed?[2]

This chapter addresses the close relationships between economic calculations, economic transactions, and economic agencies, all of which can be observed as part of economic ordering processes. This task will be accomplished through a detailed account of the introduction of the Hakon deal, a rationalization programme purporting to 'economize' the economic exchanges between a wholesaler, the Swedish firm Hakonbolaget, and its customers within the food retail trade in the late 1940s. The purpose of this programme was to realize a market without salesmen by introducing a mode of transacting based on written orders filled out by the retailers using a pre-printed goods catalogue. The account shows how the process of putting the new system into place was intimately connected to transformations in calculative practices.

After presenting the empirical case, the chapter addresses three specific issues concerning the interrelation between calculative practices and economic organizing. First, I revisit the classic argument put forward by Coase concerning the transition between different economic orders. Based on the case, I argue that neither the available alternatives, nor the methods of calculating their respective benefits can be assumed at the outset of an inquiry into a process of economic organizing. Second, I critically assess the existing preoccupation with defining the market as a starting point for such (social scientific) inquiries. I argue that, despite appearances, the present case is not about de-marketization. Third, I discuss the practical shaping of calculative agencies, suggesting that there is a simultaneous paucity and abundance of such agencies, a paradox which is an important facet of the shaping of economic orders.

Prologue – Swedish food distribution in the late 1940s[3]

In the 1940s, Swedish food retail shops were small, specialized and manually served (see Figure 1, below). According to the 1951 census, there were some 24,000 retail shops carrying food products. Among these one could find meat shops, fish shops, dairy shops, fruit & vegetable shops, grocery shops, and any combination of these in between. In addition, there were some 11,000 rural general retailers carrying a wide assortment of items including at least some food products. According to the census, the average number of employees per shop was 3.5 (af Trolle, 1963: 80–81).

Most retail shops were privately owned and were run by the proprietor. Only a few small retail chains existed, primarily in larger cities. Retailers typically purchased goods from several suppliers. Most suppliers were local wholesalers, but a few larger regional wholesalers also existed. According to the 1951 census there were 3,100 food wholesalers in Sweden, employing on average seven people each (af Trolle, 1963: 130). In addition, retailers also purchased some goods directly from producers. Attending to sales calls was an important part of everyday business for food retailers since both producers and wholesalers deployed their own travelling salesmen.

Figure 1: *A Swedish private food retail store in the late 1940s.*
(Source: From ICA's historiska bildarkiv at the Centre for Business History in Stockholm).

The death of a salesman? Reconfiguring economic exchange in Swedish post-war food distribution

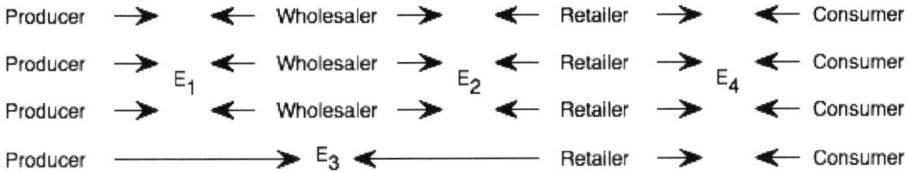

Figure 2: *A schematic illustration of the exchange situations (E1–E4) linking domestic production to consumption in Swedish food distribution in the 1940s.*

All in all, then, four exchange situations linked domestic production to consumption (see Figure 2): exchanges between producers and wholesalers (E1), between wholesalers and retailers (E2), between producers and retailers (E3), and between retailers and consumers (E4).

During the latter part of the 1940s, critical voices claimed that Swedish goods distribution was both costly and inefficient. In particular, politicians as well as industry and labour union representatives claimed that the retail and wholesale traders had been unable to rationalize their operations, as the manufacturing industries had done. One of the possible solutions suggested to spur rationalization was to increase government control through regulation.

The specific case investigated here involves Hakonbolaget, the largest privately owned wholesale company in Sweden, which took the initiative to reform the long established economic order towards the end of the 1940s. At the time, Hakonbolaget operated local offices in 28 locations across mid-Sweden, serving more than 6,600 customers (primarily private retailers). The company differed from most other Swedish wholesalers in the sense that it had been partly owned by its clients, the retailers, since its formation in 1917. By 1946, the company had 3,790 shareholding customers, who controlled considerably more than 50 per cent of the shares in the company. In addition, the company had organized a retail council in each area served by a local office, with the local director/office manager acting as secretary to the council. These councils were made up of selected retailers from each region and were used as a communication channel between Hakonbolaget and its customers.

In 1949, Hakonbolaget introduced a rationalization programme called the Hakon deal that entailed a series of changes in the interaction between producers, wholesalers and retailers (see Figure 3). Since the sought-after changes affected both the rights, obligations and abilities of all of the parties involved, a number of controversies arose in the course of realizing the programme. The contours of this re-organization process can be described as an attempt on behalf of Hakonbolaget to re-configure the way in which wholesale-retail transactions were carried out. According to the programme, the exchange between Hakonbolaget and the retailers (E2) should no longer be competitive, but should instead be co-operative. To this end, Hakonbolaget was to transform into a *purchasing centre* and the retailers into *members* associated with this centre.

© 2007 The Author. Editorial organisation © 2007 The Editorial Board of the Sociological Review   67

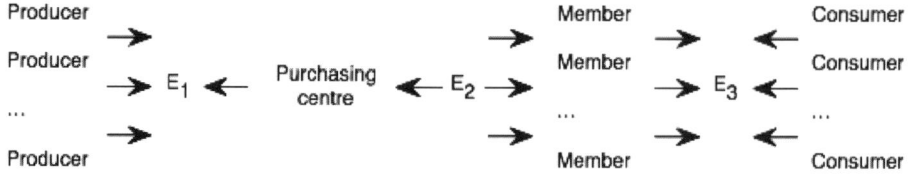

Figure 3: *The new organization of food distribution envisaged by Hakonbolaget as part of the Hakon deal.*

We enter the story during a management meeting[4] at Hakonbolaget on May 5, 1947...

The customer-contact problem

The managers of Hakonbolaget were very concerned. They appeared to have a 'customer-contact problem', in the sense that Hakonbolaget had to put too much effort into securing orders from its customers, the retailers. This was a particularly complicated claim, given that these retailers in many cases also were shareholders in the company. Since sales activities were both costly and precarious, the managers of Hakonbolaget were intent on finding some alternative and less costly form of interaction. Meeting minutes reveal how Jarl Jernunger, one of two retail advisors responsible for handling relations with retailers, viewed the situation:

> Jarl Jernunger pointed out that the retailers are strongly affected by our competitors through the advantage they have in terms of influence from salesmen through a larger total number of representatives. The customers also have a certain tendency to act according to the economic advantages offered at the point of purchase. To succeed we must achieve a definite feeling of belonging in the retailer; that Hakonbolaget is his own company. (Minutes of the managers' conference, May 5 1947) (Hakonbolaget, 1947, trans.)

Besides adding more detail to the character of the problem, several participants in the discussion quickly suggested possible solutions. For instance, it was suggested that Hakonbolaget should introduce a system of premiums to improve the purchasing fidelity of retailer clients and cut costs by reducing the number of salesmen employed. As far as the second measure was concerned, the participants agreed that this would require the creation of some other means of upholding the contact with the retailers.

Given how the retailers were perceived to act when purchasing goods, some managers thought that even more measures were needed. For instance, the head of the newly formed Organization Department, Nils-Erik Wirsäll, argued for a more encompassing change:

We must seek a solution to our contact problem that gives us improvements and cost reductions over and above that achieved by reducing the sales apparatus, for instance in terms of warehouse costs, office costs, etc. The system must give the customer an economic advantage at the point of purchase. (Minutes of the managers' conference, May 5 1947) (Hakonbolaget, 1947, trans.)

As a result of the discussion at the management meeting, two committees were formed to investigate how a 'new and more rational distribution system' might be designed – one committee was composed of middle managers in the company, the other of prominent retailers found among Hakonbolaget's customers.

Table 1: *Contributions to the turnover of Hakonbolaget from customers (shareholding and non-shareholding) classified according to annual purchases in 1946. (Source: Wirsäll et al., April 1952)*

Annual purchase per customer	Number of customers		Turnover	
	Number	% of total	MSEK	% of total
0–9,999 SEK	750 shareholders 2,429 others	47.94	10.6	8.86
10,000 SEK	3,040 shareholders 413 others	52.06	109.2	91.14
Total	3,790 shareholders 2,842 others	100	119.8	100

The two committees worked in parallel for the better part of a year. Committee members visited other European countries to study the organization of food distribution. Nils-Erik Wirsäll, who had been appointed secretary of the retail committee, provided the committees with detailed information on American wholesale-retail interaction based on a study trip he made during the winter of 1946–1947. In addition, the Organization Department supplied the committees with reports. These included time and motion studies of warehouse operations and a systematic compilation of how (much and often) clients purchased goods from Hakonbolaget (one example of this is reproduced as Table 1).

The committees presented their separate proposals in May 1948, and during the summer, a working party merged them into one. Support for the unified proposal was then sought from both the board of directors of Hakonbolaget and the local retail councils before it was presented and approved at an extra annual meeting in October 1948. It was also decided that the new programme, which from then on was known as the Hakon deal, should be introduced gradually across the company's local offices during 1949 and 1950.

Salesmen out! A new form of economic encounter

How, then, did Hakonbolaget decide to solve its customer-contact problem? An important part of the proposed solution was to reorganize the exchanges between the company and its customers, the retailers. It was suggested that through deeper co-operation, Hakonbolaget would be able to reduce its sales efforts while the retailers would be able to reduce their purchasing efforts.[5]

To underscore the difference between the proposal and the established order, Hakonbolaget was no longer to be regarded as a wholesaler, but rather as a 'purchasing centre' for its associated retailers. Similarly, the associated retailers were now to be called 'members' of the purchasing centre.

> *The co-operative plan aims at reducing the costs of the flow of goods from the purchasing centre to its members.* To do this, the present organization and the current working methods of Hakonbolaget must change so that the wholehearted support of the members can be gained. A deepened co-operation will reduce both the sales efforts of the purchasing centre and the retailers' work of purchasing. The purchasing centre can devote more time to purchasing and the retailers are given more time to do sales work. (Collin and Wirsäll, 1948: 16, trans.)

How would a deeper co-operation allow cost-reductions? The two committees argued that the salesmen did not contribute significantly to the quality of sales transactions. Salespeople were costly for Hakonbolaget and ate up the retailer's valuable time. The suggestion was to try and replace the traditional sales apparatus with organized co-operation and a clear division of labour between Hakonbolaget and its customers/members. Hakonbolaget should concentrate on purchasing goods for its members, while the members should concentrate on selling the goods to the consuming public.

Here is an excerpt of one committee member arguing in favour of the Hakon deal proposal at a meeting with a local retail council:

> B. Harne: It must be considered *wrong* that [the purchasing centre] is selling to its members at high cost instead of the members buying from the purchasing centre without any costs. (Minutes of the Ludvika retail council, September 26 1948) (Hakonbolaget, 1948, trans.)

Further, based on the investigations carried out by the Organization Department, the committees were able to show that the size and frequency of the orders received by Hakonbolaget were important cost-drivers. Considerable savings could therefore be made if the order volume received from the customers were concentrated into a fewer number of orders (see Figure 4).

How then could a more concentrated order structure be achieved? The simple solution would be to set a minimum size for each order, for instance, in terms of the number of different items ordered, ie, the number of order lines. According to the results of the time and motion studies performed by the Organization Department, this would significantly improve warehouse efficiency. However, given the heterogeneity of Hakonbolaget's customers, ranging from small, specialized rural retailers to large urban ones, this was regarded as too rigid a solution. There was an obvious risk that it would result in a loss of the small orders to competitors rather than in increased overall order size. A second alternative, then, would be to offer a premium relative to the size of each order. Although it would be a less rigid solution, the retail committee held that such

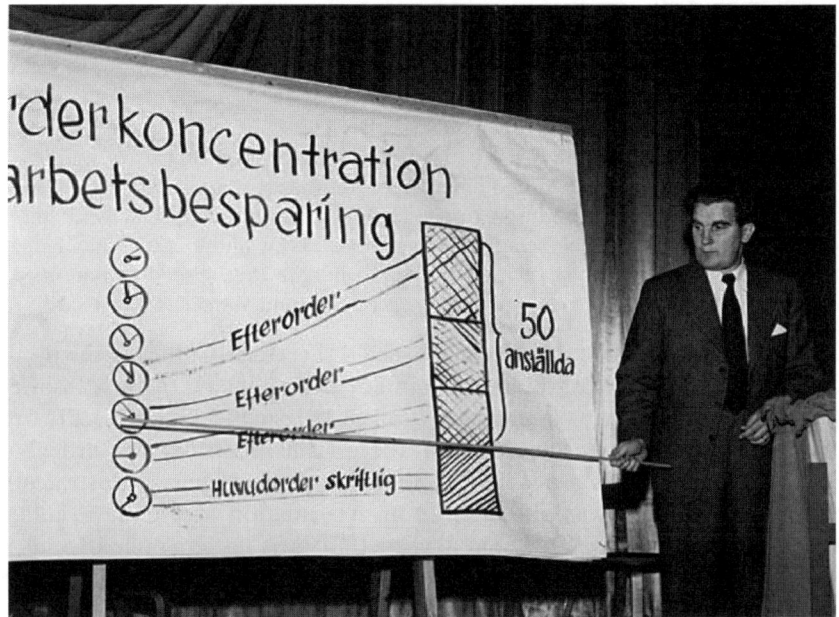

Figure 4: *Nils-Erik Wirsäll, head of the Organisation Department, presents the potential savings from a more concentrated order structure at the annual meeting in 1948.* (Source: From ICA's historiska bildarkiv at the Centre for Business History in Stockholm).

a system would encourage retailers to buy more than they really needed, eventually leading to losses in terms of spoiled goods, etc.

In the end, the committees proposed a solution based on a combination of three measures:

1) limiting the total number of dispatched orders to one per week for each retailer,
2) introducing an annual minimum-purchasing limit of SEK 5.000[6] per retailer,
3) introducing an annual progressive bonus that would encourage retailers to concentrate their orders to Hakonbolaget.

In combination, measures 1 and 2 introduced a soft version of the minimum-size-for-each-order-solution, since the average order had to amount to approximately SEK 100. The progressive annual bonus similarly introduced a soft version of the premium-relative-to-the-size-of-each-order-solution. Larger orders would result in higher bonus (at the end of the year), but retailers would not be 'punished' for occasionally placing a small order.

In addition to the measures encouraging increased order size, the committees also suggested that the procedure for placing and receiving orders should be changed. The following paragraph, from the official description of the programme, stipulates the rules that were to apply to wholesale-retail interaction as part of the Hakon deal:

> **The general purchasing rules** (the members' efforts)
> a) The member orders his goods from the purchasing centre *in writing*. The written order is made out by the member on the basis of a *catalogue* published by Hakonbolaget. [. . .] [I]n addition to the catalogue, direct contact between the purchasing centre and the members must always exist. Now and then the members must have live contact with their own company. To handle this, special contact-men will visit the members *two to four times per year*. (Collin and Wirsäll, 1948: 16–17, trans.)

A sizeable part of the programme consisted therefore in altering the mode of transacting: reducing face-to-face encounters and replacing them with interaction at a distance. Instead of relying on visiting salesmen trying to secure orders from retailers – an important part of the established economic order – the Hakon deal was based on a written order procedure. Figure 5 illustrates how the proposed solution was presented in an information leaflet to the retailers. Although not explicitly stated, the new method was to be applied to all purchases made by the retailers, with the implication that as members of the purchasing centre, they should close their doors to competitors of Hakonbolaget.

According to Hakonbolaget, there were several important differences between the new and the old methods in terms of how they organized the encounter of supply and demand. As clearly illustrated by the left side of Figure 5, in the 'old method', supply and demand met physically in the retailers' offices. Each salesman, however, represented but a part of the supply within a given region (often defined as a central village or town and its rural vicinities). Demand within the same region was represented by orders placed orally by the retailers either to the visiting salesmen or over the phone to one of the

 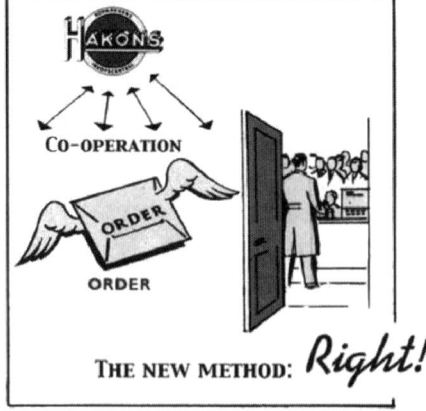

Figure 5: *Two alternative ways of organising the economic encounter between wholesale and retail trade.* (Source: Hakonbolaget, 1950, trans.)

supplying wholesalers. There was thus no instantaneous intersection of supply and demand. Instead, the intersections occurred over certain periods of time (usually one or two weeks) as the salesmen representing all wholesalers and producers made their rounds of the retailers' offices. According to the proponents of the Hakon deal, this delay was a major shortcoming of the 'old method' since it made retailers develop uneconomic purchasing practices. Rather than concentrating all order lines to *one* order from *one* wholesaler, the retailers spread them out over *several* orders placed with *several* wholesalers, largely out of some misdirected sense of fairness. Figure 5 illustrates the rhetorical tactics used to convince the retailers of the plan: spending time on salesmen reduced their contact with consumers, whereas written orders to Hakonbolaget would allow them to strengthen their contact with customers/consumers.

The proposed method modified the encounter in several ways. First, the representations of supply and demand changed. Supply was to be represented by news leaflets and a goods catalogue published by Hakonbolaget, featuring the individual products and their prices, organized into product categories, eg, dairy products, flour, sugar, canned meat, canned vegetables, hard bread, etc. Rather than being compiled by the retailers from several different sources, the aggregation of supply was now to be performed for them by their 'purchasing centre'. Proponents argued that this would give retailers a much better overview of the available goods. Demand was to be represented by the written orders, filled out on pre-printed order forms and sent in by the members on set dates to the local offices of the purchasing centre. This would provide a much better basis for planning the dispatching of orders in the warehouses. Since the catalogue listed prices, the intersection of supply and demand was reduced to a passive acceptance, or not, of the quoted price, by retail-members.

The number of actors involved in the exchange of goods was to be drastically reduced: only one seller and only selected buyers (those qualifying for membership). Pricing, the intersection of supply and demand, was transferred to a committee along with the exploration of supply. Hence, Hakonbolaget was to act more or less as *the* purchasing department for all retail-members. Some retailers voiced objections concerning this:

> Mr Georg Hammar: [. . .] Hakonbolaget may very well conjure up a grand cooperative plan, but the retailers must also think of serving their customers and complying with their wishes, supplying the goods they want. (Minutes of the Gävle retail council, September 26 1948) (Hakonbolaget, 1948, trans.)

As a whole, the proposed solution to the customer-contact problem of Hakonbolaget would reorganize much more than the contacts between Hakonbolaget and its retail customers. It would, if effectuated, reorganize a major part of the private wholesale market for food and other daily goods. It was not very surprising, then, that the programme attracted attention from competing wholesale companies. In various ways, competitors attempted to inform themselves about and counteract the impending changes, launching their own programmes as well as seeking to discredit the Hakon deal.

As the Organization Department and the six offices that had been selected as pilots were preparing for the introduction of the program on January 1, 1949, one major question remained to be answered: would it actually be possible to introduce the new way of working and divest the salesmen of their function without losing sales to competing wholesalers?

Membership rewards: reframing calculative space

As we have seen, the Hakon deal placed several requirements on retailers who wanted to remain customers of Hakonbolaget. They would have to become members and follow the stipulated purchasing rules, ie, order in writing once per week without the assistance of visiting salesmen. But, as the managers had observed already during their initial discussions, retailers tended 'to act according to the economic advantages offered at the point of purchase' (see the quote above on p. 68). That is, the calculations affecting their purchasing behaviour were highly influenced by direct situational circumstances, such as a bargain offered by a salesman. To improve the proposal's appeal, then, it was considered wise to find ways of off-setting the economic advantages offered by competitors.

To be sure, the representatives of Hakonbolaget stressed the economic benefits in their efforts to gain support for the programme among retailers. Jarl Jernunger advocated the new programme at a retail council-meeting as follows:

> Retail adviser Jernunger: [. . .] It was also pleasant to find that Hakonbolaget's travelling salesmen were so firmly rooted, as they appeared to be. One could, however, not regard the revolutionary change, which now was to be made, as an emotional issue, but as a pure issue of calculation: what did one receive? And: what did it cost? (Minutes of the Gävle retail council, September 26 1948) (Hakonbolaget, 1948, trans.)

Although no exact figures were presented, the proponents of the programme were convinced that the new order-procedure would lead to considerable cost reductions. This, in turn, would allow price cuts. At least, this was one of the major arguments made by the head of the Organization Department when he presented the new programme to the general public in an article in the leading Swedish business magazine:

> The simplified organization resulting from implementing this co-operative plan evidently results in lowered costs. This would thus allow a reduction of prices. Instead of changing the present pricing policy, which is fully competitive, the increased surplus is paid back in the form of a bonus. This gives Hakonbolaget an opportunity to lead the relatively heterogeneous circle of members (the food retail trade) towards a more rational way of thinking. (Wirsäll, 1949b: 381, trans.)

As noted by Wirsäll, price cuts would run counter to the idea behind the programme. Lower prices would be available to each and every customer/member, irrespective of their purchasing behaviour, whereas the idea behind the programme was 'to lead the relatively heterogeneous circle of members towards a more rational way of thinking.' How then, did Hakonbolaget attempt to do this?

That is, how was the calculative space configured so that the programme turned out to be attractive according to the separate calculations performed by each party?

The new requirements that were placed on the retailers-turned-members were coupled with a series of incentives that would reward them for correct behaviour. A system of premiums consisting of three bonus-scales was introduced to compensate the members for the cost reductions that would result from their new purchasing behaviour. The proposed reorganization of the encounter between Hakonbolaget and its customers was thus coupled with a change in the calculation of the economic consequences of this encounter. The calculations guiding a purchasing decision would be different for members than for those who remained non-members.[7] The system of premiums devised to compensate the retailers included:

The grounds for premiums (the efforts of the purchasing centre)
a) **Order premium.** A 1 per cent order premium is given on written orders of stock goods. This premium, calculated on the so-called bonus goods, is paid annually in the form of a savings certificate. [. . .]
b) **Member bonus.** In addition to the order premium a special member bonus is paid. This is set with reference to the total annual purchases of all goods except so called service goods. [. . .] The member bonus [. . .] is set annually by the company board and for 1949 is paid according to the following scale:

Yearly purchase in SEK	Bonus in %
5,000–14,999	1.00
15,000–24,999	1.20
25,000–34,999	1.30
35,000–44,999	1.40
45,000–59,999	1.50
60,000–79,999	1.55
80,000–99,999	1.60
100,000–149,999	1.65
150,000–	1.70

The member bonus is paid annually in the form of a savings certificate or an industrial fund certificate. The scale according to which the member bonus is calculated has been designed on the basis of thorough investigations of the purchasing centre's costs for orders of different sizes. Through this design the member bonus ought to spur members to concentrate their purchases at the purchasing centre.
c) **Hakon premium.** In addition to the member bonus a special Hakon premium is to be paid to the members, if the co-operation and the support becomes such, that the economic possibilities for this are created. When paying the Hakon premium, attention will primarily be paid to the member's purchasing fidelity and wholehearted effort for the purchasing centre. (Collin and Wirsäll, 1948: 21–22, trans.)

The *order premium* was the most straightforward of the three premiums. It expanded the frame of calculation to include the form of the transaction. By offering a bonus on each written order, the form of the transaction became associated with a direct cost consequence. Other forms of transactions with Hakonbolaget, eg, placing orders over the telephone or through salesmen, therefore became relatively less attractive as did transactions with alternative wholesale companies:

> This order premium becomes a spur for the members to try the new written order procedure. (Wirsäll, 1949b: 380–381, trans.)

The *member bonus* expanded the frame of calculation in time. When deciding on an individual order, the member was to take into account all orders he had already placed, and all orders he would place during the current year, rather than the individual order alone. This effect was further underscored by the progressive bonus-scale, which meant that later transactions would affect the final calculation of previous ones. Comments made by several retailers suggest that this was perceived as intended, ie, as giving them an incentive to concentrate as much of their purchasing as possible with Hakonbolaget:

> Mr Holm [retailer] said that precisely the fact that when the programme has been introduced, everyone must try to reach as high as possible on the bonus-scale in their own company, will become an extraordinary argument for all retailers to say no to other companies. (Minutes of the Uppsala retail council, September 23 1948) (Hakonbolaget, 1948, trans.)

The design of the member bonus might seem to run counter to the idea that large orders were more cost-effective, since it did not place any direct restrictions on individual orders. As mentioned previously, however, the rules of the programme emulated such a restriction. Provided that the member did not turn elsewhere, they were limited to one order per week.

To some extent, the member bonus also narrowed the frame of calculation. By making the bonus rate depend on the total amount that the member purchased during the year – an amount that would remain unknown until the end of the year – a final calculation became more difficult to make. This rendered a strict comparison with offers made by competing wholesalers more difficult, thus placing an obstacle between the members' demand and competing suppliers.

The *Hakon premium* differed in several respects from the other two premiums. First of all, it was conditioned on the outcome of the programme for Hakonbolaget: *if* the economic possibilities permitting it were created (whatever that meant), *then* the premium would be paid. Secondly, the members were given no clear instructions as to how the premium would be calculated, ie, who would receive what. As a ground for calculating rewards, the concept of 'wholehearted effort' was much more ambiguous than 'written orders of stock goods' or 'total annual purchases of all goods'. 'The member's purchasing fidelity' was somewhat easier to pin down, indicating that the chances of receiving a Hakon premium would increase the more a member bought from the purchasing centre. Once again, then, the premium expanded the calculation beyond the level of individual transactions.

In combination the three premiums altered the cost/benefit algorithm for members. What was to be calculated were the costs and benefits of what in modern marketing vernacular is called an 'exchange relationship' between Hakonbolaget and its customers-turned-members.

Membership did not include any formal or legal bond between Hakonbolaget and its members, except for the requirement that all members had to be shareholders in the company. Membership did, however, entail a host of additional benefits that were not directly related to orders. As a member, a retailer could: enjoy the service of the Hakon retailers' Accounting Centre (at a fee); access security for loans necessary to make investments in the store; buy equipment for the store from Retailer Service – a subsidiary of Hakonbolaget; enjoy the active efforts of Hakonbolaget to secure new retail locations for its members – eg in new housing areas; enjoy the benefits of centrally negotiated insurance conditions; and so on.

Allocating agential properties

To realize the new economic order in practice, numerous actors had to be prevented from performing activities that were linked to the old, transaction-based order. At the same time, others had to be persuaded to perform new activities.

Turning retailers into members

First of all, the programme rested on a re-configuration of the retailers. Introducing the new premiums would not be effective unless the retailers actually took them into account when making their purchases. In each of the districts where the new programme was introduced, meetings were held to introduce interested retailers to the new way of working. A still-movie called 'Defekt' was shown in order to explain the written order procedure and the new bonus-scales. In addition to holding shares, however, actually to become a member, required the retailer to apply for membership and in so doing, to declare himself willing to work according to the rules stipulated in the program.

Having been granted membership, the retailer was equipped with a Memberpackage. This included a *Member book* that stipulated the rules of the programme, a *Goods catalogue* listing the assortment of goods offered and their prices, and *order forms* and *envelopes* for written orders. Each new member was also visited by one of the new *contact-men* who were to instruct the member on how to use the goods catalogue and the order forms. The contact-man would also assist members in reorganizing their stocks in accordance with the goods catalogue. This would simplify written ordering by allowing the retailer to go through the stocks with the catalogue at hand (see Figure 7). A small sticker was also put up on the member's phone reminding him to order in writing rather than placing the order by phone to the purchasing centre (or to some other wholesaler).

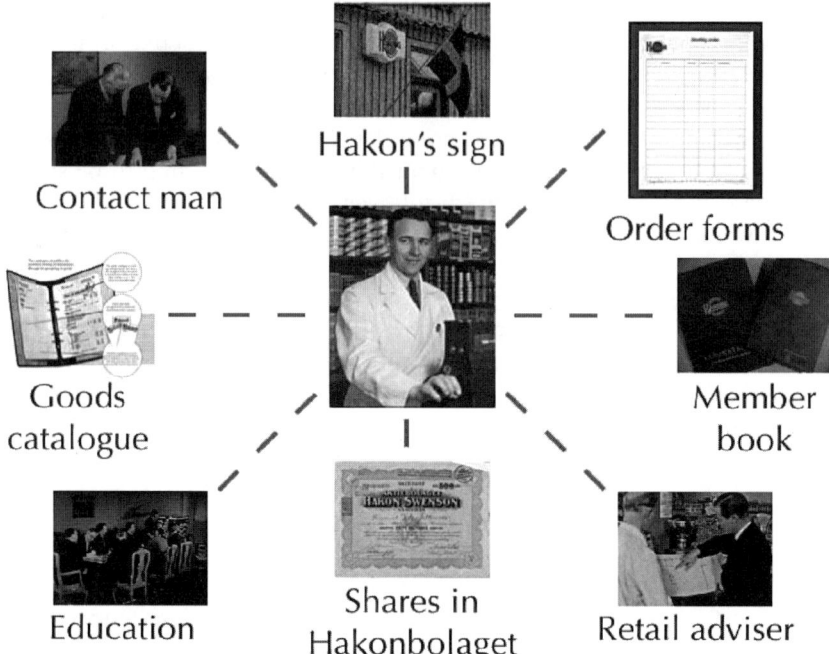

Figure 6: *Creating a Member out of a number of heterogeneous entities.* (Images courtesy of: ICA's historiska bildarkiv at the Centre for Business History in Stockholm and Nils-Erik Wirsäll.)

A member was also able to draw on the competences of a *retail adviser* for certain issues, eg, views on the assortment and store planning. In terms of marketing and sales, members were entitled to put up the *Hakon-sign* showing their customers that they were associated to Hakonbolaget. This also allowed them to benefit from the central advertisements made by Hakonbolaget in local newspapers across its territory.

New agencies within the purchasing centre

For the local offices of Hakonbolaget, which hitherto had been organized to compete with local and regional wholesalers, the new way of working also entailed considerable changes. In the introduction to the information material that the Organization Department had prepared for the changeover, the overall change in direction was clearly indicated:

> WE MUST PUSH FOR THE IDEA – NOT ONLY FOR THE GOODS. (Wirsäll, 1949a: 1, trans.)

Three distinct new agencies were created at the offices in order to handle the new programme: an order manager, a rest-order caller and a contact-man. For each of the three, fairly detailed instructions were provided:

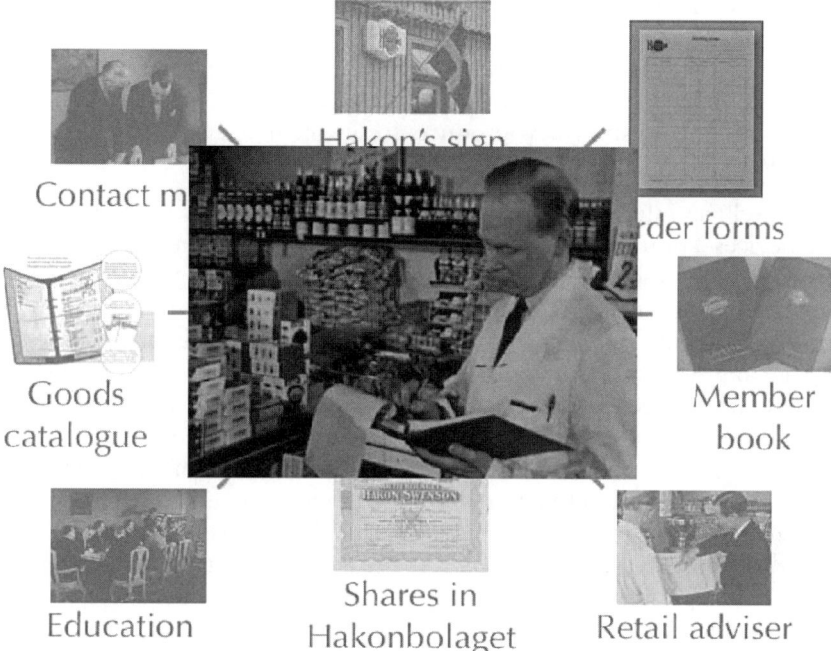

Figure 7: *A performing member preparing his written order using the goods catalogue.* (Film frame and images courtesy of: ICA's historiska bildarkiv at the Centre for Business History in Stockholm and Nils-Erik Wirsäll.)

The order manager has as his task:

1) to supervise and be responsible for handling orders [. . .];
2) to audit currently each member's turnover development [. . .];
3) to co-operate closely with the contact-man on all relevant issues [. . .]; and
4) to act to stimulate the members in general [. . .].

The rest-order caller's tasks are:

1) to notify the members quickly about any out-of-stock situations;
2) to inform the purchasing manager of existing rest-orders and their size;
3) to remember that this work must not become routine [. . .]; and
4) to act to stimulate the members in general.

The contact-man is responsible for maintaining the direct personal contact with the members. [. . .] The tasks of the contact-man primarily include:

1) To convince members of the great significance of the purchasing centre [. . .];
2) To educate on issues concerning purchasing and sales [. . .];

3) To act to strengthen the bond between members and purchasing centre [. . .];
4) To supervise that members correctly utilise the joint advertising [. . .];
5) To be the purchasing department's market researcher [. . .]; and
6) To speak about and show new products to the members.
(Wirsäll, 1949a: 31–34, trans.)

Here, as well, an internal training programme was coupled with various routines and devices. For instance, the order departments were given careful instructions on how to edit the incoming written orders before sending them on to the warehouse to be dispatched. The customer ledger was modified to keep track of each member's annual purchases of bonus-entitling goods. Report cards were printed allowing the contact-men to keep records of their customer-visits.

The final change needed to realize the new order at the local offices was to divest the salesmen of their function. This process provides a nice contrast to the creation of the members. In order to divest the salesmen of their function, their agency was transferred to and distributed among a number of new devices (see Figure 8, below). First, the printed goods catalogue was prepared. Second, a newsletter called *Hakons information* was regularly to inform the members of new items. Third, pre-printed order forms and envelopes were produced to simplify the written order procedure. Fourth, special mailboxes were put up in selected locations to ensure swift and safe delivery of the written orders to the

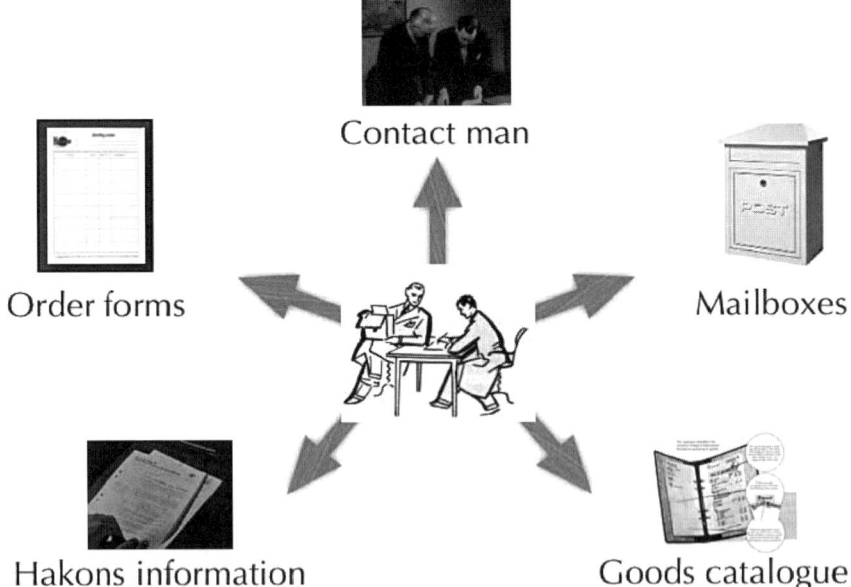

Figure 8: *Divesting salesmen by distributing agency.* (Images (except mailbox) courtesy of: ICA's historiska bildarkiv at the Centre for Business History in Stockholm)

purchasing centre. Fifth and finally, the best salesmen were appointed to the newly created position of contact-man, their task being to maintain personal contact between the members and the purchasing centre through visits two to four times a year (see the excerpt above on p. 72).

A grand plan requires hard work

Although the internal documents suggest that the managers of Hakonbolaget were satisfied with the introduction of the Hakon deal, its acceptance was not without problems. During its introduction in 1949, the company turnover dropped by one per cent. This is likely to have been considered serious at the time, given that the company had experienced a constant turnover growth since 1930! After analysing the figures, however, the managers concluded that the major cause of the drop was to be found in the sales of textiles, a group of goods that was not included in the Hakon deal. Still, several problems related to the new form of wholesale-retail interaction were identified and dealt with during the course of 1949.

To sell or not to sell

A major issue that arose concerned the very core of the programme, namely the move away from active sales measures. This had been a source of concern already when presenting the proposal to the retail councils during the autumn of 1948. Although most retailers seem to have approved of the idea, some stressed that the salesmen fulfilled important roles both for securing orders, maintaining contact with Hakonbolaget and demonstrating new products. The issue resurfaced in connection to the process of actually divesting the salesmen of their role during the introduction of the program. In the spring of 1949, reports reached the top managers that some contact-men were engaging in sales activities during their visits, despite explicit instructions not to.

During the directors' conference in June, two directors of local offices that had changed to the new way of working expressed some hesitation towards completely refraining from sales-measures. But the top managers were intent on pursuing the programme. The founder and CEO of Hakonbolaget, Hakon Swenson, argued that Hakonbolaget had taken upon itself to act as an innovator. Hence their task was nothing less than to 'reshape the way of thinking within trade'. For the contact-men this meant that they should 'increase the spread of knowledge concerning the law of the new deal'. The amount of flexibility shown by Hakonbolaget thus seems to have been rather small.

But the problem kept coming back. Not only was it difficult to exact the right behaviour from the contact-men, it also became clear that many members had not shut their doors to salesmen from competing wholesalers. Instead, they continued to purchase goods from several suppliers. Hakon Swenson again, at the directors' conference in October:

We must look at the situation realistically. We have a long way to go before we can enjoy support from the retail trade to the extent that we are entitled to. 'The significance of competition' is still cherished too much. We must therefore continue forward by use of propaganda. (Minutes of the directors' conference, October 17 1949) (Hakonbolaget, 1949a, trans.)

This cherishing of 'the significance of competition' of course meant that members still were making the old type of calculation, at least some of the time. That is, they were comparing different suppliers' offers of individual goods and placing their orders with the supplier who made them the best offer.

In their search for explanations to this development, the managers of Hakonbolaget noted that some retailers made for better members than others. In particular, they observed that former shop-managers from the consumer co-operation who had been recruited to start their own retail shop associated to Hakonbolaget generally made for better members.

> [Ex-co-op managers] are more receptive to the arguments concerning the new deal than the colleagues who have received their upbringing within the private retail trade. (Minutes of the managers' conference, June 28 1949) (Hakonbolaget, 1949b, trans.)

This observation was indirectly applicable also to the problems associated with the contact-men. For in both cases, an important part of that which went into the making of the new agencies was also an important part of the agencies connected to the old method. Salesmen and retailers were now performing as contact-men and members. Obviously, it was not that easy to divest them of their practical experience. Particularly since their behaviour was mutually supportive. The retailers-turned-members still received salesmen and compared offers; the salesmen-turned-contact-men still visited retailers and made sales-pitches.

How then, was the situation to be improved? Given that the concerned actors might not be made of the right stuff, one solution would be to replace the faulty parts. In practice, however, this was hardly feasible. Labour was in short supply and good people were hard to come by. Moreover, Hakonbolaget had no means of ousting retailers from their stores. So the managers came up with a much more practical solution: what was it that triggered the contact-men to revert to active sales-measures? What made the members receptive to such measures? After some deliberation, the managers singled out the introduction of new products as the answer to both questions. Consequently, they decided to adopt a policy of caution concerning the introduction of new products prior to the full-scale implementation of the programme in January 1950. In this way they sought to reduce the number of situations where sales-measures were likely to be called for, and taken.

Re-evaluating the programme

Adopting the policy of caution did not once and for all resolve the issue of whether to sell or not to sell. During the period 1949–1952, the managers of

Hakonbolaget repeatedly revisited the issue, the scale tilting slightly towards sales measures on some occasions and back towards a more staunch line on others. Most of the times, however, managers ended up agreeing on new efforts to increase compliance with the stipulated rules.

In 1952 a committee appointed by the managing director performed a major evaluation of the entire programme. Their final report was based on figures produced by the Organization Department as well as on a survey performed among the members of the local retail councils. The managers argued that for the first time, reliable figures showing the overall effect of the Hakon deal were becoming available. The compilation made by the Organization Department showed that the customer structure had changed in the sought-after direction. The 'small' customers were declining in importance. But the change was not very dramatic. In 1946, 3,179 customers (48 per cent) had bought for less than SEK 10,000 per year, as a group accounting for 9 per cent of the company turnover. In 1951, the corresponding figures were 2,784 customers (40 per cent) accounting for 4 per cent of the turnover.

> We can thus note a slight improvement, but still, we could reduce the number of customers by 2,784 and only lose MSEK 8.2 in turnover. (Wirsäll *et al.*, 1952: 2, trans.)

Based on these figures, the committee suggested a swift cleaning out of the customer ledgers at the local offices. It was declared that Hakonbolaget should no longer do business with customers and members who did not at least reach the set minimum purchase limit. The committee even suggested that the limit be raised to SEK 15,000.

The second source of information that the committee relied on was the survey performed among the members of the retail councils. The critical points raised against the Hakon deal in the survey almost exclusively concerned the issue of sales:

> Thus, it is held that we have not been fast enough with information concerning price changes, newly arrived goods and new products. (Wirsäll *et al.*, 1952: 5, trans.)

To some extent these views were to be expected given that the policy to act cautiously concerning new products had been established. In light of the survey, however, the committee now proposed revising the principles of the programme.

> Our ambition should be that the members also in this respect are fully satisfied with their purchasing centre. (Wirsäll *et al.*, 1952: 12, trans.)

The tone in the report was very different from that previously taken. Gone was the talk about changing the retailers 'way of thinking' and upholding 'the law of the new deal'. The major suggestion was that the rest-order callers should be given renewed training and that from now on they should concentrate on 'the task of bringing in a larger number of order-lines from each member'. Back to selling, then! In fact, it was even suggested that orders received in this way should qualify for the order-premium that had been introduced originally to reward members for the cost-reductions they created by ordering in writing.

The proposed change might give the impression that Hakonbolaget was surrendering. This is not at all the case. By this time, it was clear that the written order procedure was working. For the past two years, turnover had grown significantly and the weekly written orders from members were now the bread and butter of all local offices. Thus, reverting back to travelling salesmen was never an issue. Rather, the contact-men were to become even more of 'preachers' for the cause, rather than for the goods.

> We suggest that those [contact-men] who are considered fit to lead the member meetings are educated in meeting practices, psychologically trained, tuned up on basic accounting issues, learn to read simple balance sheets, etc. during a week this spring or summer. (Wirsäll *et al.*, 1952: 16, trans.)

Epilogue

With some modifications, such as those suggested in 1952, the Hakon deal remained the guiding principle for the interaction between Hakonbolaget and its associated retailers throughout the 1950s and 1960s. In 1964, the company formalised its co-operation with three other regional retailer-sponsored wholesale companies and formed a national retail chain called the ICA-retailers. At the same time, the Hakon deal became the guiding principle for wholesale-retail interaction also within the other purchasing centres. Gradually the purchasing fidelity of the members grew to such levels that ICA for all practical purposes was regarded as an integrated food distribution group, rather than as a loose coalition of independent retailers and wholesalers (Mattsson, 1969). As a whole, this group was reported to account for approximately 30 per cent of both wholesale and retail food sales in Sweden in 1980.

Still, my vivid recollections of a lorry from Dagab (the major competing private food wholesaler) regularly unloading goods outside the local ICA-store in my residential area in the 1970s suggest that even then, the new order was less than perfect.

Discussion

The topic of this chapter is not exactly 'the market'. Rather, the realization of the Hakon deal is about the more general process of economic organizing. This chapter, then, is concerned with the process through which markets and other economic orders emerge. Viewed as such, it directs attention to the import of efforts to alter calculative practices, and consequently to what can be called the anthropology of calculation.

In this concluding section, I will address three central issues with respect to the interrelation between calculative practices and the process of economic organizing. Firstly, I will review a classic argument put forward by Coase concerning the transition between different economic orders. Secondly, I will critically assess the existing preoccupation with defining the market as a starting point for inquiries about economic organizing. Thirdly, I will discuss the practical shaping of (calculative) market agencies.

Where did the market go?

If this chapter is a story about the process through which markets and other economic orders emerge, then, in a sense, it is Coase (1937) all over again: why are certain transactions performed under 'market'-like circumstances and others under more hierarchical conditions?

In fact, the following quote would seem to be a fairly accurate summary of the story told on the preceding pages.

> [T]he operation of a market costs something and by forming an organization and allowing some authority (an 'entrepreneur') to direct the resources, certain marketing costs are saved. The entrepreneur has to carry out this function at less cost, taking into account the fact that he may get factors of production at a lower price than the market transactions which he supersedes, because it is always possible to revert to the open market if he fails to do this. (Coase, 1937: 392)

Almost accurate. On the basis of the story about the Hakon deal, I want to raise two important objections to Coase's statement. First, my account suggests that the market may no longer be there. Over the decades that followed, other Swedish wholesalers and retailers chose to solve the problem of how to organize their economic exchanges in a similar way as had Hakonbolaget and the Hakon retailers. By 1970, then, the wholesale market for food products as it was known in the early 1950s had effectively been 'de-realized'. Rather than simply reverting 'to the open market' (or to a hierarchy for that matter), an actor might thus have to engage in (re-)constructing such a market (or hierarchy). Given the arduous efforts reported as part of the account above, as well as in numerous other accounts of similar transitions, this is far from easy. Then again, engaging in such activities may be precisely what market actors are doing, all the time.

Beyond this observation, there is a more fundamental issue at stake. In his talk about the entrepreneur having 'to carry out this function at less cost', Coase seems to take for granted that there exists an established way of performing the calculations that supposedly precedes a choice between market and hierarchy. This is not always the case. There are many ways in which to work up such calculations. Moreover, the account of the Hakon deal suggests that the establishment of such calculations are endogenous to the shaping of economic orders and that their realization involves the alignment of a complex set of materially heterogeneous elements (cf. Callon and Muniesa, 2005). In addition, it suggests that there may be many actors who are simultaneously trying to incorporate highly diverse ideas into the everyday calculations that lead up to economic exchanges. This means that interferences between multiple calculative devices are likely to be part of economic ordering processes (cf. Law and Urry, 2004; see also Sjögren and Helgesson, this volume). Thus, when taking an interest in how economic orders are shaped, the market-hierarchy dichotomy quickly becomes supplanted by a multitude of possible arrangements. Rather than the perennial paradoxes implied by this dichotomy, the issues facing market actors are likely to be dynamic and multiple in character, involving the practical management of interferences *between* calculative devices.

Draining the market concept?

Well-rooted distinctions between different economic orders, such as that between markets and hierarchies, are not likely to be so easily dismissed. Thus, there is another question that begs an answer. Isn't the story of the Hakon deal simply one of de-marketization? Indeed, by taking the established order in the 1940s as the starting point, with its competing wholesalers selling to independent retailers, the Hakon deal is easily interpreted as a case of de-marketization. Using classic distinctions it would seem that by ousting the competitors from the scene and introducing retail membership, the Hakon deal replaced the market with an organization (Brunsson, 2004).

A similar conclusion could also be drawn based on the three requirements that Don Slater has suggested for market transactions (Slater, 2002: 238): 1) that individual objects of exchange can be materially and conceptually disentangled; 2) that buyers and sellers are clearly distinguished as individual socio-legal entities; and 3) that each transaction is separated from others in terms of the obligations that they put on these parties. Viewed in this light, the Hakon deal is an effort to reorganize a set of transactions so that the third requirement no longer holds. That is, it is an effort to realize an economic order where several transactions between a specific seller and a specific buyer are considered jointly. Hence, it is a de-marketization.

Such a conclusion has its appeal, primarily by reserving some idiosyncrasies to markets as compared to other socio-economic orders. It does, however, direct attention away from, and consequently misses out on several important aspects of practical market-*ing*. (I use the term *market-ing*, here, as shorthand for all the work that actors engage in when shaping markets and other economic orders, including those activities implied by the more common term *marketing*). Scholars in industrial marketing, particularly in the markets-as-networks tradition, have for many years raised doubts concerning the usefulness of market definitions such as the one offered by Slater (Hägg and Johanson, 1982; Håkansson, 1989; Johanson and Mattsson, 1992; McLoughlin and Horan, 2002). Based on empirical observations of long-term exchange relationships in a large number of industrial sectors, they have argued that markets are often characterized by 'many hands that meet' rather than an invisible hand. Further, they have stressed the import of complementarity and interdependence rather than substitutability and independence in economic organizing processes. These are but some examples of aspects that risk being lost in analyses preoccupied with defining in principle what markets are.

Even more compellingly, such a preoccupation may be utterly unnecessary. In fact, I would argue that there is no need whatsoever to define what a market is and is not, if we are interested in economic organizing. If such a distinction is important, then the actors involved are likely to be busy doing just that as part of their efforts at economic organizing (as is readily observable in most processes of market de-regulation). Moreover, their efforts tend to do a much better job of producing convincing markets than the texts we write. It is, to restate a central tenet in the sociology of translation, by studying these actors and their efforts that we have the best chances of learning something about economic organizing (cf. Latour, 1996: 200).

From that perspective, the efforts of Hakonbolaget show that market-ing concerns not only the goods being exchanged. Although the (qualification of) goods remained an important part of wholesale-retail interaction also under the Hakon deal, as for instance the goods catalogue and the information leaflets serve to show, the emphasis clearly lay elsewhere. The major efforts were directed towards rationalizing goods distribution by reorganizing the very transactions that linked wholesale and retail trade.

Callon, Méadel and Rabeharisoa (2002) have convincingly argued that the process of qualification/requalification of goods is at the heart of the dynamics of economic ordering. The Hakon deal suggests that the form of exchange may be subject to a similar process, or stated differently, that transactions may be subject to calculations alongside goods.[8] The qualification and subsequent calculation of modes of exchange involves questions about how supply and demand meet, how prices are set, what the assortment of goods looks like, how goods are disentangled from the seller (eg, how to dispatch orders) and how they enter into the world of the buyer (deliveries and use). You could say that Hakonbolaget sought to replace the list of comparable entities so central to calculations in the competitive order, with a list of associated entities including time spent on purchasing, quality of the resulting assortment, stock-keeping costs, benefits of store planning and joint advertising, and direct premiums for certain behaviour.

This general point is also well known from classical marketing literature, where the emergence of middlemen, such as wholesalers and retailers, has often been explained in functionalistic terms as a consequence of their economizing effects on transactions, eg, the number of transactions and the search costs, and their value creation, eg, offering assortments rather than single goods (see, eg, Alderson, 1966). Indeed, an abstract version of these very insights concerning the role of intermediaries seem to have been reinvented more recently as economists have begun to show an interest in market making and market microstructure (cf. Spulber, 1996). While these ideas were clearly present in the Hakon deal, the efforts of Hakonbolaget provide a nice illustration of the idea that: '[A]ll framing thus represents a violent effort to extricate the agents concerned from [the network of interactions in which they are involved] and push them onto a clearly demarcated stage which has been specially prepared and fitted out' (Callon, 1998a: 253).

By creating a metrological system capable of re-presenting the various activities performed within the warehouse as well as the cost consequences of different purchasing behaviours, Hakonbolaget emerged as a new centre of calculation (cf. Callon, 1998a; Latour, 1987). By introducing a number of new calculative devices, eg, the goods catalogue, the bonus scales and the order forms, the calculative competences of both its local offices and its retail customers were altered so that they could account also for the form of transaction. A member was still able to compare goods and reach decisions as to what to buy, although the various lists of entities had been reduced to what was to be found in the goods catalogue edited by Hakonbolaget. In this sense, the efforts of Hakonbolaget can be seen as an attempt to become a market provider for its members, rather than a market actor among others. Viewed in this way, the story of the Hakon deal is one of market (re)making rather than de-marketization.

The difficult practice of shaping market actors

A final insight offered by the account of the Hakon deal is that economic organizing and the emergence of economic orders are closely connected to the formation of economic (calculative) agencies. And this connection is somewhat of a paradox. On the one hand, suitable buyers and sellers are not simply available off the shelf, as (many) economists would have it. On the other, buyers and sellers are so readily available that it creates problems for actors who engage in economic organizing.

It is clear that the proponents of the Hakon deal engaged in shaping several new agencies as part of their efforts to realize the new order. Agencies such as the new Hakon retailer, aka 'the member', and the contact-man did not exist prior to the implementation of the new programme, but were brought into being in the process. At the same time, it is equally clear that there was an ample supply of buyers and sellers already taking part in the situations that Hakonbolaget sought to reorganize.

Stated more generally, we find buyers and sellers everywhere. They are so common that almost any attempt to reorganize economic transactions will have to make use of materials already involved in performing other buyers and sellers. The reasoning is somewhat akin to one of the basic tenets of the embeddedness position developed by Granovetter, ie, that economic behaviour and institutions are constrained by ongoing social relations (Granovetter, 1985, 1992). Here, however, the key issue is that actors who engage in attempts to realize an envisioned economic order are constrained by the embeddedness of heterogeneous elements into actor-networks performing *other* economic orders (cf. Callon and Law, 1995, 1997; Callon, 1998a).

What this amounts to is that economic orders are performed by agencies that have overlapping constitutions. The consequence is clearly illustrated in the story of the Hakon deal: the overlaps between the configurations of a member and a retailer, and between a contact-man and a salesman, made it difficult for Hakonbolaget to exact the correct performance in specific exchange situations. Preventing alternative agential configurations from performing, and alternative calculations from being made, thus becomes a major issue for actors who are trying to realize a particular economic order. At the same time, the decision by Hakonbolaget to resume active sales again indicates that these overlapping agential constitutions also may be an important source of resilience and dynamics in processes of economic organizing.

Concluding remarks

Three concluding remarks can be made to summarize the discussion. Firstly, the process of economic organizing is not primarily one in which actors select, based on an existing calculative algorithm, the solution that renders them the highest benefits. Rather it is a process through which such solutions, and the calculative algorithms that go with them, are being shaped. The presence of simultaneous efforts by different actors to give direction to the process of economic organizing suggests that such processes can be characterised by multiplicity. Secondly, and relatedly, inquiries that start out by assuming that there is a finite number of economic orders possible, are necessarily handicapped at the outset. In principle, there is no such limit and our chances of knowing more about the available alternatives are not improved by assuming that there is. Thirdly, the practical realization of economic agencies is likely to be an important, yet paradoxical, facet of economic organizing. On the one hand, the performance of a particular calculative algorithm requires assembling a specific agential configuration, which seldom will be readily available. On the other, the practical realization of such a configuration is likely to disrupt many other on-going agential configurations, rendering the performance of any specific one both problematic and precarious.

A final comment on the continued efforts of Hakonbolaget and its associated retailers to render economic encounters calculable through the Hakon deal, might be addressed to Bauman (1992): economic orders are seldom pure, but not for the lack of trying.

Notes

1 This chapter is a considerably revised version of a paper originally presented at the 4S conference in Paris, August 2004. It has benefited greatly from comments supplied by the editors of this volume as well as by Claes-Fredrik Helgesson and Franck Cochoy.
2 These questions are all at the heart of the debate triggered by the publication of *The Laws of the Markets* (see Callon, 1998b; Callon, Méadel and Rabeharisoa, 2002; Miller, 2002; Slater, 2002; Holm, 2003). Although inspired by these efforts, this chapter focuses more narrowly on the interrelation between various aspects of calculation and economic organizing.
3 I offer this prologue since most readers are likely to be unfamiliar with Swedish food-distribution in the 1940's. It adds some points of reference to the story told in the remainder of the chapter. This main story was compiled from my reconstruction of the modernization of food distribution in post-war Sweden (Kjellberg, 2001) using the methodological principles of the actor-network approach (see eg, Callon, 1986; Latour, 1987; Law, 1994). The story is based on archive material collected from Hakonbolaget, from private archives of former employees, from deposits made at the Library at the Stockholm School of Economics and at the Swedish National Archives.

4 There were two types of bodies involved in policy making within Hakonbolaget during these years: the directors' conference and the managers' conference. The directors' conference was a regular series of meetings held approximately four times a year where the top central managers and district office directors of Hakonbolaget met to discuss general issues related to company operations. The managers' conference, which also met approximately four times a year, was a wider body including also middle level managers such as the office managers at the affiliate offices.

5 The whole programme offers an interesting variant of what Kotler and Levy have called demarketing, defined as 'that aspect of marketing that deals with discouraging customers in general or a certain class of customers in particular on either a temporary or permanent basis' (Kotler and Levy, 1971: 75). By reducing their sales efforts and instead opting for co-operation, Hakonbolaget employed demarketing tools for marketing purposes! I thank Franck Cochoy for pointing this out to me.

6 Adjusted for inflation between 1947 and 2007, and converted into euro, the proposed purchasing limit corresponds to roughly €10,000/year. For the retailers associated to Hakonbolaget it corresponded to between two and ten per cent of their annual turnover.

7 To qualify for membership, a retailer had to own *shares* in Hakonbolaget. This was not a very tough requirement since most of the large customers already were shareholders, see Table 1.

8 In a sense then, efforts such as the Hakon deal anticipate the advent of various modern-day frameworks, among which the Williamsonian transaction cost analysis perhaps has been most influential (eg, Williamson, 1994). Indeed, the calculative space created through the Hakon deal would be one example of precisely the kind of framework that Coase assumed to already be in place in his discussion on the nature of firm and the cost of utilizing the market (Coase, 1937).

References

af Trolle, U. (1963) *Distributionsekonomi I*, Malmö: Hermods.
Alderson, W. (1966) 'Factors governing the development of marketing channels', in B. E. Mallen (ed.), *The marketing channel: A conceptual viewpoint*, New York: John Wiley & Sons.
Bauman, Z. (1992), *Intimations of postmodernity*. London: Routledge.
Brunsson, N. (2004), 'Marknad, organization och reform', in C.-F. Helgesson, H. Kjellberg and A. Liljenberg (eds), *Den där marknaden*. Lund: Studentlitteratur.
Callon, M. (1986), 'Some elements of a sociology of translation: Domestication of the scallops and the fishermen of St-Brieuc bay', in J. Law (ed.), *Power, action and belief: A new sociology of knowledge?* London: Routledge & Kegan Paul.
Callon, M. (1998a), 'An essay on framing and overflowing: Economic externalities revisited by sociology', in M. Callon (ed.), *The laws of the markets*. Oxford: Blackwell.
Callon, M. (ed.) (1998b), *The laws of the markets*. Oxford: Blackwell.
Callon, M. and J. Law (1995), 'Agency and the hybrid collectif', *South Atlantic Quarterly*, 94(2): 481–507.
Callon, M. and J. Law (1997), 'After the individual in society: Lessons on collectivity from science, technology and society'. *Canadian Journal of Sociology*, 22(2): 165–182.
Callon, M., C. Méadel and V. Rabeharisoa (2002), 'The economy of qualities', *Economy and Society*, 31(2): 194–217.
Callon, M. and F. Muniesa (2005), 'Economic markets as calculative collective devices', *Organization Studies*, 26(8): 1229–1250.
Coase, R. (1937), 'The nature of the firm', *Economica*, 4(4): 396–405.
Collin, G. and N.-E. Wirsäll (eds.) (1948), *Hakonbolaget – köpmännens inköpscentral, Medlemsbok*. Västerås: AB Hakon Swenson.
Granovetter, M. (1985), 'Economic action and social structure: The problem of embeddedness', *American Journal of Sociology*, 91(3): 481–510.
Granovetter, M. (1992), 'Problems of explanation in economic sociology', in N. Nohria and R. Eccles (eds.), *Networks and organizations*. Boston (Massachusetts): Harvard Business School Press.

Hakonbolaget (1947), *Minutes of the managers' conference*. Västerås: AB Hakon Swenson.
Hakonbolaget (1948), *Minutes of the retail councils*. Västerås: AB Hakon Swenson.
Hakonbolaget (1949a), *Minutes of the directors' conference*. Västerås: AB Hakon Swenson.
Hakonbolaget (1949b), *Minutes of the managers' conference*. Västerås: AB Hakon Swenson.
Hakonbolaget (1950), *Hakonsgiven: En revolution inom svensk varudistribution*. Information leaflet. Västerås: AB Hakon Swenson.
Holm, P. (2003), 'Which way is up on Callon?' *Sosiologisk årbok* (1): 125–156.
Håkansson, H. (ed.) (1989), *Corporate technological behaviour, co-operation and networks*. London: Routledge.
Hägg, I. and I. Johanson (1982), *Företag i nätverk*. Stockholm: SNS.
Johanson, J. and L.-G. Mattsson (1992), 'Network positions and strategic action: An analytical framework', in B. Axelsson and G. Easton (eds), *Industrial networks: A new view of reality*. London: Routledge.
Kjellberg, H. (2001), *Organizing distribution: Hakonbolaget and the efforts to rationalize food distribution, 1940–1960*. Stockholm: The Economic Research Institute.
Kotler, P. and S. J. Levy (1971), 'Demarketing, yes, demarketing'. *Harvard Business Review*, 49(6): 74–80.
Latour, B. (1987), *Science in action: How to follow scientists and engineers through society*. Cambridge (Massachusetts): Harvard University Press.
Latour, B. (1996), *Aramis, or the love of technology*. Cambridge (Massachusetts): Harvard University Press.
Law, J. (1994), *Organizing modernity*. Oxford: Blackwell.
Law, J. and J. Urry (2004), 'Enacting the social', *Economy and Society*, 33(3): 390–410.
Mattsson, L.-G. (1969), *Integration and efficiency in marketing systems*. Stockholm: Norstedt.
McLoughlin, D. and C. Horan, C. (2002), 'Markets-as-networks: Notes on a unique understanding', *Journal of Business Research*, 55(7): 535–543.
Miller, D. (2002), 'Turning Callon the right way up', *Economy and Society*, 31(2): 218–233.
Slater, D. (2002), 'From calculation to alienation: Disentangling economic abstractions', *Economy and Society*, 31(2): 234–249.
Spulber, D. F. (1996), 'Market microstructure and intermediation', *The Journal of Economic Perspectives*, 10(3): 135–152.
Williamson, O. E. (1994), 'Transaction cost economics and organization theory', in N. J. Smelser and R. Swedberg (eds.), *The handbook of economic sociology*. Princeton (New Jersey): Princeton University Press.
Wirsäll, N.-E. (1949a), *Den nya Hakonsgiven*. Internal report. Västerås: AB Hakon Swenson.
Wirsäll, N.-E. (1949b), 'Den nya Hakonsgiven', *Affärsekonomi*, 1949(8): 379–398.
Wirsäll, N.-E., O. Kihlgren, V. Eriksson, E. Gotborn and A. Lundgren (1952), *Hakonsgiven, Noveas betänkande*. Internal report. Västerås: AB Hakon Swenson.

Struggling to be displayed at the point of purchase: the emergence of merchandising in French supermarkets

Sandrine Barrey

Introduction

Merchandising is a management tool that has been progressively mastered by retailers.[1] Retailers use this tool to facilitate the encounter between supply and demand, by controlling the presentation of products at the point of purchase. This chapter focuses on the conditions under which merchandising has emerged as a market device, as well as on the evolution of relationships between retailers and manufacturers regarding its implementation. The stakes are high when it comes to mastering merchandising, since capturing customers and controlling the appropriation of a share of the profits in 'big box' retail is directly affected by the final phase of merchandising. The first part of the chapter analyses the conditions under which merchandising emerged, the forces underlying technical transformations, and trends in the division of labour between manufacturers and retailers concerning its control. Next, the chapter examines the processes whereby merchandising was stabilized around a definition made common to multiple market professionals, who were all set on finding fresh outlets for their activities.

Merchandising developed in France over a period of only 20 years even though its accommodation required a large number of changes. Retracing this evolution requires investigating the progressive accumulation of equipment involved in the selling process. The method I have chosen here is a comprehensive examination of one major professional journal for retailers in France: *Points de Vente* (Points of Sale). The journal's date of first issue, 1962, corresponds to French manufacturers' first attempts at merchandising. Concrete examples of the tool's implementation in French supermarkets and of the opinions expressed by professionals are reported in the journal, which enables us to study the arrival of merchandising in the mass distribution sector, and its successive appropriations/transformations by market professionals. To clarify and complete the empirical evidence, a less systematic review of other professional journals (such as *LSA* or *Linéaires*) was conducted, as well as of management handbooks. Further empirical support was drawn from interviews with mass distribution professionals who experienced the changes in this domain first-hand. Finally,

© 2007 The Author. Editorial organisation © 2007 The Editorial Board of the Sociological Review. Published by Blackwell Publishing Ltd, 9600 Garsington Road, Oxford OX4 2DQ, UK and 350 Main Street, Malden, MA 02148, USA

the analysis of a single French case of the implementation of merchandising tools by a leading food processor, France-Glaces Findus, is used to demonstrate the efforts made by a one firm to 'make its mark' on the market via a process of 'context-building' as a means of developing its business.

Merchandising takes hold: a current runs through the aisles

The concept of merchandising appeared for the first time in American manuals intended to formalize certain practices (Douglas, 1918; Copeland, 1927). In France, a similar process of formalization took place much later, although the founding principles of merchandising as a management science were applied there well before the English term came to encompass the set of techniques that it does today. To be convinced of this, one need only recall Emile Zola's (1984 [1883]) description of the 'modern' merchants of the 19th century, of whom Aristide Boucicaut – founder of the department store Bon Marché in Paris – is probably still emblematic. Boucicaut was a specialist in the display of goods at the point of purchase. He had already foreseen the advantage of stacking goods to create the effect of mass (Zola, 1984: 91), and had even conceived of 'drowning' products without much attractiveness – like shawls in summer – amidst far more lively shelves to promote their sale.

Curiously, the practice of merchandising initially concerned the makers of products (manufacturers) rather than those who distributed them (retailers). Leaders in the French market, such as L'Oréal and Gervais-Danone, were the first to undertake merchandising actions in the early 60s (Seret, 1985). It is by analysing the characteristics of a new form of selling, known as 'self-service', that we might better understand why manufacturers were the first to show an interest in this new type of product management.

Merchandising: a manufacturers' initiative

Self-service is characterized by the display of all goods available for sale in plain view of the customer: buyers have free access to all products and can choose among them without any direct human intervention channelling that choice. Of course, advertising and packaging are 'silent sellers' (Pidlitch, 1963; Strasser, 1989; Cochoy, 2002), but once these mediators had been circumvented by modern merchandising methods, manufacturers no longer had the same proximity to retail outlets that they had enjoyed previously. The advent of self-service selling did away with salesperson support through product promotion. All of the goods for sale became rivals, were equally faced by the customer, and all of them had to 'sell themselves' on their own. Not, of course, in the sense of 'selling themselves alone', since behind technical mediations like packaging and brand there are numerous human beings, but in the sense of 'selling themselves in the absence of direct human support'. It was then that the arrangement of products in the retail display space became an important stake for manufacturers who wanted to maintain control 'at-a-distance' over the sale of their products.

Consider this history through the firm France-Glaces Findus, a major player in the frozen foodstuff sector. The presentation here is based on the firm's application, in 1998, for the 'jury's special prize' awarded by the Institut Français du Merchandising (IFM), the main professional association in the field of French merchandising. I have chosen to analyse France-Glaces Findus (its application file) for three reasons. First, because it was actually awarded the prize by the IFM, which means that it had all the qualities *expected* by the relevant authorities. Second, the application file presents a succession of the firm's devices for managing retail display space, in fine detail. Finally, the application file also reports a healthy amount of qualitative and quantitative data from INSEE (France's national institute for statistics and economic surveys) on consumer behaviour in the frozen foods section. Through this case study, we will see how this manufacturer made use of a particular context and seized upon elements of it, to advance within its own business.

The appearance of merchandising at France-Glaces Findus can be explained by the consumption habits of the time, as well as by the supermarket's facilities for selling this particular type of product, frozen foodstuff. On the demand side, the frozen food market was still in its infancy in the early 60s. The supply of frozen products was limited to vegetables and fish, since, despite the development of the sector, the use of frozen products still bore strong negative associations in the domestic sphere. For example, ice-creams remained a special treat to be consumed outside of the home. To develop their markets, a manufacturer's primary challenge was to convince customers, who still bought and ate their ice-creams in ice-cream parlours, to buy it directly from supermarkets. The goal was not just to make the customer discover a product they had not thought of, but it was also to persuade them to change their consumption and usage habits. Between 1963 and 1972, France-Glaces Findus hired 15 'product demonstrators' who travelled throughout France presenting Findus frozen products at the points of sale, teaching consumers how to use them. In the early 70s, the firm witnessed an explosion in the demand for frozen foods, stimulated by manufacturing's on-going innovation. With the help of their product demonstrators, France-Glaces Findus slowly managed to transform 'consumers of ice-cream outside the home' into customers who bought ice-cream from supermarkets. This change went hand-in-hand with other changes, especially widespread household acquisition of deep-freezers (Herpin and Verger, 1988: 60).

If, on the demand side, possession of a deep-freeze was the condition *sine qua non* for developing the frozen food market, it was equally important for the supermarket intermediary to have the required facilities. Although supermarkets had invested in freezers, according to France-Glaces Findus, these did not satisfactorily display their products, which tended to be overlooked in the mass of other frozen foods. In order to sell its goods from the best possible conditions, the firm had to take charge of the management of retail display space. This was the objective when it created a merchandising service within the firm, in 1973. The action logic was the promotion of products at a distance, via intermediate objects. Procedures set up by the firm disseminated the advertising efforts nationally, right into each point of purchase. During the 70s, the firm developed its first point-of-sale promotions to support the material presentation of its frozen foods and ice-creams in retail outlets. It activated the frozen food department of supermarkets by choosing the position of promotional operations, and by offering clear signposts, accompanied by information, to customers. In and of themselves, these procedures were nothing new. They were more of an extension of the logic behind attractive packaging, which had become so common that even a handsome product might drowned out in the ocean of supply were it not highlighted in some additional way. Making a product stand out in the display space required not only words and pictures, but also a kind of plot. Until the mid-80s, the general mission of point-of-sale campaigns was limited to promoting products off the shelves or out of specific display cases (Debaussart, 1989: 52).

In order to 'act at a distance' and affect the point of purchase, however, France-Glaces Findus had to garner the involvement of actors with the closest physical 'ties' to the shop, that is, of the retailers. Hence, for the merchandising to be effective, manufacturers also needed to develop 'selling aid' for their retailer counterparts. Offering such an aid for promoting France-Glaces Findus products required modifying communication methods upstream. Instead of sales reps dealing with the frozen-food department manager at supermarkets, actual manufacturer specific salespeople were deployed on the retail floor. France-Glaces Findus launched two programmes with this objective. The first programme was designed to 'enrol' retailers. It trained sales representatives on ways of convincing the retail sales force to move away from the act of 'selling', and accept 'having someone else sell' in their place.

The second programme created tools to aid rather than displace the existing retail sales force. One of these tools was a 'grid', a guide for organizing the display spaces, which on one side, indicated an optimal assortment (of the products that the distributor was supposed to have), and on the other, the manufacturer's suggestions for how they should be displayed. Translated onto this 'grid', the retail display space became more coherent in the eyes of department managers who now simply had to follow their 'lists'. For the managers this little tool was a veritable 'cognitive artefact' (Norman, 1991). By offering them a large amount of diverse information of a varied nature on the same written medium, from different sources,[2] the 'grid' reduced the need for internalization or learning, and, in effect, expanded their capacity for memorization. Beyond the cognitive amplification achieved by the loading of material onto a 'centre of calculation', the manufacturer's action logic engaged a crucial dimension of design: the transcription of the shelves on the grid highlighted its own products in the retail display space by allocating them a larger 'facing'[3] than rival products and an optimal place in the display space (usually at the average consumer's eye level).

The manufacturers' intrusion, from a distance via objects and via people at closer proximity, did not seem to disturb the retailers, at least not until the late

70s. A retailer's job still consisted of selling products manufactured by other firms in mass quantities, and for that purpose all of these tools were certainly helpful. The evolution of the organizational, legislative and competitive contexts, however, soon compelled supermarkets to take over an activity that, they would come to feel, had been left in the hands of manufacturers for too long. In this sense and, paradoxically so, it was the efforts of manufacturers that ended up arming retailers with the very equipment they needed to bypass them.

Three reasons for retailers to take over merchandising at the point of purchase

An organizational factor: centralizing the physical distribution of products

In the mid-70s, mass distribution adhered more to a logic of purchasing than to a logic of selling. Retailers seldom manipulated the products they purchased. In fact, the success of the discount system depended on mass procurement from suppliers. Moreover, the growth of firms and the extension of sales networks soon created the required conditions for achieving greater efficiency at a logistic level (Colla, 1997: 15), where the search for higher profits encouraged greater productivity in a part of the organization that still generated very high costs (Moati, 2001: 187). Efforts to reduce the costs of logistics started in the mid-70s, as a former buyer for a regional trading group explains:

> I started working in a supermarket 27 years ago [. . .] Suppliers were on their knees! We did whatever we liked, or almost! And plus, it was interesting, we did everything: I bought my products, we had no purchasing centre. And then afterwards, I worked for a chain of small urban supermarkets. The group had just bought over a food distributor with chain stores, and there I was a buyer on a regional purchasing centre, because we were starting to organize purchases for fresh produce; and so there I worked at regional level, to supply supermarkets, but I was also negotiating with firms. Those were really the good times. We started to buy fresh foods in bulk, and you can imagine the spate of discounts . . . those were really the good times! (Richard, product coordinator, 'Ultra-frais')[4]

The creation of 'super purchasing centres' shrank distribution costs since the price per square meter, per product, was lower than that of supermarkets (Colla, 1997: 15). The development of these purchasing platforms would also radically alter relations between retailers and firms. Not only did it reinforce retailers' negotiating power with suppliers, by forcing them to make less frequent but larger deliveries, but in centralizing purchasing it also created a distance between the agents involved – suppliers and supermarket department managers – who had often interacted until then. It forced them to work via a third type of organization that had not previously existed, that is, through trading groups and warehouses. These new mediators, 'obligatory points of passage' for manufacturers, increased the product maker's zone of uncertainty, since it no longer had direct access to the sales figures of the supermarkets that commercialized its products. Since relevant data hardly reached them any more, many suppliers had to stop giving merchandising advice, as was the case, for example, for cleaning product manufacturers in the early 80s.

Paradoxically, it was when trade was industrialized and became distant from 'pure' market logic – by organizing its sales according to warehouses and regional purchasing centres – that retailers obtained the most advantageous market effect, since these centres enabled them to take over the merchandising function. Additionally, the gradual saturation of retailers' growth potential further prompted them to turn to take an interest in merchandising.

The end of extensive growth

On 27 December 1973 the Royer Act (law 73-1193, articles 28-34), a French law oriented towards the trade and the craft industry, was passed. According to this law, new supermarkets had to obtain authorization from the departmental commercial urbanism commission (CDUC) prior to opening. The aim of the law was to protect 'small traders' from the growing competition of large retail chains, a clear and unequivocal objective that was stated in its first four articles. It was necessary to avoid 'wastage of commercial facilities' and to prevent 'small enterprise from being crushed'. The effectiveness of this law, however, has been limited. First, the number of points of sale over 1,000 m authorized to open or expand started to decline from 1989 onwards. Second, the law had unintended consequences such as the proliferation of new supermarkets on the outskirts of towns and cities, as well as by a string of corruption affairs (Cliquet and Des Garets, 2000). Expansion through the race for new openings continued to guarantee retailers' profits. The conquest of market share consisted quite simply of rapidly occupying the field and of 'picking-up' customers wherever they were.

With time, the gradual saturation of the French commercial scene and the coexistence of several rival groups in the same geographic area led consumers progressively to diversify their shopping habits. The retailers' aim was no longer to *find customers*, by offering them products 'within their reach', but was rather to *bring them* into supermarkets by selling them 'better products cheaper'. It should be noted that the success of mass distribution was, in large part, based on the reduction of manufacturing firms' power, much to the benefit of consumers. Retailers strove to obtain the lowest possible prices for consumers, on the basis of the virtuous circle of 'small margins, low prices, high volumes', and by committing themselves fully to 'the struggle against high prices' and the richness of manufacturers' offers (Barrey, 2004: 147–168). Hence, capturing the customer required the creation of the retail group's own image, which was achieved via more personalized stores and shelf displays. In this new *décor*, manufacturers' merchandising became increasingly invasive as their heterogeneous point-of-sale promotions compromised the coherence of the retailer's own vision for the commercial space:

> We refuse [. . .] studies that benefit suppliers, advertising objects, packaging such as giraffe products [. . .]. (A sales group manager, cited in Romec, 1989: 92)[5]

> It seemed unacceptable for us to be reduced to entrusting our retail display space to manufacturers. [. . .] We had to stop being subjected to marketing and to take care of it ourselves! (Hervé Motte, manager of the trading group of Auchan, cited in Rebeix, 1985: 62)

Retailers had indeed started to become aware of manufacturers' potential capacity for 'action at a distance'. The idea of defending the consumer's interests against attempts at enrolment launched by suppliers was a powerful foil to manufacturer's promotional devices at the point of purchase. The new life breathed into retailers' brands provided yet another additional encouragement for retailers to take the merchandising of their products in hand.

A competitive factor: the development of distributor brands

The invention of 'free products', a line put out by the Carrefour group in 1976, revived the dynamic of distributor brands in France, but the revolution was stopped before its completion. Private label production was limited to products that sold well, and therefore accounted for only a small percentage of supermarket sales (Barrey, 2004: 73–112). Unlike distribution groups that have been exploiting distributor brands for a long time (eg, firms like Casino, Migros, Marks & Spencer), most French supermarkets were largely unfamiliar with the techniques required by a genuine distributor brand policy:

> They tried to capture a share of the industry's value added without really understanding that they also had to integrate a part of the functions normally fulfilled by manufacturers, especially the marketing function. (Thil and Baroux, 1983: 74)

Overall, new products kept arriving on the market. There were 'low cost' and 'no name' products launched to compete with bottom-of-the-range products of competitors, especially those of deep discounters who had just entered the market, openly claiming that their products were 'not quite as good' as brand-name products, but corresponded perfectly to consumers' demand for low-priced goods. These 'no name' products started to compete seriously with private labels (distributor brands). Likewise, their presentation (black writing on white labels) was similar to that of private label products, which tended to confuse customers (Thil and Baroux, 1983: 80). Even though there was ample evidence that cheap products did correspond to a consumer segment, this new trend obliged retailers to structure their own product lines better. From 1985, most of them started printing their names on distributor brand products such that:

> [. . .] distributor brand products of the second generation, 'clones' of brand-name products, sold at a substantially lower price, with attractive packaging featuring the distributor's brand name. (Moati, 2001: 270)

By printing the distribution group's name clearly on product labels and by improving their quality – that is, by redefining benchmark qualities[6] – retailers endeavoured to personalize and to enhance relationships with customers at their points of sale. Distribution lines were re-structured into three price segments:

national brand products; distributor brand products, on average 20 per cent cheaper than national brands; and 'first price' products (Thil and Baroux, 1983: 82). This tripartite segmentation demonstrates retailers' engagement with a market logic that had not yet been developed when private brand products were initially launched. But the logic was also profit-related. Retailers discovered the function of brand proliferation that had until then been used by manufacturers, multiplying their products within the same range. The more brands a distributor had in the various product families, the more market share it took over from manufacturers. With these new products, retailers no longer tried only to sell 'the most products present at the point of purchase' but also, if possible, to sell 'the most private brand products' for which margins were greater than those of national brand products (Sordet, Paysant and Brosselin, 2002: 76).

In 1985, the products with the best position in the retail display space, that is, national brands, were still those that sold the fastest (Lévy, 1985). As retailers asserted themselves by developing their own brands, they also took over the complete management of their retail display space. Henceforth, those products that 'sold best' were used as loss leaders to channel customers towards the distributor's brand products.

Clearly, it was the simultaneous appearance and combination of organizational and competitive factors that encouraged retailers to take over merchandising from manufacturers. This does not mean that context was imposed across all of the market actors in a mechanical and homogeneous way. What I try to show here is how certain actors grasped elements of this context to promote their own interests. This process of re-contextualization through the changing of hands of merchandising allows us to revisit a classical thesis in market sociology that treats the asymmetry of power between retailers and manufacturers. Retailers' power over producers, especially when it is a matter of analysing the modalities of benchmarking their products, is often explained by the progressive concentration of retail distribution:

> [. . .] the five leading trading groups control almost all the points of sale of food products (the retailers' strength stems from their concentration which uniformizes definitions of consumers). (Dubuisson-Quellier, Méadel and Rabeharisoa, 1999: 150)
>
> At a time when 80% of food products are bought from supermarkets, fish tends to have a particular place since it is found both in specialized shops – of which there are fewer and fewer – and in supermarkets. [. . .] Mass distribution uses this privileged access to consumers to back up its demands on suppliers, in the name of the customer being king. (Debril, 2000: 439)

These analyses account for trends in the distribution sector towards centralization and concentration, which partly explains retailers' power over manufacturers in terms of 'the laws of the market' (Dupuy and Thoenig, 1986). It is important to emphasize, however, that alongside this 'quantitative' power of negotiation (related to the weight in turnover generated by possible markets), there is also power that stems from a more 'qualitative' mastery of management devices, as explored here, in terms of control over the commercial space and of effective ways of presenting products.

The intent to take over an activity that had previously been left to manufacturers was concretized by the creation of posts for merchandisers within commercial firms. Even if Casino remained a pioneer in the field of merchandising in France, it was soon joined by its competitors. In 1987, Carrefour, for example, created merchandising manager posts per sector and per region, and since 1982 Euromarché has also had a merchandising department (Le Blanc and de Chaumont, 1989: 86). This new management mode, however, remained largely a pragmatic activity, largely ill-defined at the professional level. Merchandising was either taken care of by the trading group, or it remained the responsibility of each point of purchase, as in firms with less centralized structures, as were Carrefour and Auchan at that time. In these cases, merchandising was the department managers' job. With regard to the management of merchandising services, firms also opted for a great diversity of solutions, instituted from the marketing division all the way to the purchasing division (Le Blanc and de Chaumont, 1989: 87).

To acquire control over the retail display space, retailers also had to rely on other agencies. 'Control over the territory' required 'investments in forms' (Thévenot, 1984; Desrosières, 1998). Merchandising equipment was generated from agencies outside distribution. The first tools arrived via the Institut Français du Merchandising (IFM), a think-tank founded in 1972 by consultants and professionals (initially mainly manufacturers), to focus on this new management approach. This institute organized 'seminars for research and technique' with the aim of promoting the development of merchandising techniques. What happened within the IFM in 1986 reveals the detour that mass distribution was taking in order to master merchandising. The institute created an independent arm for studying retailers' merchandising, which more and more retailers joined. An initial impulse had been equally given in 1971 by the publication of a manual by Jean-Emile Masson and Alain Wellhoff, *A la Découverte du Merchandising* (published by Dunod). For ten years, this remained the only management book to cover merchandising comprehensively. The next one, by André Fady and Michel Seret, was only published in 1981 (Fady and Seret, 2000 [1981]). In the end, the retailers' take-over of the management of retail display spaces gave rise to a new group of market professionals in search of fresh outlets for their activities.

From merchandising to a market for display management devices

The advantage of identifying key points in the evolution of merchandising is that it enables us to see merchandising techniques being rationalized as this management method became adapted by several groups of professionals: first panel survey institutes – which quickly interested retailers with the launching of new market measurement devices – followed by manufacturers, who also adjusted their methodological recommendations to suit retailers' needs in order to remain in the race of merchandising share.

The survey institutes: new merchandisers 'at a distance'

In an increasingly competitive commercial environment, firms and retailers have had to master their knowledge thoroughly. The survey panel is a tool that responds to this need. A panel is 'a permanent sample of individuals, consumers, households, shops, firms, etc., built to represent the environment under study. Panel members are questioned at regular intervals on the same subject or on different subjects' (Opsomer, 1987: 14). This definition clarifies the generic method although says nothing about the various logics that can underpin the actual construction of panels. For a long time these tools have functioned as market barometers enabling firms to monitor the life of their products, and the way in which the products are received by consumers, so they might better develop their offering. They have also become a decision-making tool for conscientious retailers who wish to segment their departments to fit customers' needs. Hence, an historical analysis of panel survey institutes cannot be separated from that of the practice of merchandising. This history reveals the birth of a new market: a market for merchandisers.

The Nielsen company, founded in the USA in 1929, is at the origin of the first retailer distributor panel, which was designed to solve stocking and storage problems. being experienced in the retail trade at that time (Opsomer, 1987: 13). It was only in 1954 that STAFCO (*Statistiques Françaises de la Consommation*) set up France's first consumer panel. There are, in fact, two basic types of panel available to those who might want to assess the 'temperature' of the market – distributor panels and consumer panels. Today two firms share most of the panel market in France: AC Nielsen and IRI-Secodip. The former was originally the specialist of distributor panels while the latter, spawned in 1968 by a merger between STAFCO and CECODIS (*Centre d'Etudes de la Consommation et de la Distribution*) started off as an expert in consumer panels.

For many years, the main customers of survey institutes were industrial firms. Data obtained from distributor panels provided information about sales to consumers, the number of purchases made by supermarkets, knowledge of their stocks and other information relative to the quality of the distribution of a product and of its rivals. Consumer panels like those of Secodip or INSEE provided additional information obtained from distributor panels via on-going measurements of consumer behaviours and trends in eating habits. All of these panels were modernized in the 80s to meet manufacturers' increasing needs for a detailed knowledge of the markets in which they operated.

In the mid-80s, when retailers took over the merchandising at their points of sale, panel survey institutes regarded them as an expansion opportunity. To manage the assortment and positioning of products, retailers would demand very precise data on the products they were selling. Of course, they already had a means of obtaining those data from tills and/or warehouses, owing to the commercialization of the bar code in France by GENCOD in 1972 (followed by the creation in 1977 of the European Article Numbering Association), which gradually allowed optical scanning technology to develop. Yet, even if the collection of these data was simplified by optical scanning, their exploitation was extremely time-consuming. Moreover, although suppliers also possessed these data, they manipulated in ways that suited themselves:

> [Retailers no longer accepted] the *eenie-meenie-minie-moe* formula: the one where the supplier draws peremptory recommendations from a magic machine fed by uncontrollable data. (Boudet, 1985)

Panel survey institutes were able to present themselves as neutral protagonists. To nurture relations with retailers, however, they had to find the way of 'interesting' them (Callon, 1986). In 1985, Secodip's buyout of the distributor panel INTERCOR (Opsomer, 1987: 47) laid the foundations for such a strategy. By launching market studies based on a distributor panel (until then the privileged domain of its rival Nielsen) Secodip wanted retailers to take notice of its activities. It supplied sales figures for all brands present at the points of sale, whereas Nielsen distributor panels – still intended only for manufacturers at that time – lumped together the brands of manufacturers who were not customers in a category called 'other brands'. Nielsen's counter-attack to Secodip was swift indeed. It engaged in the construction of a consumer panel, launching the SCAN 5000 panel in January 1986 (Opsomer, 1987: 30). The particularity of the Nielsen panel compared to Secodip's was in the data collected from consumers at the point of purchase. 5000 homemakers, placed on the panel, were equipped with a card containing their socio-demographic characteristics, which identified them at the time of purchase and recorded in detail the products that they bought.

The purpose of panels had changed. They became tools to monitor consumers' behaviours regarding the group's entire offer, as well as for monitoring the different brands' behaviours in relation to the distribution channel. It was thus that 'marketing tools' for manufacturers were transformed into practical 'merchandising tools' for retailers.

In the mid-80s, the merchandiser's trade was reconfigured. Once retailers detected an advantage in applying this new management science, the leading merchandising consultancy firms (ie, BCMW Merchandising, CERCA, Vepro Conseil, Best Seller) started to advertise in the journal *Points de Vente* (aimed at distribution professionals). Once retailers found themselves in a position of strength, and mastered the adjustment of supply and demand flowing through the retail display space, they began to create markets and missions for panel survey institutes. The institute's techniques for characterizing the market, already tried and tested on manufacturers, barely needed to be changed. The panel survey institutes had simply to adapt their techniques to questions that were immediately comprehensible to retailers, an adaptation that often rested on a single parameter (for instance, monitoring the behaviour of all of the brands in a product family on the shelves of all of the channels of distribution).

What had become of manufacturers' merchandising? Although a few advertisements for their own merchandising service still appeared in *Points de Vente*, manufacturers (ie, Onno Bretagne, Fraimont, C.G. COQ, Vittel, Pernod, Gama

Nova, etc.) lost the place that they had a few years earlier. They continued to consider merchandising as a tool for selling or marketing only their own products, even though it was highly integrated into their marketing function. Manufacturers' merchandising managers had nothing more than a consultative role among the purchasers of mass distribution (Comte, 1985: 52). To maintain their remote control over product sales, they had to adjust by aligning their interests with those of the retailers.

Counter-merchandising by manufacturers

The 'action at a distance' of manufacturers on the point of purchase, via intermediate objects (elaborate packaging, point-of-sale promotions, suitable furniture, etc.) had become insufficient. Manufacturers' dream of selling directly to the consumer, without going through retailers, no longer coincided with the desires of retailers who, for their part, dreamt of selling their own brands in the absence of competition. If manufacturers had not entirely disappeared from the merchandisers' market then it was probably because they retained some assets. Although their merchandising recommendations remained occasional and focused on their own products, panel survey institutes sold them information that enabled them to draw comparisons between different groups of product consumers within the same geographic sector – something that retailers were unable to do:

> What distributor would be able to finance all of the marketing studies, the detailed performance analyses, the studies of buying behaviours for each of the products that it distributes? (Seret, 1985: 57)

Rather than confining themselves to this logic of 'action at a distance', manufacturers adopted another logic, by becoming their own 'spokespersons', and representing their own products among retailers. They supported the physical presentation of products in the retail display space, producing the figures to back their arguments up. They also opted for 'customized' merchandising efforts that tailored recommendations for retail groups: 'your shop occupies a surface area of so much, belongs to this group, is situated in that region, so here's how you should construct your retail display space'. Simulating the force of sales on laptops for supermarket department managers came to replace the use of the cardboard grids. While some firms acquired the leading software packages to ensure that none of their retailers would be neglected,[7] others opted for more specific products developed by consultancy firms (Cappelli, 1993). France-Glaces Findus opted for the latter, which by this time had armed itself with a new know-how of merchandising based on the computerized studies of retail catchment areas. This manufacturer chose 'Optifroid', a software package that enabled it to undertake complete, customized studies for retailers, through which it allocated the number of 'facings' for each benchmark product, according to the distributor's performance indicators and decisions. France-Glaces Findus had clearly understood that by proposing customized merchandising to retailers it could, if not entirely recover its role as a privileged adviser, at least maintain certain key relationships with retailers. The retailers agreed to this partnership, in exchange for specific answers adapted to each point of purchase.

From the early 1980s, articles published in *Points de Vente* attest to a reversal in the relationships between manufacturers and retailers. The time had come for the development of forms of partnership likely to provide satisfactory solutions for all of the actors. Born in the USA in 1985 as part of the 'Efficient Customer Response' trend (Waldman, 1999), 'Category Management' is one of these initiatives aimed at instituting a partnership between food producers and retailers. The manufacturer helps the distributor to develop the category of products in which their own are present, with the objective of maximizing the end consumer's satisfaction.

Retailers' wish to work with the 'captains of category' (that is, with people responsible for constituting a set of categories for products and then for implementing them on the shelves) was translated into various forms of cooperation with manufacturers. The Casino group, which had been experimenting with category management since 1992, stated in late 1998 that it wanted to develop a 'captainship' (Boudet, 1998: 8). The idea was to create and nurture a privileged relationship with specific suppliers chosen for their ability to endow Casino's categories with a 'strategic interest' (Simonnet, 1993: 14) able to meet the performance standards expected by the group. The contractual relationship did not end there, since the distributor would give the appointed 'captain' access to select internal data. The same year, Carrefour opted for another mode of cooperation, which involved selling its own data to the two panel survey institutes AC Nielsen and IRI-Secodip. In so doing, the group hoped to obtain the recommendation of many firms (since everyone would have access to the group's data). It would thus be able to provoke competition by pursuing the leads most likely to meet its objectives.

Irrespective of the mode of cooperation, behind the appearance of partnership the supplier-distributor relationship remained lopsided. With both the case of Casino and of Carrefour their category manager could be replaced at any time, and the right to participate in the construction of a category was never guaranteed. Whereas Casino made its suppliers pay for the status of captain (Boudet, 1998: 8), those firms that wanted to contribute suggestions to Carrefour had first to buy the group's internal data from panel survey institutes. Despite its position as a subordinate, manufacturers stood to gain: firstly, because they were finally able to obtain data allowing them a more detailed knowledge of the retail group's markets; secondly, because they obtained the possibility of influencing the arrangement of categories in a way that was favourable to themselves, as well as to the merchandise on its own shelves. This explains the one-upmanship of suppliers and the general internalization of this new responsibility (by the creation of 'category managers' posts in manufacturing firms). The ultimate winner was still often the distributor since the suppliers all ended up neutralizing each other's effects.

Once the panel survey institutes had adapted the tools they used to characterize the market to meet retailer's needs, manufacturers were able to manipulate their own data and offer their retailers customized recommendations. The manufacturers found themselves in a somewhat paradoxical position from that point forward as the following definition of merchandising from a 1988 issue of *Point de Vente* suggests: 'Merchandising is considered as a set of techniques, generally proposed by a manufacturer, that facilitated the encounter between products and consumers through an adequate offer in terms of choice and presentation.' This means that manufacturers had been placed in a position to do some of their retailer client's work for them. Even if they did not initially have this objective, the integration of these new activities was the condition *sine qua non* for developing any sort of dialogue with retailers. This asymmetrical relationship was reinforced by the idea that the risks were not identical for the two parties. While one placed its entire stake on a benchmark product or product range, the other, a general dealer, could offset local losses by gains made elsewhere. Above all, the distributor could allow itself to try out all of the solutions proposed by the manufacturer and to opt for the best one without taking too many risks. There is evidence of this in the example of a distributor who wanted to apply the Pareto law[8] to the jam and canned fruit product family (Lévy, 1985: 62–63). Noting that these figures did not 'stick to' the ideal curve, they tried to reframe them by playing on the assortment:

> Do away with what? Logically, the least profitable. Consider the profitability analysis: the figures designate victims. People decide. They bring in another more dynamic brand, and another factor: price. [. . .] It's a gamble. (Lévy, 1985: 63)

To be sure, this was a gamble, but a very measured one. The simulation made it possible to act by trial and error. Each drop in performance due to decisions that were made could quickly be rectified by the distributor who, as the ultimate step on the merchandising scene, could always decide to promote one product rather than another (Barrey, Cochoy and Dubuisson-Quellier, 2000).

Conclusion

This history of merchandising shows that its take-over by retailers cannot be considered as an automatic adjustment of commercial organizations to a changing environment. On the contrary, I have shown the processes through which the different market professionals used the competitive context and organizational changes to advance in their own action logic. The historical perspective has the advantage of highlighting the fact that the battle was not won in advance. In effect, no organizational model of merchandising used by retailers seems to have prevailed.

Throughout this chapter, I have borrowed concepts from actor-network theory such as 'interessement', 'enrolment' and 'translation' (Callon, 1986, 1991; Latour, 1987, 1996) to describe the conditions under which merchandising emerged, as well as the evolution of relationships between retailers and suppliers around the control of its implementation. The genesis of merchandising shows us that retailers were not the only ones attempting to 'align' the various parties' interests. Manufacturers on their own were the first to try to align retailers' interests, via a 'remote' control of their products at the point of purchase. But, when this form of 'promotional' merchandising became invasive, retailers swiftly refused the attempt at enrolment. This kind of model has the twofold advantage of, firstly, accounting for both multilateral harnessing processes – processes which are similar to those that David Martin has observed in his study of the birth of France's organized financial options exchange (Martin, 2004) – and secondly of accounting for the emergence of distribution merchandising that has prevailed as a common denominator in the merchandising practices of all the actors engaged to any extent in controlling the market.

What are the processes through which retailers' merchandising prevail? Retailers' take-over of the management of retail display space created new markets and tasks for panel survey institutes. The 'new' tools set up by these institutes also interested manufacturers who saw them as a means to maintain relations with retailers. Retailers' merchandising was progressively and accumulatively rationalized on the basis of the different action logics of the collectives who found it interesting to keep an eye on the actions of these distributors. Saying that merchandising was rationalized does not mean that management devices had evolved towards a more logical future or methodological progress. Although we can observe a rationalization of methods and procedures (for example the grids that replaced demonstrators) that leaves more place for measurements and calculability, this can hardly be a proof of measurement being rational *per se*. It rather echoes a belief in measurements in the form of figures, already common throughout the distribution world. When merchandising changes hands, it is the retailers who define the criteria of performance management in supermarkets. This way of measuring performance has become the common denominator among almost all panel survey institutes (whose tools become neither more complex nor rational but are adjusted to the parameters decreed by the retailers) and among manufacturers who seize these new technical means to retain some of the expertise among the retailers. This struggle over the control of these particular 'market devices' which are located closer to the market, is also a fight for the control of the appropriation of a part of profit.

Notes

1 This chapter is based on Barrey (2005). I would like to thank Liz Libbrecht for her wonderful work in translating the first version of this text. I also want to thank Martha Poon for her precious help brought at the time of the final reading of this text. I am also grateful to Michel Callon, Yuval Millo and Fabian Muniesa for their helpful comments and suggestions. Of course, all remaining errors, in the form as well as in the content, are mine.
2 The 'grid' objectified both objectives of profitability (quantitative parameters such as gross income and turnover) and the calculation of the 'coverage in sales days', which encompasses the most qualitative information from the point of purchase (quantities sold), the supplier (delivery frequency) and the storage places (knowledge of secure stock).

3 'Facing' refers to the number of identical products visible to the consumer on the façade of the retail display space.
4 All interviews were carried out in French.
5 The translation of this quotation, like the following ones, is my own.
6 In the well-known example of 'free products' that became 'Carrefour products' in 1985, the terms of reference were based on the results of tasting panels set up to establish the quality perceived by customers. Carrefour also asked producers to set up a system of self-control on their supplies and their production lines. (Internal information brochure of the Carrefour group, 'Evolution des MDD').
7 Procter & Gamble equipped itself with both Spaceman and Apollo in order to provide each of its clients with a customized service (Cappelli, 1993).
8 15% of the assortment is to account for 60% of the turnover, 25% of the assortment for 25%, and the remaining 60% for 15%.

References

Barrey, S. (2004), *Le travail marchand dans la grande distribution alimentaire: La définition des relations marchandes*, PhD Thesis, Université Toulouse II.
Barrey, S. (2005), 'Du merchandising des fabricants au merchandising des distributeurs, ou le bricolage collectif d'un dispositif de gestion du marché', *Economies et Sociétés*, 39 (4): 625–648.
Barrey, S., F. Cochoy and S. Dubuisson-Quellier (2000), 'Designer, packager, merchandiser: Trois professionnels pour une même scène marchande', *Sociologie du Travail*, 42 (3): 457–482.
Boudet, A. (1985), 'Le merchandising, une évolution permanente', *Points de Vente*, (292): 53.
Boudet, A. (1998), 'Les vrais enjeux du category management', *Points de Vente*, (744): 8–15.
Callon, M. (1986), 'Some elements for a sociology of translation: Domestication of the scallops and the fishermen of St-Brieuc Bay', in J. Law (ed.) *Power, action and belief: A new sociology of knowledge?* London: Routledge.
Callon, M. (1991), 'Techno-economic networks and irreversibility', in J. Law (ed.) *A sociology of monsters: Essays on power, technology and domination*. London: Routledge.
Cappelli, P. (1993), 'Les logiciels de merchandising se perfectionnent', *Points de Vente*, (516): 48.
Cappelli, P. (1995), 'Des logiciels pour mieux vendre', *Points de Vente*, (604): 24.
Cappelli, P. (1996), 'Logiciels de merchandising: Vers la réalité virtuelle', *Points de Vente*, (663): 56.
Cliquet, G. and V. des Garets (2000), 'Réglementation des implantations commerciales et stratégies des distributeurs', *Actes des 15èmes Journées des IAE*, Biarritz-Bayonne.
Cochoy, F. (2002), *Une sociologie du packaging ou l'âne de Buridan face au marché*. Paris: Presses Universitaires de France.
Colla, E. (1997), *La grande distribution européenne*. Vuibert, Paris.
Comte, E. (1985), 'Les déçus du merchandising', *Points de Vente*, (284): 52.
Copeland, M. T. (1927), *Principles of merchandising*. Chicago: AW Shaw.
Courage, S. (1999), *La vérité sur Carrefour, l'épicier planétaire aux 2 millions de clients par jour*. Paris: Assouline.
Debaussart, M. (1989), 'La PLV sous le signe de la créativité', *Points de Vente*, (357): 52–53.
Debril, T. (2000), Mareyage et grande distribution: Une double médiation sur le marché du poisson', *Sociologie du Travail*, 42 (3): 433–455.
Desrosières, A. (1998), *The politics of large numbers: A history of statistical reasoning*, Cambridge (Massachusetts): Harvard University Press.
Dubuisson-Quellier, S., C. Méadel and V. Rabeharisoa (1999), *Consommateurs et produits alimentaires: La construction des ajustements*, research report, Ecole des Mines de Nantes / Ecole des Mines de Paris.
Dupuy, F. and J. C. Thoenig (1986), *La loi du marché*. Paris: L'Harmattan.
Douglas, A. W. (1918), *Merchandising*. New York: The Macmillan Company.

Fady, A. and M. Seret (2000 {1981}), *Le merchandising: Techniques modernes du commerce de détail.* Paris: Vuibert.
Herpin, N. and D. Verger (1988), *La consommation des Français.* Paris: La Découverte.
Latour, B. (1987), *Science in action: How to follow scientists and engineers through society.* Cambridge (Massachusetts): Harvard University Press.
Latour, B. (1996), *Aramis or the love of technology*, Cambridge (Massachusetts): Harvard University Press.
Le Blanc, M. and A. de Chaumont (1989), 'Faut-il se doter d'une cellule merchandising', *Points de Vente*, (357): 86–88.
Lévy, G. (1985), 'Quand l'informatique pose les problèmes', *Points de Vente*, (292): 60–64.
Martin, D. (2004), 'Dérives d'un produit, arrimages d'acteurs: La captation de tous par tous aux fondements du Monep', in F. Cochoy (ed.), *La captation des publics: C'est pour mieux te séduire, mon client.* Toulouse: Presses Universitaires du Mirail.
Moati, P. (2001), *L'avenir de la grande distribution.* Paris: Odile Jacob.
Norman, D. (1991), 'Cognitive artefacts', in J. M. Caroll (ed.), *Designing interaction: Psychology at the human-computer interface.* Cambridge: Cambridge University Press.
Opsomer, C. (1987), *Les panels: Leur pratique, leurs utilisations.* Paris: Chotard et Associés.
Pilditch, J. (1963), *Le vendeur silencieux.* Paris: Compagnie Française d'Editions.
Rebeix, F. C. (1985), 'Merchandising, les panels à l'heure informatique', *Points de Vente*, (84): 59–62.
Romec, R. (1989), 'Le merchandising des fournisseurs, une question de confiance', *Points de Vente*, (357): 89–93.
Seret, M. (1985), 'Le merchandising des producteurs: Hier, aujourd'hui, demain', *Points de Vente*, (292): 54–57.
Simonnet, V. (1993), 'A quoi sert le category management?', *Points de Vente*, (514): 14.
Sordet, C., J. Paysant and C. Brosselin (2002), *Les marques de distributeurs jouent dans la cour des grands*, Paris: Les Editions d'Organisation.
Strasser, S. (1989), *Satisfaction guaranteed: The making of the American mass market.* New York: Pantheon Books.
Thévenot, L. (1984), 'Rules and implements: Investments in forms', *Social Science Information*, 23(1): 1–45.
Thil, E. and C. Baroux (1983), *Un pavé dans la marque.* Paris: Flammarion.
Waldman, C. (1999), 'Efficacité et limites du category management', *Revue Française de Gestion*, (124): 115–121.
Zola, E. (1984 {1883}), *Au Bonheur des Dames*, Editions Fasquelle, Paris.

A sociology of market-things: on tending the garden of choices in mass retailing

Franck Cochoy

Introduction

In its attempt to challenge economic explanations of market choices, the (now not so) 'new economic sociology' proposed to investigate the social (Granovetter, 1985), cultural (Zelizer, 1985; Abolafia, 1996) and political (Fligstein, 1996) 'embeddedness' of market behaviour.[1] This research effort has been very useful in fleshing out economic exchanges, moving their investigation beyond abstract structures and stylized actors. The new economic sociology has given sociologists some robust tools and efficient theories for investigating the richness and humanity of economic activities and processes. Since it tends to reduce market realities to their human dimensions (networks, ideas and institutions), however, this perspective ends up neglecting the role of objects, technologies and other artefacts in framing markets (Chantelat, 2002).

Michel Callon's *Laws of the Markets* (1998) may be seen as an attempt to fill in this gap. Callon proposed as a focus, the technical and intellectual devices shaping market exchanges. To a certain degree, this programme may be presented as a fourth contribution to the new economic sociology paradigm, a contribution that insists on the 'cognitive/technological' embeddedness of markets. Yet this would only be accurate if Callon and his colleagues could be said to think of a market reality as being 'embedded' in some kind of social context! In the very same way that Bruno Latour refuses the idea of an 'ever there' 'social stuff' encompassing everybody and everything, preferring to define the word 'social' as an association process mixing and connecting human and non-human matters and issues (Latour, 2005), one might consider that for 'ANT-driven' economic sociology 'market' and 'social' realities are neither separated nor subject to the precedence of the other. Rather they are both combined and produced through 'socio-economic' action.

In this chapter[2] I propose, to follow along the latter perspective, to move from a sociology of marketing – ie, of how market knowledge 'performs' economic action (Cochoy, 1998) – to a sociology of 'market-things' – ie, of how commercial objects, frames and tools equip consumer cognition (Cochoy, 2004). In other words, I suggest abandoning *market theories* and opening our eyes to *market matters*. Instead of looking for the explanation of market choices in classical or innovative 'backstage' mechanisms, such as cultural-political-social constructs or theoretical frameworks, I intend to show that markets may *also* be traced at the immediate ground level of ordinary transactions. (The two approaches are of course neither exclusive nor contradictory). In order to accomplish this, I will concentrate on 'interobjective' (Latour, 1996) relationships occurring between consumers and market devices in the supermarket.

The perspective being proposed is supported by similar endeavours that precede it, such as studies of situated consumer cognition (Lave, Murtaugh and de la Rocha, 1984), some market ethnographies (Knorr-Cetina and Bruegger, 2000, 2002), and more recently the theory of markets as 'calculative spaces' (Callon and Muniesa, 2005). Callon and Muniesa's expression rather nicely insists on the fact that economic cognition, far from being abstract and purely cerebral, is always *situated and equipped*. It is my conviction that the spatial/material properties of market operations may be even more crucial than their calculative dimension. Even when exchanging goods does not immediately imply computing (goods may be given, stolen, or chosen routinely, blindly, etc.), it always involves moving them from one point to another, through a wide range of physical channels and equipments. These range from traditional bazaars (Geertz, 1978) and flea markets (Belk, 1991) to the electronic screens, sites and networks of financial markets (Callon, Licoppe and Muniesa, 2003) and e-shopping (Licoppe and Picard, 2005).

Even if some markets are highly sophisticated (as financial ones might be), most of them are quite mundane and 'down to earth' – just like supermarkets. This chapter investigates the supermarket through the use of the 'garden' metaphor.[3] This metaphor evokes soil, plants, tools and enclosures, but it also outlines all of the work that should be done to encourage purchasing. As I have already put it, shedding light on market labour[4] and space moves us a little bit away from theories of markets. But this does not mean that nothing is performed by market professionals and their spatial activities. To the contrary, through the study of the 'gardening of choices' in supermarket settings, we observe that performation is not only about the enactment of some *ex-ante*, given theories. It is also about the formation of knowledge through situated exchanges and practices. In other words – and in supermarkets at least – performation is better defined as 'performance'. As we will see, what is 'performed' is what is played, directed, staged (or rather gardened in this case). The market performance is about those very local and material events and devices that 'make us do things' (Latour, 1999), but that, in so doing, also make actors think differently, be they consumers, producers or retailers.

Supermarket cycles

By visiting the material space of the supermarket, I propose to make visible 'what everyone sees and still doesn't see'. I will only comment upon things that are in plain sight, and I will try to outline in these observations some elements, issues and processes that, even if not always noticed, nevertheless redefine the skills, activities and identities of consumers. To meet this objective, I will set aside an omniscient, cartographic point of view, and adopt instead the modest and 'naturalist' position of the passing stranger, the shopper, or the wanderer. Rather than looking for hidden backstage mechanisms behind the observed phenomena, rather than calling for some external knowledge in order to increase the understanding of the field, I will try to begin simply from the surface of behaviours and things. In order to give some depth (of field) to my perspective, however, I will displace my point of view and proceed from particular 'optical' positions, alternating the observation sites. That is, I will rely on pairs of photographs for the purpose of grasping the dynamics and implications of supermarket objects through anamorphosis (ie, adopting extreme angles of vision) and stereoscopic effects (ie, systematically looking not at one but at two pictures of the same site or topic).[5] This method is consistent with the garden metaphor which invites us to take the supermarket not as a palimpsest whose layers should be scraped off one after the other, but as a landscape, as a space, as a set of clumps and paths that we have to visit with curiosity, fondness and attention, from the right position and at the right time.

Thanks to automobiles (Strasser, 1989), big retail returned to the old site of medieval markets at the cities' outskirts (Braudel, 1981). In so doing, contemporary supermarkets remind us of the extent to which markets, just like gardens, build bridges between cities and the open country, between sites of consumption and spaces of rural production. The supermarket has displaced the market not only geographically but also in terms of built space. When consumers enter a supermarket they are no longer in the public space of the street. They penetrate instead a curious house everyone can visit and leave, without revealing their identity, but also a house where circulation is restricted: we must first deposit or wrap up previous purchases before entering, we go out with a full trolley (provided you have paid for its contents) or perhaps with an empty one (provided you pass a human or electronic security check), and, of course, you do not steal or grab things and eat them on spot.

The historical cycle is supplemented by a seasonal one. In commercial sites as well as in open nature, activities follow a seasonal pace: wine fairs occur in autumn, toys appear in the winter, gardening happens in spring, sales take place during the summer. A short day cycle also intervenes. Everyday, supermarkets experience an alternation between two 'dances in a ring' which are astonishingly symmetrical: the night work of the very special 'gardeners' who 'clean' the aisles, 'pick out' the products on the shelves, 'set up' the general display of goods; and the activity of the day shoppers who roam through all of the aisles, pick up the products and thus 'undo' the entire scene that was built for them (see Pictures 1 and 2). Having once been authorized to take some photographs before the opening of a supermarket, I was surprised by the nocturnal agitation and disorder. Here and there, positioned in the aisles and in front of end displays, some well-stocked trolleys were waiting, as if some clients were already in their midsts.

Pictures 1 and 2: *Night and day.* (All photographs by Franck Cochoy)

But I soon realized that, curiously enough, the same trolleys were being independently filled by several people. The issue at stake was not to buy, but to collect the aborted choices of the day before, to reassemble products abandoned in the middle of the shelves, far away from their initial 'success' of having been selected.

What was also striking was the congestion induced by cardboard boxes, pallets, rubbish, and the numbers of people rushing all over the place. I noticed that the supermarket's attendance in the early hours is close to that which it faces during the quiet hours of the day. The pallet carriers and telescopic ladders joined the trolleys of abandoned goods, but this time the 'consumers' were retailers. Retailers place and tidy up products while consumers pick and mix them up. Retailers come and go repeatedly from the back of the shop to the same aisles, while consumers move from one aisle to the next. Yet in each group, one could clearly observe the same commitment, the same silence, the same meticulous orientation towards the shelves.

The parallel between the two temporally differentiated scenes became even more striking when the speakers announced at half past eight in the morning, that 'the shop opens in thirty minutes'. Meaning: everything should be finished before shop opening. As for Cinderella, it is necessary to leave on time and not to forget anything left behind her: tape, torn up boxes, garbage, etc. The announcement was identical to the one that would be given in the evening, varying only the verb 'close', and the tone of politeness granted to visitors. Supply is obviously the mirror of demand. But the rule is that neither one nor the other should meet each other directly (or at least, that they meet as little as possible). The supermarket succeeds in performing in some way the liberal, market-view of the world reported by Karl Polanyi:

> Vision was limited by the market which 'fragmentated' life into the producers' sector that ended when his product reached the market, and the sector of the consumer for whom all goods sprang from the market. The one derived his income 'freely' from the market, the other spent it 'freely' there. Society as a whole remained invisible. (Polanyi, 1971 {1944}: 258)

The supermarket gives anthropological content to the cultural scheme outlined by Polanyi, but it does so without reproducing it exactly. With the supermarket, what Polanyi says is simultaneously true and false. It is true, since the perfect dissociation between supply and demand eventually becomes possible within the supermarket (or the 'hypermarket', to speak literally of a 'superlative market'). It is also false, since in this case the market is not the same any more: the birth of mass retailing should be taken neither as the advent of a market without merchants (du Gay, 2004), nor as the triumph of a local auto-regulative bidding system described in Marie-France Garcia's strawberry market (Garcia-Parpet, 2007). In the supermarket, the distributor's presence and action is constant even if very discrete and remote. And prices and offers do not fluctuate on the spot, but are set in advance.

This 'time discontinuity' is crucial, for two reasons. Firstly, it shows that 'free markets' rest on managerial voluntarism. Paradoxically enough, *'laissez-faire'* has to be 'done': supermarket gardeners work hard both to render themselves as invisible as possible (in acting at night and in delegating their skills to market-things) as well as to organize a space were consumers may feel free and move freely. Secondly, time discontinuities between night and day open up a space for 'pragmatic management'. Night 'suspends' not only consumer behaviour on the demand side, but also managerial science on the supply side. Nocturnal supermarket activity performs management not as textbook knowledge, but as situated practice: through its pragmatic gardening activity, supermarket staff shows us that market framing is about adopting the consumer's point of view 'physically' rather than 'intellectually': in moving at night into the very space and position consumers will occupy during the day, the supermarket gardeners experience the consumers' own gestures with their senses and bodies. They thus anticipate consumers' possible actions and impressions, and frame the scene accordingly.

The 'presence' of the shop, as a place but also as an actor distinct from supply and demand, leads us to reconsider the dynamics and implications of 'self-service'. At first glance, the very mundane self-service device may be taken as a scenography of the theoretical market, since it hardens the free-market scheme. In a supermarket, circulation, calculation and decision-making are meant to be free.[6] Everyone can come in and go out without further explanation. Consumers can examine the entire range of available products in a common unit of place, time and action. They can evaluate and manipulate objects directly, freely activate their preferences, make choices without any human intervention or material constraints – that is, they can fulfil the ultimate dreams of the liberal economy, dreams that only undergraduate textbooks in economics dare to convey, alongside the sociological critique of some 'fantasized' economics!

But who are 'they'? What is the supply they face? What do their exchanges really rely upon? In the supermarket, the central actors of market economics seem to have been removed. On the one hand, the producer rarely intervenes directly, but is rather represented by the products and/or by the work of the aisle managers. On the other hand, the consumers themselves are not as present as one might believe. When I see someone wandering around with a shopping list, I quickly understand that the one who shops is not necessarily the one who consumes. The shopper either acts as the representative of someone else or as an entity larger than herself[7] (when they are not the author of the list, as it is evidenced when they call someone on their cellular phone for explanations). Or do they split their own identity in two, when they oppose their intentions as a consumer to her immediate experiences as buyers.

As a consequence, the buyer should not be taken for the consumer, just as the big retailer should not be confused with the producer. Self-service presents itself not as the encounter between supply and demand but rather as the confrontation of two mediations, two delegations which are commissioned by the production and consumption sides. In order to understand the social dynamics of self-service, we therefore have to study the particular contribution of these two mediations (and their articulation) to the accomplishment of exchanges.

The nocturnal scene reported earlier helps us to identify the fundamental drives of self-service, along with the horticultural metaphor. The alternate ballets of retailers and buyers may for instance take us back to the strategy of an 18th century exceptional 'gardener-marketer': Antoine-Augustin Parmentier. In France, Parmentier is famous for being the man who succeeded in making French people consume potatoes. He met this objective by cultivating them on a field given to him by King Louis XVI, and by placing guards all around (except at night). This stratagem made potential thieves think that the mysterious product cultivated there was precious, and enticed them to robbery during the hours when the field was not kept. Self-service professionals, just as Parmentier with his potatoes, set up a garden whose guards vanish (in the day, this time) in order to let the buyers go in and take as much advantage as they can of the windfall of an abundant and 'open' supply. Budgetary constraints are expelled as far as possible: payment certainly does occur but only at the end and all at once, after everything has been gathered without any precise idea of the total amount (prices are marked only on shelves and not on products themselves). This confirms the point about the necessary *'faire laissez-faire'* we already mentioned: there is no such a thing as a market without organization, no choices are possible without preliminary framing not only of these choices, but also of the freedom of the framed actors (Cochoy, 2007). Last but not least, the final virtue of this scene is to help us understand that the same space is surrounded by different populations with their respective activities – populations and activities that now deserve a closer examination.

The work of the visitor

The absence of a direct, physical encounter between supply and demand in supermarket settings forces the sociologist to make a detour through the objects that play a mediating role in markets: we must question the meaning and the functioning of a commercial world where human eyes do not cross, but rather slide towards the edges, towards the tops or bottoms of the shelves (or towards the exit!) (see Picture 3).

The supermarket space reminds us of streets, subways or train stations (Augé, 2002). It looks like a typically urban place where everyone goes their own way, has their eyes turned towards their own horizon, even if they sometimes look for a point of reference to know where to go or what to do. In the shop, however, the visual objective is not a vanishing point located beyond the circulation of people. Rather, the visual objective is the set of objects that surrounds the circulating people. Buyers do not look in front of themselves but to the sides, and behind each other, while all the while looking at the shelves. Eyesight in supermarkets does not seem to be particularly prone to intersubjectivity. People do not look at each other but make themselves busy (du Gay, 2004). Yet the absence of interaction is not experienced as a moment of embarrassment as in the closed and oppressive space of elevators. On the contrary, this absence of human

Franck Cochoy

Picture 3: *Face to shelf.*

interaction finds a natural derivative in the general interobjectivity that establishes itself between buyers and products.

Face-to-face interaction between clients and vendors (Prus, 1989) is replaced by a 'face-to-shelves' relationship analogous to the 'face-to-screen' pattern analyzed by Karin Knorr-Cetina and Urs Bruegger (2000, 2002) in financial markets. Acknowledging the material, industrial and delegated character of market interactions in self-service environments is probably better achieved through a sociology of cognitive equipment (Cochoy, 2002) than through classical interactionism. Each 'face-to-shelf' interaction is abutted by a 'face-to-list' interaction. An initial 'face-to-list' launches the buyers' attempt to establish a fragile correspondence between their purchase intentions and the differentiated offer of the shelves (Cochoy, 1999). Afterwards, a symmetrical 'face-to-list' leads the distributor to adjust his offer according to scanner data as best as he can (Barrey, Cochoy and Dubuisson-Quellier, 2000). But of course, one should not forget the other very complex coordination that happens in between, implicating faces, shelves, lists, as well as the multiple principals and their agents of each of these (Barrey, 2001).

Producing a supply in self-service involves asynchronous, delegated and mediated interactions. These interactions, equipped with objects and scripts, involve both adventure and calculation, planning and exploration. Such operations and gestures largely rely on scriptural, symbolic and material registers and thus on a scrupulous setting up of the commercial space.

The work of the distributor: tending to the volume of choices

On the opposite side of the 'buying eye', we find not only objects, but also an array of professionals who manipulate these objects. Aisles managers for example obviously take advantage of the hybrid interactions between people and products. They do so by arranging cognitive supports, by providing multiple 'choice devices'. Grasping the knowledge and action patterns of these particular professionals does not require relying on backstage information. I can simply start from a close examination of products and shop furniture, reading at their surface a great deal of the concerns of these 'commercial gardeners'. This does not exclude more direct and complete observation of market professionals (Barrey, Cochoy and Dubuisson-Quellier, 2000) which, as good landscape architects do, distribute commercial information along the vertical, lateral and depth axes that are open to our eyes.

Pictures 4 and 5: *Up and down.*

Sticking to my front stage investigation, it is the 'vertical axis' that I first encounter when entering an aisle (Pictures 4 and 5). In the upper part of this axis, large boards clearly indicate the alleyway's contents. For instance, the board I am facing mentions very explicitly, in very large and readable characters, the type of items gathered underneath: 'sandwich bread', 'brioche' and 'fruit juice'. On either side of this board, smaller ovoid signs placed along the shelves provide more details about the product offering: 'individual pre-sliced brioche', 'plaited brioche', etc. Such boards place us in front of a purely informative realm that ranks and distributes an asset of perfectly understandable, monosemic and denotative indications. The main rubric (which implicitly refers to breakfast), is divided into particular rubrics (brioches, beverages), along a functionalist taxonomical logic (close to a botanist's?). This way of proceeding is also close to a market ideal of pure and perfect information: whether we adopt the point of view of the ordinary consumer or even the critical stance of the most suspicious sociologist, it would be very difficult not to admit that the distributed means of signalling, hanging above our heads, are aimed at informing us rather than at manipulating us. They are obviously designed to help the consumer quickly and surely identify and locate their preferred objects, to assist them in going 'straight to the goal' – towards *their* goal, and not towards the one that someone else may have defined. (This is somewhat accompanied by ulterior motives, since buying quickly allows buying more!). Now, perfect information soon meets other dimensions which add to it but that also counterbalance its importance and significance. First, we should notice the optional and peripheral character of such 'aerial' signalling. Informative boards are not like tolls, gates or obligatory checkpoints. They are not constraints but rather resources, they provide possible cognitive supports that anyone can rely on or ignore as they see fit. The remote position of such information in the upper part may correspond exactly to that: the place of something that goes largely 'above our heads'. Consumers raising their eyes in search of this information are not that common in supermarkets. Some have incorporated the map of the shop during their repeated visits and others favour a systematic exploration of every aisle, thereby rendering the quest for directional supports useless. Many ignore, or at best forget, such signalling devices. It is as if consumers would activate (unconsciously?) the action scheme of the city dweller and the country walker; that is, they activate the behaviour of a subject who first pays attention to the objects in front of her. Now, when examining what lies at eye level in the supermarket, the consumer looks at the lower part of the vertical axis. And when she looks at it, she encounters much more than just clear informational transparency.

As soon as I enter the aisle and look straight in front of me, I abandon the vertical axis in order to engage into the lateral one. Do I leave the realm of transparent information in order to meet products directly? Not yet, not really. In following the lateral axis, I do not see the aisle from head on, but encounter them in profile (Pictures 6 and 7).

And as soon as I look to the aisle in profile, I discover not the products but rather cards, signs, and flags that function a little bit like thumb indexes. These

A sociology of market-things: on tending the garden of choices in mass retailing

Pictures 6 and 7: *Profile and full-face.*

indexes show me not the full-range but rather a selection of products: 'World cuisine', 'Carrefour product', 'Reflets de France', 'tea time, 9 euros 49 cents', 'new' (see Picture 6). Elsewhere in the shop, similar indexes also designate 'promotion', 'lowest price', 'customer card', etc. Unlike the aerial boards presented above, these lateral flags operate a double deviation: they attempt to stop my eyes on such or such product (which I may have not noticed otherwise) and to attract my attention on this or that aspect of its dimensions (that I may have not spontaneously considered, or that I may even ignore until now).

Let's take an example. When I read the flag 'Carte Pass' (Carrefour customer card), I learn not only that this product is subject to a price reduction but also that I need the shop's card in order to benefit from it. The flag's trick is double: it succeeds both in showing members what they should buy to benefit from their status, and to non members what they lose in not joining up. All of these sorts of flags show new ways of grasping the products. In the process, we learn that preferences, far from always preceding the act of purchase, are largely constructed along the immediate interaction with products that praise their own properties (sometimes we do not even suspect the existence of these properties, see below).[8] Finally, let us note the constant zeal of aisle managers in renewing not only the products they introduce on the shelves, but also the ways in which they present them. The highly rationalist slogan reading 'At Carrefour, our prices are frozen until the summer', which followed the shift to the euro currency in the first semester of 2002, was later replaced with the more seductive campaign for the new Carrefour product range 'J'aime' ('I love') in January 2003. After playing on a calculative logic, Carrefour attempted to activate the consumers' hedonic drives. I realize the extent to which the market space arranges not only objects but also my inner configuration. I discover that the art of *'achalandage'* (Grandclément, 2003) activates a plurality of cognitive schemes that are embedded in my self (Cochoy, 2007). This art plays on reason and passion, calculus and feelings, concepts and affects.

Finally, when I face the aisles – when I look at the 'depth axis' – I do not see the flags anymore, since their edge becomes invisible through this angle of vision. Now that aerial boards are forgotten and flags are eclipsed, now that no obstacle comes to hamper my vision, I might believe that I am finally in a position to see the products and to finally reach my goal. But not quite, yet. What I take as the products are actually paper faces, boxes, packaging. Packaging is to products what clumps are to flowers. In the very same way that in a flower garden we are charmed by a chromatic assemblage before being able to name the species composing it, in a supermarket we are first attracted by colourful blocks rather than by the brands which constitute these blocks.[9] The place assigned to a product induces an implicit judgement about this product, as does the height and breadth of the display space devoted to it. The upper, lower, side or centred positioning of a product in the supermarket shelve works as a podium, or rather as a target, whose centre is generally reserved to the product the shop managers try to highlight. Most of the time, this space is occupied by the retailer's private brand.

Facing the package clump that I like (or that attracts me), am I able to access the product I am looking for (or that is pointing at me)? No, still not yet! Just as the bee first has to get over the flower's corolla to take the nectar it covets, the supermarket customer first has to go through product packaging in order to consume it, and extract from it the satisfaction they wish for. Packaging changes the product, the consumer and the producer all at once. It changes the product since, in hiding what it shows and showing what it hides, packaging transforms the qualification of the product. It helps attribute new characteristics to products, be they intrinsic (eg, a particular ingredient) or extrinsic (eg, a customer service). Packaging changes the producer, who is now able to understand product development not only through his technical skills, but also through the packaging of competitors. Packaging changes the consumer too, since it makes them discover the invisible dimensions of products, for instance the presence of a guarantee or of an additive that they could not have identified without the mediation of the box. In other words, the consumer learns to exchange their preferences for new references. Hesitating between two products is seeing them as similar, as indistinguishable along any *ex-ante* criteria. The solution to such a problem does not rest on the consumer's internal or previous preferences, but on packagers' ability to propose some distributed references which consumers may then take as their possible new preferences, that is, as a means of differentiating the products (Cochoy, 2002, 2007).

Thanks to observations of merchandising and packaging, I understand that I will never reach the product, or at least not here, *in* the market. Such is the paradox: in the modern supermarket, references are the things that are being bought, not products. Monetary signs are exchanged for market words and images. Evaluating the adequacy of such references to their substantial counterpart is postponed beyond transaction, in the realms of production and consumption. Since I cannot move further to the product, since I stumble over an impassable paper, a glass or a plastic barrier, since I understand that my exploration of the commercial space stops at the last mediation, I wonder if my shopping journey is truly over. Might I have left some important aspects aside and should I rewind the film of my visit?

This introspective flashback is not useless. It makes me realize that I have only accomplished a very short route. I have only visited one or two aisles. I could have turned off elsewhere, taken other directions, scrutinized many things – I could have completed the examination of the aisles' diversity and multiplicity. Let me leave packaging and come back upstream. Or, better, let me extend the packaging metaphor to the garden metaphor and see the extent to which the supermarket, as a product, is itself subjected to a packaging process. For the shop works as a physical envelope for the market, and transforms commerce in the very same way that a greenhouse modifies the plants growth. Marketplaces, as any other public arenas (Latour, 2004), are matters of 'air conditioning' and atmosphere management (Chung, Inaba, Koolhaas and Tsung Leong, 2002; Grandclément, 2004). In order to make sense of such a transformation, let's have a look at another pair of pictures (Pictures 8 and 9).

On the left, the wine aisle (Picture 8). This aisle goes far beyond the classical tabular ranking of bottles' in rows (in line) and their names (in column). Large paper boards hanging from the ceiling simulate the vaults of a cellar, lined with other items of rustic decoration. On the right, the health and beauty aisle (Picture 9). Here again, the display of products breaks with the standard

Pictures 8 and 9: *Wine and Heath & beauty.*

organization of the other aisles. This space is closed on three sides, giving the impression that one is entering a restricted room. The white frame that surrounds the whole scene channels customers' eyes towards the interior. Smaller furniture, a special cash register, a shiny floor which contrasts with the dull and colourless floor tiles of the rest of the shop – all these create the atmosphere of a snug and familiar bathroom.

This new way to organize supermarket aisles – known as 'retail universe management' in French professional vernacular – recreates sites of production (wineries) and consumption (bathrooms), and thus moves us away from a place of pure exchange. In this respect it contributes to the 're-enchantment' of consumption evoked by George Ritzer (1999). By not gathering products along a commercial taxonomy, as elsewhere in the shop, but along the same rationale we use at home, 'retail universes' do not, however, necessarily break with marketing logics. This is not a post-modern occurrence, in which the marketplace would have turned into a pure space of sociability. On the contrary, these universes are designed to reinforce the channelling of consumers towards pure commercial dynamics.

Setting 'retail universes' consists in 'wrapping-up' the shop, caring for its 'packaging', transforming the sale space into a product. With such 'retail universes' we do not consume the product anymore but rather we consume the commercial space itself. Consuming the shop is a possible substitute for a purely utilitarian consumption: the supermarket experience can be justified in terms of leisure more easily. The retail universe becomes to supermarkets what leisure gardens are to vegetable growing. On the other hand, favouring free 'visual consumption', encouraging not only strictly purchasing behaviour but fostering a personal relationship with the shopping place contributes to settling the consumer into a 'regime of familiarity' (Thévenot, 2001) – and possibly also into a regime of reciprocity. The *décor* of the store might be perceived as a gift to which the consumer is meant to correspond through purchasing. It is as if the shop's landscape gardeners had invented a sort of a 'theory of efficient *décor*', combining the drives of the Maussian gift and the old dynamics of Elton Mayo's human relations, or even the lessons of the more recent Goffmanian sociology of service relations, into a theory which insists on the civility exchanges which are necessary to the co-production of services in intersubjective commercial or administrative contexts (Joseph and Jeannot, 1995). The development of these 'retail universe' merchandising techniques obviously bets on a 'postponed' consumption, a consumption that relies on a long-lasting loyal relationship to the store, where the free enjoyment of a familiar place comes to encourage or anticipate future purchases (Barrey, 2004).

Hopefully, my journey has comes to its end. I have scrutinized the distant and alternating articulation of supply and demand. I have gone through the supermarket in every direction. I have explored the framing of (either actual or postponed) consumption choices. But I might still have missed something. While I thought that all views were limited and channelled towards the 'inside' of the commercial scene, three strange windows (one still close, another rather clandestine, and a third wide open) keep on pointing me towards something I have missed in the 'outside' – an outside which is now different from the one I started from.

Three windows to (re)orient the consumer towards political issues

The first window opens towards the French countryside. This window was opened in the supermarket in spite of retailers. It is a fragile window, which now seems to be closed, or even walled up. Under the social pressure of farmers fighting against the gap between producers' and retailers' prices, this window was once built and opened with a rule issued by the government in August 13th, 1999, which imposed, for two months at least, the labelling of both the production price and the retail price of some fruits and vegetables. This rule turned consumers into judges in a commercial quarrel and somehow introduced a new way for them to evaluate products, too. Moreover, this effort also anticipated a new kind of competition: the initial intention of the rule (ie, to transform individualistic consumers into consumer-citizens able to evaluate the fairness of 'trading margins' in the retailing sector) turned ever so slightly into a call for more 'commercial transparency'. The tension between producers and retailers has died down ever since this episode. The authorities' voluntarism has gotten slack, and this first window was thus closed after its two months validation period. It did, however, let fresh air blow through the supermarket, an air which seems to spread through a second window.

This second window opens on several types of relationships that can occur between consumers and producers: fair trade, organic food, GMO-free food, or environment protection. The 'fair trade' movement (Cochoy, 2004) opens a discrete window directly on the surface of products. The Max Havelaar label, for instance, guarantees that 'the coffee you'll consume was bought *directly* from *small producers* at prices higher than world rates, after a partial financing of their harvests'. This label works as a window aimed at opening consumers' eyes to farming issues in southern countries. It attempts to foster a political consumption (Micheletti, 2003) in which everyone works, at their own level, for a fair allocation of profits in distribution channels. This device may be seen as a global and voluntary equivalent of the French regulatory measure mentioned above. Its promoters expect that its non-mandatory character will (paradoxically) support its visibility and success, through the development of competition based on better ethical commitment.

The third political window is the largest, most visible and spectacular one. It first half-opened at the shop's entry, in the context of a temporary commercial show which took place in March 2002 in the very French supermarket I have been walking you around in. The shopping mall was transformed into a 'living farm', with real animals such as a calf, and even a real 'gardener', with a straw hat, apron, trolley and flowers (see Picture 10). The third window opens completely, in a more serious, solid and lasting manner at the back of the supermarket, in the 'quality channel' of the meat aisle. In the latter, I observe a terracing of perspectives: in front of me lies the packaged meat (see Picture 11). Meat is clearly visible under the plastic film, well described through references to price, quality, origin and traceability guarantees. A little bit farther, I see the butchering chain which precedes the display of products. Finally, in the back, some windowpanes grant me visual access to the cold room, to the carcasses and to other pieces of meat. The scene just stops of a final window, which would open onto the farms, rendering the overall effort of transparency complete. In fact, the cattle were nevertheless already there in some way, with the quiet calf near the shop's entry, bringing into surrealism the modern requirement for product traceability.

This kind of 'visual marketing', which consists in setting up a 'transparent' staging of a product's distribution path, is an obvious attempt at clearing away the foolish fears of consumers – a hole is pierced in the shop's walls so they can see beyond. Emphasis on traceability invites consumers to base their choices on safety issues and even to exchange taste (or 'older' concerns of the like) for precaution (Cochoy, 2001).

Through these three windows, I see how well mass retailers monitor and adjust to market evolutions, just as farmers from the old days looking at moon's phases or clouds' shapes. To promote GMO-free foodstuff, sustainable development, or product traceability is to follow the wind (opinion streams), seasons (fashion) and temperatures (more or less 'hot' crises), at least to some extent. The three windows point in different directions, but these directions all turn the consumer towards the 'outer world'. They try to take the consumer out of the realm of pure price economics and immediate satisfaction. They propose different relations between consumers and producers, between 'the city' and 'the country'. They connect to other values, to other concerns.

Pictures 10 and 11: *From calf to veal.*

Conclusion

At this point in my journey, I see to what extent the supermarket appears as an ambivalent soil – closed on itself but also opened to the outer world, prone to civic values but also to managerial ones, transparent but also full of 'captation' traps.[10] This soil can lock the visitor up inside a consumerist dimension, but it can also reveal formerly hidden characteristics of products, from their production and distribution circuit to their ethical and political contents. Tending the garden of choices may of course involve social networks, cultures and institutions. But it also rests upon some very mundane, immediate and material 'market-things' such as boards, flags and shelves. Behind such things, the same gardening of choices also relies on the professional skills and actions I tried to read (rather than unveil) at the surface of supermarket sight. Here we meet the methodological – or rather optical – stake of this chapter. My aim is not only to describe and unfold the supermarkets logics, but also to do so along a particular way of handling marketing realities. I propose to leave large interpretative frameworks as well as backstage investigations at the door of the supermarket, and to focus on the difficult challenge of helping everyone 'see what they see and still do not see'.

Social scientists often investigate social realities for which 'special' access is required. They need to make considerable efforts to find the right path to the data, or at least to some reliable informants. Moreover, the resulting work does not always address (or interest) a potential readership of first-hand specialists in the studied field. This is not to cast suspicion over this kind of research: scientific research is a professional activity with its rules and ethics which deserves the same respect and trust as any other social activity – not less and not more! In these cases, giving a descriptive account of the topic at stake is already an important achievement – although it is not always the primary aim[11] – since this account provides a useful 'first' depiction of an 'unknown' reality. Further discussions may focus on the possible biases, oversights, mistakes, misinterpretations of this account, but rarely on its 'trivial' adequacy to the field under scrutiny.[12]

The situation is radically different with the study of very mundane objects, such as supermarkets. Actors – but also the fellow researchers – are both informants and analysts. Everybody knows the field by heart, as a research agenda or at least as a weekly experience (I confess I am personally unable to separate the two). That's probably why most monographs dealing with such fields tend to quickly leave aside superficially descriptive aspects to focus instead on theoretical implications – such as Daniel Miller's highly suggestive *Theory of Shopping* (Miller, 1998) – or to look for something 'hidden' behind data that deserves to be 'unveiled'. In this latter case, market ethnographers tend to favour the critical stance, either in its most classical way – as for instance, Maurice Duval (1981) does in and his fascinating ethnography of street pedlars – or in a more subtle manner – like Michèle de la Pradelle (2006) in her marvellous ethnography of the farmers' market at the small French town of Carpentras.

De la Pradelle's study aims at disclosing the reality of industrial supply and false peasants lying behind a façade of tradition and authenticity. But it also reveals that all actors, far from being fooled, are well aware of the merchants' tricks. They simply prefer to behave as if such 'backstage realities' did not exist, in the very same way children know that puppets have their puppeteers, but also know that they will appreciate the show better if they pretend they do not – see Goffman (1986) for a similar analysis. As a consequence, in de la Pradelle's book, the only real façade is that of critique: in a spectacular reversion of critical studies, the only naïve persons who deserve to be informed about the dark side of the world are de la Pradelle's readers – ie, the specialists of social critique who have long grounded their professional credentials on their ability to open the eyes of poor credulous citizens on the obscure processes that work behind 'common knowledge' appearances.

In my own ethnography, I propose to go (methodologically and analytically) a little bit farther than de la Pradelle, although I am proposing not to go (physically) as far as she does. My bet is that a market ethnography may also be fruitful even if rather restricted to 'mere surfaces', acting as though 'back-aisles' explorations were not necessary to understand what is at stake in a supermarket.[13] In neglecting backstage mechanisms, I do not fight against other interpretations. I simply attempt not to follow the larger route that most research already follows, in order to see if one might not learn something new in first looking at market-things before looking behind them.

Notes

1 See Philippe Steiner's (2002) excellent review.
2 This chapter is a translated, updated and 'upgraded' version of a paper formerly published in *Ethnologie Française* (Cochoy, 2005).
3 I am not alone in believing in the virtues of such a metaphor. Hans Kjelberg and Claes-Fredrik Helgesson recently showed how considering markets as landscape gardens may improve their understanding (Kjellberg and Helgesson, 2007).
4 Sophie Dubuisson and I pleaded elsewhere that, as soon as it focuses on market professionals, marketing devices and exchange management, economic sociology does not need to be considered as something essentially different from a regular branch of the sociology of labour (Cochoy and Dubuisson, 2000).
5 I thank Anne Querrien for her documentary help, Sandrine Barrey, Michel Callon, Catherine Grandclément, Hans Kjellberg, Bruno Latour and Jean-Claude Thoenig for their reading of previous versions of this text, and the director of the supermarket 'Carrefour Portet-sur-Garonne' who gave me the authorization to take the pictures illustrating this chapter.
6 These operations are also reversible: most supermarkets reimburse the products that consumers bring back without asking anything other than a proof of purchase and that no adulteration has been made to the returned product (this reversibility of purchases is a premium supplement to the perfect competition that the theory do not even require).
7 The marketer Wroe Alderson presented the buyer as an 'organized behaviour system' (Alderson, 1958).
8 Of course, some of these flags may only produce their immediate effect thanks to a preliminary work aimed at making them understandable (advertising campaigns, distribution of leaflets, etc.).

9 Colour codes serve to identify the characteristics of some products like coffee (black for Arabica, red for mixtures, blue for decaffeinated, etc., at least in the case of France).
10 The capture or 'captation' of consumers articulates two apparently contradictory hypotheses. The first is that the consumer's trajectory is predictable (it follows a particular action scheme or disposition). The second is that with the help of *ad hoc* devices – *'dispositifs'* in French – any trajectory, even predictable, may be cut, seized, or even replaced with another 'cognitive program' or disposition (Cochoy, 2003).
11 I believe that theory-less or un-analytical 'sociography' should be considered as respectable as sociology.
12 For instance, when Callon and Rabeharisoa (1999) discuss Peneff's (1997) ethnography of surgery work, they do not question the excellence of the description (which they praise for its precision and vividness), but rather they challenge its theoretical standpoint (surgery as a 'butcher' work) which led the author to forget the patient as 'living flesh' and to neglect other crucial elements such as the anaesthetist's role.
13 I admit I have occasionally transgressed this rule in referring to supermarkets' night life, or in bringing here and there some additional information into my 'superficial' exploration of market pictures.

References

Abolafia, M. (1996), *Making markets: Opportunism and Restraint on Wall Street*. Cambridge (Massachusetts): Harvard University Press.
Alderson, W. (1958), *Marketing behaviour and executive action*. Homewood (Illinois): Richard D. Irwin.
Augé, M. (2002), *In the metro*. Minneapolis: University of Minnesota Press.
Barrey, S. (2001), 'On ne choisit jamais seul: La grande distribution des choix', *Consommations et Sociétés*, (1): 25–38.
Barrey, S. (2004), 'Fidéliser les clients dans le secteur de la grande distribution: Agir entre dispositifs et dispositions', in F. Cochoy (ed.), *La captation des publics: C'est pour mieux te séduire, mon client*. Toulouse: Presses Universitaires du Mirail.
Barrey, S., F. Cochoy and S. Dubuisson-Quellier (2000), 'Designer, packager et merchandiser: Trois professionnels pour une même scène marchande', *Sociologie du Travail*, 42(3): 457–482.
Belk, R. W. (ed.) (1991), *Highways and buyways: Naturalistic research from the Consumer Behavior Odyssey*. Provo (Utah): Association for Consumer Research.
Braudel, F. (1981), *Civilization and capitalism* (3 volumes). New York: Harper and Row.
Callon, M. (ed.) (1998), *The laws of the markets*. Oxford: Blackwell.
Callon, M., C. Licoppe and F. Muniesa (2003), 'Présentation', *Réseaux*, 21(122): 9–12.
Callon, M. and F. Muniesa (2005), 'Economic markets as calculative collective devices,' *Organization Studies*, 26(8): 1229–1250.
Callon, M. and V. Rabeharisoa (1999), 'De la sociologie du travail appliquée à l'opération chirurgicale: Ou comment faire disparaître la personne du patient', *Sociologie du Travail*, 41(2): 143–162.
Chantelat, P. (2002), 'La nouvelle sociologie économique et le lien marchand: Des relations personnelles à l'impersonnalité des relations', *Revue Française de Sociologie*, 43(3): 521–556.
Chung, Ch. J., J. Inaba, R. Koolhaas and S. Tsung Leong (2002), *Harvard Design School guide to shopping: Harvard Design School project on the city 2*. Cambridge (Massachusetts): Taschen.
Cochoy, F. (1998), 'Another discipline for the market economy: Marketing as a performative knowledge and know-how for capitalism', in M. Callon (ed.), *The laws of the markets*. Oxford: Blackwell.
Cochoy, F. (1999), 'De l'embarras du choix au conditionnement du marché: Vers une socio-économie de la décision', *Cahiers Internationaux de Sociologie*, 106: 145–173.
Cochoy, F. (2001), 'Les effets d'un trop-plein de traçabilité', *La Recherche*, 339: 66–68.
Cochoy, F. (2002), *Une sociologie du packaging ou l'âne de Buridan face au marché*. Paris, Presses Universitaires de France.

Cochoy, F. (2004), 'Is the modern consumer a Buridan's donkey? Product packaging and consumer choice', in K. Ekström and H. Brembeck (eds), *Elusive consumption: Tracking new research perspectives*. Oxford: Berg.
Cochoy, F. (2005), 'L'hypermarché, jardin d'un autre type aux portes des villes', *Ethnologie Française*, 35(1): 81–91.
Cochoy, F. (2007), 'A short theory of "the captation of publics" or the Little Red Riding Hood revisited', *Theory, Culture and Society*, forthcoming.
Cochoy, F. and S. Dubuisson-Quellier (2000), 'Introduction. L'étude des professionnels du marché: vers une sociologie du travail marchand', *Sociologie du Travail*, 42(3): 359–368.
Cochoy, F. and C. Grandclément (2005), 'Publicizing Goldilocks' choice at the supermarket: The political work of shopping packs, carts and talk', in B. Latour and P. Weibel (eds), *Making things public: Atmospheres of democracy*. Cambridge (Massachusetts): MIT Press.
de la Pradelle, M. (2006), *Market day in Provence*. Chicago: University of Chicago Press.
du Gay, P. (2004), 'Self-service: Retail, shopping and personhood', *Consumption, Markets and Culture*, 7(2): 149–163.
Duval, M. (1981), 'Les camelots', *Ethnologie Française*, 11(2): 62–86.
Fligstein, N. (1996), 'Markets as politics: A political-cultural approach to market institutions,' *American Sociological Review*, 61(6): 656–673.
Garcia-Parpet, M.-F. (2007) 'The social construction of a perfect market: The strawberry auction at Fontaines-en-Sologne', in D. MacKenzie, F. Muniesa and L. Siu (eds), *Do economists make markets? On the performativity of economics*. Princeton: Princeton University Press.
Geertz, C. (1978), 'The bazaar economy: Information and search in peasant marketing', *American Economic Review*, 68(2): 28–32.
Goffman, E. (1986), *Frame analysis: An essay on the organization of experience*. Boston: Northeastern University Press.
Grandclément, C. (2003), 'How to describe the specificity of large retailers' activities? A proposal through "achalandage devices"', Workshop on market(-ing) practice in shaping markets, Stockholm School of Economics, Skebo (Sweden), June 14–16.
Grandclément, C. (2004), 'Climatiser le marché: Les contributions des marketings de l'ambiance et de l'atmosphère', *Ethnographiques.org*, (6): http://www.ethnographiques.org/.
Grandclément, C. and F. Cochoy (2006), 'Histoires du chariot de supermarché: Ou comment emboîter le pas de la consommation de masse', *Vingtième Siècle*, (91): 77–93.
Granovetter, M. (1985), 'Economic action and social structure: The problem of embeddedness,' *American Journal of Sociology*, 91(3): 481–510.
Joseph, I. and G. Jeannot (1995), *Les compétences de l'agent et l'espace de l'usager*. Paris: CNRS Editions.
Kjellberg, H. and C.-F. Helgesson (2007), 'On the nature of markets and their practices', *Marketing Theory*, 7(2): 137–162.
Knorr Cetina, K. and U. Bruegger (2000), 'The market as an object of attachment: Exploring postsocial relations in financial markets', *Canadian Journal of Sociology*, 25(2): 141–168.
Knorr Cetina, K. and U. Bruegger (2002), 'Traders' engagement with markets: A postsocial relationship theory', *Culture and Society*, 19(5–6): 161–186.
Latour, B. (1996), 'On interobjectivity', *Mind, Culture and Activity*, 3(4): 228–245.
Latour, B. (1999), 'Factures/fractures: From the concept of network to the concept of attachment', in *Res*, (36): 20–31.
Latour, B. (2004), 'Air-condition: Our new political fate,' *Domus*, (868): 40–41.
Latour, B. (2005), *Reassembling the social: An introduction to actor-network-theory*. Oxford: Oxford University Press.
Lave, J., M. Murtaugh and O. de la Rocha (1984), 'The dialectic of arithmetic in grocery shopping', in B. Rogoff and J. Lave (eds), *Everyday cognition: Its development in social context*. Cambridge (Massachusetts): Harvard University Press.

Licoppe, C. and A. Picard (2005), 'Choisir entre plusieurs techniques de fixation des prix: Acheter sur catalogue et enchérir sur un même site de commerce électronique', *Economie Rurale*, (286–287): 71–88.
Micheletti, M. (2003), *Political virtue and shopping: Individuals, consumerism, and collective action*. New York: Palgrave Macmillan.
Miller, D. (1998), *A theory of shopping*. Cambridge: Polity Press.
Peneff, J. (1997) 'Le travail du chirurgien: Les opérations à coeur ouvert', *Sociologie du Travail*, 39(3): 265–296.
Polanyi, K. (1971 {1944}), *The great transformation: The political and economic origins of our time*. Boston: Beacon Press.
Prus, R. (1989), *Pursuing customers: An ethnography of marketing activities*. Newbury Park (California): Sage.
Ritzer, G. (1999), *Enchanting a disenchanted world: Revolutionizing the means of consumption*. Thousand Oaks (California): Pine Forge Press.
Steiner, P. (2002), 'Encastrement et sociologie économique', in I. Huault (ed.), *La construction sociale de l'entreprise: Autour des travaux de Mark Granovetter*. Colombelles: Editions EMS.
Strasser, S. (1989), *Satisfaction guaranteed: The making of the American mass market*. New York: Pantheon Books.
Thévenot, L. (2001), 'Pragmatic regimes governing the engagement with the world', in T. Schatzki, K. D. Knorr Cetina, and E. von Savigny (eds), *The practice turn in contemporary theory*. London: Routledge.
Zelizer, V. A. (1985), *Pricing the priceless child: The changing social value of children*. New York: Basic Books.

A market of opinions: the political epistemology of focus groups

Javier Lezaun

Introduction

Provoking a conversation among a small group of people gathered in a room has become a widespread way of generating useful knowledge.[1] The focus group is today a pervasive technology of social investigation, a versatile experimental setting where a multitude of ostensibly heterogeneous issues, from politics to economics, from voting to spending, can be productively addressed.[2] Marketing is the field in which the focus group has acquired its most visible and standardized form, as an instrument to probe and foretell economic behaviour by anticipating the encounter of consumers and products in the marketplace.[3] But whether they are used to anticipate consumer behaviour in a laboratory-like setting, or to produce descriptions of political attitudes, conversations elicited in the 'white room' of the focus group are relevant to a striking range of objects of social-scientific inquiry.[4]

The observation of contrived groupings of research subjects in 'captive settings' is of course a familiar source of knowledge in the social sciences, but there is something peculiar to the focus group as a research technology. In focus groups, knowledge is generated *in the form of opinions*. Moreover, a *group* dynamic is used to bring into existence a series of relevant *individual* opinions; the peculiar form of social *liveliness* of the focus group is meant to 'produce data and insights that would be less accessible without the interaction found in a group' (Morgan, 1988: 12). Both the productive qualities and methodological quandaries of the focus group originate in its special form of liveliness. The peculiar politics and epistemology of a focus group conversation derive from the tension implied in using a group to engender authentically individual opinions. Moderators are in charge of resolving this tension: they must make the conversation conducive to the expression of private and idiosyncratic views, while preventing the focus group from rising to the status of a 'collective;' they are called to structure a process of interaction conducive to the elicitation and elucidation of the most private of views, while reducing to a minimum the residuum of 'socialness' left over from the process. As a professional group moderator describes it:

> We talk to ourselves all the time. Most of these inner thoughts never surface. They reflect the same kind of internal dialogue we have when we stand at a supermarket shelf to select paper towels or stop to take a closer look at a magazine ad for a new cell-phone service or decide whether to use a credit card to pay for gas. Our running commentary is often so subliminal that we often forget it's going on. As a focus group moderator, I reach out to consumers in my groups and try to drag that kind of information out of them and into the foreground. What I do is a kind of marketing therapy that reveals how we as consumers feel about a product, a service, an ad, a brand. (Goebert, 2002: viii)

Researchers hope to externalize the silent 'running commentary' of consumers by means of an intently managed group discussion, to translate a series of inaudible monologues into a visible conversation. They provoke an exchange so as to bring to light the inner qualities of consumers.

Knowledge about people is extracted from the opinions elicited from them – opinions that are freely expressed by the subjects, yet structurally incited by the setting.[5] Those opinions are then selected, categorized and interpreted by the focus group researcher and fed into production and marketing strategies. 'Illustrative opinions' are filtered from the wealth of talk generated in the discussion, to be quoted verbatim or paraphrased in the research reports circulated to clients and other relevant audiences. Thus, opinions generated in the 'white room' are read, interpreted, and discussed by managers and marketers who were not present in the original conversation and are in no position to directly assess their authenticity or relevance. The statements produced in the unique environment of the focus group enter a long chain of quoting and rephrasing, and reverberate into other actors' market strategies. The ultimate product of a focus group conversation is a series of tradable opinions – statements that are generated in an experimental setting but can be disseminated beyond their site of production. Opinions elicited from focus group participants thus help constitute particular marketplaces.

Producing opinions of such value and mobility is a highly complex technical process. A focus group can generate a multitude of objects that, while seemingly identical to relevant opinions, are in fact radically different kinds: *false* opinions, *induced* judgments, or *insincere* beliefs, all of which appear profusely in the course of a focus group discussion – especially in a poorly run one. These deceptive statements must be sorted out and expunged so as not to lead researchers and their audiences astray. The task of the moderator is to manage the focus group discussion so as to limit the proliferation of irrelevant or inauthentic viewpoints; to foreground tradable opinions against the background noise that is inevitably generated in the experimental situation.

The purpose of this chapter is to draw attention to some of the strategies utilized by focus group moderators to carry out this task of extracting tradable opinions out of experimentally generated conversations. In so doing, we can regain a proper appreciation of the extent to which categories such as 'relevant opinion' or 'consumer preference' are problematic – and not simply or primarily to the external observer, but to the actors who are professionally trained to elicit and recognize them, the focus group moderators.

My account will be limited in a number of important ways. The manufacture of opinions in a focus group starts with the assembling of a group of adequate research subjects and a meeting with one or more moderators, but the 'focus group chain' comprises a long sequence of exchanges and analyses beyond this initial encounter. This chapter, however, will only investigate the initial experimental moment, when research subjects and moderators come together in the physical setting of the focus group 'white room.' Moreover, I will analyse this encounter solely from the perspective of the moderators: my analysis is based on the moderators' own technical literature – the training manuals, methods handbooks, autobiographical accounts, and other documents in which they lay out their own philosophy of 'good practice' and a portrayal of the 'good moderator.' I do not attempt to examine the focus group discussion from the point of view of the research subjects, nor will I draw extensively on analyses of the patterns of interaction between subjects and moderators that actually emerge in a focus group, a dimension of the focus group encounter that others have studied at some length (Myers, 1998 and 2004; Myers and Macnaghten, 1999; Puchta and Potter, 1999 and 2003). The chapter is thus limited to descriptions of the craft of moderation that professional moderators have put into writing.[6] Through this literature, I try to reconstruct an ideal *moral epistemology* of moderation. In particular, I try to capture the *political constitution* of an experimental setting in which individual attitudes are elicited and market behaviour is routinely anticipated.

The chapter is organized around three themes, all of them topics that social scientists have frequently raised in relation to the production of scientific knowledge under experimental conditions: 1) the distinction and balance between naturalness and artificiality in the focus group setting, and the embodiment of this distinction in the moderator's skills and abilities (or, rather, in the *accounts* that moderators give of their own craft); 2) the co-production of knowledge and particular forms of social order, or the political constitution of the focus group – a constitution that ideally, I will argue, takes the form of an *isegoric* assembly; and finally, 3) the role of material artifacts and the physical arrangement of the setting in the organization of the 'focus group chain' as a technology of knowledge production. The chapter concludes with a call to make the production of *opinions* a proper object of sociological investigation, in the same way that the creation and circulation of *knowledge* has long occupied a central place in the agenda of sociological research.

Chameleonic moderators

A fundamental dichotomy runs through the technical literature on focus group 'facilitation' and serves as an object of interminable reflection for moderators:

should the focus group be seen as a natural phenomenon, closely resembling a naturally occurring (or 'casual') conversation, or should it rather be treated as the highly artificial outcome of an experimental intervention? Moderators' opinions on this issue obviously vary. Some emphasize the similarity between the kind of conversation they hope to encourage, and naturally occurring talk. 'The moderator,' one argues, 'should be viewed by the group as the authority figure in the room but also as the type of person with whom they would like to have a casual conversation' (Greenbaum, 1988: 51). 'The frequent goal of focus groups,' another stresses, 'is to conduct a group discussion that resembles a lively conversation among friends or neighbours, and most of the problems come from topics that fail to meet that goal' (Morgan, 1988: 22). The productive liveliness of the interaction depends, according to this view, on a successful replication of the conversational patterns of friends or neighbours. Yet, as Agar and MacDonald point out, 'it is not automatic that a group of strangers will have a 'lively conversation' about anything' (Agar and MacDonald, 1995: 78), and in fact many moderators choose to emphasize the seemingly opposite view: that whatever takes place in a focus group should be understood and analysed as the result of a radical experimental intervention, that the focus group is a highly artificial product – from which, however, valid knowledge about the natural world can be extracted. A historian of the focus group form puts it as follows:

> While agreeing that focus group research patterns itself on field studies – 'natural' contact with people – in actual fact, they have by their 'falseness' – the deliberately constructed contact with people – much more in common with the experimental situation of the laboratory than is usually acknowledged. There is no reason to consider this as 'wrong', we cannot consider focus group discussions as consisting of naturally occurring meetings which just happened to be organized by the researcher or sites of natural conversation. The presence of the moderator reduces even further the naturalness of the exchanges that occur. (Morrison, 1998: 180).

Judging from the body of literature analyzed for this article, the view of the focus group as an artificial encounter is more widely held among practitioners (or, rather, among the authors of methodological texts), but the recognition of artificiality is often accompanied by caveats and justifications that suggest a structural orientation towards the model of a casual, natural conversation as the regulatory ideal for their practice. Moderators can and will explain the departure from naturalness as inevitable and useful, but in addressing the differences vis-à-vis naturally occurring talk they highlight the relevance of the latter as the ideal of talk to which they aspire. In other words, while most moderators will readily acknowledge that the focus group is not a natural setting, very few will be willing to give up the claim to conduct a 'naturalistic inquiry' (Morgan and Krueger, 1993: 8).[7] One could argue that focus group moderation is to them akin to an Aristotelian 'perfective art' – an intervention that, by removing the obstacles in their way, 'perfects natural processes and brings them to a state of completion not found in nature itself' (Newman, 2005: 17).

Whether they choose to emphasize the naturalness or the artificiality of the focus group in the descriptions of their trade, most moderators would nevertheless argue that, in the practical conduct of a focus group, both dimensions need to be tackled and made compatible; that the strength of the focus group as an engine for the production of tradable opinions rests precisely on the ability to combine these apparently contradictory dimensions; and that the point at which these trends are unified is *in the very figure of the moderator*. This is paradoxical, since, as was pointed out in the quote above, it is the very presence of the moderator that renders the situation hopelessly artificial. Yet, in their methodological writings, particularly in the portrayals of the 'good moderator' put forward in the technical literature, one finds a pervasive effort to combine in the kaleidoscopic identity of the moderator the apparently irreconcilable demands of naturalness and artificiality. This combination of conflicting qualities surfaces in long, colourful descriptions of the moderator's *persona*:

> The best facilitator has unobtrusive chameleon-like qualities; gently draws consumers into the process; deftly encourages them to interact with one another for optimum synergy; lets the intercourse flow naturally with a minimum of intervention; listens openly and deeply; uses silence well; plays back consumer statements in a distilling way which brings out more refined thoughts or explanations; and remains completely nonauthoritarian and nonjudgemental.[8] (Karger, 1987: 54)

In these characterizations, the moderator *embodies* – in his skills but also through his personality – the conflicting burdens of objective detachment from, and natural empathy with the research subjects. Moderating is always more than a science – or a set of easily formalizable techniques:

> Mastering the technique of moderating a focus group is an art in itself, requiring the moderator to wear many hats and assume different roles during the course of even a single focus group. He or she has the unenviable task of balancing the requirements of sensitivity and empathy on the one hand, and objectivity and detachment on the other. (Stewart and Shamdasani, 1990: 69)

The prevalence of artistic metaphors is worth noting here and in other instances:

> The moderator is often compared to an orchestra conductor, in that he or she sets the tone for the session and directs it in such a way that the research objectives are achieved. Further, an effective moderator will do a great deal of preparation in advance of the groups, as does an orchestra leader before conducting a symphony. (Greenbaum, 1998: 73)
> The moderator also must have a sense of timing – timing for the mood of the group and the appropriateness of discussion alternatives. Like the actor who takes too many bows, the moderator also must know when to wrap up the questioning and move on to the next issue, but not prematurely. (Krueger, 1994: 101)

It is also, and crucially, an art mastered only by the few:

> Conducting focus groups that result in useful information, insights, and perspectives requires both science and art. And in my experience, only a handful of practitioners

understand the science and can intuitively grasp the art of conducting them (Bostock,1998: vii–viii).

The tension between the natural validity of the product the focus group strives to generate and the experimental nature of its extraction is thus translated into multidimensional portrayals of the 'good moderator,' of the skills and personality traits best attuned to this research practice. The tension is not resolved, but rather given a new form in the self-discipline of a moderator simultaneously capable of both attachment and detachment, of leading a natural conversation and generating experimental observations at the same time.

The emphasis in the technical literature on the *personality* of the moderator, in addition to his technical skills, as the key to a successful focus group is a relatively new phenomenon, likely connected to the professionalization of focus group research and the effort to market the value added by moderators. In the descriptions of focus group moderation offered by the pioneers of the trade one finds a very different tone. In their seminal 1946 article on 'focussed interviews' (the term they coined for the technique), Robert K. Merton and Patricia Kendall placed the emphasis on the recurrence in the focus group situation of specific patterns of interaction, and on the fundamental teachability and transferability of the techniques necessary to manage these typical situations:

> A successful [focussed] interview is not the automatic product of conforming to a fixed routine of mechanically applicable techniques. Nor is interviewing an elusive, private, and incommunicable art. There are *recurrent* situations and problems in the focused interview which can be met successfully by *communicable* and *teachable* procedures. (Merton and Kendall, 1946: 544–545; emphasis added)

One detects in their descriptions a view of the moderator as a *technician* of sociological investigation. 'We have found,' Merton and Kendall continue, 'that the proficiency of all interviewers, even the less skilful, can be considerably heightened by training them to recognize type situations and to draw upon an array of flexible, though standardized, procedures for dealing with these situations' (Merton and Kendall, 1946: 545). Hence the term 'interviewer,' which Merton, Kendall and other members of the Bureau of Applied Social Research used throughout their writings to refer to the moderator of a discussion. 'Interviewer' emphasizes an essential continuity between different research interventions – from asking standardized questions drawn from a questionnaire, to the managing of a group of research subjects. The 'focussed interview' could be applied to individuals as well as to 'groupings,' and it always involved a recurring question-and-answer pattern of interaction.[9] The conception of the moderator as interviewer represents the polar opposite of the open-ended, idiosyncratic practices denoted by names such as 'facilitator,' or 'qualitative research consultant.' To the social-scientific pioneers of the group discussion, the interviewer is above all a trainable *instrument* of social research, rather than the chameleon-like master of an arcane art of conversation.[10]

Orienting the subjects' reflexivity

If moderators incorporate in the descriptions of their craft an array of diverse traits and features, including a strong element of self-discipline, they devote most of their technical literature to the management and disciplining of others: their research subjects. The self-discipline of the moderator and the disciplining of subjects are but the two sides of the same coin. In both cases the question is, once again, how to strike an adequate balance between naturalness and artificiality. In the case of the research subjects, the key to this balance is the proper management – the incitement, orientation and taming – of their reflexivity.

In short, the fundamental problem for moderators is how to turn the research subjects *away* from the experimental features of the setting. That is, how to prevent subjects from explicitly attending to their peculiar context, the focus group 'white room,' so that their actions – in this case, the opinions they express – are not direct responses to their being in that particular setting and can be projected beyond their site of production. Moderators have to steer the participants' inevitable contextualization of their own situation and statements (Myers, 2004: 56–66), and neutralize the attention they are bound to pay to the experimental nature of their grouping.

The technical literature addresses this general problem through a series of 'type situations' to be tackled by the well-trained moderator. Perhaps the most obvious example of a participant's orientation towards the experimental setting is the problem of *sabotage*. Sabotage is a reflexive response, and a highly disruptive one at that. It occurs when, for whatever reason (because they dislike the research question, or the way the moderator goes about extracting their opinions, or simply their being there) participants actively try to upset the proceedings of the focus group. Dissatisfaction with the experimental situation can be expressed in a multitude of ways. In some cases, research subjects avail themselves of the mechanisms of the focus group to generate a disruptive outcome – for instance, by expressing what, from the point of view of the moderator, will turn out to be a series of useless or irrelevant opinions.[11] More frequently, sabotage is in the moderators' literature equated with a lack of respect for the basic etiquette of civilized conversation. Bullying other participants, showing excessive aggressiveness in stating one's own views, or trying to monopolize the conversation are all ways of contravening the rules under which the focus group is conducted. 'There are some people who just are unpleasant,' a moderator remarks. 'They must be removed if they become intimidating to other members of the group' (Morrison, 1998: 211). The techniques used to deal with this kind of behaviour run the gamut from withdrawing eye contact, in the hope of silencing the offending participant, to directly removing the disrupting individual, or even calling off the meeting.

Unproductive or disruptive reflexivity is sometimes not a matter of participants behaving badly, but of the researchers enrolling the wrong kind of participant. This is the case with the 'professional respondents': people who either make a living out of participating in focus groups, or simply enjoy them too much and manage to participate in too many. They represent a serious problem because they are too familiar with the setting. While detecting and weeding out these 'repeaters' is nowadays largely a matter of computerized screening of research subjects, the moderator must always be on the look-out for signs of excessive familiarity or comfort on the part of the research subjects. Research subjects that appear too relaxed or gregarious are to be treated with suspicion. 'Sometimes a focus group feels fishy,' a moderator notes:

> Respondents who are supposedly strangers immediately are highly talkative, grabbing food across the table. Sometimes, the respondents' conversation indicates they are repeats. They talk about the last time they were at the facility, the fact that the refreshments are different this time, or compliment the moderator on being 'better than the other ones' – a compliment we'd rather not get. (Langer, 2001: 70)

The repeater's familiarity with the focus group setting generates a sense of ease and naturalness that is at odds with the ability to extract tradable opinions from him. Familiarity is, like the conscious sabotage, a form of orientation towards the specific features of the focus group setting – an orientation characterized in this case by fluency and skill rather than by awkwardness or aggressiveness, but equally detrimental to a proper balance between artificiality and naturalness.[12]

A third situation, more subtle and widespread, is not related to the kinds of individuals who take part in the discussion, but to the kinds of opinions they express. Merton and Kendall described this in their 1946 article as the problem of *direction*: the process by which the actions of the moderator end up 'modifying the informant's own expression of feelings.' When this occurs, '[t]he interview is no longer an informal listening-post or 'clinic' or 'laboratory' in which subjects spontaneously talk about a set of experiences, but it becomes, instead, a debating society or an authoritarian arena in which the interviewer defines the situation' (Merton and Kendall, 1946: 547).

For Merton and Kendall, 'directed' opinions were those not spontaneously expressed in the research subject's own 'frame of reference.' This is why moderators must be careful to use 'nondirective techniques' and to give the research subject 'an opportunity to express himself about matters of central significance to him rather than those presumed to be important by the interviewer' (Merton and Kendall, 1946: 545). It is the possibility of generating nondirective outcomes that makes focus groups a more adequate technology to elicit authentic opinions than polling and other highly formalized research tools. This is a central tenet of the moderators' epistemology, going back to the foundational uses of group interviews by Merton and others: 'in contrast to the polling approach, [the focussed interview] *uncovers what is on the subject's mind* rather than his opinion of what is on the interviewer's mind, and 'it permits subject's responses to be placed in their proper context rather than forced into a framework which the interviewer considers appropriate' (Merton and Kendall, 1946: 545).

The moderators' technical literature also discusses the issue of 'direction' as the problem of 'moderator demand,' defining it along similar lines to the 'experimenter demand' in experimental psychology: situations 'where the respondent or subject guesses what is going on, realizing what is expected of him or her and 'helping' the experiment along by performing in ways that they think the experimenter would like' (Morrison, 1998: 182). Most participants in a focus group are certainly going to realize that *something* is going on, if not *what exactly* is going on. As Myers argues, a focus group is in fact 'two hours of "What is it that's going on here?"' (Myers, 2004: 56). The focus group meeting is a highly contrived occasion, and research subjects are obviously aware that the fundamental purpose of their being there is to get them to talk about matters of relevance to the researcher. More often than not, they will try to be 'helpful.' While it might seem the polar opposite of sabotage, helpfulness is, from the point of view of moderators, a similarly disruptive orientation towards the experimental nature of the encounter. As Morrison writes:

> I have certainly experienced such situations where answers have been given that the respondent has imagined would suit the client. People like to be helpful, at least if they have been asked along to be a member of a group specifically set up to help with some research . . . [I]t is 'natural' to help by providing considered helpful answers to questions if one has been asked to help with some research. (Morrison, 1998: 186)

This is why, rather than being a negative quality, non-direction needs to be actively engineered into the behaviour of the moderator and into the responses he elicits from the research subjects. Moderators need to forestall the natural propensity to help. Research subjects will always try to anticipate what is expected and desired from them, and are very likely to act (ie, express views) on the basis of these assumptions. The task of the moderator is thus much more complicated than simply letting the conversation run its 'natural course,' or leaving respondents to their own devices. He or she has to manage the expectations of participants carefully so as to generate nondirective outcomes that are conducive to the research. The role of the moderator is thus to *provoke* preconceptions that would suit her research purposes, without allowing research subjects to be conscious of their own helpfulness. The moderator must, through self-discipline and the careful management of information, elicit what Merton described as the 'self-betrayals' and 'self-revelations' of the research subjects. He must tame and channel the subjects' unavoidable awareness of the research situation towards goals beyond their grasp.

Influence: the moderator as political philosopher

In his study of jury deliberations, Harold Garfinkel analyzed the rules of judgment that jurors were expected to use in producing a legal decision (Garfinkel, 1984). He discovered that, while jurors simultaneously entertain everyday and official rules of social judgment, they use the 'official line' to produce retrospective accounts of the decisions they arrive at, and of the process by which they arrive at them. The focus group shares important similarities with the jury setting – another experimental setting designed to generate relevant opinions – but it presents even more telling differences. Focus group participants are seldom asked to justify their opinions on the basis of a set of official rules. They will normally be asked by the moderator to *elaborate* upon and develop their opinions, to extend their contributions by pursuing the ramifications of their initial statements, but this is quite different from being asked to produce accounts of their opinions in accordance with a set of formalized procedures. A second, even more fundamental difference between juries and focus groups is that, while jurors are asked to abandon their everyday patterns of judgment in reaching legally relevant opinions, the participants of a focus group are expected to come into the experimental situation with all their preconceived (if, perhaps, not yet thought out or articulated) attitudes and beliefs. While a juror's reasoning is ideally interchangeable with that of any other juror, the opinions of a focus group participant should be personal and idiosyncratic, generated according to a 'natural,' not an 'official,' logic of opinion-making. For it is only through the adoption of an everyday repertoire of judgment and talk that the desired liveliness of the focus group can be achieved.[13]

The expected idiosyncrasy of individual opinions raises a fundamental practical problem for the moderator: the matter of *influence*. Not, as in the case of direction, the influence of the moderator herself on 'the informant's own expression of feelings,' but rather the influence of other focus group participants on the authenticity of individual opinions. After all, focus groups bring subjects into contact with one another on the assumption that the dynamic of their interaction will favour the generation of individual opinions. Yet, at what point does the group dynamic produce opinions that are no longer genuine and individual but simply the effect of processes of influence among participants? When is the influence of some members, or of the group as a whole, significant enough to render the judgments expressed by its members inauthentic? In other words, when is the product of a focus group simply a 'focus group discussion,' a series of opinions produced for and by the occasion, and not a series of genuine viewpoints? As one researcher puts it:

> The effectiveness of focus groups depends on the interactions among the participants. But these same interactions can (and frequently do) also impede the effectiveness of focus groups, under any of several circumstances. An opinion 'leader' may emerge who influences the inputs of the other participants. As a result, the discussion will reflect the opinion leader's views more than their own. (. . .) In other cases, a very strong-willed person may intimidate some of the other participants, who subsequently say as little as possible for fear of alienating this person. Sometimes, a few participants realize that they do not express themselves as well as the others and withdraw from the discussion for fear of looking stupid. (Greenbaum, 1998: 143)

These are all scenarios in which the dynamic of the focus group gives rise to misleading objects: insincere beliefs, induced judgments, opinions produced under the influence of others or only for the purpose of the research at hand. Some critics see in this quandary an insoluble paradox, a contradiction in terms that fundamentally limits the usefulness of focus groups as a valid instrument of investigation: evidence that 'what is often witnessed [in focus groups] are group attitudes and not the individual expression of an attitude' (Morrison, 1998: 185)

To proponents of focus group research, however, the problem of influence is not an impossible contradiction at the heart of their methodology, but in fact simply an issue of 'quality control,' to be effectively addressed by the managerial skills of the moderator.[14] The techniques in which moderators must be proficient are precisely 'those that seek to maximize the benefits and minimize the limitations of group dynamics by properly controlling them' (Greenbaum, 1998: 110).

Yet, the term 'quality control', with its technical undertones, can be misleading, for what moderators articulate in their reflections on the problem of influence is not simply a purely technical understanding of 'quality,' but their implicit political philosophy. Discussions of the problem of influence are the touchstone on which moderators formulate an image of the social order most conducive to the expression of authentic individual opinions. By discussing the counterproductive aspects of the group situation, they provide a procedural definition of the ideal 'small moral world' of a focus group, a space of talk in which contradictory forces are kept in an artificial balance so as to generate the conditions for a fruitful exchange of genuine individual opinions.

Broadly speaking, and allowing for multiple differences of nuance and emphasis, the focus group is designed (and the moderator trained) to generate an *isegoric* situation. Classical Greek thought described isegoria as the condition of *equality in the agora*, understood as equality in the ability to express one's own opinions. Isegoria would not describe what we might understand today as 'freedom of speech,' the liberty to say whatever is on one's mind (that 'freedom' could rather be described, as I will argue below, as the virtue of parrhesia, which is often uncomfortably close to the vice of loquacity, an excess of speech that sometimes expresses a lack of authenticity). Isegoria refers to the formal conditions of an assembly in which citizens would have an equal share in the debate in the agora; it describes the quality of a space in which every member of the community is granted the right *and* the obligation of deliberative participation.[15]

In the focus group, the research subject does not enjoy anything resembling 'freedom of speech,' for his or her speech is constrained by the objectives of the research and limited to the topics of discussion presented by the moderator. But the moderator nevertheless aspires to make the proceedings isegoric, in the sense that every research subject is not only allowed, but enticed and incited to form views and express opinions, and that any tendency towards a monopolization of the powers of argument (let alone overt intimidation) is strictly curtailed.[16] Using an altogether different metaphor, but expressing a similar view, the role of the moderator in bringing about isegoria is also described in terms of 'diplomacy':

The moderator must provide an element of balance in the focus group by diplomatically shifting the conversation from the active talkers to those who have said less. It is a dangerous mistake to assume that silent participants are agreeing or not thinking. If the moderator does not successfully solicit the opinions of less talkative participants, some valuable insights may be lost. (Krueger, 1994: 76)

Even excesses in rhetoric need to be limited in the focus group. While arguments often need to be drawn out to their ultimate consequences, rhetorical persuasion is dangerous because it tends to produce 'group attitudes,' and not 'the individual expression of an attitude' – a collective, rather than a collection of individual opinions. In the focus group, the moderator addresses the need to strip statements of their rhetorical quality through a series of directive techniques. As Puchta and Potter have shown in their analyses of focus group discussions, moderators visibly ignore – for instance by not writing down – statements directed by one participant to another, and persistently redirect participants to speak to the moderator, so as to generate 'freestanding opinions,' rather than contextually specific responses to other participants' statements. Moderators 'display attention (that is, visibly attend) to freestanding opinion formulations and display disattention to (explicitly) rhetorically embedded formulations' (Puchta and Potter, 2002: 351). By inciting non-rhetorical formulations of participants' opinions, moderators not only try to generate formally egalitarian conditions of deliberation. They also anticipate the need to produce a retrospective account of the focus group discussion stripped of its contextual specificity, an account that often relies heavily on the reproduction of *illustrative* quotes, which can be circulated far beyond their site of production and signification (Krueger, 1994: 167; Puchta and Potter, 2002: 360).

The ability of moderators to manage processes of influence, rhetoric and persuasion among participants should remind us that, in the focus group, isegoria among research subjects is compatible with an unequal distribution of the powers of speech between subject and moderator. In fact, from the point of view of the moderator the achievement of this equality in speech is simply the result of his own 'isegoric skills,' of his or her ability to maintain the evenly distributed liveliness of the interaction by preventing the concentration of talk and influence. We have seen in previous sections the importance that moderators grant to maintaining their authority vis-à-vis the group, their emphasis on the need to adopt a 'style of leadership' that would guide the subjects toward a productive exchange of opinions. The focus group is in this sense closer to the confessional or the pedagogical models of elicitation than to the ideal of the democratic assembly. The goal of the moderator is to benevolently (forcefully, yet imperceptibly) lead the focus group to a useful outcome (of which their subjects are ignorant). And, as I noted before, a fundamental objective of the moderator's techniques is to prevent the emergence of a 'collective' out of the group dynamic – to protect the individuality of the opinions expressed by each participant. 'The moderator,' one of them argues, stressing this point, 'is a bit like a puppeteer, controlling the action, yet hoping panelists don't see her pulling the strings' (Goebert, 2002: 35).

The opposite of an isegoric assembly is one in which some participants remain silent, and it is these silences – whatever their cause – that moderators aim to dissolve. 'The facilitator,' a moderation manual states, 'must not just avoid domination of the group by individual members, but must also seek to encourage contributions from the most timorous' (Bloor *et al.*, 2001: 49). Thus, in the focus group setting isegoria implies that the elicitation of speech among participants must be evenly distributed, and that every member of the group must be given the encouragement and opportunity to express his or her opinions.

The logic behind this organization of talk is a purely utilitarian one. If elicitation is not evenly distributed, 'valuable insights may be lost.' In other words, any and every insight is potentially *valuable* to the moderator and her clients. 'The focus group,' one moderator writes, 'rests on the deceptively simple premise that consumers can impart valuable information' (Goebert, 2002: 32). Not only that: *every* participant is a potential source of value. If the moderator is to fulfill his productive mission, he 'must truly believe that the participants have wisdom no matter what their level of education, experience, or background.' (Krueger, 1994: 101) The 'deceptively simple premise' that value can be extracted from people by inciting them to formulate views and judgments, explains why the economy of discourse of the focus group is one of almost unrestricted proliferation. After the focus group meeting the researcher will have to code the multiplicity of opinions and screen out those considered irrelevant or inauthentic, distilling the most important trends into a report that quotes or paraphrases the opinions considered most representative or illustrative. But the larger the number of opinions expressed by the research subjects, the more likely that moderators and researchers will be in a position to mine valuable insights from the discussion. This is why alternative opinions must be encouraged and dissent actively promoted. The moderator continuously 'heads off premature agreement' between participants and works against their tendency to avoid direct disputes (Myers, 2004: 126).[17] The goal is to maximize the power of the focus group to generate multiple and heterogeneous viewpoints.

Given this economy of speech, it is not surprising that truthfulness, as a characteristic of the statements produced by participants, is strikingly absent from the moderators' reflections. Judging from their technical literature, opinions cannot be true or false – they can either be genuine or induced, frank or contrived. In this sense, the focus group is not only isegoric, but also a space of *parrhesia*, a form of speech in which 'there is always an exact coincidence between belief and truth' (Foucault, 2001: 14). Parrhesia is often translated as 'free speech,' but etymologically it simply means 'to say everything.' In the focus group, the goal is to elicit a *complete* record of the participant's own 'frame of reference,' not to ascertain the 'objective' quality of his views. The function of the moderator is to turn every participant into a *parrhesiastes*, in Foucault's words:

> Someone who says everything he has in mind: he does not hide anything, but opens his heart and mind completely to other people through his discourse. In parrhesia,

the speaker is supposed to give a complete and exact account of what he has in mind so that the audience is able to comprehend exactly what the speaker thinks. The world 'parrhesia,' then, refers to a type of relationship between the speaker and what he says. For in parrhesia, the speaker makes it manifestly clear and obvious that what he says is his own opinion. And he does this by avoiding any kind of rhetorical form which would veil what he thinks. (Foucault, 2001: 14)

Foucault points out in relation to *parrhesia* that 'truth-having is guaranteed by the possession of certain moral qualities.' In the focus group, true opinions – that is, opinions that can be circulated as authentic and actionable – are guaranteed by the moral qualities of the *moderator*, and by the proper ordering of the research subjects and their discussion. This is a curious reformulation of the Socratic method, in which a good moderator, armed with the proper techniques of interrogation, is able to extract truthful opinions from the assembled research subjects – where 'truthful' means, once again, a correspondence with the subject's authentically held beliefs.

I have so far argued that in conducting a focus group, moderators must grapple with fundamental questions of political philosophy: the right style of 'leadership,' the adequate form of authority (and the limits to its exercise), the role and dangers of rhetoric, the mechanisms of elicitation, silencing, and exclusion. All these issues come to the fore in the moderators' discussions of the problem of influence. We can analyze the focus group as a sort of laboratory polity – an experimental and transient community in which a particular notion of the proper social order must be instantiated. The focus group is in this sense a practical application of political philosophy, and the moderators' reflections on good practice represent the articulation of an ideal social order. This social order is isegoric, rather than egalitarian: it grants every member of the assembly an equal opportunity to express his or her views but their talk is always steered towards the goals of the moderator. The 'deceptively simple premise' underlying this practice is fundamentally utilitarian: the assumption that if a larger number of opinions can be extracted from research subjects, the moderator will gain more valuable insights into the modes of judgment and behaviour of consumers. Over and over again moderators emphasize this fact: that the purpose of the focus group is to extract *value* from the discussion with research subjects. In the microcosms of the focus group, then, political organization and knowledge production are one and the same thing. The focus group is an instrument of knowledge production, but also a 'small moral world' that must be properly ordered so as to maximize this function.

One-way mirrors and the focus group chain

The philosophies of moderation articulated by moderators undergo their materialization in the choice and arrangement of the particular physical setting in which the focus group takes place. As noted above, focus groups are examples of 'white room' settings – well-demarcated, closed spaces, designed to facilitate the interaction of research subjects and their observation by researchers, while isolating all of them from external influences. The design of this locale, and of the artefacts with which it is furnished, is part and parcel of the focus group methodology. In fact, the lack of adequate facilities is a major challenge to the usefulness of focus groups as a reliable instrument of knowledge production, and moderators sometimes complain that 'the weakest link in the focus group chain is probably the facility.'

In the last two decades, however, as the use of focus groups has become widespread in commercial market research, the 'physical plant' of focus groups has improved a great deal. 'What was a mom-and-pop operation has become big business,' an American researcher notes. 'A number of corporate chains are opening up more and more facilities around the country. Modern facilities are often large, well-appointed, and even glamorous' (Langer, 2001: 54–55). The 'upgrade' of facilities has not been an even process, and the peculiarity of the setting often reflects divergent methodological choices and a differential access to resources between professional moderators, who use the focus groups for market research, and those, mostly social scientists, who employ it for scholarly purposes. Users of the focus group for marketing research often criticize the material arrangements of social scientists, and vice versa. Sometimes, this is combined with different 'national styles' in the conduct of focus groups. An American market researcher describes as follows the kind of facility often used in other countries:

> In a number of countries, focus groups are often still conducted in private homes, out of necessity or choice. In the United Kingdom, for instance, there are a growing number of viewing 'studios,' but many British researchers insist that the living room environment is the best in making respondents feel comfortable. They disapprove of what they see as the sterility of U.S. facilities. I don't agree, at least for groups done in the States. When I've done focus groups in a 'living room' setting (a real home or facility), I found that strangers squooshed onto a sofa together did not seem comfortable physically or psychologically. It is also difficult to control the inevitable side conversations. (Langer, 2001: 56)

The focus group setting encompasses thus a variety of possible sites, and the variability is a reflection of vernacular methodologies, the level of material resources, and even national preferences.

Perhaps the most identifying and controversial element of the focus group setting is the mirrored window that separates the research subjects and moderators from the back room so that clients and researchers can observe the proceedings while remaining themselves invisible.[18] The physical separation of those directly participating in the focus group discussion (moderator and research subjects) from those observing and recording it raises the question of the real-time and *in situ* communication between the moderator and her clients (or fellow researchers) in the back room. But it also generates broader questions about the relationship between moderators and clients, and the embeddedness of the 'white room' discussion in the 'focus group chain.'

The real-time communication between clients and moderators is a perennial problem and a pervasive issue in the moderators' literature. The old practice of passing written notes from the back room, by which clients used to communicate their reaction to the ongoing discussion, is almost unanimously rejected by moderators today. Such an obvious external intervention into the discussion 'disrupts the flow of conversation' and undermines the moderator's position of authority vis-à-vis the research subjects:

> One of the main reasons why focus groups work as a research technique is that the moderator is the *authority figure* in the room. (...) I have found that when notes are passed into the room from the clients, the moderator loses the position of authority since it becomes obvious to the participants that the people in the back are really in control. Often, the participants begin to talk to the mirror rather than to the moderator, since they feel the more important people are behind the mirror. (Greenbaum, 1998: 50)

The alternative of having the moderator regularly leave the room to ask for instructions is even worse. In general moderators are keen to limit contact with clients throughout the course of the focus group. It is easy to understand that the moderator's strenuous efforts to become the benevolent 'authority figure' in the room can be easily upset by 'overzealous clients,' and generally by any intervention that makes visible to the research subjects the larger setting of which the focus group discussion is just a part. When instructions are passed from the back room, it becomes clear to the participants that the moderator is himself the object of observation and moderation by people hiding behind the mirror. The experimental features of the setting – the first- and second-order processes of observation to which participants are being subjected – become then glaringly apparent, perturbing the *natural* course of an *experimental* conversation.

This leads some moderators, particularly those using focus groups for social scientific research, to reject the presence of clients and invisible observers altogether. For these moderators, the increasing technological sophistication of the research apparatus, particularly visible in the United States, is a hindrance, rather than an enabling element.

> In America market researcher technocratising focus group research has even progressed to a state where the moderator might be equipped with an ear-piece to receive instruction from the client. One can understand this in terms of the moderator-client relationship in market research, but even so to have a client watch focus group in operation is damaging to the method. If one has moderator demand, one now has client demand. (Morrison, 1998: 222)

Thus, discussions over the mirrored window and other physical arrangement of the focus group address, implicitly or explicitly, the relationship between moderators – the technicians of elicitation that produce the raw material of the research – and the clients and users of the knowledge being generated. An important dimension of this relationship is the theatrical aspect of the focus group. The mirror gives rise to a multidirectional game of observation and attribution in which research subjects, moderators, and invisible observers are entangled. As an American moderator puts it:

> For better or worse, there is a theatre aspect to a focus group conducted in front of the one-way mirror. Observes are unobserved themselves, watching strangers interact. The moderator is highly aware of having two audiences to keep involved and pleased. One of the charges made against focus groups is that they are 'entertainment' for the back room. (Langer, 2001: 103)

The danger of trying too hard to entertain the back room is often mentioned in the moderators' technical literature. 'I have observed moderators who spend a disproportionate amount of time during the session trying to be funny or clever for the basic purpose of generating a reaction from observing clients,' one moderator notes (Greenbaum, 1988: 52). Yet the theatrical gaze is multidirectional and can be highly stimulating for the moderator. While the one-way mirror allows an invisible audience to observe the performance of the moderator and his subjects, it also reflects this performance back to himself, and to the people assembled in the 'white room.' 'Somebody once asked me what I like best about being a moderator,' one moderator remarks. 'It's the entertainment value. The one-way mirror is a little like a proscenium arch. Part of the reward is the exuberance I feel in front of the mirror when things are going well or the anxiety when they aren't going the way the client – and I – thought they might' (Goebert, 2002: 34).

The one-way mirror invites assumptions on both sides of the wall. Sometimes it gives clients a sense of immediacy to the minds of the research subjects, or so moderators think. 'The most beguiling aspect of focus groups,' one moderator argues, 'is that they can be observed in action by clients and creative people hidden behind a one-way mirror. Thus, the planners and executors of advertising can be made to feel that they are themselves privy to the innermost revelations of the consuming public. They *know* what consumers think of the product, the competition, and the advertising, having heard it at first hand' (Bogart, 1995: 67). At other times, moderators interpret the invisibility of the observers in the back room as a sign of shyness, or even fear, on the part of their clients – a perception that emphasizes the authority of the moderator *beyond* the 'white room' itself:

> Clients are apt to see that one-way mirror as a wall that protects them from their customers. In some instances, it becomes the clients' last refuge against reality. I was doing sessions with principals from a new dot.com company, one of whom asked me if he should wait until the group started before going to the bathroom, which was located across from the waiting room. Why? He didn't want any of the panelists to see him. In truth, no one would have known who he was, but advertisers and marketers cling to a deep-seated fear of confronting the people who might buy and use their stuff. (Goebert, 2002: 26)

Yet, regardless of the motives attributed to the unobserved observers, moderators perceive and resent their presence – invisible as it might be – as a form of control.[19] In a certain way, the mirror makes real and evident (if also physically invisible) the dictum that 'the moderator is the *instrument* in a focus group interview' (Morgan and Krueger, 1993: 6). This idea may in theory be acceptable to facilitators, but it must also be made imperceptible during their encounter with the research subjects. The mirrored window gives a material form to this ambiguity.

Conclusion: the political constitution of market opinions

Despite being a key *resource* in social-scientific and marketing research, opinions are a neglected *object* of investigation. Researchers spend a great deal of effort explaining why people have the opinions they have, or using those opinions to explain other social phenomena, yet they have devoted very little attention to how something comes to be counted as an opinion, to the conditions of possibility for something to become an 'opinion.' Opinions are too often treated as unproblematic objects, unmediated expressions of people's beliefs or values.

The relatively unproblematic status of opinions is surprising, given the fact that knowledge and knowledge claims are routinely subjected to intense analytical scrutiny. We have sophisticated accounts of the manufacture of technical and scientific knowledge, for instance, and of the instruments and technologies through which it is created, certified and circulated. Opinions, as the example of the focus group hopes to make clear, also have an instrumental history. They are generated in a highly mediated fashion and through complex technologies of investigation, yet they do not seem to merit the same analytical treatment and are often addressed as if they somehow *emerged* from individual preferences. The famous distinction between *episteme* and *doxa* is maintained, albeit in a curiously inverse fashion: we have come to understand valid knowledge as an entity in need of an explanation, but the existence of a field of opinions still appears to us as a natural phenomenon, a function of actors' beliefs.

In the focus group chain, individual opinions are manufactured as such – as peculiar entities, different from knowledge claims. They are treated as materializations of personal viewpoints and certified as expressions of individual beliefs. Among many other things, focus groups produce experimental representations of consumer attitudes and opinions on market products. The 'focus group chain' is, in its most refined and standardized form, a machinery for the elicitation of individual opinions and for their integration into marketing strategies.

This chapter has focused on the techniques of moderation and the self-understandings that moderators bring to bear on the task of generating those opinions. I have tried to discuss these techniques and self-understandings, not only as methodological prescriptions but also as a peculiar epistemology of moderation and, moreover, as instantiations of a particular notion of political order. The technical literature of moderators is infused with moral and political issues. It discusses authority, rhetoric, exclusion, influence, equality. The focus group is thus a kind of laboratory polity, an experimentally assembled and transient community organized to extract knowledge about people – particularly about their behaviour in the marketplace – from the opinions they express. And it can only do so if it endows the group with a particular political constitution. According to the moderators, this constitution is based on a personal, even artistic, style of authority and self-discipline on their part, an isegoric distribution of speech among the subjects, and a high degree of autonomy vis-à-vis clients and audiences. From the point of view of moderators, tradable opinions about the market are best manufactured in these 'small moral worlds,' where they can handle their subjects with a combination of conversational virtuosity, a skilful application of technique, and an isegoric political philosophy.

Notes

1 I would like to thank Chi-ming Yang, Catherine Grandclement, and the editors of this volume for many insightful comments on an early version of the argument.
2 The genealogy of the focus group as a technique of social investigation crisscrosses into a variety of domains, beginning with the early uses of the 'focussed interview' by Robert K. Merton, Patricia Kendall, and other researchers associated with Paul Lazarsfeld's Bureau of Applied Social Research (BASR). The fluidity of the focus group form, its relative cost-effectiveness and versatile nature, allowed the members of the BASR to move quite effortlessly between social-scientific and marketing research – from investigations into the effects of war-time propaganda films on the morale of US troops to analyses of the most efficacious marketing strategy for a brand of toothpaste. Deployed in a variety of contexts and for a multitude of purposes, the technology of the focus group soon underwent numerous changes. For a detailed history of the BASR and its methodological innovations see Converse (1986).
3 Robert K. Merton commented critically on the spread and multiplication of the 'focussed interview' beyond social-scientific research, and he rued its elevation in the marketing sciences to the status of almost infallible truth-finding machine. He noted that 'during the passage from Morningside Heights [the site of Columbia University and Lazarsfeld's BASR] to Madison Avenue the focussed interview has undergone some sea changes of the kind I've been in a position only to hint at: the quick would-be conversion of new plausible insights into demonstrable gospel truths' (Merton, 1987: 560).
4 The term 'white room' is borrowed from Cicourel (1996).
5 For an analysis of another instrument of social scientific investigation, the opinion poll, see for instance Osborne and Rose (1999).
6 Finally, the chapter is also limited in that it is restricted to British and American sources. One should expect a fair degree of variability across different cultures of social research, and the existence of distinct vernacular forms in other countries and literatures.
7 The distinction between 'natural settings' and 'naturalistic inquiries' is drawn from Lincoln and Guba (1985).
8 The image of the chameleon is more common than one would expect: 'A good moderator knows how to be a chameleon, relating to people across the socio-economic spectrum by modifying dress, body language, and vocabulary' (Langer, 2001: 31).
9 The term 'focus group' was a misnomer, according to Merton, if only because, from a sociological standpoint, the congregation of research subjects hardly constituted a 'group.' It was merely a 'grouping' (Merton, 1990: xix).
10 In the 1940s, Merton and his collaborators analysed transcripts of focus group discussions precisely to discover these teachable patterns of interaction between moderators and interviewees and train future researchers. Their study of these transcripts resembles the kind of analysis of talk conducted, with a very different purpose, by Conversation Analysis scholars (Myers, 2004; Puchta and Potter, 2002).

11 This sort of sabotage is not unique to focus groups, but appears in all kinds of social experiments. Sagoff (1998) describes the case of an economic experiment in which research subjects were asked to value environmental qualities by putting a price (or compensation) on their loss (eg, how much would a pollutant have to pay to compensate for a loss of visibility due to an emission). About half of the participants 'required infinite compensation or refused to cooperate' with this portion of the exercise.

12 Of course the perils of familiarity also affect moderators, particularly professionals with a wealth of experience in eliciting opinions on any given topic. 'A disadvantage of using a professional group moderator,' Greenbaum writes, 'is that this person may not be able to address the subject at hand in a totally objective manner because of prior experience with the subject (or a closely related one) during a previous focus group assignment. I have found during my career as a moderator that I do not forget the material covered in a group session for a long time, and it is not unusual to use information learned from a focus group to help direct the discussion in a subsequent session.' (Greenbaum, 1988: 48) The solution to this problem is, according to moderators, a high degree of self-discipline, the ability to treat every group session as if it were unique.

13 Among the rules of the 'official line' that jurors are expected to adopt, Garfinkel lists the following: (6) 'For the good juror, personal preferences, interests, social preconceptions, ie, his perspectival view, are suspended in favor of a position that is interchangeable with all positions found in the entire social structure. His point of view is interchangeable with that of 'Any Man'. (8) 'The good juror suspends the applicability of the formulas that he habitually employs in coming to terms with the problems of his own everyday affair' (Garfinkel, 1984: 109). None of these rules apply to focus groups – in fact, the focus group is founded on the opposite expectations.

14 While the focus group largely centers on the production of oral opinions, it is interesting to note that 'quality control' procedures often rely on writing to assess the authenticity of views, or the degree to which the group dynamic has altered the views of individuals. Writing, as opposed to group talk, is the space where the ultimate meaning of the stated opinions can be recovered. Greenbaum argues that 'the best way a moderator can help the participants say what they really think and feel rather than be influenced by each other is to have them write down their opinion before sharing them with the group' (Greenbaum, 1998: 144). Krueger, on the other hand, recommends a final writing assessment, in which research subjects 'clarify' inconsistent views expressed in the course of the discussion. 'If the participant does not have the opportunity to explain the differences, it is nearly impossible to determine what to do with the comments.' (Krueger, 1994: 80) Writing can also be used during a group discussion to 'quiet down the group enthusiasm so the moderator can get the discussion back on track.' (Greenbaum, 1988: 65)

15 Thus, in the chapter I use the terms 'isegoria' and 'isegoric' differently from most of the existing commentary on the concepts and their use in ancient Greece (see for instance Griffith, 1966). I am interested in the form of organization of an assembly in which the powers of speech must be evenly distributed so as to generate the maximum value for the audience – in this case, the moderator and her clients. My use does not include the notion of 'freedom of speech,' nor a notion of *justice* in the distribution of speech, which are central to the principle of isegoria as instantiated in the Athenian agora. The focus here is exclusively on the condition – or, in the focus group, the imperative – of equal participation. I owe this caveat to Emmanuel Didier.

16 Pursuing a similar argument, Silver (1990) has traced the pervasive use and theoretical significance of small groups in American sociology to the 'theories of community' of religious congregations. The focus group shares the assumption that 'central features of total societies are best or uniquely understood by investigating properties of small-scale interaction between persons.'

17 This is not the same as encouraging polarization, a well-known effect of poorly run focus groups. As Morrison points out, 'polarization of thought is of particular concern to the clients of market researchers since if what is being measured is an effect of group membership then it is not a good predictor of attitudes and behaviour in the natural setting of everyday life outside the parameters of the focus group' (Morrison, 1998: 183).

18 The increase in the use of focus groups in the production of commercially relevant knowledge has been accompanied by the creation of facilities explicitly designed to facilitate the interaction between researchers and their clients. The sophistication of the back room and the observation equipment has grown accordingly. 'Many back rooms today are built for 20 observers, often theatre-style with stepped-up levels for better viewing. There are adjoining lounges with phones and closed-circuit TV for viewing . . . Some have booths so clients and moderators can make private calls because the facility is their office-on-the-road' (Langer, 2001: 55).

19 The struggle for control of the focus group extends beyond the management of the discussion, to other stages in the 'focus group chain.' For instance, the use of recording equipment is generally intended as an aid to the research, but it also serves to make the moderator accountable. Videotapes or transcripts of the focus group allow clients and outsiders to 'reverse' the process of analysis, probing the connections between the interpretations offered by the researchers and the evidence generated in the course of the discussion.

References

Agar, M. and J. MacDonald (1995). 'Focus group and ethnography'. *Human Organization* 54(1): 78–86.

Bloor, M., J. Frankland, M. Thomas and K. Robson (2001). *Focus Groups in Social Research*. London: Sage.

Bogart, L. (1995). *Strategy in Advertising*. Lincolnwood (Illinois): NTC Contemporary.

Bostock, R. (1998). Foreword in T. L. Greenbaum, *The Handbook of Focus Group Research* (2nd edition), Thousand Oaks, London, New Delhi: Sage Publications.

Cicourel, A. (1996). 'Ecological validity and 'white room effects': the interaction of cognitive and cultural models in the pragmatic analysis of elicited narratives from children'. *Pragmatics & Cognition* 4(2): 221–264.

Converse, J. (1986). *Survey Research in the United States: Roots and Emergence*. Berkeley: California University Press.

Foucault, M. (2001). *Fearless Speech*. Los Angeles: Semiotext(e).

Garfinkel, H. (1984). *Studies in Ethnomethodology*. Englewood Cliffs (New Jersey): Prentice-Hall.

Goebert, B (with H. M. Rosenthal) (2002). *Beyond Listening: Learning the Secret Language of Focus Groups*. New York: John Wiley & Sons, Inc.

Greenbaum, T. L. (1988). *The Practical Handbook and Guide to Focus Group Research*. Lexington (Massachusetts): Lexington Books.

Greenbaum, T. L. (1998). *The Handbook of Focus Group Research*. Thousand Oaks, London, New Delhi: Sage.

Griffith, G. T. (1966). 'Isegoria in the Assembly at Athens', in E. Badian (ed.) *Ancient Society and Institutions*. Oxford: Basil Blackwell.

Karger, T. (1987). 'Focus groups are for focusing, and for little else'. *Marketing News*, August 28: 50–55.

Krueger, R. A. (1994). *Focus Groups* (2nd Edition). Thousands Oak, London, New Delhi: Sage Publication.

Langer, J. (2001). *The Mirrored Window: Focus Groups from a Moderator's Point of View*. Ithaca (New York): Paramount Market Publishing, Inc.

Lincoln, Y. S. and E. Guba (1985). *Naturalistic Inquiry*. Beverly Hills (California): Sage Publications.

Merton, R. K. and P. L. Kendall (1946). 'The Focused Interview'. *American Journal of Sociology* 51(6): 541–557.

Merton, R. K. (1987). 'The Focussed Interview and Focus Groups: Continuities and Discontinuities'. *Public Opinion Quarterly* 51(4): 550–566.

Merton, R. K. (1990). Introduction to R. K. Merton, M. Fiske and P. L. Kendall, *The Focussed Interview: A Manual of Problems and Procedures* (2nd Edition). New York and London: The Free Press.

Morgan, D. L. (1988). *Focus Groups as Qualitative Research*. Newbury Park (California): Sage Publications.
Morgan, D. L. and R. A. Krueger (1993). 'When to use focus groups and why', in D. L. Morgan (ed.), *Successful Focus Groups: Advancing the State of the Art*. Newbury Park (California): Sage Publications.
Morrison, D. E. (1998). *The Search for a Method: Focus Groups and the Development of Mass Communication Research*. Luton: University of Luton Press.
Myers, G. (1998). 'Displaying opinions: topics and disagreement in focus groups'. *Language in Society* 27(1): 85–111.
Myers, G. (2004). *Matters of Opinion: Talking about Public Issues*. Cambridge: Cambridge University Press.
Myers, G. and P. Macnaghten (1999). 'Can focus groups be analysed as talk?', in R. S. Barbour and J. Kitzinger (eds), *Developing Focus Group Research: Politics, Theory and Practice*. London: Sage Publications.
Newman, W. R. (2005). *Promethean Ambitions: Alchemy and the Quest to Perfect Nature*, Chicago: University of Chicago Press.
Osborne, T. and N. Rose (1999). 'Do the social sciences create phenomena?: the example of public opinion research'. *British Journal of Sociology* 50(3): 367–396
Puchta, C. and J. Potter (2002). 'Manufacturing individual opinions: market research focus groups and the discursive phsychology of evaluation'. *British Journal of Social Psychology* 41(3): 345–363.
Puchta, C. and J. Potter (2004). *Focus Group Practice*. London: Sage Publications.
Sagoff, M. (1988). *The Economy of the Earth: Philosophy, Law, and the Environment*. Cambridge: Cambridge University Press.
Silver, A. (1990). 'The curious importance of small groups in American sociology', in H. J. Gans (ed.), *Sociology in America*. Newbury Park (California): Sage Publications.
Stewart, D. W. and P. N. Shamdasani (1990). *Focus Groups: Theory and Practice*, London: Sage.

Performance testing: dissection of a consumerist experiment

Alexandre Mallard

Introduction

The consumer press is a key player in today's markets.[1] On the one hand, it contributes to shaping the demand side through recommendations and advice given to the public concerning the quality of various products and services. On the other hand, it tends directly to influence the supply side through a series of operations targeted at firms or public authorities, which are visible enough in the public sphere to generate decisions that carry economic consequences. These operations include the denunciation of dishonest manufacturers, alerts concerning dangerous products, court cases to trigger changes in legal decisions on consumption, etc. As the commercial success of periodicals and magazines specializing in various domains of consumption and the multiplication of 'consumer' columns in national dailies show, this approach is not the hallmark of consumerist magazines. Nowadays, offering information on new products and criticizing the innovations circulating in the market are relatively common exercises. Yet consumerist magazines in the strict sense of the term, like *Que choisir* and *60 millions de consommateurs* in France, retain a particular position in the press as a whole. This position is related as much to the specific nature of the point of view they wish to represent, as to their goal of promoting a rational conception of consumer choice.[2] In practice, this ambition of consumerists is based largely on a particular exercise: the comparative testing of products and services.

Social scientists have paid little attention to the way in which this type of consumerist information is produced. For researchers interested in the consumer press, the production of comparative information on goods and services is conceived as a painstaking activity at best, and at worst, as a kind of craze with limited effects on customer behaviours. Scholars usually suggest that comparative testing constitutes the reasonable side of a press characterized, above all, by protest journalism (Pinto, 1990); one that most often reports on unrealistic comparisons never encountered in the consumers' real life (Marcus-Steiff, 1977);

or that does not influence their opinions in any substantial way (Aldridge, 1997). Whatever the empirical evidence provided to support this kind of criticism, the practical processes of producing comparative information on product performance have been relatively ignored. Yet it seems to me that these processes are worthy of investigation because they reveal many interesting aspects of the micro-politics of value (Appadurai, 1986) that underpin the circulation of commodities in contemporary markets. Through an experimental approach, consumerist testing elaborates the nature and properties of economic goods that usually stand in opposition to those promoted by market suppliers. As with any deconstruction, this invites us to reflect on the logic of construction itself and, more generally, to question the way in which various actors compete for the qualification of economic goods in the market.

I propose to investigate in detail the processes that give birth to comparative tests, in order to show the originality of the consumerist approach to quality evaluation. In the first section, I will briefly review the resources available in the realm of the social sciences to characterize consumerist information, and specify a frame of analysis rooted in an economic sociology perspective. In the second part I will study the construction of comparative tests from this frame. I will deliberately ignore the reception of test results by readers, focussing instead on the work carried out by the professionals who perform comparative testing in order to illuminate the practical operations they bring into play and the troubles they encounter. I will suggest that this practice – a relatively rich and fairly original one – aims to define a particular position for the consumer, one in which his or her ability to choose is subject to a specific form of what I call 'disengagement' from the market.

A perspective for understanding comparative testing

The sociology and economics of consumerist information

Even though consumption has been widely studied by sociologists, their approach leaves little room for discussing the role consumerist information plays in consumption practices. Baudrillard (1998), for instance, argues that goods are no longer characterized by their value or their properties but by the signs they represent. This conception undermines the importance of information obtained through comparative tests as goods are defined, to a large extent, in relation to their performance and not to the semiology of which they partake. Similarly, Bourdieu's emphasis on the social logic of distinction tends to restrict the question of evaluating goods to the exercise of taste (Bourdieu, 1984). The rationality of consumer choices – in so far as this expression can be used to denote processes that are as unconscious as they appear in the theory of the *habitus* – is embedded in a social context largely untouched by public information on goods and services. As a whole this perspective is of little help in understanding the impact of performance tests on consumers' opinions.

In contrast, economists have shown a great deal of interest in the information necessary for accomplishing an economic exchange. Yet the way in which consumer theory has taken consumerist information into consideration remains complex. Indeed, economics has spent a lot of energy to delineate the relationship between information on prices and quantities but it usually encounters difficulties when dealing with information concerning quality – which is precisely the information produced by comparative testing. The failure of economic theories to integrate product quality as a relevant variable has been criticized for a long time and solutions have been proposed to improve the neo-classical model in this respect (Eymard-Duvernay, 1989). For example, Lancaster (1966) has proposed to split goods up into their constitutive characteristics: each good is then seen as a combination, as a 'basket', of different characteristics that can be qualified (for instance, through the use of consumerist tests). Although Lancaster notes that these characteristics – the only relevant variables for informing the consumer's choice – are objective properties, he says nothing about the devices and practices used to reveal them or about their modes of appropriation and interpretation by economic actors.

Consumerist actors as prescribers

In contrast, cultural theory of consumption tends to consider that appraising the performance of products and services falls mainly under the realm of arbitrary judgement disconnected from the goods themselves, while economics rely on an objectivist definition of performance. The former places little value in investigating the modes of production and appropriation of consumerist information (why bother since that's not where the consumer's choice is made?), while the latter raises the question without providing the means to answer it (the analysis of consumerist know-how remains outside the economic model). I suggest shifting the perspective slightly by focusing on the role of prescribers (Hatchuel, 1995).

An analysis in terms of prescription stresses the action of mediators that 'fit' the space separating suppliers and customers and participate in the structuring of their relations. This perspective leads us to take into account the existence of a plurality of prescribers in the market, as well as the mechanisms of competition between them. Consumer magazines are by no means the only actors to propose information on the quality of goods and services, and it is important to identify what differentiates these materials from other categories of prescribers: advertisers, public authorities, consultants, distributors, etc. This question runs through Alan Aldridge's research (Aldridge, 1994; Aldridge, 1997) on British consumer unions. Following a British sociological tradition strongly influenced by Marxist critique (Keat *et al.*, 1994)[3], he considers the issue of consumer power and authority in relation to the other actors in the market.

In a study devoted to the magazine *Which*, the British equivalent of the French magazine *Que choisir*, Aldridge investigates competition in the market for information on products and services. He compares consumerist magazines and specialized magazines that also publish advice and information on goods.

In comparison, consumerist publications are characterized by their independence from manufacturers, especially in financial terms. Magazines affiliated to independent consumer unions (eg, *Que choisir*) or to public institutions (eg, *60 millions de consommateurs*, created by the Institut National de la Consommation) do usually not appeal to advertisement in order to remain autonomous from manufacturers.

This independence is not the only difference between these two types of prescribers. Aldridge (1994) identifies several other points: first, consumer organizations relate to a form of depersonalized authority rather than to the charismatic authority usually mobilized by specialized magazines; second, their product evaluation is based on scientific analysis rather than on connoisseurship; and, lastly, they portray consumption in an austere light, as opposed to specialized magazines' implicit emphasis on consumption as an hedonistic activity. More generally, Aldridge contrasts the consumerists' ascetic and critical discourse with the proliferation of 'promotional discourse' accompanying goods and encouraging consumption. With regard to financial services and investment advice, his analysis (Aldridge, 1998) plays down the real effectiveness of consumerist methods in the empowerment of the consumer. This powerlessness shows the difficulty of holding a key position in a context marked by the influence of more pre-eminent forms of prescription (especially advice by financial experts and investment clubs).

Consumerist prescribers in the process of qualifying goods

Alan Aldridge's research is suggestive of the reasons why the notion of prescription for the study of consumerist activity might be interesting, since it emphasizes the capacity to produce and transmit information on the goods traded, *in a specific way*. I propose to take this research question further and to consider the task performed by consumerist prescribers from the point of view of qualifying goods. As Callon *et al.* (2002) show, the process of qualifying commodities that lies at the heart of competition in modern markets operates through the attribution of particular positions and competencies to economic actors. From this perspective, the distinctive feature of prescribers is not that they provide information that would be more objective than that disseminated by producers. This would merely boil down to the traditional *mise en scène* of the transaction provided by economic theory, resorting to notions like imperfect information or bounded rationality in order to explain the mediating role of prescribers. It is rather that prescribers offer alternative modes of engagement between consumers and goods – and therefore, between consumers and suppliers. Prescription supports the ability to calculate – in the extensive sense defined by Callon and Muniesa (2005) – in the making of market choices, an ability which is not necessarily concentrated on the individual actor and can be distributed among several actors and material settings.

From this perspective, let me briefly examine the performance test published in a consumerist journal. Two interesting features immediately appear, which provide a preliminary understanding of the way the consumerist prescription alters the consumer's engagement in the market. First of all, the act of reading a performance test in a consumer magazine is designed to shape a situation of consumption choice prior to the economic transaction as such. Yet this type of distilled situation is actually rare in the realm of consumption, for the constitution of information intended to guide choices is most often rooted in the interaction with market actors and networks. Consumerist activists like to recall that the consumer's capacity to choose from within traditional trade institutions is more restricted than market professionals usually claim: even when they are confronted by countless products sold in the supermarket, consumers are already in the shop where everything has been done to organize their route and lead them to the purchasing act, from the packaging of products to the salesperson's smile, through to the arrangements of the shelves or the choice of background music.[4] Consumers are already *engaged* in the commercial act. In contrast, using the terms of a distributed cognition specialist (Hutchins, 1995), I would describe the consumerist magazine device as carrying out a 'pre-computation' of the purchasing act: choose first, then (maybe) buy. It aims to separate the emergence of choice and the purchase and to distribute them to two different time-frames and situations.

The second striking feature relates to the rhetoric of testing itself. The very idea of setting up a sort of experiment, with all of the quasi-scientific characteristics this entails, tells us much about the way consumerists consider the correct attribution of qualities to economic goods. Social scientists like to say that one of the first steps in the development of a scientific approach is to fight against 'prenotions'. Similarly, consumerists want the consumer to get rid of any prenotion that blurs a correct understanding of the commodities, and in particular the prenotions transmitted by other economic actors. Of course, as the sociology of scientific knowledge has extensively shown, there is no scientific project without a related political device. As we will see, the consumerist testing apparatus is not bare of political significance.

As a whole, we can consider the consumerist's goal as precisely opposite to that of the actors on the supply side: it aims to *disengage* consumers from the market infrastructure[5] – to the point where it may even advise them simply to cancel the planned transaction and to not buy. The market abounds with equipment enabling consumers to calculate so that they can shape their preferences (Canu and Mallard, 2006) and escape the paradox of too much choice (Cochoy, 2002). Consumerism would like to replace this equipment by the apparatus of comparative tests, that is, a quasi-scientific setting of prescription designed to allow the consumer to make a choice without engaging emotionally in market devices – and possibly without even buying. Yet this ambition entails various costs and requires a specific kind of work, with regard to the identification of the economic goods to qualify, to the construction of a representation of the supply and to the defence of a discourse of autonomy *vis-à-vis* the market. I will focus on these points throughout my examination of the practical achievement of performance testing.

Investigating consumerist work

Let me now outline the empirical material I will mobilize for this purpose. It is based on a survey of performance tests concerning telecommunication products and services that were published in *60 millions de consommateurs* and *Que choisir* in the end of the 1990s.[6] I examined the comparative tests run on telecom products (faxes, mobile phones, Internet subscription, phone cards, cordless phones, etc.) in 1997, 1998 and 1999 and tried to determine the work that lay behind those tests. Like many other activities, comparative testing is standardized. The main ethical principles (eg, 'Tested products have to be bought in conditions comparable to those of the average consumer') are found in the French standard NF X 50–005. These rules form a framework of legitimacy for consumerist magazines that distinguishes them from rival prescribers.[7] Testing, however, is of course more complex in practice than the rules depicted in the standard, and only a dialogue with professionals enables a thorough understanding of this work.

Performing a comparative test in a consumerist magazine requires the collaboration of two different types of actors: first, the engineers of the test centre working with the magazine, in charge of designing and monitoring the performance tests usually sub-contracted to test laboratories; and, second, the journalists or market researchers who play only a small part in the design of the technical testing protocol but who are key in drafting the final reports and writing up the results in articles. I met the managers of test centres and the engineers participating in the tests concerned.[8] The data concerning the more journalistic part of this activity are partly drawn from this survey and partly from a former survey undertaken in 1997, on the role of consumer organizations in controversies over water quality (Mallard, 2001).

All in all I was able to collect general information on testing, supported mainly, but not exclusively, by examples from the telecommunication sector. In the end of the 1990s, the liberalization of this sector extended the scope of competition to a wider range of goods, thus lending a new dimension to the question of choice. Yet all situations of consumption are obviously not identical with regards to choice. It is worth noting that much of the information provided here applies, on the whole, to household appliances.[9] The examples I use in the analysis below pertain largely to telecommunications products and services but also, here and there, to other consumer goods.

Comparative tests on telecommunication products and services: elements of a practice

As historians and sociologists of science have shown, the significance of an experiment never lies only in the technical achievement of the test itself. For instance in their seminal study of Robert Boyle's experiments on the properties of air, Shapin and Schaffer (1985) pay as much attention to the technical design of the air pump, as to the various social, political, literary practices that were mobilized to constitute an audience for these experiments, and to disclose their results far beyond the laboratory. Similarly, I think that in order to take the measure of performance testing, it is necessary to examine the entire process from the elaboration of the experiment to the publication of results in the consumerist journal. I will focus on five successive categories of operation comprising a comparative test: the preliminary market analysis; the identification of the goods that takes place through the sample's construction; the formulation of criteria for the tests; the formatting of the results; and the presentation of results to the manufacturers concerned.

Analysing the market and informing the consumer: a matter of qualification and critique

Let me begin with an obvious fact: to inform the consumer, consumerist workers have to be informed themselves. Like scientists investigating a new field, the consumerist workers have to constitute their expertise for each new subject, and a comparative test usually starts with a data collection phase. Engineers and journalists have to update their know-how regularly by reading the specialized literature and by reviewing a subject each time the magazines plans an investigation. The engineer in charge of the test, possibly in collaboration with the journalist or market researcher concerned, carries out a preliminary study and sometimes even questions professional experts in the field – who will cooperate in the exercise more or less willingly.

This phase is extremely important because it initiates the mechanism of deconstruction and reconstruction of the economic environment supporting the design of a test protocol that will ultimately prove relevant and legitimate for the magazine's readers. In order to provide their own representation of what the market is made up of, consumerists have to gather various pieces of information, discuss their relevance and rearrange them in a new combination that they will pass onto the readers. Indeed, consumer magazines aspire to train readers, not just to inform them. As Hatchuel (1995) would put it, they are not content to supply information, the utility of which is known to readers in advance (a prescription of facts). Rather, they define criteria that readers did not know about and were unable to formulate (a prescription of judgement). Prior to the presentation of tests themselves, this ambition requires the elaboration of products and services as well as their contextualization. Thus, reading articles presenting performance tests is an effective way of seeing the task of market analysis that consumerist workers perform at the beginning of each new test. In these articles, it appears that economic goods are (re-)qualified at three different levels: at the level of the technology, of the possible uses of the technology, and of the market actors that are involved in its circulation.

On the technical side, articles explain the way objects work or the way they are made, list the services they offer, distinguish between useful functions and gadgets, and so on. In a test on phone-faxes, for instance, the difference between thermal transfer and laser or ink jet technology is explained. With regards to use, the consumerist magazines describe practices (eg, 'What does *surfing the web* mean?') and answer a number of questions that users are likely to ask ('Should you insure your mobile phone?').[10] Finally, a significant proportion of information provided relates to market actors' behaviours and exchange mechanisms: the strategies and range of actions of the main actors (manufacturers, distributors, service-providers, etc.) are identified, the consumer is warned about usual traps to avoid, about possible bargains and bad deals, price trends and market share are qualified, etc. For instance, in the telecom market the ambiguous role played by service providers working as intermediaries between operators and customers is regularly discussed in articles on mobile phones. Indeed, consumerist magazines consider these actors – the intermediaries – to be parasites in the market relationship, as providing no real service and as needing to be treated with caution.

An important aspect involved in this multifaceted analysis is the identification of the traded good itself. The telecom sector is interesting in this respect since many goods are combinations of products and services. Depending on the good's 'perimeter', its performance and associated costs will vary. The case of mobile phones, for example, is generally meticulously investigated in consumerist magazines. The slightest comparison is an opportunity to take into account not only the performance of the telephone itself but also of its battery, subscription rates, call rates, and the various options that combine to make a whole. Here, consumerists prompt consumers to question what is really involved in the act of buying and using a good, against the definitions provided by the suppliers' promotional information.

This work of constituting and providing information to the reader, a necessary preliminary step in the construction of understandable and legitimate comparisons, has a polemical and critical objective. It sometimes makes it possible to suggest that what the supplier wants to sell to consumers does not match what the consumers will eventually have to pay. More generally, it proceeds from a critique of the market, the flip-side of providing information. One can even suggest that the specific nature of the information produced by consumerism stems from a dual construction of the critical stance: consumerist magazines aim both to reveal the hidden properties of consumer goods and to denounce injustices in the market. The first part of the work is performed by the engineers who construct the comparative tests, while the second part is carried out mainly by the journalists. They contextualize the tests in the critical context of consumerist discourse and sometimes do field studies resembling investigative journalism applied to the market. Even if it generates multiple tensions, the link between these two activities of qualification and critique (and the subsequently sometimes complicated relationships between the journalists and the engineers) distinguishes the originality of consumerists' ambition: to challenge not only the quality of goods but also the trust that one can have in the different categories of prescribers and in their modes of engagement in the market.

Identifying and collecting consumer goods

I shall now examine the practical constitution of the sample of products that will be submitted to the test. At first sight, this step seems mundane, but in fact, it conceals many tensions and difficulties that are emblematic of the *episteme* of performance testing. In the previous section, I alluded to the fact that consumerists discuss the perimeter of the goods that have to be tested. The delicate question of the identification of the supply lies at the heart of the operation. In order to highlight the significance of this operation, let me compare this task with the work of an entomologist interested in testing the reaction of insects to a new insecticide designed to kill a species of harmful butterflies. The entomologist has to catch the insects in the natural environment and bring them to the laboratory, where he can perform the test. Before he departs to the fields with his net, the entomologist needs a way to recognize the butterflies belonging to the particular species concerned. He will use a classification, which makes possible the identification of the butterflies that are relevant for the test, and he will discard the ones that are not concerned. The consumerists' job is quite analogous: he has to identify a particular category of goods, catch them 'in their natural environment' and bring them to the laboratory in order to test their performance.

In the domain of consumption, the equivalent of the natural classification used by the entomologist is segmentation. As economists know, segmentation is a tool that helps to solve the first problem of the consumer theory: identifying the goods that are substitutable for one another, whose quantities can be added up to calculate the total amount available in the market. Commodities may be dissimilar but comparable in the sense that they fulfil analogous functions for the consumer. These will be put in a given segment. Yet as anthropology has shown – see for instance Kopytoff (1986) – there is nothing straightforward or neutral about assembling separate goods into a category. Therefore, the consumerists usually scrutinize the segmentations proposed by suppliers or inscribed in technical standards. My survey shows that segments devised by marketing professionals can be at least partially ignored during the testing.

If, for instance, the market analysis has revealed that many consumers in the general public buy products that suppliers target at professionals, these products may be included in the test sample: the opposition between 'products for professionals' and 'products for the general public' will not be taken as such in the constitution of the sample. Segmentations based on technical criteria are likewise critically examined. The test managers try to see which segmentation is developed from the point of view of use. For example, it might be possible to segment the refrigerator market according to the number of compressors each fridge comprises, but this is of little relevance to the consumer whose interest when buying a fridge rather refers to its capacity. In other cases, a technical segmentation can match a segmentation that is meaningful for the user. A case in point is washing machines, where the spinning speed corresponds to the price variable:

> 'It may seem strange that we segment the market by saying 'Que Choisir tests washing machines that spin at over one thousand revs per minute'. However, there's an almost perfect correlation between the price of a product and its spinning speed. So, in the end, as far as I'm concerned it amounts to testing products with the same spinning speed.' (Interview with the testing manager at *Que choisir*.)

The next step is selecting the goods. The influence of this phase in the overall structure of a test can vary from case to case, depending primarily on the degree of competition in the market under consideration and on the speed at which products evolve. Two phenomena are particularly interesting here: the pressure of time, and the dilemma of variety reduction.

Let me come back to the comparison with the entomologist. For his experiment to be valid, he has to bring the butterflies to the laboratory, alive. No test of the insecticide's efficiency will be possible with dead butterflies. It is the same with the performance test: all the goods tested have to be 'alive', in that they must still be being sold when the magazine article is published. The demand for up-to-date products is central to the spirit of comparative testing, since this experiment does not bear on the respective performance of different technical objects but rather on the assessment of different purchasing options. Test managers have to select products that are already available when the test is scheduled and that will still be available – and preferably in line with current tastes – when the results are published. Due to the time needed to perform the tests, however, a few months may separate these two points in time, during which products are withdrawn from the market and innovations are introduced. A telephone handset that has not been available in the market for over two months may be a 'product', but it can no longer stand as a 'good' in a comparative test. The market is a shifting entity, constantly evolving, whereas the comparative test needs to 'freeze it' in order to produce a photograph that can be valid at two different times.

Controlling variety also has important effects on the test. What is at stake is to determine which good can be included in the comparison and which do not belong. It sometimes proves necessary to reduce the commercial offer in order to reach an acceptable size for the sample. The offer may be so vast and complex that for practical reasons or for cost considerations it is unthinkable to test all possible products. In 1998 the magazines *60 millions de consommateurs* and *Que choisir* published test results at the same time (in November and December, respectively). In total, 27 telephone models were tested: 21 by *Que choisir* and 10 by *60 millions de consommateurs* but only 4 of them were featured in both samples. Under such circumstances, it is not surprising that the final ranking of the products differs significantly from one magazine to the next – even when both achieve good quality assessments. In some cases the magazine articles even point out that the reader has to take this factor into account in appraising the test results.

Many of the tensions outlined here come from the very nature of the comparative test as a device with ambitions to represent. Using Pinch's (1993) terms, there must be a similarity, a possible projection, between the situation of choice as it is simulated in the test report and the one that is really experienced by consumers when they are shopping. An analogous requirement is present in the entomologist's practice: the act of killing a series of butterflies in the laboratory has no particular relevance in itself, and makes sense only because these butterflies represent other butterflies present in the natural environment, that will be eradicated if the insecticide is disseminated outside the laboratory. It is interesting to note that the requirement of similarity and projection, which is so important for consumerists, does not concern other market actors as much. Retailers do not have to carry out a representational process: the available offer, that is, *their* offer, is precisely the one the buyer will find in the shop's shelf space. In a sense, specialized magazines leave it up to manufacturers and distributors to fill their advertising space with lists of products and prices, thus constituting a representation of the offer available in various places. Mail order selling must put together an offer, contextualize it in a representative device and keep it available, but the rules and process mobilized to do so probably do not face the constraint of representativeness that consumerists aim for. Comparative testing set up a fictitious point of view on the supply which is available nowhere as an actual juxtaposition of rival goods but which has to be realistic enough to include what buyers may possibly find if they enter into the market. Organizing the 'pre-computing' of buying is, in the final analysis, a complex and somewhat strange task, especially when one is not engaged in the business of commercial distribution.

Devising criteria and trials

Once the goods have been identified and purchased in shops or supermarkets (taken from their 'natural environment'), they are ready to be submitted to the tests. But devising the criteria and trials themselves proves to be a tricky task in comparative testing. What comes to mind are the words of Lancaster who, with regard to relevant characteristics, wondered how many people would choose their car depending on the colour of the engine. This suggests, among other things, that it is very difficult to propose a general definition of the relevance of a criterion of quality. I will limit my comment here to a few pragmatic points and resources mobilized in devising criteria and tests.

Tests of solidity and security probably constitute the basic components of a large array of comparative tests. They point to traditional background know-how, rooted in a long history of consumerist practice. Blacklisting products that fail to withstand shocks during use is a traditional feature of performance tests, one probably inherited from the industrial practice of quality control where these practices originate (Gabriel and Lang, 1996; Winward, 1993). Attention to product safety has also become a systematic concern, since the Corvair affair that made consumerism '*à la Nader*'[11] popular. The engineers that I met consider that, whatever their importance, criteria of this kind are neither the most interesting nor the most distinctive of the consumerist approach. According to them, the most specific dimension of their work today relates to the way they take use into account.

The predominance of use in identifying relevant criteria for the consumerist evaluation calls for comment. In reflecting about the nature of the commodity in the capitalist economy, one may think, firstly, of the Marxian distinction between use value and exchange value. Whereas traditional economics (be it neo-classical or Marxist) has been very absorbed with determining the exchange value of goods, consumerist actors consider investigating use value to be of main concern. Secondly, one may notice that considering use implicitly or explicitly means taking into account the user's social identity. The choice of representing one or another category of user has a political significance. Hence, consumerist tests usually testify on behalf of particular categories of users who may statistically represent minorities but who still deserve consideration. In a test of telephone handsets, they will for example scrutinize the size of buttons, in order to qualify the product's appropriateness for the elderly and the partially sighted.

Even if the design of criteria and trials for testing use is undoubtledly culturally and politically laden, one should not conclude that it is arbitrary. Consumerist actors claim to have a privileged access to the consumer's irreducible point of view concerning use. Hence, although they share this know-how with other specialists – manufacturers, standardization engineers – they downplay the abilities of these other actors to interpret and assess the consumers' view correctly. One may ask, then, what kind of approach supports the correct qualification of use. Indeed, the notion of usage is at least as general and as cumbersome as that of 'quality'. The measurement of object properties and the identification of scenarios of predictable interactions with users will not be enough to qualify use (Thévenot, 1993). It appears that a peculiarity of the consumerist approach may lie in a comprehensive approach to what constitutes the context of use. It rests on a sound knowledge of the entire trajectory of the user-product relationship:

> 'We put ourselves virtually in a user's position and imagine the context or contexts of use of the product. We imagine the trajectory of the product, that also includes the phase of the intention to buy, the purchase itself, the installation, the putting into service, the use, with different modes every time, and then even the scrapping of the product or the failure scenario.' (Interview with the test manager of *Que choisir*.)

Consumerists follow the biography of the good after it is bought and de-commoditized (Kopytoff, 1986) in order to identify relevant trials to which it will be submitted. The approach assumes certain kind of projective attitude into the user's position, the legitimacy of which is largely based on the fact that everyone can naturally accede to that position (after all, are we not all users?). Knowledge mobilized to construct the tests, however, goes far beyond this intimate knowledge of users' practices. Here again, the information collected during the market analysis phase plays an important part because this makes it possible to identify relevant non-trivial criteria or, on the contrary, useless criteria. As the test manager at *Que choisir* noted, 'when you know that do-it-yourself tools are used for a few minutes a year only, you don't expect a drill to work for several hours continuously in the endurance tests'. It is through this type of investigative process that the test protocols emerge. The most interesting evaluation criteria and associated tests will be determined at each stage.[12] Tests for evaluating criteria may vary fairly widely and the whole paraphernalia of trials in quality evaluation can be mobilized: standardized tests, determining the physical properties by means of a measurement tool, appealing to individual experts (eg, for ergonomy), collective expert or to user panels (eg, for the sound quality of a mobile phone), and so on.

Let me note, finally, that the consumerist tradition has a longstanding experience in the field of services – insofar as the service can be reduced to the set of contracts and rates linking the consumer to the service-provider. Years of studying service regulations and struggling against unfair conditions have helped shape a set of skills that can be applied to widely diverse sectors (banks, insurance companies, public services, etc.) and are one of the main drivers of court action to defend consumers. The most useful tool here is the double-entry comparative table that summarizes, for each supplier, the proposed services along with their costs and a qualification of the related contractual commitments (eg, minimum length of subscription). The limit of this approach is that it addresses more directly the promises of services rather than their quality as such, as can be seen in tests devoted to mobile telephony or Internet access plans. The comparative tests that *Que choisir* and *60 millions* have run on these subjects in the period under scrutiny have focused mainly on product evaluation, with a secondary, qualitative or exploratory analysis of related services (hotline, on-line services, etc.) or, on an even more complex subject, the quality of the telecommunication network strictly speaking.

Indicating the choice or choices

Consumerist performance testing is commonly seen as an exercise aimed at selecting the best product on the market. Yet carefully reading the consumerist press suggests a less clear-cut reality. A performance test does not look like a demonstration that is able to reveal the best of all products and to calculate the optimal quality/price ratio. In fact many articles show a relative indecision, or tension, between two ways of accomplishing rational choice from the consumerist standpoint: as a) the discovery of the best product or service ('given a series of criteria, there is an intrinsically best good that wins'), or as b) the identification of the plurality of possible answers to the consumers' needs and desires. The magazine articles therefore often propose contrasting approaches to the issue of choice. It is interesting to look carefully at the 'literary devices' that these articles mobilize in order to outline the test results, in the same way as Shapin and Schaffer (1985) examined the experimental accounts written by Robert Boyle to communicate the facts discovered within his laboratory to the external world.

Let me examine how the best choice is presented. The most usual device is a ranking of products and the attribution of grades to them, for instance on a scale from 0 to 20. Such a system indicates an unambiguous order of preference. In the two magazines considered here, the grades are calculated on the basis of a linear weighting, with the use of restrictive criteria: a bad score for one of the criteria – eg, a safety flaw – brings down the overall grade. In this type of approach, setting the respective weight of each criterion has significant consequences for the results. Grades and ranking may be altered substantially simply by changing the balance between the different parameters. How are the underlying trade-offs made? It seems that for each of the two magazines, principles of weighting are adopted prior to the tests and their relevance is re-examined and adjusted *ex-post*. Depending on the grades and ranking obtained for the different products, the engineers may discuss their validity and perform computer simulations to test their sensitivity to the weighting coefficients. This pragmatic approach, which relies on the testing professionals' experience and know-how, allows them to qualify the robustness of weighting functions and to discard arbitrary results.

Other literary devices bring into play more circumstantial situations of choice. Test managers confess they would like to have a more flexible medium than the magazine, allowing them to take into account the variability of consumer preferences. They imagine interactive terminals in public places or internet websites where consumers could themselves express their preferences and obtain a 'personalized best choice' in return. A very traditional medium of communication, the magazine nevertheless affords certain opportunities to take this variability into account. Two different kinds of literary devices are used, one being centred on the product and the other on the consumer. In the former case, the magazine indicates the product(s) that, notwithstanding the grade obtained for the test, get(s) the best evaluation according to a particular criterion. The diversity of possible choices relates here to the diversity of criteria that can be conceived of to qualify the product. In the latter case, the readers are given a choice of user profiles, each of which is associated with a suitable product. For instance a section devoted to choosing the best mobile phone rate proposes several use scenarios similar to the following one: 'On average, you phone twice a day, essentially for family reasons. And you like to be contactable all the time'. For each scenario, the reader is prompted to choose the corresponding rate. The idea here is to offer the reader a figure for projecting his or her own identity or needs so that questions on the criteria themselves no longer need to be answered.

What conclusion can we draw from the fact that the magazine resorts to various literary settings in the publication of the consumerist experiment's output? For test managers, this indecision is a response to the readers' various expectations. There is, on the one hand, the feeling that 'consumers like clear, straightforward advice' and, on the other that, 'depending on the consumer, certain criteria may be more important than others and that one should not single out a given product'. What is important to me is that test managers and above all journalists seem to have a deep understanding of the cognitive processes that underlie the consumer's making of choice. They know that readers have unequal interpretative capabilities and that information must be transmitted through distinctive formats. Moreover, they rightly feel that the proliferation of mediations is an efficient way to shape the judgement concerning a good's quality: a persuasive prescription is not always the one that says 'Buy this product!' Instead, they prefer juxtaposing and illustrating various forms of embodiment of the relation between the consumers and the goods. In some sense, this plurality ratifies the idea that consumption involves different ways of filling in the gap between evaluation (product qualification) and action (buying).

Keeping manufacturers at a distance

Consumerist testing has developed an attitude of keeping distance from manufacturers. Although consumerist magazines need the cooperation of firms to obtain information on products and services, they are very careful not to be taken over by the commercial point of view. When results are received, they follow strict protocols in order to involve manufacturers without letting them have the last word. Before the final publication, each manufacturer will receive the results of the tests concerning its product – but it will not by privy to those of competitors. If ever a dispute arises concerning the results, possible explanations are sought together with the causes of divergence. Whenever manufacturers' arguments are acceptable the magazine may – although rarely does – publish a comment that in light of these arguments, puts certain results into a different perspective.

The aim of this preliminary procedure is, among other things, to avoid unpleasant surprises at the moment of publication. Situations of disagreement may persist, however, and may give rise to varying degrees of conflict: verbal dispute by phone, mail, registered letters, requests for court action to suspend the publication, or even outright prosecution. The latter occurs only rarely, which highlights the importance of a dialogue with manufacturers in the preliminary information phase. *60 millions de consommateurs* has been sued ten times in its 20-year existence and has lost only once. Another area of tension between consumerist magazines and industry relates to the appropriation of comparative test results by manufacturers for promotional purposes. In the consumerist world two policies exist in this respect, found in the two French magazines considered here.

Que choisir (like the British magazine *Which?*) does not want its results to be used by manufacturers and refuses to grant authorization to be quoted in this respect. According to the test manager at *Que choisir*, this deontological rule helps avoid having consumerist information misused in a context over which the magazine has no control:

> 'We always remind our readers that the test results are valid only when they are published and during the period that just follows: their lifetime is short precisely because in the market products largely evolve with time.' (Interview with the test manager of *Que choisir*.)

What is at stake once again, is the capacity of the goods tested in the magazine to represent accurately the goods that the consumer will actually find in the shops. Here the consumerists wish to distinguish themselves very clearly from a certification process, which usually has more resources to check up on the compliance of products with standards over time. I shall add that *Que choisir*'s policy on the question of quotation probably also originates in the necessity of preserving their image as observers untouched by the vicissitudes of commerce. Such purification clearly contributes to the credibility of consumerism as an institution that is uncontaminated by the interests and strategies of economic actors.[13]

In contrast, *60 millions de consommateurs* (like the German magazine *Test*, associated with the Warentest Foundation) does allow its results to be quoted by producers. This position relates to a more comprehensive policy implemented since 1987 by the INC (Institut National de la Consommation), a policy which, according to the test manager, had not really proved successful and was scheduled for amendment at the time of the survey. The original purpose of this policy was to reinforce the authority of the INC's as a test centre that would be also respected by manufacturers through a more formal testing approach. The model used was German, where the periodical *Test* had a very wide readership and where test results were quoted extensively by manufacturers. The system, however, was not very successful in France. In a spirit of control over the information supplied, the way to proceed in order to quote test results had been codified very precisely in a standard of the AFNOR (Association Française de NORmalisation, the French standardization organization). The manufacturer was allowed to mention only an overall qualitative assessment based on the comparative test result, without any indication of grade or rank and without any reference to rival products. This system proved unattractive to manufacturers who were unable to incorporate it in their promotion:

> 'If we wanted to subvert the system it would be easy. We receive requests daily, to quote results, all the time. But the manufacturers are limited by the little normative information sheet, which isn't useful for advertising, it's not promotional enough' (Interview with the test manager at the INC.)

Moreover, certain forms of competition with certification institutions (which were being reorganized in France at about the same time) probably contributed to weakening this device. Consumerist testing was confronted here with quality assessment as it is viewed in the certification system – a system in which manufacturers are more directly involved.

Conclusion

The sociology of the consumerist work outlined in this chapter is based on an analysis of one of its most emblematic activities: comparative testing. The chapter aims not so much to describe in itself the social and organizational context in which the defenders of consumers act, as to demonstrate the processes through which a very particular representation of consumption choices is produced. It is by reconstructing the challenges and practical constraints governing the fabrication of consumerist information that the specific character of this information becomes visible. The hypothesis followed throughout this chapter is that in performance testing there is as a dynamic of disengaging the consumer from the market. I will briefly sum up the different efforts that consumerist actors have to make to produce a situation of disengaged choice.

As the survey presented shows, consumerists perform work similar to that of the marketing specialists, but turned the other way around. To be in a situation to reveal what can be done with products and the cost one should pay for them, it is first necessary to take the place of the usual spokespersons of the modern market. Consumerist actors accuse those who manage supply of being much too engaged in the market to be considered as reliable prescribers of the best choices. In order to make this denunciation legitimate they need in turn to constitute their own credibility. Deposing of the established spokespersons is a laborious task – it is the alpha and the omega of journalists' critical work. But instating themselves as credible spokespersons is equally difficult – and the engineers' contribution is essential. This is why it is important to recall that the goal of reflecting the specific point of view of the consumer is far more than a mere claim or a formal justification of consumerist discourse. The inquiry on the consumer's point of view is embodied in a series of procedures and practices, and supported by a multitude of operations and know-how constituting the trade of performance testing specialists.

The investigation suggests that the task of testing is a somewhat exhaustive one. Firstly, it implies a process of collecting and centralizing data about the market which is not trivial for a number of reasons: because there is, *a priori*, no pre-existing standardization procedure nor place for the concentration of data relative to the market; because the manufacturers cooperate to a greater or lesser degree in the transmission of important data; because it is necessary to check the veracity of producer's statements through field inspections at retail shops. Drawing on this information, consumerist actors re-order and re-describe the sometimes messy sphere of supply – that is, they animate it with categories of their own, which are not systematically borrowed from the definitions that producers give.

Secondly, performance testing involves the constitution of a link of representativeness, of drawing similarities and the possibility of projection between this sphere and a particular place of experiment. This requires identifying and collecting entities that can prove fragile, unstable and sometimes short lived: that is, the economic goods. At this stage of testing, the definition of what constitutes the goods will be critically examined and the way in which consumers segment the market through their consumption habits will be taken into account.

Thirdly, consumerist actors carry out the attribution of qualities to the goods through an experimental process which is quite sophisticated and which intertwines various points of view. As opposed to technical definitions of objects and the anticipation of buyers' assumed needs, consumerist actors seek the actual use of goods, considered as a point of access to their ultimate truth. They do not systematically restrict points of view on the question of quality and can be forced instead to multiply them, perhaps to the extent that uses and consumers are multiple. As a whole, the consumerist evaluation of products and services is not simply a trial of objects, in charge of distinguishing their intrinsic characteristics. It aims to construct differences between goods, through a relatively detailed exploration of their worlds, a testing of their qualities, a redefinition of their shapes and extension, and a composition of criteria of judgement.

In so doing, consumerists end up representing the issue of choice in a way that is quite distinctive, when compared against other representations provided by market professionals. As a representational device the comparative test is at first sight very similar to many other tools used in the organization of trade and in the *mise en scène* of competition (catalogues, prospectuses, supermarket shelves, sales arguments, specialized press benchmarks, etc.). As our study shows, however, its elaboration incorporates a whole series of situated hypotheses, decisions and values. In this sense, performance testing offers us a striking example of a socio-technical process that makes possible the attribution of particular qualities to consumer goods: even if these qualities and the logic of attribution are, as always, highly negotiable, they are not contingent in the sense that they embody a specific politics of consumption characterized by the figure of a consumer disengaged from the market.

This approach naturally raises questions about the impact of tests, from the point of view of their reception by the general public, by political decision-makers, and by the suppliers themselves. It seems likely that, apart from a more or less hypothetical impact on the general public, comparative tests have 'indirect' effects of prescription on various actors of supply, especially distributors and manufacturers. For instance, the survey enables us to assume that, as with the mobile phone, telecom operators, anticipating a potential effect on buyers, are attentive to the results of consumerist tests when they have to select the models around which they plan their packages. More in-depth investigations should be undertaken fully to answer the question of impact. To conclude, it should be noted that the research I have presented points to another direction for research, stemming from the notion of disengagement that I have placed at the heart of my reflection. There is no operation of disengagement that does not imply other forms of engagement. It seems particularly interesting to investigate how the move from disengagement vis-à-vis the market to modes of more political engagement typical of consumerist associations takes place, for example towards defending the interests of consumers or of the environment. An analysis of forms of criticism and denunciation of inequalities or imperfections of markets – which, I noted earlier, constitutes the work of consumerist journalism – seems to be an interesting starting point to address this issue.

Alexandre Mallard

Notes

1 An earlier version of this chapter has been published in French (Mallard, 2000). The present version has largely benefited from the editors' comments.
2 In France, three magazines are concerned: *Que choisir*, *60 millions de consommateurs* and *Test Achat* (the latter is available only to subscribers). Throughout this chapter I use the term 'consumer magazine' to refer to these particular magazines and not to the vast range of magazines and newspapers that publish reports or special sections on consumer products.
3 The persistence of this frame of analysis and its relative sturdiness probably owes a lot to the deregulation of markets and public services in the UK in the 1980s. This trend might have resulted in patterns of relations between buyers and sellers more strongly characterized by the power struggle than is the case in other national contexts.
4 The theme of the consumer's uncontrollable desire and temptation generated by the market environment is recurrent in the consumerist literature. Aldridge refers to a set of practical advice given by the magazine *Which?* in an article bordering on self-parody, to help consumers resist the sirens of consumption and to not allow themselves to lose control over their own actions: keep strictly to your shopping list, wear earplugs so that you don't hear the coaxing music, walk to the supermarket and take a basket rather than a trolley *physically* to limit your buying power, avoid taking along children who will push you to buy, do take along a stick to help you to reach the cheaper products placed higher up in the shelf space, etc.
5 It is of interest that based on a similar uncoupling of situations of choice and consumption, we find here the exact opposite of the difficulty experienced by promoters of e-commerce trying to find ways to engage the virtual consumer. In an e-commerce situation the consumer can leave the transaction framework at the click of a button. With the current upsurge of e-commerce, the role of various intermediaries in consumers' engagements in market transactions is being re-examined.
6 Throughout this chapter, I will emphasize the many convergences that exist between the two magazines investigated (*Que choisir* and *60 millions de consommateurs*), without examining in detail significant points of divergence that would need further work.
7 For instance, a controversy was started in the magazine *Que choisir* on tests performed by the FNAC, one of the most powerful retail companies for technology products in France. The controversy revolved around the question of the compliance of the FNAC testing protocols with the methods recommended in the norm.
8 When the survey was made, *Que choisir* employed seven engineers and *60 millions de consommateurs* six, specialized in various areas of consumption (agri-food, chemicals, household appliances, electronics, etc.). The five individuals that I met, who all worked on telecom products, were qualified engineers and had 5 to 12 years of experience in this field.
9 It also stands to reason that the socio-demographic profile of the readers of comparative tests plays an important part in their impact. As noted, I excluded the issue of tests results'reception from this study. It is nevertheless possible to clarify some of the conditions. According to the journalists, most *Que choisir* subscribers are middle-aged or retired, with average or substantial buying power. There is a large percentage of teachers and middle and senior managers, and more home owners than tenants. Most live in the provinces in average-sized towns, as opposed to Paris and other cities.
10 Use-related aspects receive more attention when dealing with new products. Note that the propensity to represent or promote new uses (found far less in consumerist magazines than in specialized ones) differs in the two magazines concerned. At *Que choisir* the journalists' mission seems to be less to provide information about new products (they consider that suppliers make enough of a fuss on their own) than to alert the readers of fraud and abuse hidden behind novelties. In *60 millions de consommateurs*, in contrast, articles fairly often gently promote new products and innovations.
11 In this affair, one of the most sensational in the history of US consumerism, Nader, a lawyer, accused car manufacturers of having a criminal attitude since they sold vehicles that had not been designed to guarantee their drivers a minimum of safety.

12 Other requirements also play a role in designing tests for a collective of magazines. This is the case for ICRT (International Consumer Research and Testing), a consortium of European organizations to which the magazine *Que choisir* belongs. The issue of the cultural relativity of the definition of quality might be raised, as this definition is embodied in the diversity of national behaviours and habits. Although this applies in any branch of activity, it is obviously highly sensitive in such cases as food technologies (eg, the French, Italians and Swiss easily agree on criteria for testing coffee percolators, but agreement on the subject is more difficult to reach with other European partners). In a test on mobile phones, for instance, the importance of the 'low battery' alarm was a subject of disagreement between ICRT participants.

13 In the same way, Aldridge stresses that the magazines refuse to endorse the manufacturer's sales strategies, due to a form of pure aversion to the market. He also suggests a complementary, more critical analysis: consumerist magazines have to ensure themselves of a monopoly on the distribution of their own information, to guarantee their independence based essentially on income from sales.

References

Aldridge, A. (1994), 'The construction of rational consumption in Which? Magazine: The more blobs the better?', *Sociology*, 28(4): 899–912.

Aldridge, A. (1997), 'Engaging with promotional culture: Organized consumerism and the personal financial services industry', *Sociology*, 31(3): 389–408.

Appadurai, A. (1986), 'Introduction: Commodities and the politics of value', in A. Appadurai (ed.) *The Social Life of Things: Commodities in Cultural Perspective*, Cambridge: Cambridge University Press.

Baudrillard, J. (1998), *The consumer society: Myths and structure*, London: Sage.

Bourdieu, P. (1984), *Distinction: A social critique of the judgement of taste*, London: Routledge.

Callon, M. and F. Muniesa (2005), 'Economic markets as calculative collective devices', *Organization Studies* 26(8): 1229–1250.

Callon, M., C. Méadel and V. Rabeharisoa (2002), 'The economy of qualities', *Economy and Society* 31(2): 194–217.

Canu, R. and A. Mallard (2006), 'Que fait-on dans la boutique d'un opérateur de télécommunications? Enquête ethnographique sur la mise en référence des biens marchands', *Réseaux* 24(135–136): 161–192.

Cochoy, F. (2002), *Une sociologie du packaging, ou l'âne de Buridan face au marché*, Paris: PUF.

Eymard-Duvernay, F. (1989), 'Conventions de qualité et formes de coordination', *Revue Economique*, 40(2): 329–59.

Gabriel, Y. and T. Lang (1996), *The unmanageable consumer: Contemporary consumption and its fragmentations*, London: Sage.

Hatchuel, A. (1995), 'Les marchés à prescripteurs', in A. Jacob and H. Warin (eds), *L'inscription sociale du marché*, Paris: L'Harmattan.

Hutchins, E. (1995), *Cognition in the Wild*. Cambridge, Massachusetts, MIT Press.

Keat, R., N. Whiteley and N. Abercrombie (eds) (1994), *The authority of the consumer*, London: Routledge.

Kopytoff, I. (1986). 'The cultural biography of things: Commoditization as process', in A. Appadurai (ed.), *The social life of things: Commodities in cultural perspective*, Cambridge: Cambridge University Press.

Lancaster, K. J. (1966), 'A new approach to consumer theory', *Journal of Political Economy*, 74(2): 132–157.

Mallard, A. (2000), 'La presse de consommation et le marché: Enquête sur le tiers consumériste', *Sociologie du Travail*, 42(3): 391–410.

Mallard, A. (2001), 'L'action des consommateurs dans les controverses sur la qualité de l'eau', *Environnement et Société*, (25): 7–21.

Marcus-Steiff, J. (1977), 'L'information comme moyen d'action des consommateurs', *Revue Française de Sociologie*, 18(1): 85–107.
Pinch, T. (1993), '"Testing – One, two, three...Testing!": Toward a Sociology of Testing', *Science, Technology and Human Value,* 18(1): 25–41.
Pinto, L. (1990), 'Le consommateur, agent économique et acteur politique', *Revue Française de Sociologie*, 31(2): 179–199.
Shapin, S. and S. Schaffer (1985), *Leviathan and the air-pump: Hobbes, Boyle and the experimental life,* Princeton: Princeton University Press.
Thévenot, L. (1993), 'Essai sur les objets usuels: Propriétés, fonctions, usages', in B. Conein, N. Dodier, L. Thévenot (eds), *Les objets dans l'action*, Paris, Edition de l'EHESS.
Winward, J. (1993), 'The organized consumer and consumer information co-operatives', in R. Keat, N. Whiteley, N. Abercrombie (eds), *The authority of the consumer*, London: Routledge.

Framing fish, making markets: the construction of Individual Transferable Quotas (ITQs)

Petter Holm and Kåre Nolde Nielsen

For sale: fish quota

If it so happened, one crisp and beautiful day in April, that you surfed into the site www.kysttorget.no and clicked on 'For Sale: Miscellaneous', you would, among the offers of flag poles, crab traps and used ice machines, find ads like this one:

Entered: 28.03.2005
Quota 9–10 m
gr 1 i Nordland for sale
Phone: 75 . . .

The quota that is on offer, which would cost you in the order of NOK 1.0–1.3 million if you got the bid[1], is a right to fish a specific amount of a certain kind of fish. '9–10 m' is the length of the fishing vessel in relation to which the quota is defined. 'gr 1' is short for Group1, a basic category of fishing vessel defined within the management system for the coastal cod fishery in Norway. There are two such basic categories (Group1 and Group2), the first targeting full-time professional fishermen, the second reserved for part-timers. In 2005, the quota for a Group1 vessel of 9–10 meters would have been 65380 of 'cod equivalents.'[2]

As the above suggests, the commodity we have before us is a complex thing. Every phrase in the ad, including the date at the start and the phone number at the end, is packed with significance. While you, the model reader of this chapter, have no problem with the numbers that frame the ad (date and phone number), you are not pre-equipped with the lexicon required to decode the meaning of its key concepts. We shall try to turn this quality of the tradable quota into our advantage. Still, we would not be surprised if you, at this point, see the quota and the cod as just another case of fishy objects. At the end of the chapter, however, you will learn to appreciate these things in all their intricate beauty.

Let us begin with the obvious. The ad indicates that a market for fish quotas exists. From the specifications in the ad (9–10 m; gr 1; Nordland) and the rule systems these refer to, we understand that the fish quota is a legal construct. Without a formal apparatus to define and produce the fish quota as a stable bundle of entitlements, there could be no quota markets. It is through the legal definition and an extensive work of socio-technical framing that the quota becomes stabilized to such an extent that it can be treated as property.

As commodities go, fish quotas are not unique. Even if you start with the simplest and most natural item you can think of – say, a bale of cotton – you will quickly find that this must also undergo considerable amounts of framing before it is fit for the market (Caliskan, 2004). One reason why fish quotas are interesting is that they are emerging right now. Like CO_2 emission quotas or music in mp3 format, fish quotas did not exist 20 years ago. At that time, there would be no ads comparable to the one with which we started. Instead of having fishing measured in, and restricted by, specific quotas, there was reasonably open access to the fishing grounds. If you were registered as a fisherman and had access to an appropriate vessel, you could steam out, throw in your gear and hope for a lucky catch.

Something has happened to the fish and the fishermen. Twenty years ago, there was open access and fish were common property. The fisherman was a kind of hunter. Today, access has been closed. Fish, or at least fish quotas, have become property. The fishermen have turned into quota owners and property managers. In this chapter, we want to examine the trajectory that has transformed the fish and the fisherman. How is it possible for un-caught fish to become private property in a socially binding way? What kind of framing is capable of producing fish quotas as tradable objects? What ingredients – besides the fish – go into the stew and make property rights?

Cooking up quotas

In order to make a market for fish quotas, a number of different ingredients are needed. The proliferation of qualifications needed in our attempt to describe the object that featured in the internet advertisement above, demonstrates this. If the market is seen as stew, its production can reasonably be attributed to some sort of cook. Or can it?

In general, the notion of a cook fits well into the terminology of actor-network theory (ANT). Instead of playing into an understanding of the scientist-entrepreneur as a thinker, safely lodged in the world of ideas, the metaphor of the cook allows us to focus on the practical skills and materialities that science requires. Rather than the cleaned up surfaces of ready-made science, the cooking imagery brings us back to the messy process of science in the making. With the scientist as a cook and the laboratory as a kitchen, we keep up an interest in the raw materials used, how these are prepared, the devices it takes and the practical work undertaken, while not forgetting the heat from ovens, the accumulating stacks of dirty pots and pans, and the pressure from hungry customers. We also understand that a theoretical account of the process, rendered as a recipe in a glossy coffee-table book, is of limited help if the right ingredients, a well-equipped kitchen, and the appropriate skills are lacking.

The candidate for a cook that we could have in mind is indeed a kind of scientist, namely a resource economist. The recipe in question is known by the acronym ITQ, short for Individual Transferable Quotas. The object featured in the ad with which we started is exactly the intended outcome of an ITQ recipe. The question before us is whether economists held an orchestrating agency, if they somehow directed the chain of events that ended with our ad. Can we single out the resource economist as the cook behind the stew cum quota market?

We shall reveal up front that our answers to these questions will be in the negative. If you are an ITQ fan or, more generally, believe in the healing powers of economics, this may of course come as a disappointment. What is more problematic, at least from a writers' perspective, is that this revelation threatens to suck the dramatic tension out of the story. Why would a tale about tradable fish quotas be of interest in a volume dedicated to the traffic between market theories and market practices if it turns out that such traffic is scarce? Our answer is to take advantage of the expectation, in part reinforced by this book, that there will be interaction between theories and the realities they describe. Instead of the first-order task of demonstrating that such interaction takes place, which within the covers of this volume approaches a commonplace, we move to the second-order task of mapping this interaction in more detail. What are the roles of economists and economic theories here? How do they play off against other agencies and devices? Under which circumstances will market models get to frame the phenomena they describe? In order to make good on these promises for our chapter, the first task is to show why the resource economists and the ITQ model were plausible candidates for the roles as recipe and cook, even if they turn out to be fit for the lesser tasks in our culinary story.

Inspired by neoclassical economic theory, the recurrent problems of managing fisheries are diagnosed in terms of overexploitation and dissipation of sizeable resource rents within resource economics. This is because the fisheries are (or used to be) common property and hence subject to market failures. Because no-one owns the fish, no-one cares (enough) for their health and survival. Hence, the fisheries commons has to be closed and property rights installed. This can be achieved in many ways. Within the ITQ model, the main device is an individual quota that can be bought and sold on the market. On the conditions that the quotas form stable and easily transferable property rights, this system will solve the problems of overexploitation and overcapacity.

So we have a cook and a recipe. Is there also a corresponding stew? Yes there is. Since its inception in the 1970s, the ITQ model has proliferated in the world of fisheries. As scientific products go, this one must be deemed a success. Not only has it flourished within certain academic arenas, supporting a hastily growing body of theoretical literature. It has also been put to work as an actual policy instrument. In their 'global overview of marine fisheries' of 2003, Garcia and Moreno (2003) cite an estimate that about 10 per cent of the world's marine catch was taken under ITQ systems, with more fisheries becoming subjected to ITQs systems every year. Francis Christy, credited with the first ITQ proposal in 1973, observed that his creation, 20-odd years later, was doing well: 'The transition to property rights regimes in fisheries is occurring with a speed which, I think, is not fully appreciated. The process is inexorable' (Christy, 1996: 288). The claim here is not just that ITQs are out there, but moreover that the credit for them belongs to resource economists. In a special issue of the *Journal of Environmental Economics and Management*, James Wilen asked: 'What differences have we [resource economists] made?' (Wilen, 2000: 306). While his answer is handsomely modest in general, he claims one feat: 'the profession's most important policy achievement must surely be its influence on getting the ITQs on the agenda as a viable policy instrument' (Wilen, 2000: 321).

In Wilen's account, the introduction of ITQs is a clear case of economic theory performing the economy. In Iceland, for instance, the ITQ system resulted from '. . . bold policy innovations in an economic setting in which fisheries were important . . .' (Wilen, 2000: 322). This assertion is backed up by a footnote which presents an Icelandic economists and ITQ proponent as one of the 'architects' of the 'Iceland program'.[3] Even though academic critics of the ITQ model are reluctant about the depth and success of the transformation, they certainly think that the economists and their models have played an important part in it (Helgason and Pálsson, 1998).[4]

From a 'performativist' viewpoint, the ITQ model looks like the perfect exemplar. Just like the case of the strawberry market studied by Garcia-Parpet (2007), turned into the paradigmatic example of performativity by Callon (1998), it's all there: a textbook model, an invention of economics taking the leap into reality and theory guiding reality. Hence, economists are the constructors of market phenomena, and not just as their analysts.

A clear cut case? As it turns out, there are divergent interpretations of the ITQ case. Replying to the question whether the ITQ system in Iceland is a result of a grand design or of a historical accident, Matthíasson (2003: 16) leans towards the latter: 'The history of the regulatory exercise clearly shows that ITQs are a last resort choice. Hence, the introduction of the ITQs can hardly be claimed to be the result of a grand design'. Even Arnason (1993: 206), although credited by Wilen as the 'architect' behind the Icelandic ITQ system, is opposed to the notion of 'grand design' here.[5]

In the case of New Zealand, the importance of economic design seems clear. But even if we accept that, we are left with a number of questions with regard to the conditions for and qualifications of such an event. What exactly is the role of economists and economic models when a theoretical entity materializes and makes it in reality? How can we know that a phenomenon before us is playing out a script composed by economists? How can we distinguish between 'strong' performativity, where the script directs reality and its more 'whiggish' relatives, where the script is adjusted post hoc to account for the facts?[6]

As we shall see, the Norwegian ITQ case is ideally suited to address these types of questions. In Norway, a master plan for the introduction of ITQs was actually constructed on the basis of economic theory. But in contrast to what happened in New Zealand and Iceland, this plan met heavy opposition, and the ITQ model was rejected as a formal policy. Nevertheless, this did not prevent quotas from being traded by fishermen, as demonstrated by the ad with which we began. Here, then, the model was rejected, while its practices were accepted. What can this tell us about performativity and about the interaction between economic theory and economic life?

When we set out shortly on our search for the trajectory that led to the ITQ market indicated by the ad above, we will keep the following question in the back of our minds: can the market in fish quotas be accounted for with – or without – reference to some master plan? We shall frame our examination as one concerning the role of the ITQ model as a market device. Can the ITQ model be considered among a number of different devices that can be mobilized and may play a role in framing and formatting the quota market?

Something not quite open getting not quite closed

A fundamental condition for the formation of a market is restricted access. As long as there is open access to fishing grounds, there will be no market in fish quotas. No fishermen would be able to sell a right to fish, if such a right was granted to all who might want it. Hence, the closure mechanisms that render the right to fish exclusive to some extent is the first ingredient that goes into the pot in which a market for tradable fish quotas is cooked. While closure mechanisms might be thought of as a *sine qua non* market device, we need to pay careful attention to the specifics of how such closing came about. For this ties in with how the quota could be further qualified on its path to being finalized as the commodity featured in the opening ad.

The day that the Norwegian fisheries commons shifted from being fairly open to becoming fairly closed is an event we can date quite precisely to Tuesday April 18th 1989. Until then, the Norwegian coastal cod was open to the extent that no market had formed with regard to access. It is correct to refer to the coastal fishing grounds of Norway as late as the 1980s as 'a commons' (or a nested system of commons), to the fishermen as 'commoners' and to the fish as 'common property.' Note that these labels should not be taken to imply the absence of culture and regulation, as in the usage made famous by Garrett Hardin (1968; see McCay and Acheson, 1987). The commons we write about here was not a social vacuum; it was a positively defined and cultured social space (Johnsen, 2004). When we insist on its openness, it is only in a specific and relative sense: the fishery commons was open in ways that made it impossible for a market in access rights to form.

This changed in 1989. The immediate background for the closure of the coastal cod fisheries of Norway on that crisp and cruel Tuesday was a resource crisis. In May 1988, ACFM[7] dramatically revised its assessment of the cod stock, concluding that it was in much worse shape than previously thought. Growth rates for young cod were found to be about half of those estimated the previous year. The overestimated growth rates had been used in the stock predictions that were underlying the scientific stock advice of 1987 on which the 1988 TAC

(Total Allowable Catches) was based. The weak growth rates of the young cod were linked to a collapse of the capelin stock, an important prey species of the cod in the Barents Sea. Not only was the cod stock biomass much lower than expected but also the mortality rates produced by the fishery were much higher than had been previously considered. In fact the internationally agreed 1988 TAC of 530.000 tons (for Norway, Russia and third countries) was now expected to inflict almost twice the mortality on the stock compared to what had been anticipated when the TAC was decided in 1987. Consequently, the fishery scientists recommended that the fishery should be 'reduced as far as possible' for the remaining half of 1988 towards the level of 325.000–363.000 tons and also recommended the 1989 TAC to be in the range of 330.000–370.000 tons (ACFM, 1988).

While this recommendation was followed, it nevertheless marked the beginning of the crisis. In 1989, the low TAC combined unhappily with a rich fishery[8], and the quota was quickly fished up. The traditional Lofoten fishery came to a full stop in mid April, at a time that used to be the peak of the season. The 1989 season had ended before a number of vessels even had started fishing.

The appearance of a fisheries Leviathan

In the story of April 18th, the ground zero of Norwegian fisheries, we encountered a number of strange entities, like 'stock assessment,' 'fishing mortality', 'TAC' and 'ACFM.' As we shall see, the creatures that now enter the scene comprise the underlying flock of measurement and intervention devices that made it possible to close the commons. They constitute part of the social machinery that allows property rights to stick to slippery fish. Since we are more interested here in the use of these instruments, than in their invention, we shall go easy on the details.[9]

In our account of the closure, we encountered one agency that took the role of adviser ('fishery scientists' working in the Arctic Fisheries Working Group and ACFM, bodies within ICES), and another, conspicuously anonymous, that received and acted upon such advice. Let us start by revealing the identity of the latter, the Leviathan in action here: the Joint Norwegian-Russian Fishery Commission (JNRFC). This commission, comprised of bureaucrats, scientists and interest group representatives from the two countries, meet once a year to negotiate the regulation of shared fish stocks. One of the key issues for the commission is to decide the size of the TAC for the Northeast Arctic cod stock. An overly important part of the legal and political environment in which a commission like this functions, is the new oceans regime. This regime was negotiated in the 1970s, and became codified with the UN Convention of the Law of the Sea (UNCLOS) in 1983. A major principle of UNCLOS is the right and obligation of the coastal states to manage the living marine resources within 200 mile exclusive economic zones (EEZ). The JNRFC[10] was established in 1975–76 in conjunction with the setting up of EEZs by Norway and the USSR. Since the Northeast Arctic cod resides on both sides of the boundary between the Norwegian and Russian EEZs in the Barents Sea, it is considered a shared Norwegian-Russian resource (50-50 ownership, as reflected in the TAC distribution), and it is managed jointly.

How can we characterize the powers of this fisheries Leviathan? On the one hand, it is not difficult to find reasonable assessment criteria by which the Joint Commission is an utter failure. One such criterion would be an effective monitoring and control system, the absence of which is demonstrated by a sizable amount of illegal fishing. On the other hand, the Barents Sea, on a global scale, represents a kind of success: the marine ecosystem here has not been emptied out, as has happened in a number of other similar ecosystems around the world. In this context, it must also be pointed out that the Joint Commission has proved much more potent than its predecessor, NEAFC. The two Commissions belong to opposite sides of the regime shift. NEAFC was a creature of the Mare Liberum, a regime by which the fundamental practice for marine resources was open access. Within this legal framework, NEAFC carried the extremely difficult task of managing an open international commons with no effective mechanism to police against free-riders. If you're looking for a case where the logic of 'the tragedy of the commons' is played out as Hardin imagined, NEAFC would be an excellent choice (Underdal, 1980).

Compared to NEAFC, the Joint Commission, born of the new oceans regime, based its authority on firmer legal and political grounds. Within the EEZs, the political power, and the capacity of the two states to enforce it, could be mobilized directly behind the Commission's decisions. When the Lofoten fishery was closed in April 1989, this was directly related to the recent regime change. At this point, the notion of the coastal states as resource managers had become much more than a theory of international law. The appropriate institutional and organizational mechanisms – including the JNRFC – had been established. By the end of the 1980s, the role of the state as fishery manager had become so well-established that the closing of the Lofoten fishery could be successfully undertaken, despite the deep crisis and massive criticism that this triggered.

The mundane technical apparatus that allowed for the efficacy of the fishery Leviathans like the Joint Committee is quite simply a measuring device, a tool for fish counting. Invoking the metaphor of a well-known scientific instrument, we can call it a fish stock 'macroscope'. Like the microscope, this is an instrument for making objects, which you cannot see with the naked eye, visible. In contrast to the microscope, though, the reason fish stocks are not directly observable is not that they are too small, like microbes, but that they are distributed over large areas, and are submerged at that. Fish stocks can become observable and be measured only with the installation of a network of standardized data collection procedures and the invention of statistical models that make sense of the data. The invention and institutionalization of a new such fish counting tool during the 1960s and 1970s contributed crucially to the effectiveness of the Joint Committee. With the stock assessment macroscope in place, the fisheries Leviathan could become powerful because he now could see and measure the object to be managed: the fish stock.

Virtual Population Analysis and Total Allowable Catch

Unlike trees in a forest, fish are hard to count, at least directly. In order to measure a fish resource, the stock must be modelled. The Virtual Population Analysis (VPA) has, since the 1970s, been a preferred assessment model for the purposes of fisheries resource management. VPA is an age structured model which operates by assessing the loss of individuals from each age class (or cohort) as it projects through time. By this model, the stock size in a year is the sum of individuals across cohorts present in the stock that year. Here is a stripped-down account of how this is accomplished.[11]

A basic 'catch equation' relates the cohort's loss of individuals in a year to catches by the fishery and to nature's toll. The VPA models the cohort projection as an exponential decrease, where the total mortality is divided between mortality due to fishing, denoted 'fishery mortality', and the mortality due to other causes, collectively summed up as 'natural mortality'. In practical terms, data on landings is used as a proxy for the catches, while the natural mortality can be assessed by a number of different methods. Unfortunately, however, the number of unknowns is too large for the catch equations for each cohort progression step to be solved directly. In practice, this problem is handled by way of 'tuning' the VPA, ie, by way of calibration procedures drawing on other sources of information, typically abundance indices (Catches per Unit of Effort) from either standardized scientific surveys, or by information from the fishery (eg, from log books). While tuning narrows down the interpretive flexibility of the cohort matrixes, the results of the assessment exercises remain sensitive to modelling choices (Darby and Flatman, 1994). Fish counting by way of VPA is not an exact science, and is sometimes referred to as 'guesstimation.'

The story of the development of VPA to assess fish stocks is a long-winded one. We skip over decades of hard work and go directly to the landmark achievement of Beverton and Holt (1957), which still holds a status as a sort of 'principia mathematica' for modelling exploited fish populations. Beverton and Holt brought a century of work into fruition by modelling the yield from a stock as a function of growth rates, natural mortality, and fishing mortality. In 1965, the modern VPA was born as Gulland turned Beverton and Holt's yield function into an explicit age structured model (Ulltang, 2002).

The VPA turned into a tremendous success. Within about 10 years it had become the dominant assessment method in the North Atlantic fisheries. One reason for this success is the way the VPA as a population assessment tool linked into a practical intervention mechanism: the VPA offers an analytical ground for the fish quota. We have, in other words, returned to the instrument with which we started: the Total Allowable Catches or TAC. As the historian Rozwadowski (2002: 188) puts it, the VPA fits the TAC as 'hand in glove.'

Once the VPA has been used to estimate the present sizes of the individual cohorts, the underlying 'catch equations' of the VPA can, on the basis of some further estimations and assumptions, be turned into a forward looking mode. This transformation is necessary, of course, since a TAC as an intervention mechanism represents the part of the stock that will be removed by next year's fishery. In the predictive mode, the catch equations allow for the calculation of a set of relations between future catches (ie, TAC levels) and their expected effects on the stock. This is called a 'catch prediction'. It is in this sense that the 'TAC is at the end of the VPA calculation' (Rozwadowski, 2002: 190). Hence, we should not be too surprised that the TACs became the dominant intervention mechanism within fisheries management during the 1970s, in the same decade as VPA became the dominant assessment tool. The VPA and the TAC fit each other as two parts of the same instrument. We call it the 'TAC Machine' (Holm and Nielsen, 2004).

The scientific advice, on which most of these TACs are decided on, is produced by way of VPA based assessment methodology. The scientific advice is based on data collection and modelling procedures with VPA-based TAC decision making in mind. Furthermore, allocation of fishing opportunities between nations and between fleets is grounded in TAC-VPA metrology. Surveillance and control efforts are focused on the enforcement of the TAC. In summary then, the TAC holds an integrating position in the whole system of modern fisheries resource management, including data collection, stock assessment, management decision making, allocation mechanisms, regulation procedures, and enforcement. The TAC Machine is the engine around which the fisheries management is constructed, and without which the annual management cycle would come to a standstill.

Returning to Lofoten

We are now in a better position to understand what happened on April 18, 1989. On this date, the share of the TAC allocated to the coastal cod fishery was fished up. As a consequence, the fishery was closed. Despite all appeals to the historical rights of the fishermen, despite Lofoten's position as the little people's sanctuary and despite the grossly unfair distributional consequences of the closure, the fisheries Leviathan had grown too strong to overturn, and it stood its ground. For the first time, the concern for the cod stock counted more than the concern for the fishermen exploiting it. And it was the TAC Machine that made all the difference.

For us, this is only the beginning of the story that ends with the market in fish quotas. The events of the 1989 season turned out to be a mind-shattering experience, effectively summarized and made available in the collective memory in form of the slogan 'Never Again the 18th of April!' The main problem of the 1989 season that the fishermen collectively agreed should be avoided in the future at all costs concerned the re-distributional consequences of a competitive fishery within a small but enforced TAC. Under a competitive system, the larger and more modern vessels would win out simply because they could start earlier. Being vulnerable to harsh winter conditions, the smaller vessels were, in effect, kept out of the competition. In order to avoid the unfairness of a mid-season stoppage, Individual Vessel Quotas were introduced from 1990.

Under IVQ, the coastal fleet was divided in two parts, Group1 and Group2, where Group1 vessels got individual vessel quotas and Group2 vessels continued within a competitive regime. The main criteria for allocating the vessels among the two groups were historical catch records and 'cod dependency'. Group1 was intended for the vessels carrying full-time professional fishermen, and it was consequently allocated the major part of quota for the coastal cod fishery. If a vessel had landed more than a minimum quantity (depending on the vessel length) in at least one of the years 1987, 1988 or 1989, it would qualify for a Group1 vessel quota, obtaining a predefined length specific quota. The vessels not qualifying for Group1 could register for Group2 to compete for a relatively small joint quota.[12]

With the definition of a Group1, and by that a limited number of fishing vessels with individual quota allocations, the formation of a market in access rights suddenly seems much closer at hand. The social production of an enforced TAC represents a real and substantial restriction to the fishery. Access had become a scarce and valuable asset. With the parcelling out of the TAC in the form of individual vessel quotas, an interest in finding ways of trading such quotas soon manifested itself. Returning to our cooking metaphor, we could say that by 1990, the basic ingredients for our stew, the quota market, were already simmering in the pot.

A recipe: ITQs are proposed . . .

A formal system for the market-based allocation of fish quotas was proposed in 1991 (Anon, 1991) and we shall refer to it as a model for Individual Transferable Quotas, or ITQs. The ITQ model is an invention of resource economics that can be located within the tradition of neoclassical economic theory.[13] While the development of the underlying thinking of this fishery management model can be traced back to the work of Gordon (1954) and Scott (1955) (see Squires *et al.*, 1995), the first mature ITQ model was launched by Christy (1973) and Moloney and Pearse (1979). As the name 'Individual Tradable Quota' indicates, the quota intervention mechanism was designed to regulate fishing on the basis of scientific fish stock assessments introduced above, constitutes a starting point for the model (Gissurason, 2000). If implemented and enforced, the TAC would place a limit on the biomass harvested from the stock. The fundamental management objective of the TAC is to achieve optimal biological exploitation of the resource. The simplest way to implement the TAC is to allow free access and competitive fishing until the TAC is finished and then close the fishery – as splendidly exemplified by the 'April 18th' situation we discussed above. While this system, known as 'Olympic fishing', may solve one major problem, namely biological overexploitation, it creates a couple of new ones. Importantly, the system generates fleet overcapacity. The race for fish translates into a fish technological 'arms race': investments in newer and more effective equipment and bigger vessels, generating more and more surplus fishing capacity. From the perspective of society (or the 'tax payer', as economists prefer to put it) this is a waste. The resource rent is squandered on excessive fleet capacity. Moreover, overcapacity, in combination with the low profitability that it is the source of, makes fisheries management extremely difficult. This is because it generates political pressure to set TACs above scientific recommendations. In addition it invites fraud, eg, 'black landings' or 'high-grading' of catches.

It is here that the ITQs come in. Instead of the Olympic model, the manager can split the TAC up into small packages and allocate them (as gifts or by auction) to fishermen as individual quota rights, for example in the form of individual vessel quotas (IVQs). An IVQ system allows the fisherman to plan their fishery and hence to minimize costs while maximizing quality. They can fish when the prices are good, avoid bad weather, and so on. In the long run, they can invest in vessels that maximize their profit from the given quota. Instead of the overcapacity produced by Olympic competition, individual quotas would produce a better fit between harvest capacity and resource base.

An additional efficiency boosting advantage is obtained if the fishermen are allowed to trade the quotas. The fisherman, now a (rational) quota owner, will consider whether he will be better off doing the fishing himself, or selling the quota to someone else. If the market works according to theory, the quotas will flow to the most efficient fishermen because, all else being equal, they will be able to pay the best quota price.

When the Ministry of Fisheries presented its ITQ proposal in 1991, practical experience with the model was as important as its theoretical beauty.[14] Therefore, the proposal (known as the Green Paper) provided an overview of management systems elsewhere in the world. In the case of New Zealand, the ITQ model was evaluated as a success (Anon, 1991). The evaluation in the case of Iceland, the second ITQ pioneer, was less clear-cut, but ended up in the positive (Anon, 1991: 39).[15] One of the critical factors, said the Green Paper, was the extent to which the fishermen agreed to and wanted it: 'The ITQ systems with the greatest success [have been implemented with] extensive consultations with the industry' (Anon, 1991: 39).

As the Green Paper hinted at, but was in general was shy of bringing up, the introductions of ITQs have been intensely controversial wherever this has been attempted.[16] In Iceland, New Zealand, Australia, Canada, and South Africa, the battles continue to this day (Arnason, 2000; Helgason and Pálsson, 1997; Hersoug, 2002). In the US, the Congress put an embargo on ITQs in 1996. And as we shall see shortly, the Norwegian ITQ proposal suffered a similar fate.

... and rejected ...

Despite the attempts to anchor the ITQ model in important and legitimate objectives for the industry, it was received with suspicion and fear. The Green Paper and the ITQ model quickly made traditional enemies forget their differences and mobilize a counter-attack. After a swift but intense battle, the ITQ proposal was ritually killed and buried with proud fanfare.

The Green Paper was sent on hearing in June 1991 and the ITQ proposal also led to intense activity in the Labour party that was in office and would continue on after the election. In February 1992, the National Council of Labour went against the proposal (Moldenæs, 1993), sealing its fate. When the Ministry issued the White Paper in June 1992, the proposal had been withdrawn with reference to the barrage of negative reviews from the industry.

> The majority of the stakeholders are very sceptical towards transferable quotas even if the system is modified with restrictions. The most important arguments are that the system will lead to concentration of quotas and a centralization of the industry, which will make it difficult to realize the policy objectives of employment and [maintenance of a decentralized] settlement structure. Many of the stakeholder groups fear that the system will result in Norwegian fishing rights being bought up by European fishing companies. Several of the stakeholders point out that the introduction of transferable quotas with restrictions in all likelihood will be an irreversible process and that the restrictions will be temporary (Anon, 1992b: 126–127).

While this summary somehow does not convey the intensity of the industry's near unanimous rejection of ITQs[17], it identifies three of its main arguments against the model: quota concentration, centralization and the possibility of a European takeover. In conclusion, the ITQ model as a formal and explicit management system was rejected by an almost unanimous industry. Seen as a political object, it carried too much negative symbolic baggage. It contrasted too radically with the traditional political epistemology of the sector, which was anchored in the open-access commons, the fisherman as community carrier, and anti-capitalist rhetoric (Holm, 1995; Nilsen, 2002). When the Ministry, perhaps under the influence of the liberalist spirit of the times, suggested the ITQ model as a solution to the management problems, the sector quickly took cover in orthodoxy. The Government went with the flow and shifted its sponsorship from ITQs to reasonably unrestricted access within a total quota. This was also sanctioned by the Parliament, where only the right-wing parties stuck with the original proposal (Anon, 1992a).

... but quotas are traded anyway

Following unusually strong and consistent advice from the industry, the Parliament rejected the ITQ model, but it also wanted a return to the open access regime of yesteryear. The Parliament's wishes are not always carried through in practice, though. In the case of the coastal fisheries, the established IVQ regime was going to be gradually transformed into an ITQ system. Ironically, the fishermen, whose organizations were emphatically battling the ITQ model in the political arena, were quietly engaging in the practice of buying and selling quotas.

Formally, monetary quota transactions did not happen. The transfer of quotas from one fisherman to another depended on a decision from the fisheries authorities. When the conditions for approving the sale of the vessel were otherwise fulfilled, the authorities would normally permit the quota right to be transferred with the vessel. In practice, this made monetary transaction possible, as the price paid for the quota formed part of the price paid for the vessel. Sometimes, this would become very obvious, as when a vessel with quota were sold from one party to another one day, and the vessel without the quota was sold back the next – for a fraction of the price. Hence, a market was established and thrived during the 1990s – in spite of the absence of a formal recognition of it.

The bundling of the quota with the vessel and the absence of any official recognition of the quota transactions raises the question about the sense in which we can talk about a 'quota market'. There is little doubt that a quota carried a price, which could be cashed in if need be. But while money no doubt changed hands, a question remains about the identity of the items these sums would buy: did the sale establish the buyer as a quota owner? Does the informal quota market feature transactions in property rights to fish? In the Norwegian context, these questions were framed within a controversy over the privatization of fishery resources. On the one hand, critics claimed that the quota market meant that the fish were increasingly owned and controlled by a small elite, and that the status of fish as a common resource was threatened. On the other hand, defenders of the system argued that the absence of legal recognition of quota transactions meant that there were no private property rights for fishery resources, and therefore that the fishery resources were still held in common.

There is of course some truth in both of these positions. The stew we have called a quota market was now boiling at full steam, and a number of different cooks were in contention, stirring things up. If the proof of the stew, like the proverbial pudding, is in the eating, let's wait until it has cooled down a little. Hopefully, this will have happened when we arrive at the concluding section below. For now, we will concentrate on one of the major ingredients, the device called a vessel quota.

A vessel quota is a quite complex and dynamic entity. As a legal entitlement fixed to a specific vessel and a vessel owner, it gives this pair access to a specific fishery. At the outset, the quota puts a cap on the size of the catch the vessel can take. The actual size of the catch that a quota can realize, though, is dependent on a number of things. Firstly, it is a reflection of the size of the TAC, which is set annually on the basis of scientific assessments. Secondly, it is a reflection of the size of the vessel, as measured by length. Thirdly, it is a reflection of the 'availability' of the fish.

This third point needs some further explanation. When fish are plenty and they are biting willingly, finishing a given quota will be relatively easy for most vessels. Sometimes, though, the fish are hard to catch. When this happens, many vessels will not be able fish their allocated quota and the TAC may not be finished up. While this might be ok with the fish, it is unacceptable for other interested parties, among them the processing industry, which will not receive the expected amount of raw materials. In response to this problem, the vessel quota is combined with a total quota so that the sum of the vessel quotas is larger than that of the total quota. This is called 'overregulation', implying that the vessels, on average, will not be able to finish their allocated quota. Under conditions of low availability and large overregulation, there is a return to the competitive fishing of yesteryear, and the efficient vessels with the better crews will have a great advantage. Since the size of a vessel is one important component in getting to the fish, low availability usually rewards the larger vessels over the smaller ones.

The conditions that had led to the closing of April 18th 1989 involved, as you may recall, a low TAC combined with good availability. By the mid-1990s, this shifted around to a situation characterized by a generous TAC and low availability. In comparison with the meticulously calculated and 'fair' distribution of vessel quotas, this meant a substantial redistribution of catch opportunities from smaller to larger vessels. While this happened within the short term flexible framework of overregulation, it also had long term structural effects. This could happen because the size of the quota followed the size of the vessel. By extending the vessel, or replacing a smaller vessel with a larger one, a fisherman could gain an advantage in the race for fish. The rewards on size, together with a government sponsored program, encouraged building and using a new 'robust coastal vessel' prototype. This resulted in extensive investments in newer and larger vessels, for which quotas could be sought by way of the informal quota market.

As all of this suggests, the vessel quota during the 1990s was a highly volatile entity. The entitlements it would carry were dependent not only on the size of the stock, but also on the vessel size, a parameter that the vessel owner could influence. The quota's sensitivity to traits in their natural and social environment would perhaps be of little concern if this was not combined with their mobility by market transaction. At this stage, then, the quota was a 'mutable mobile', the movement of which produced massive overflows in Norwegian fisheries. This became painfully clear when the availability of cod again improved at the turn of the century. With an ironic twist, the IVQ system in combination with the informal market had produced overcapacity instead of curtailing it. The time was ripe for reform.

Instead of a concerted reform process, the rebuilding of the quota system happened as an aggregate of several semi-independent events. Since we are particularly interested in the quota as a commodity, we will concentrate on only one of these events, namely the attempt to redesign the quota market so that it would help reduce the fishing capacity instead of boosting it. First, we should note that loosely coupled to this tentative at reform were a series of less conspicuous reforms to reduce the volatility of the quotas. One of these was the introduction of the so-called Finnmark model, by which the quota transfers were banned between size groups, so that larger vessels would not compete directly with smaller ones. Another was the decoupling of the quota size from the vessel size. If a quota was transferred from a smaller to a larger vessel, the quota allocation would remain the same. A third was the introduction of a mixed fisheries quota, by which the quota would be defined not only with regard to cod, but also including the two other main species targeted by the coastal fleet (haddock and saithe). Together, these reforms helped stabilize the quota, making it more immutable. On top of this came the introduction of a formal system for quota exchange.

Let us see how the appearance of the vessel quota reconstituted the fishermen as political as well as economic agents. The major political factor in Norwegian fisheries was the Fishermen's Association. Established in the 1920s, this organization became a value-rational political institution, focused not only on the narrow economic interest of the fishermen. The fishermen's organization turned itself into a defender and caretaker of the values of the good life on the coast, as embodied by the small-type coastal fishermen (Holm, 1995). Reflecting the common resource it lived by, the Fishermen's Association was, in principle, open. In practice, of course, it was more open to some than to others. This worked well as long as most people, at least when correctly gendered, could go the grade, from apprentice to fisherman, mate, and then skipper and vessel owner.

When the vessel quota system entered the picture in 1990, it had severe consequences for the Association. According to the qualification procedure for the IVQ system, which relied on catch records the previous three years, the skippers and owners of the most active vessels received most of the quotas. These people were precisely those who were the most likely to be in responsible positions within the Fishermen's Association. In this way, the Association had, as a matter of fact, suddenly become an association of quota owners. Gradually, it also changed its ideological position and its practical politics so as to fit such an identity (Holm, 2003; Holm *et al.*, 1998). The first step in that direction was a shift in position with regard to the IVQ system. When the resources had returned, around 1995, and the time had come to change back to open access, the Association had already changed its stance. Thus when the Ministry proposed a system that would formalize quota transferability, described in the next section, the Association was among its most active supporters.

Formalizing a quota market

In March 2003, the Fisheries Minister proposed measures that would formalize a system of transferable quotas in the coastal cod fishery (Anon, 2003). While this was not a fully developed ITQ system, the new measures, which entered into force in January 2004, created a legal framework for a substantial part of the informal quota market. Instead of, or perhaps we should say in addition to, a half-hidden and under-managed practice, the quota market was now organized and made to work for explicit and politically sanctioned purposes.

The measures, which became known under the name of the Structural Quota system (SQ), constituted a programme for allowing both permanent and temporary quota transfers among vessels. A number of different conditions were specified for such quota transfers. For coastal vessels between 15 and 27.99 m, a quota can be transferred from one vessel to one or more other vessels on condition that:

- the donor vessel is destroyed
- the receiving vessels have participation rights to the same fishery as the donor vessel
- transfers are allowed only among vessels within length groups of 15 to 20.99 m and 21 to 27.99 m respectively
- transfers are allowed only among vessels registered within the same county for at least one year
- 20 per cent of the quota in question is withdrawn and redistributed among all of the vessels within a vessel group
- one vessel cannot have more than 3 vessel quotas.

Vessels below 15 m are not (yet) allowed to participate in the system. Instead, there is a buy-back programme for this group. The quotas bought out and destroyed within this programme are redistributed among all of the vessels within the group.

All these restrictions contribute to the boundary conditions by which the market in fish quotas is defined. On the one side, the formalization of the market by way of such restrictions is part of the process that turns the quota into property and transforms fishermen into fish owners. On the other side, these specifications come about, at least partly, as an attempt to control the barrage of overflows produced in the informal and partly hidden market. The restrictions on how many quotas one vessel can have (max 3), is designed to prevent quota hoarding and the upsurge of 'quota lords.' The restriction on transfers between size groups is designed to prevent the big guys from eating the smaller guys. The restriction on transfers across county borders is designed to prevent geographical concentrations, and in particular the movement of quotas from the poorer and more fish dependent north to the richer south. It is in the struggle with these issues, all of which are intensely political and can be traced far back in the Norwegian fisheries discourse, that the quota becomes qualified and takes shape as a commodity.

The time has come for us to end our story. This does not mean that we have reached some kind of a natural cut-off point in the chain of events. The market for quotas continues to evolve and new chapters could have been added endlessly. We could have continued, for instance, by following up on the newest proposals from the Department of Fisheries and the newest regulations issued by the Directorate of Fisheries, representing the ongoing attempts to dam up the variety of overflows that are being incessantly produced within the ITQ frame. We could have explored the latest scientific evaluations of the economical efficiency of the IVQ/SQ system, its impact on fleet capacity, and its demographic effects on coastal societies. We would also have liked to investigate the interaction between the formal and informal market; whether the distinction between them is appropriate, how they complement – or compete with – each other and so forth. In particular, we would have taken pleasure in plunging into questions about when, how and to what extent quotas become property – for example the extent to which ownership of quotas means that the fish itself are privatized. Last but not least, this theme is interesting because it seems to have an almost unlimited capacity to stir up public controversy. Just as the market is not completed but evolving, so is our understanding of how it all works. But our allotted space is up and we need to wrap things up.

The art of quota cookery

Our narrative has been one of transformation and reconfiguration. At one point in time, the Norwegian coastal cod fishery did not contain a quota market. Then something happened. At the end of a series of events the sector had changed. The Norwegian coastal fishery now included a quota market, and things never would be the same again.

We have tried to explain how the quota market came about. Given the complexities of the story we are not sure whether we have succeeded. A number of different materials went into the stew and they combined in unexpected and volatile ways. Perhaps it would be appropriate to wrap it all up in the literary genre of a recipe?

> *ITQs à la Lofoten*
> *This is a delicious stew based on the traditional ingredients of a conventional coastal fishery. It offers a rich historical flavour of coastal community and colourful folklore that combines nicely with the bitter zest of modern capitalism, giving it a lovely piquant and contrasting bite. It is a stew full of surprises.*
> *You'll need:*
> *A reasonably healthy fish resource, preferably cod, but other valuable groundfish species will also serve. Avoid mixed fisheries, as this will tend to spoil an ITQ recipe.*
> *A heterogeneous coastal fleet, sizes 6–29 m. Rinse out trawlers, which don't combine well with conventional coastal gear and will tend to make the stew fall apart. (Hint: trawlers make excellent ITQs when prepared separately.)*
> *2–3000 well seasoned fishermen of mixed ages and dispositions. Don't be too picky. Inferior exemplars will boil off in the process while rational and competitive ones will grow into really crunchy capitalistic enterprises.*
> *In addition, you will need a cooking device, preferably a TAC Machine that will not crack under pressure. Place all ingredients in the TAC Machine and seal tightly. Simmer for 10–15 years. (Note that the ingredients at the outset will not fit into the machine,*

and that there will be overflows. This is normal.) Slice the TAC into individual quotas. IQs should be of variable size and fit with the size range of the fleet. In order to avoid having the larger chunks dominate, it may be necessary to split the stew according to size components.

The IQs will at the outset be quite fragile. You may have to add appropriate legal emulsifiers to stabilize them and to enable them ripen into ITQs. Stir lightly. Don't let any controversies get too hot, as this may trigger political intervention. Skim overflows regularly. Serve slightly chilled...

While this rendering works as a recap of the story and may hence substitute for a conventional summary, it is difficult to take it seriously as a recipe. This is because the position of agency it assumes, an ITQ cook, is such an unlikely character. Or more precisely, it is a recipe designed primarily for reading and contemplation, not for replication in practice. Its proper place is within the glossy covers of a coffee-table book, not in the heat of the kitchen. The story shows that, even though an 'ITQ cook' may be a plausible character in the New Zealand case and, to some extent, for Iceland too, this is not so with regard to Norway and its coastal cod. If there is an agency that may have pretensions towards a cook-like position in our story, it is the character we have called the Fisheries Leviathan, the Joint Norwegian-Russian Fisheries Commission (JNRFC). On the basis of the scientific assessments provided by fisheries scientists and the politico-legal authority provided by Russia and Norway as coastal states under UNCLOS, the JNRFC annually serves up fishing opportunities certified as TACs. Pressing the last juice out of the culinary metaphor, we could say that the TAC is a pie that can easily be sliced up and shared out among hungry contenders. In this case, it makes sense to talk about a recipe (the rules for scaling and certifying the TAC) because it comes paired with a cook. In the case of 'ITQs à la Lofoten', neither side of such a pair was present. The closest we come to a recipe is the Green Paper from 1992. The closest we come to an ITQ cook was the Fisheries Ministry that had commissioned it. I f the ITQ proposal had been accepted, we might have worthy candidates for both roles. It wasn't and we haven't.

Instead of a master plan, by which a pre-existing agency created order, the story of ITQs in Norway lends itself to be told in terms of a co-construction of agencies and of (market) devices. Note the plural. Instead of one Leviathan and a single master plan, several agencies and different devices were set in circulation. While we do not intend the following to comprise an exhaustive list of the co-constructions of this sort implied in our story, it will illustrate the diversity of mechanisms at work. It may also demonstrate the difficulty in keeping up a strict division between agency and device; between cook and recipe.

The first device on such a list must be the TAC Machine, constituting and being constituted by the coastal states as the empowered Leviathans of the new Oceans regime. The TAC Machine serves as a market device in more than one respect. It is by the operation of the TAC Machine that access to the fisheries is produced as a scarce resource. The TAC Machine also provides the metrology by which the quotas are singularized as commodities.

The second device is the entity produced and circulating within the TAC machine, the TAC itself, which, when sliced up and shared out as individual quotas (IQ) proved to be an extremely potent and volatile device. It came with the capacity to transform a range of agencies, as well as to introduce new ones. One example here is the changing role of the fish, which we have referred to under the constant term 'availability'. As explained, the availability of fish, being dependent on a variety of environmental conditions (including weather conditions), interacted with the IVQ system with unpredictable but weighty consequences.

On a practical level, the IQs had immediate repercussions for the fishermen, including the planning of fishing operations, the investments in equipment and vessel, crew size and composition, etc. In addition, the market value of the quota itself gave the fishermen access to a new type of agency, namely as actors in a quota market. As we have seen, the introduction of transferable quotas also transformed the political agency of fishermen. Instead of coastal custodians – visitors in an open commons – they became resource owners, and as such they became motivated to protect their private gains. We witnessed this by the change in the makeup of the Fishermen's Association, transforming it from an institution dedicated to the values of coastal communities, into an instrument, a vessel for the vested interests of quota owners.

Together, the TAC Machine and the IQ transformed fishing from a way of life to a way of making a living. It goes almost without saying here that this process made the sector as such more manageable. By offering new and effective management options, the TAC and the IQ helped strengthen the agencies that were positioned as managers. To some extent, this was of course intentional. As the story demonstrates, however, the practical work of making the quotas fit for such a task proved to be quite difficult. For instance, the economists' promise that individual quotas, particularly if these were set up as transferable commodities, would reduce overcapacity, proved overly optimistic. The way the quota system was set up probably contributed to building up capacity instead of reducing it. Turning this around required a lot of tinkering with the quota design, as well as linking it systematically to a buy-back program. In order to control the overflows, a new frame, the SQ system, had to be superimposed on the IQs. At the end of this story, we may think we begin to see the contours of a Leviathan, a manager in a position to monitor and control the sector by way of quota markets. But such a position, it would seem, is authorized by the market as much as it is the market's author. In our story, it is actually more appropriate to say that it was the stew that made the cook, rather than the other way around.

The analysis of the lengthy and complex construction of the Norwegian fisheries quota market contributes to a better understanding of the role and dynamics of market devices. It also allows tackling the role played by economists in this case, even if this aspect was not addressed at length in this chapter. To what extent and in what sense can the emergence of the ITQ market be ascribed to the activities of this particular profession? Because the ITQs represent the paradigmatic contribution of resource economists to fisheries management, the mere existence of an ITQ market suggests that this profession must have played a strong performative role. Such an inference is not without merit. Indeed, Wilen's account of the introduction of ITQs in New Zealand and in Iceland seemed quite persuasive in this respect (Wilen, 2000). What then, about the case we have examined here?

While the story about ITQs in Norway is clearly not one in which economists perform their model in a straightforward way, this does not mean that these agencies and devices did not play a role. The agency of economists is in little doubt with respect to the Green Paper and the first ITQ plan of 1992 and the strong rejection of the plan does not mean that economists did not have any role to play. Quite to the contrary, the allergic reaction to the ITQ model, at least in combination with the acceptance of the practice of buying and selling quotas suggests a more complex answer. Within the framework of Norwegian fisheries policy, where anti-capitalist rhetoric had been strong for well over a century, the market-oriented ITQ model did not go down well, even though it promised to work wonders. In this situation, the economists played the rather unpleasant role as anti-hero and as object of despise. In order for the ITQ model to fit in – under a different name – it had to be 'ritually rejected'. Traces of such anti-heroism remain in the naming practice with respect to the quota market. Since the more accurate and conventional label 'ITQ' had so much negative political and cultural baggage, more clumsy ones, 'structural quotas' and 'structuration', have gained.

As time went by, however, and the practices of the quota market gained legitimacy, the economists were allowed to play a more substantial role. When the structural quota program was devised, economists emerged as self-evident experts and advisors since they are in command of the terminology and calculation tools needed to understand and control the market. This was forcefully demonstrated in January 2006 when a government task force was set to evaluate and redesign the SQ system (Anon, 2006). The only expert group within the task force was that of the economists. While the task force can hardly count as a cook (it is more like a committee of prospective cookbook authors), it seems safe to conclude that the quota market authorizes the economist as an important and legitimate expert as it settles in.

Economists were indeed among the cooks that prepared the stew we have called a quota market. But it took much longer than they expected, and it didn't turn out quite the way they wanted it to. Accounts (be they critical or self rewarding) that put too much emphasis on the direct role of resource economists in this transformation carry the risk of oversimplifying the story and even leading to inaccurate interpretations. In the Norwegian case at least, the contribution of economists, at some point criticized by other actors at stake, was inscribed in a wider movement they hardly mastered. They certainly were not alone in the kitchen.

Notes

1 This quota price, an estimate suggested to us by S.A. Rånes (Norwegian Institute of Fisheries and Aquaculture Research), corresponds to 120 000–150 000 EUR (exchange rates of November 2006).
2 The 'cod equivalent' refers to a conversion system that allows fishermen some flexibility in substituting one kind of fish for another.
3 'One of the architects of the Iceland program was Ragnar Arnason. [. . .]. In 1979, Arnason was instrumental in suggesting that the Icelandic herring quotas be made transferable, and he was also heavily influential in the subsequent program designs for Iceland's IQs in Capelin in 1980 and the Demersal [i.e. bottom dwelling] fisheries in 1984.' (Wilen, 2000: 322).
4 '[A]n attempt was made to transform the reality of fishing in Iceland to bring it into accord with the virtual reality of neo-classical economics expressed in the model of ITQ-management' (Helgason and Pálsson, 1998: 118–119).
5 '[T]he course towards a complete ITQ fisheries management system in Iceland has evolved more by trial and error than by design' (Arnason, 1993: 206), a statement later mimicked by Runolfsson (1999: 111). Yet some passages in Arnason's writing indicate a stronger role of ITQ theory in the process leading to Iceland's ITQs: 'The fact that these concerns [to improve the economics of fishing and to conserve fish stocks] could be translated into an untested theoretical system for fisheries management that has radically altered the institutional framework of the fishing industry and upset traditional social equilibria at a considerable political expense is quite intriguing . . .' (Arnason, 1996: 71–72).
6 Callon (2007: 316) defines performativity as when a discourse 'contributes to the construction of the reality that it describes'. With 'strong' performativity we here have in mind the situation when a contribution of a particular (scientific) agency amounts to an orchestrating role in performing the reality. For a related discussion on the topic of the performativity of economics, see Holm (2007) and Mirowski and Nik-Khah (2007).
7 The Advisory Committee on Fisheries Management of the International Council for the Exploration of the Sea (ICES). ICES is 'the organization that coordinates and promotes marine research in the North Atlantic' (www.ices.dk).
8 A rich fishery is not by itself a reliable indicator of a strong fish stock. Had it been, there would be little need for scientific stock assessments. Catch Per Unit of Effort, a measure of how much is fished from a standardized effort (eg, one trawl-hour), varies both with environmental and ecological conditions, as well as with changes in fishing ability though technological improvement and learning. Accordingly, CPUE indexes are known to have increased even while stock sizes were actually declining (Hilborn and Walters, 1992; McGuire, 1997; ACFM, 2000).
9 For a more detailed account of the institutionalization of the modern fisheries management regime, see Holm and Nielsen (2004). The authors currently work on a more refined and presentable account of this transformation.
10 The commission was first named the Norwegian-Soviet Fisheries Commission. The EEZs of Norway and the USSR were established in 1977.
11 For an introduction to basic VPA, the reader may turn to Hilborn and Walters (1992).
12 Although comprising the majority of coastal vessels, Group2 was on average (1990–1999) only allocated about 10% of the total coastal cod quota. In addition to its smallish economic significance, however, Group2 served an important symbolic role, since it could stand as a proof that the fishery commons had not been closed.
13 The ITQ literature is massive. For a recent overview, see Shotton (2000a, 2000b, 2001).
14 For the Green Paper's interpretation of the ITQ theory, see Anon (1991: 96–99).
15 The relative lack of improvement in economic performance under ITQs in Iceland was explained with reference to 'the restrictions put on the system' (Anon, 1991: 49).
16 One reason for New Zealand's departure from the rule here is that its fishery, before a 200 mile EEZ was established in 1977, was relatively small. Hence, the ITQ system was not introduced

as a massive reform of a traditional system, but could be developed in pace with the development of the sector (Hersoug, 2002).

17 The only stakeholder group supporting ITQs was NHO/FNL, the organization of the fish processing industry.

References

ACFM (1988), 'Report of the Advisory Committee on Fisheries Management' in ICES Cooperative Research Report 161. Copenhagen. ICES.
ACFM (2000), 'Report of the Advisory Committee on Fisheries Management' in ICES Cooperative Research Report 242. Copenhagen. ICES.
Anon (1991), 'Høringsnotat om Strukturen i Fiskeflåten'. Oslo: Ministry of Fisheries.
Anon (1992a), 'Innstilling S. Nr. 50 (1992–93)'. Oslo: Stortinget.
Anon (1992b), 'St.meld.nr. 58 (1991–92): Om struktur- og reguleringspolitikk overfor Fiskeflåten (Strukturmeldingen)'. Oslo: Ministry of Fisheries.
Anon (2003), 'St.meld.nr. 20 (2003). 'Strukturtiltak i kystfiskeflå6ten'. Oslo: Ministry of Fisheries.
Anon (2006), 'Strukturvirkemidler i fiskeflåten'. Norges offentlige utredninger 2006: 16. Oslo: Departementets servicesenter.
Arnason, R. (1993), 'The Icelandic individual transferable quota system: A descriptive account', *Marine Resource Economics*, 8(3): 201–218.
Arnason, R. (1996), 'On the ITQ fisheries management system in Iceland', *Reviews in Fish Biology and Fisheries*, 6(1): 63–90.
Arnason, R. (2000), 'Property rights as a means of economic organization', in R. Shotton (ed.), *Use of Property Rights in Fisheries Management. FAO Fisheries Technical Paper 404/1*. Rome: FAO.
Beverton, R.J.H. and S.J. Holt (1957), *On the Dynamics of Exploited Fish Populations.* London: Her Majesty's Stationary Office.
Caliskan, K. (2004), 'Realizing the price in world markets: The prosthetic and actual worth of a bale of cotton', working paper.
Callon, M. (1998), 'Introduction: The embeddedness of economic markets in economics', in M. Callon (ed.), *The Laws of the Markets*. Oxford: Blackwell.
Callon, M. (2007), 'What does it mean to say that economics is performative?', in D. MacKenzie, F. Muniesa and L. Siu (eds), *Do Economists Make Markets? On the Performativity of Economics*. Princeton: Princeton University Press.
Christy, F. (1973), 'Fishermen's catch quotas'. Occasional paper 19. Kingston (Rhode Island): Law of the Sea Institute.
Christy, F. (1996), 'Thalassorama: The death rattle of open access and the advent of property rights regimes in fisheries', *Marine Resource Economics*, 11(1), 287–304.
Darby, C.D. and S. Flatman (1994), *Virtual Population Analysis: Version 3.1 (Windows/DOS) User Guide*. Lowestoft: Information Technology Series. Ministry of Agriculture, Fisheries and Food.
Garcia, S.M. and I.L. Moreno (2003), 'Global overview of marine fisheries', in M. Sinclair and G. Valdimarsson (eds), *Responsible Fisheries in the Marine Ecosystem*. Rome: FAO.
Garcia-Parpet, M. (2007), 'The social construction of a perfect market: The strawberry auction at Fontaines-en-Sologne', in D. MacKenzie, F. Muniesa and L. Siu (eds), *Do Economists Make Markets? On the Performativity of Economics*. Princeton: Princeton University Press.
Gissurason, H.H. (2000), 'The politics of enclosures with special reference to the Icelandic ITQ system', in R. Shotton (ed.), *Use of Property Rights in Fisheries Management. FAO Fisheries Technical Paper 404/2*. Rome: FAO.
Gordon, H.S. (1954), 'The economic theory of a common property resource: The fishery', *Journal of Political Economy*, 62(2): 124–142.
Hardin, G. (1968), 'The Tragedy of the Commons', *Science*, 162(3859): 1243–1248.
Helgason, A. and G. Pálsson (1997), 'Contested commodities: The moral landscape of modernist regimes', *Journal of the Royal Anthropological Institute* 3(3): 451–471.

Helgason, A. and G. Pálsson (1998), 'Cash for quotas: Disputes over the legitimacy of an economic model of fishing in Iceland', in J.G. Carrier and D. Miller (eds.), *Virtualism: A New Political Economy*. Oxford: Berg.
Hersoug, B. (2002), *Unfinished Business: New Zealand's Experience with Right Based Fisheries Management*. Delft: Eburon.
Hilborn, R. and C.J. Walters (1992), *Quantitative Fisheries Stock Assessment: Choice, Dynamics and Uncertainty*. New York: Chapman and Hall.
Holm, P. (1995), 'The dynamics of institutionalization: Transformation processes in Norwegian fisheries', *Administrative Science Quarterly* 40(3): 398–422.
Holm, P., S.A. Rånes, and B. Hersoug (1998), 'Political attributes of rights-based management systems: The case of individual vessel quotas in the Norwegian coastal cod fishery', in D. Symes (ed.), *Property Rights and Regulatory Systems in the Fisheries*. Oxford: Fishing News Books.
Holm, P. (2003), 'Which Way is Up on Callon?', *Sosiologisk årbok*, 8(1): 125–156.
Holm, P. (2007), 'Which way is up on Callon?', in D. MacKenzie, F. Muniesa and L. Siu (eds), *Do Economists Make Markets? On the Performativity of Economics*. Princeton: Princeton University Press.
Holm, P. and K. Nielsen (2004), 'The TAC Machine', working paper.
Johnsen, J.P. (2004), *Fiskeren som forsvant?* Trondheim: Tapir.
Matthíasson, T. (2003), 'Closing the open sea: Development of fisheries management in Four Icelandic fisheries', *Natural Resources Forum*, 27(1): 1–18.
McCay, B.J., and J.M. Acheson (eds.) (1987), *The Question of the Commons: The Culture and Ecology of Communal Resources*. Tucson (Arizona): University of Arizona Press.
McGuire, T.R. (1997), 'The last northern cod', *Journal of Political Ecology* 4(1): 41–54.
Mirowski, P. and Nik-Khah, E. (2007), 'Markets made flesh: Performativity, and a problem in Science Studies, augmented with Consideration of the FCC Auctions', in D. MacKenzie, F. Muniesa and L. Siu (eds), *Do Economists Make Markets? On the Performativity of Economics*. Princeton: Princeton University Press.
Moldenæs, T. (1993), 'Legitimeringsproblemer i fiskerinæringen: En studie av utformingen av en Stortingsmelding.' Tromsø: LOS Notat Norut Samfunn.
Moloney, D., and P. Pearse (1979), 'Quantitative rights as an instrument for regulating commercial fisheries', *Journal of the Fisheries Research Board of Canada*, 36: 859–866.
Nilsen, R. (2002), *Makt og motmakt på kysten*. Oslo: Makt- og demokratiutredningen 1998–2003.
Rozwadowski, H.M. (2002), *The Sea Knows no Boundaries: A Century of Marine Science under ICES*. Seattle: ICES in association with University of Washington Press.
Runolfsson, B. (1999), 'The Icelandic system of ITQs: Its nature and performance', in R. Arnason and H. Gissurarson (eds.), *Individual Transferable Quotas in Theory and Practice*. Reykjavik: The University of Iceland Press.
Scott, A. (1955), 'The fishery: The objectives of sole ownership', *Journal of Political Economy* 63(2): 116–124.
Shotton, R. (ed.) (2000a), *Use of Property Rights in Fisheries Management. FAO Fisheries Technical Paper 404/1*. Rome: FAO.
Shotton, R. (ed.) (2000b), *Use of Property Rights in Fisheries Management. FAO Fisheries Technical Paper 404/2*. Rome: FAO.
Shotton, R. (ed.) (2001), *Case Studies on the Allocations of Transferable Quota Rights in the Fisheries. FAO Technical Paper 411*. Rome: FAO.
Squires, D., J. Kirkley, and C.A. Tisdell (1995), 'Individual transferable quotas as a fisheries management tool', *Reviews in Fisheries Science*, 3(2): 141–169.
Underdal, A. (1980), *The Politics of International Fisheries Management: The Case of the Northeast Atlantic*. Oslo: Universitetsforlaget.
Ulltang, ø. (2002), 'Realizing the basis for overfishing and quantifying fish population dynamics', in E.D. Andersen (ed.), *100 Years of Science under ICES: A Symposium held in Helsinki 1–4 August 2000*. Copenhagen: ICES Marine Science Symposia 215.
Wilen, J.E. (2000), 'Renewable resource economists and policy: What differences have we made?', *Journal of Environmental Economics and Management*, 39(3): 306–327.

Making things deliverable: the origins of index-based derivatives

Yuval Millo

Introduction

Index-based derivatives: financial contracts that use financial market indices as their underlying 'assets' are currently amongst the most commonly traded financial contracts (BIS, 2006).[1] Furthermore, the introduction of index-based derivatives is considered by many as the single most significant development in contemporary financial markets (Chance, 1995; Arditti, 1996; Kolb, 1997a, 1997b). The use of index-based futures has become a standard practice in the financial world and today banks, pension funds, insurance companies and governments hold portfolios that include index-based derivatives. In fact, index-based contracts have become such an indispensable feature of the global financial system that it would be safe to say that there are many millions in the West who own, either directly or indirectly (even unknowingly), index-based derivatives.

In spite of their ubiquity in the financial world, index-based derivatives represent a fundamental ambiguity. Derivative contracts, as their name implies, derive their prices from the prices of a variety of assets, such as agricultural commodities, precious metals, currencies and many others. The contract themselves, (eg, futures contracts), state the terms of future transaction: price to be paid and time for the delivery of assets. In contrast with physical and deliverable assets, market indices are the products of mathematical procedures applied to market data. Hence, index-based derivatives are contracts written for 'strange assets', assets that do not have straightforward physical characteristics, and therefore cannot be delivered, upon buying and selling, in a similar manner to physical assets. This fact raises an interesting historical and sociological question: how did it happen that these abstract mathematical entities became the basis for the most popular financial contract of our time? More specifically, how did the non-physical and non-deliverable nature of market indices change in such a way that allowed indices to serve as a basis for the popular derivative contract we know today? This is the question that this chapter discusses.

Economic sociology has paid little attention so far to the evolution of index-based contracts. Several sociologists refer to the role that index-based contracts play constructing hedging positions and to the way in which they are used in arbitrage trading (for example, Beunza and Stark, 2004; MacKenzie, 2006). Yet, there exists no published sociological work that traces the social history of this market and analyses the evolution of index-based derivatives and the network of institution in which this processes unfolded. This chapter is hoping to be a first step in recognising the importance of index-based financial instruments as a topic for sociological investigation.

How are we to conceptualize index-based derivative contracts sociologically? The empirical material in this chapter suggests that the question of the qualification of index-based derivatives – that is, the process through which the derivatives gained their particular qualities – may provide a useful entry point. The qualification process can be described as an interactive (network-like) process that involves not only various actors located in different organizations and institutions (the staff of commodity exchanges, commodity traders and financial regulators), but also the products themselves.

The notion of product qualification is related to the work done by Geoffrey Bowker and Susan Leigh Star (Bowker and Leigh Star, 1999). Bowker and Leigh Star analyse classificatory systems and trace the ways in which they were embedded into bureaucratic infrastructures and become part of the taken-for-granted reality of organizational structures. Using detailed case studies, Bowker and Leigh Star outline several general historical heuristics along the lines of which classificatory systems come about and how their legitimacy is being proposed and contested. This process of institutionalisation is a vital part of the organizational implication of the qualification process. That is, it describes how the intra- and inter-organizational spaces internalise categories-making rules and practice. Complementarily, this chapter focuses on qualification practices and their performance and less on the resulting structures of such actions. In fact, by focusing on the action-related dimensions of product qualification, this chapter tries to strengthen one of Bowker and Star's more provocative conclusions, the futility of separating between actors and the structure in which they operate. In addition, by regarding qualification as a dynamic process, this chapter refers to a specific theory of action: the Actor-Network theory (ANT), and more specifically, to the work about qualification done by French sociologists Michel Callon, Cecile Méadel, and Vololona Rabeharisoa (2002). As we will see in the discussion below, ANT and the specific form of qualification proposed by Callon capture the dynamic nature of the process. That is, according to Callon qualities of a product are not simply assigned to it, but instead are the outcomes of multiple interactions, including, as we see in the empirical case, the products themselves.

In order to analyse this process, involving heterogeneous entities, we need first to assume that it does not operate in a linear fashion, but rather in network-like one. That is, the various actors that shape the products do not operate one after the other, but rather interact with each other, and products are shaped through these interactions. A second assumption that stems from the interactive and networked perspective of product qualification is that the various actors may promote different and even conflicting ideas about the desired shape and function of the product. As a result, the qualification process should be regarded less as a centrally orchestrated effort, and more as an emergent, and potentially a competitive one. In this respect, it can be expected that any set of qualities attached to a product through the interaction of actors may be challenged by alternative sets of qualities that other actors, or coalitions of actors, propose. Lastly, the networked nature of the qualification process places the evolution of markets themselves in a new light. In particular, the relations between the products and the markets in which they are traded may need to be re-examined.

If qualification is a process in which take part different actors whose conflicting worldviews clash, can we assume that the market itself does not change as a result of such process? In other words, should not we consider qualification not only as a process that takes place in the market and affects products, but also as a process of qualification *of* the market itself? This perspective departs from Granovetter's influential approach, which insists upon the structural embeddedness of markets (Granovetter, 1985) and tends to bracket off the content of economic goods. In certain aspects it echoes Zelizer's notion of multiple markets and her seminal work about the creation of 'types of money' that can be seen as a description of a multifaceted process of product qualification (Zelizer, 1989). In fact, this chapter expands Zelizer's work by focussing on the controversial dimension of the (networked) process of qualification.

As mentioned before, the notion of qualification developed in this chapter is related to a concept presented in an influential paper by Callon, Méadel, and Rabeharisoa (2002) as well as by Callon and Muniesa (2005). The motivation behind the analytical effort in this chapter and the one behind Callon's paper are similar: an effort to understand where products come from. These similarities, however, are limited to the contours of the theoretical approaches, while the contents are significantly different. Callon suggests that qualification operates through the continual creation and recreation of relations between the evolving products and existing products. The temporary outcomes of these comparative exercises are performed each time the qualified product is bought and sold. This schematic framework is a very powerful conceptual tool, because it allows us to treat products as a chain composed of connected qualification attempts. Yet, the qualification of financial products includes aspects that call for broadening and reconfiguration of existing concepts in economic sociology. The relationship between the products and their attached practices are different in financial markets, the markets described in this chapter, from those that exist in most other markets that empirical works in economic sociology describe. In the cases of products such as wine bottles or cars, for example, there is a visible distinction between the practices of trading, in which the qualities of the products take part in constructing the prices of the products, and between the practices through which the qualities are established and tested. In the case of financial products, like index-based derivatives, no such distinction exists; a crucial part in the qualification of financial products is performed on the trading floor. Namely, the way financial products 'behave' in the market is not only a trial of their qualities, but the market is also one of the arenas where these qualities are formed and attached to the product. As the empirical material in this chapter shows, the *practices* through which the qualities of financial products were performed had a dramatic impact on the evolution of the markets.

The construction of deliverability: early history of commodities futures

Derivatives are financial contracts whose market price, as their name implies, is derived from the price of another asset that underlines the derivative. Agricultural commodities, shares and stock indices are just some of the most common entities for which derivative are designed. The central claim that this chapter makes is that to understand the social dimension of derivatives in general, and index-based ones in particular, it is necessary to trace the development of the links between the underlying entities and the derivative contract. It is vital to understand the nature of the qualities of the underlying assets and how these qualities are embedded into institutionalized market mechanisms, practices and conventions. This dynamic historical process through which the qualities of the underlying assets are linked to the derivative contract – the qualification of the contract – is central to the analysis of index-based contracts. To analyse the complex historical process of the qualification of index-based derivatives we need to trace the evolution and the influence of two key factors in the markets where these financial contracts were first traded – the commodities futures markets: (1) the deliverability of underlying assets and (2) the nexus of connections between the futures exchanges and the regulatory establishment.

The first American market to trade derivative contracts, the Chicago Board of Trade (CBOT), started trading in 1848. The commodities-based contracts (known as 'forwards') traded in the CBOT specified the terms of mutual obligations of the buyer and the seller to, respectively, deliver and pay for a specified amount of product (of a certain quality) on a set date. For example, a typical contract might include the obligation to deliver 20 tons of potatoes of a given variety and of a given quality at a given date in return for a set amount. The terms of each contract had to be negotiated by the buyer and seller: the date in which delivery of the agricultural product was to take place (the contracts' 'expiration date'), the exact nature and quality of the product and the price to be paid for the product on delivery. Hence, since forward contracts were designed for the needs of the two specific parties to the future transaction and they had little use outside the particular setting.

Three years after its inception, in 1851, the CBOT took a revolutionary step and standardized the bilateral forwards. The standardized forward contracts, which came to be known as 'futures', were templates that included the terms of the contract and all that was left for the parties to negotiate was the contract's price. Any futures contract bearing the same expiration date and underlying asset became interchangeable with any similar contract, regardless of the identity of the trader who bought it initially. By standardizing the contracts, the time-consuming stage of negotiations over the details of the contracts was eliminated and the trading process became faster and more efficient. There was a more far-reaching implication to contract standardization, however: the standardization made the contracts *themselves* tradable, thus relieving the traders from the necessity of owning the underlying agricultural products on which the contracts were based. In other words, the traders could buy and sell the contracts and, when the expiration date was approaching, offset their obligations by acquiring contracts that were the 'other side' of their transactions. For example, a trader holding a contract requiring her to buy 500 bushels of corn at the end of the month would offset her obligations by buying a contract requiring her to sell the same amount and the same type of corn at that date.

After the standardization of the contracts the CBOT and futures trading witnessed a long period of growth. The popularity of futures trading gave rise to bets that were made on the prices that the market would quote. In the late 1880s, that practice of betting on futures' prices gained popularity and by the end of the century, there were numerous shops that sold contracts that were based on CBOT-traded prices of agricultural futures (Fabian, 1990). CBOT regarded those establishments, commonly known as 'bucket shops', as illegitimate competition. First, the bucket shops were piggybacking on information that originated from the CBOT (where the prices were determined) and offered no compensation for that service. Second, by betting on futures' prices the bucket shops were taking potential customers from the CBOT and thus were denying commissions to CBOT members. During the last years of the 1890s and the early 1900s, CBOT went on a fierce legal battle against the bucket shops, at the end of which, after several landmark court cases (Ferris, 1988) the operation of the latter was declared illegal and was effectively terminated.

The main argument that the CBOT used in its legal struggle against the bucket shops was that contracts that did not include a specific obligation for the delivery of the underlying assets (i.e., were settable only through the payment of cash), could not count as legitimate commercial contracts but were essentially gambling. The carefully constructed CBOT's argument struck a chord with broader anti-gambling emotions in the American society and following this initial success, the association between cash-settlement and gambling did not remain limited to institutions like the bucket shops, but was extended, at least implicitly, to all other possible cash-settled contracts (Fabian, 1990). A lobbying effort by the CBOT also brought about a change in Illinois' gambling laws, forbidding the trading of cash-settled contracts and allowing only contracts that included the option to deliver the goods. The changes in Illinois laws were followed by a number of other Midwestern states (Cronon, 1991). Moreover, the notion about the similarity between cash-settlement and illegal betting, in its wider form, became a common argument against the trading of financial contracts and even against the immoral nature of financial markets in general. For example, bucket shops were mentioned in the Congressional debates in the early 1930s that led to the establishment of the SEC (Shapiro, 1984).

Yet, although assets' deliverability was a milestone in the establishment of CBOT as an economic and political institution, the actual performance of assets' delivery has all but disappeared from CBOT. The enormous success of standardized futures eroded the importance of deliverability. Over the decades since the introduction of standardized futures in the mid 19th century, the ratio of traders who actually took part in a delivery of assets on expiration of the futures contracts dwindled constantly. By the 1950s the vast majority of futures contracts were not settled in delivery: most estimates were that only in 3 to 5 per cent of transactions did products actually change hands (Clark, 1978; Markham, 1987). The rest of the transactions were settled by offsetting the obligations in the contracts through buying/selling 'opposite' contracts. This yawning gap between the volumes of futures trading and actual deliveries of the assets on the basis of which the contracts were written was not merely an evolving feature of agricultural futures exchanges like the CBOT. In effect, the discrepancy between trading futures and delivery became one of the main growth engines for futures market. Nominally, each futures contract was backed up by the underlying agricultural product in the amounts and qualities specified in the contract. Futures trading grew about a 100-fold in the first century of CBOT (Tamarkin, 1993). In practice, therefore the volume of futures contracts traded made it impossible for delivery of assets to taken place for more than a fraction of the futures contracts. It would be safe to say that such phenomenal growth would not have been possible had all the transactions ended up in delivery of the agricultural products.

This short analysis of the historical path of futures markets shows that the deliverability of the underlying asset was crucial for the legitimacy of futures, and indeed was embedded in the coded norms of gambling laws. While the concept of deliverability became crucial to futures markets, however, the actual practice in the markets rendered deliverability and indeed the sheer physicality of assets irrelevant. Moreover, it was crucial for the growth and prosperity of futures exchanges that deliverability would be possible in principle, but that it would not be performed in practice in all but a tiny minority of the transactions.

Regulators and exchanges in the network of qualification

By the 1960s, the tension between deliverability-in-principle and market practices has become an inherent part of the futures market. Yet, in the following few years that reality was about to change. In 1969–1971 the agricultural commodities markets witnessed a period of low trading volume (Yamey, 1985). That period coincided with the gradual demise of the currencies' gold standard; a process that allowed currency exchange rates to float with less regulatory intervention and turned currencies into a much more risky asset than they had been previously. The futures exchanges, whose members were struggling due to the slow grains market, saw the more volatile currencies markets as a promising business opportunity and in spring 1971, Leo Melamed of the Chicago Mercantile Exchange (CME), the CBOT's archrival Chicago futures exchange, began to promote a plan for trading futures contracts based on foreign currencies (Melamed, 1988). Melamed's initiative, the International Monetary Market (IMM), an exchange that traded futures based on currencies, commenced trading in April 1972. The volatile currency markets contributed to high volumes in currency futures and following this initial success other agricultural futures exchanges developed similar contracts. Within months, the commodities regulator, the Commodity Exchange Authority (CEA) in the Department of Agriculture, received notices from several other American commodities exchanges about their intentions to apply for permissions to trade futures on non-agricultural products (R* interview).

Currency futures broke the virtually exclusive association that futures had had for over a century with agricultural products. In addition, non-agricultural futures signalled that the futures exchanges were aiming to expand their potential customers' base by attracting investors from the general business community and in particular from the financial sector. These trends created a challenge for the regulatory process related to approving new contracts. Non-agricultural futures were an unknown territory for the Department of Agriculture and following the success of futures on currencies concerns were raised among the futures exchanges that the regulatory approval of contracts might be slowed considerably due to lack of knowledge. The severity of the regulatory challenge was manifested in the form requesting information about proposed contract that was sent to the CME by the Commodity Exchange Authority when permission to trade currency futures was sought. That form asked, among other things, about the size, location and condition of the warehouses in which the underlying commodities would be stored (Melamed, 1988).

These growing concerns about the suitability of the existing regulatory regime led CBOT in early 1973 to initiate an intensive lobbying offensive in Washington intending to persuade the American Congress to change the commodities regulatory structure. Concerns about the CEA's suitability to regulate the evolving futures world were not the only reason for the lobbying campaign. Since futures contracts were no longer associated exclusively with agricultural products there were now potential candidates to be transferred to another regulatory authority, one more suitable for the regulation of financial products. The possibility that the CBOT was particularly concerned about was that the American Congress would define futures on financial products as securities and consequently transfer the regulation of the contracts to the Securities and Exchange Commission (SEC).

The CBOT's concerns were not without basis. The same weak trading period in grain markets in the late 1960s that motivated the CME to develop the currency futures also drove the CBOT to fund research into the possibility of trading options on stocks.[2] Options, being underlined by stocks, were regarded as securities and thus the SEC was given jurisdiction over that contract and the CBOT's proposal to trade stock options in an organized exchange underwent a long and exhaustive approval process by the SEC. The regulatory process took more than three years and acquired considerable effort by a team of lawyers and the exchange staff. Following those events, when the commodities exchanges' lobbying effort succeeded in bringing about a Congressional hearings about the future of futures regulation, it promoted one message above all others: financial futures should not be regulated by the SEC. R*, at that period a CBOT lawyer who was heading the lobbying effort in Washington:

> [. . .] the CBOT people said: 'Damn! We're not gonna go through all that again [referring to the protracted approval process of stock options]. We're gonna make sure that whatever agency comes out of that Congressional process, for the futures community, has exclusive jurisdiction over everything and nobody else is going to torment us for three years the way these guys did three years ago. (R* interview)

The main argument of the lobbying team was that the CME's currency futures opened the floodgates to a new torrent of financial futures and soon futures based on a variety of financial products would be proposed. That situation, the argument continued, may lead to an 'administrative hell' in which an exchange that would offer, say, futures on Treasury bills, crude oil and orange juice would have to go through separate approval procedures with the Treasury Department, with the Department of Energy and with the Department of Agriculture. Moreover, whenever a change to the contracts would be necessary, each of the agencies that regulated the underlying assets would have to be notified. Hence, the argument concluded, in a world where futures were no longer limited to agricultural products, regulation according to the underlying products was no longer feasible. Instead, the exchanges' lobbying mission suggested that a new agency would be created that would have exclusive regulative authority over all futures contracts. In other words, a new principle of regulatory taxonomy was presented: regulation based on the type of contract instead of one based on the type of the underlying commodity.

The lobbying efforts were successful and in May 1974 the American Congress amended the Commodity Exchange Act (CEA) of 1936 and facilitated the creation of a new regulatory agency – the Commodity Futures Trading Commission (CFTC). The meaning of this new legal structure was that the CFTC was given exclusive rights over the regulatory approval of futures contracts. In other words, since futures could not be traded without such an approval the CFTC became an obligatory point of passage in the topology of the qualification network. That is, in the regulatory reality that was put in place by the 1974 Act, the CFTC has become an indispensable part of any path connecting a potential underlying asset, an exchange and a tradable futures contract.

The broad regulatory definition of futures created a conceptual blur between non-agricultural futures and between securities, and created uncertainty regarding the regulatory domains of financial markets. For example, being the exclusive regulator of futures the CFTC had jurisdiction over futures written on any asset, including, potentially, securities. The SEC, however, already had exclusive jurisdiction over securities. This may lead to the following dilemma: if futures on securities were to be proposed, which of the two, CFTC or SEC, would regulate them?

Such a qualification challenge was not merely hypothetical. In October 1975, the CFTC approved an application by the CBOT to trade futures on a financial product – mortgage-backed certificates known as GNMA's (US GAO, 2000: 5).[3] At the same time, an application by the CME was pending to trade futures on Treasury Bills (Johnson, 1976), and several of the other 12 American commodity exchanges also had applications for the trading of futures on Treasury bills at various stages of completion. It was the common opinion among the SEC's staff that futures on GNMA's would erode the distinction between securities and commodities. This was a trend that the SEC observed with much concern as it threatened its regulatory territory. This potential conflict between the interests of the two regulators would have had serious implications for the qualification of financial futures. Futures could not be traded without a regulatory approval and such an approval was not likely to be given while the regulatory identity of the contracts was disputed.

The challenge to the qualification of financial futures was embedded in a broader, deeply-rooted rivalry between the two regulators. It is true that the immediate issues that troubled the SEC's staff were related to the threatening possibility that the SEC's jurisdictional turf would be limited as a result of the new broad definition, but the concerns were also underpinned by a more general perception about the nature of commodities markets and their regulation. A senior staff member of the SEC's division of market regulation in the mid 70s described the SEC's staff attitude to the CFTC:

> The CFTC has always been a horrible regulator. [. . .] People who moved from the SEC to the CFTC thought that the CFTC was the end of the world. They were dealing with a bunch of dinosaurs over there. They just could not get them to understand the need for any kind of regulatory oversight. (M* interview)

The views, common among the SEC's staff, that the SEC was a better regulator than the CFTC and that its staff was more professional than that of the new regulator should not be dismissed merely as a sign of inter-regulatory rivalry. These views belong to a broader perception that contributed to the shaping of qualification struggle between the two regulators. G*, who was the chief economist of the SEC when the CFTC was established, described the common view about commodities futures at the SEC:

> Commodities were just . . . they smelled, you know. Commodities were really viewed like gambling. [. . .]. It's like saying: 'when people put those quarters in the slots, that is really an investment' and you [the SEC] got to regulate the casinos. I think it's a cultural thing. (G* interview)

This quote encapsulates both the nature of qualification and the contours of the qualification conflict that took place in the inter-regulatory sphere. As the history of markets for agricultural commodities indicates, assets gain their relative positions in the market and their qualities through the market practice.

Hence, if commodity trading is comparable to gambling, and the actual practice of trading is compared to pulling the handle of a slot machine, then the massage is clear: futures cannot be used for conducting sound, calculable investment and trading them is equal to the entirely luck-determined practice of gambling. This is not the entire message, however. At the time, the SEC and the CFTC were engaged in a struggle over the definition of futures contracts and the struggle was, in many respects, a zero-sum game. Any regulatory 'territory' lost by one regulator would have most likely be given to the other one. In this light, the quote above, and the common opinion about commodities should be regarded as an implicit opinion about the SEC, as much as it was a direct opinion about the CFTC. That is, if commodities trading is equal to gambling, then securities trading, the other activity in this dichotomy should be seen as legitimate investment.

Such views underlined the conflict about the qualification of futures. Yet, for the SEC, having a decisive impact on product qualification was not the ultimate goal. Qualification was seen as a step towards the more important goal, to distinguish its regulatory domain from that of the CFTC. The SEC, established in the early 30s, was the more well-established of the two regulators and had better chances to recruit influential supporters and to impose its definition. Given that the CFTC had exclusive statutory rights over regulation of all futures, however, and since the definition of commodities included financial products, the separation between the two regulatory fields of securities and commodities no longer existed. In this situation, the SEC's staff knew that in order to avoid the threat of having its regulatory domain taken over by the CFTC, the boundaries between the regulatory areas would need to be reconstructed.

This insight motivated the staff of the SEC to promote a message according to which there is a need to maintain the distinction between securities, the exclusive domain of the SEC, and between the types of assets that could be served as underlying for futures. Internal discussions in the SEC took place in the months after the American Congress passed the amendment to the Commodity Exchange Act and in December 10, 1975, Roderick Hills, the chairman of the SEC sent a letter to the chairman of CFTC suggesting that:

> Both the CFTC and this Commission should be concerned, not with bare questions of jurisdiction, but with a number of important questions relating to the integration of our capital markets [. . .]
> Can a meaningful distinction be drawn [. . .] between securities options [. . .] and futures contracts [. . .] and if so, what is it? (Hills, 1975)

The two regulators were not the only actors involved in the political struggle. Due to the dense network of ties between the organizational actors, the debate over the shape of qualification had important implications for the exchanges. The futures exchanges, which were regulated by the CFTC, wished to expand their catalogue of contracts, and not to transfer to the stricter regulatory regime of the SEC. CBOT, the leading futures market of the time, directed an additional lobbying effort aiming to persuade the American Congress to incorporate into the Futures Act a wide as possible a definition of underlying assets, so as to include as many potential financial assets under the jurisdiction of the CFTC. R*, one of the leading commodities lawyers at the time coordinated CBOT's lobbying effort. R*:

> I was looking for something that I thought would capture everything that one could think of and did not include securities [. . .] I could not say securities because it would have alerted the SEC. So we used this phrasing So we used this phrasing – 'services, rights and interests' – I borrowed it from a uniform commercial code, and crossed our fingers and hoped that the courts will see it as broad enough, which they did. (R* interview)

The regulatory compromise solved the discursive aspect of the qualification process but the disputes over market practices did not end. The following six years, between 1974 and 1980, witnessed a long chain of 'border incidents' between the SEC and CFTC that flared around the regulatory approval processes of futures contracts based on financial assets, contracts that could be interpreted as being securities. In several cases, securities exchanges sued commodities exchanges for trading financial futures contracts, claiming that the futures contracts were actually securities in disguise and that the futures exchanges were illegally expanding their trading territory at the securities exchanges' expense. As a general rule, the SEC and the CFTC provided advice and support to 'their' exchanges that were involved in cases, but mostly remained out of the courtrooms themselves. One exception was a court case related to the GNMA-based contracts mentioned earlier. CBOT traded GNMA futures since 1975 with considerable success. In 1981, there were approximately 2,293,000 sales of the contract, each representing $100,000 in unpaid mortgage principal (Board of Trade of City of Chicago v. SEC. 1982: 25,719). In early 1981, the Chicago Board Options Exchange (CBOE) submitted an application to its regulator, the SEC, to trade options on GNMA's. The CBOT, fearing that options on GNMA's would compete with its lucrative futures contract, sent a complain to the SEC and when, later on, the SEC approved CBOE's option contract, the CBOT filed a petition, objecting the approval, at a Federal court of appeals. The GNMA's case brought the two regulatory agencies into a direct confrontation in court. The court case resulted in a call by one of the judges for commencement of negotiations between the two parties:

> I did not appreciate seeing two federal agencies expend their time and resources fighting a jurisdictional dispute in court. I believe their efforts would be more wisely spent in utilizing their expertise to reach a solution, which they would jointly recommend to Congress. (Board of Trade of City of Chicago v. SEC. 1982: 25, 737).

The GNMA's case exposed the full extent of the regulatory struggle to the public and forced the SEC and the CFTC to start negotiations over the regulatory qualification of futures contracts.

As we shall see, the talks between the SEC and the CFTC that followed the court case discussed above eventually decoupled the exclusive link between derivative contracts and deliverable assets. Before we return to the historical narrative, however, a brief explanation about index-based contracts may be necessary. Stock indices are mathematical averages of the market prices of set groups of stocks at a given time. For example, a list of 500 stocks complied by Standard and Poor (S&P) is used as a basis for the S&P 500 index. On their own, indices are little more than mathematical representations of markets' price levels. In contrast, when incorporated into financial contracts, like futures or options, stock indices can serve as a useful market tool. Index-based futures contracts require their owners (buyer) and its seller to pay or receive an amount of money proportional to the difference between the index level at the market on expiry and the index level stated in the contract. These contracts allow market participants to protect their holding against sudden drops in prices. For example, a contract that would grant its owner, say, $25 for each index point below a certain value at a certain date could serve as a safety net for investors. Similarly, a contract that would pay its owner $25 for each index point above a certain value would make a good device for profit-seeking traders who hope to gain from increasing prices. Index-based contracts would also have a significant advantage over contracts written on the basis of individual assets. Index-based contracts, being based on a relatively general 'prices generator' – the index – were less specific. That meant that as long as a person's portfolio is correlated with the price movements of the whole market, a derivative contract based on a market-wide index could be used to protect against losses to that person's portfolio.

These attributes explain why index-based contracts were attractive for investors. In addition, the nature of the assets underlying index-based contracts – indices – made them attractive from an organizational perspective. The SEC approved only a limited number of stocks to be used as bases for options. Consequently, as option trading became more popular, competition among exchanges for available stocks increased and so did the motivation of futures exchanges (regulated by the CFTC) for the approval of index-based futures.[4] Unlike stocks, indices represented a virtually infinite source of underlying assets and a promising source of growth for the exchanges. Index-based contracts also carried with them the promise of a light organizational burden as they allowed the exchanges to write one type of contract per market-wide index, instead of writing contracts on many individual stocks, thus their maintenance required less organizational resources than single stock contracts.

As promising as indices were, the deliverability problem stood between the exchanges and the realisation of index-based contracts. Index-based contracts could not guarantee the delivery of goods – such deliverable goods simply did not exist! Because no exchange of goods and funds was possible, index-based contracts could only be settled through the transfer of cash (cash settlement) and this was illegal in most American states. Indeed, as discussed earlier in the chapter, the evolution of commodities markets and the establishment of the notion of deliverability were contingent on each other.

Yuval Millo

Deliverability and Witching Hours: the contracts in the qualification network

The contrasting arguments of the SEC and the CFTC that evolved in the period leading to the GNMA case framed the range of qualification options in such a way that left the two regulators little choice other than to cooperate. Futures were put under exclusive jurisdiction of the CFTC, yet the products on which the indices were based – the stocks – were regulated by the SEC. This situation led the two regulators to the realisation that in spite of the rivalry between the two agencies the cash-settlement issue should be solved co-operatively. Even the more militant among the SEC staff realised that cooperation was necessary. For example, H*, a senior staff member of the SEC who was involved in the discussions, described SEC's the situation:

> [We r]ecognized that our legal positions were less than strong. [. . .] The SEC dealt with a very weak legal hand (H* interview)

In the Spring of 1981, while the GNMA case was still discussed in court, John Shad and Philip Johnson were appointed as the chairs of, respectively, the SEC and the CFTC and according to Johnson, even before he took up office in Washington he contacted Shad and they both agreed to meet and discuss the overlapping regulatory areas of the two agencies (R* interview).[5]

Although it was essential to solve the deliverability issue, tackling it proved difficult. Delivering the underlying was the practice through which the distinction between legitimate financial contracts and illegitimate, illegal, gambling was performed. As such, deliverability performed a crucial part of the contract qualities – their legality. From this legal and social perspective, doing away with the contractual obligation to have a delivery and replacing it with cash settlement would have amounted to obliterating the distinction between financial markets and casinos. Hence, the dilemma that the Shad and Johnson faced was: how could the heads of the two most important financial regulatory agencies in the US decide suddenly that cash-settlement was different from gambling, after their agencies have been condemning the practice since they were formed?

Shad and Johnson considered an approach that would circumvent the problems rather than tackle them directly. They simulated a scenario in which index-based contracts would include an obligation to deliver the assets. For example, if sellers of index-based futures would choose to exercise their contracts and deliver the underlying assets they would have to buy the stocks that composed the index that underlined the contract. Considering that indices are composed of any number of stocks ranging from 30 (Dow Jones) to a few hundreds (Standard and Poor's 100 or 500), and also that many series of futures would expire at the same date, deliveries of the underling assets would certainly result in sudden demands for stocks, leading to sharp surges in prices. Following such a scenario, Shad and Johnson understood that even if a fraction of index-based contracts would be settled by delivery, then the consequential transactions might still cause extreme volatility in the securities markets; a situation that both parties did not want to induce:

> We didn't want this great flood of demand for stocks . . . He [Shad] didn't want it. He had this notion of 'witching hours' in the options markets, triple witching hours. He said: 'I don't need this kind of thing over here in the stock index side and I don't think my guys [SEC staff] care so let's just cash-settle everything. We decided that any index should be cash-settled.' (R* interview)

The 'witching hours' R* referred to were the last trading hours before the expiration of stock options. These contracts were written typically for periods of one month, three months, or six months and usually expired at the end of trading at the third Friday of the month in which the contract expires. Due to these standard time intervals, four times a year (on March, June, September and December) there occurred mutual expiration of the contracts. On those dates, at the hours before expiration, participants in stock markets witnessed huge price movements that seemed to be completely unrelated to the known information about the stocks. Such waves of sale and buy orders, frequently amounting to tens of millions of dollars, did not only leave the traders bewildered, but also caused significant losses to many veteran traders (Stein, 1986). These periods, immediately prior to the expiry of the contracts, came to be known as witching hours in the Wall Street parlance. The reason for this moniker was that market participants realized that during these near-expiration periods markets tended to display behaviour that was dramatically different from what was normally expected. It was gradually understood that usual patterns of trading did not hold true on those Fridays, and the markets behaved as if they were put under a mysterious spell.

Shad and Johnson's simulation exercise brought to the fore the role that deliverability played in the qualification and the realization of index-based contract. Shad and Johnson showed that the environments of deliverable assets and the non-deliverable assets were incompatible. According to the deliverable assets worldview, the absence of a delivery clause from financial contracts meant that those contracts were no different from betting. In contrast, in a market where index-based contracts are traded, an obligatory delivery would be equal to inviting a market crash. Therefore, what was a condition of the legal existence of trading in the deliverable assets world became unbearably dangerous in the world of non-deliverable index-based contracts.

This conceptual reconfiguration of the meaning of cash-settlement was a step in the creation of a new 'language game' in its Wittgensteinian sense (Lyotard, 1984). The two regulators created a constitutive language act (Barnes *et al.*, 1996) and by so doing, by assigning a new discourse to the situation they resolved a century old concept. Namely, by connecting the trading practice of delivering underlying assets with the new index-based contracts, obligatory delivery was denounced as irrelevant and even dangerous. It has to be noted that although crucial for qualification, the interaction between the regulator was not the only site where index-based futures were born. The new environments in which financial futures and options were traded and the products themselves, the financial derivatives, gave the regulators with the essential vocabulary. Shad and Johnson were able to use the notion of 'witching hours' as a discursive tool in their discussions because such phenomenon had existed in organized options markets for several years before they met. Actors who traded financial futures and options created a new market nexus of practices and norms, constituting a new lingual and communicative medium, which was later recruited by the regulators. Together, this network of connections among traders, exchanges and regulators qualified index-based derivatives and turned the non-deliverable into tradable assets.

Discussion

The ability to design derivatives on the basis of market indices is arguably one of the reasons behind the explosive growth of these markets in the last decades and is an integral part of contemporary financial markets. Unlike other entities that are tradable assets in their own rights, however, indices are merely the products of mathematical procedures. Therefore, a crucial element in the qualification of index-based derivatives was the construction of the indices as legitimate underlying assets. As we saw, the qualification of index-based derivatives depended on a concentrated effort by a heterogeneous forum of agents (exchanges and regulators) that together transformed the cultural, political and practical aspects of commodities trading into qualities that were assigned to the new financial contract. This analysis serves as a basis for a more general discussion regarding financial markets. In particular, it raises a number of interesting questions. This concluding section will address two of them. First, the case of index-based derivatives illuminates the complex nature of the network of heterogeneous actors that constitutes contemporary financial markets, and in particular the connections between financial regulators and exchanges. Second, the dynamic process through which index-based derivatives were qualified raises the more general issue of the nature of agency in evolving market networks.

The qualification of index-based derivatives reveals the dense nexus of connections between regulators and exchanges. If a commonly accepted worldview were to be applied to this case then the various actors involved would probably be classified as belonging to one of two archetypical groups: regulators and regulated. A good example for the application of such a dichotomy to financial markets is the characterisation of financial economist Merton Miller (1986) of the constitutive powers of financial regulators. Miller suggests that many of the sophisticated financial derivative products existing today were developed because financial entrepreneurs were trying to break away from regulation.[6] According to Miller, new and innovative financial products did not fall under the existing regulatory definitions and thus allowed their users to be free from regulatory constrains such as reporting, or compliance with strict risk-mitigation practices. The 'action-reaction' hypothesis makes an implicit assumption about the nature of the financial entrepreneurship process. According to this assumption the regulators and the entrepreneurs are locked in an endless symbolic tennis game: the financial entrepreneurs launch a new type of product, which challenges the abilities of the existing regulatory regime, and the regulators react by changing the regulations.

As index-based derivatives show us, such sequential, bilateral model is inaccurate. Instead, we saw how regulators and exchanges form and dissolve coalitions that cross the boundaries between regulators and regulated. Ian Ayers and John Braithwaite offer an alternative to the mutually excluding division between regulation and deregulation, a dichotomy they regard as arbitrary and contrived (Ayers and Braithwaite, 1992). In their analysis, Ayers and Braithwaite predict that in complex fields, such as financial markets, the relations between regulators and regulated would tend to shift from a pattern of command and control, in which the regulators dictate to regulated the regulatory goal and the means through they are to be achieved, to an interactive pattern they refer to as 'enforced self-regulation'. In the second phase, the regulatory goals are still chosen by the regulator, but the ways in which they are attained are dependent on the expertise of the regulated. The 'enforced self-regulation' scheme assumes implicitly that there is a separation between the 'what' element of regulation, the value-based, normative demands that underline the regulatory practice, and the 'how' element, the means through which these demands are tackled. Andrew Leyshon and Nigel Thrift (1996) follow a different disciplinary path but offer similar conclusions: they suggest that there is a discursive plurality in the interfaces between regulators and corporations, which brings about frequent changes in the content and boundaries of the economic system. If we add this insight to the hypothesis about enforced self-regulation, we see that complex regulatory fields, like the one that evolved around derivatives markets, call for very different analytic perspectives from the ones that divide the institutional agents to regulators and regulated. Instead, as the historical description implies, in an environment where it is necessary for the institutional agents to co-operate in order to influence the shape of the regulatory action, the nature of the ties among the various actors is as important as their motivations.

This theoretical perspective, which assumes that there is a dynamic, multifocal regulatory environment, sets the stage for a concept of a more decentred regulation, such as the one offered by Julia Black (2001, 2002). According to Black, regulation is not a process that the state or its agents activate, but it is rather an outcome, or multiple outcomes, of interactions among actors. This approach differs radically from command and control approaches not only because it distributes the regulatory action among the agents but also because it also detaches the responsibility for the regulatory process from a single agent, or a group of agents, and transfers it to the *relations* among the different actors.

In other words, the question 'who regulates?' is replaced by the question 'how is regulation performed?' This question, which according to previous theoretical approaches to regulation was seen as a technical derivative of the worldview of the regulator, has moved to the fore. Since no single agent performs the regulation, but instead it is seen as an emerging organizational, political and, more recently, technological phenomenon, it cannot be reduced to a string of pre-determined procedures. Instead, the network of connections through which regulatory activity takes places should be regarded as the organizational infrastructure where rules, practices and procedures evolve and take shape. As the case of index-based derivates shows us, such a network includes the various interfaces between the actors, as well as the material and technological artefacts that they use.

The qualification process also raises questions about the nature of agency in financial markets. If we use the historical narrative in this chapter as a possible answer for the question: 'who created index-based contract?' we would find that the answer is far from straightforward. The regulators did not create the market for index-based contracts on their own because the options traders were the ones who developed the new conceptual meaning of non-delivery contracts. In particular, it was the notion of 'Witching Hours' that motivated Shad and Johnson to relinquish the demand for delivery. Similarly, it cannot be argued that the exchanges were the ones responsible for the creation of index-based contracts because, as the data show, critical parts in the qualification process took place within organizational settings in which the exchanges had relatively little influence.

A possible answer to the question of who created the first index-based derivatives can be that the network of connections that makes up the market is responsible for their creation. In other words, qualification provides us with an explanation why we should regard markets as a case of networked, distributed agency. This concept is taken from Marvin Minsky (Minsky, 1986). Minsky argued that intelligent action should be conceptualized as a large system of agencies that can be assembled together in various configurations. Edwin Hutchins (Hutchins, 1995) followed Minsky and expanded the concept to systems that include both humans and material objects. Hutchins showed that in a complex techno-social network the attribution of exclusive decision-making capacity to one actor would not be accurate. In such networks (Hutchins analyses aircrafts and boats), no single actor is the 'commander' while the rest are 'subordinates'. Instead, whole network of humans and machines makes the decisions and performs the practices. In accordance, it can be said that the creation of markets for financial derivatives, a process that included a string of interpretations and decisions, could not be reduced to a simple 'action-reaction' narrative between the regulators and the exchanges. Indeed, the data shows us that each of the agents had a set of goals that was distinctly different from those of the rest. Instead, the connections between the differential actors were responsible for the transformation of index-based contracts from general concepts to tradable products.

Notes

1 I would like to thank Daniel Beunza, Michel Callon, Donald MacKenzie, Phil Mirowski, Fabian Muniesa and Alex Preda for their kind and insightful comments on various versions of this paper. All remaining mistakes are mine.
2 For a detailed discussion of this historical process see MacKenzie and Millo (2003).
3 Government National Mortgage Association pass-through certificates were known in short as GNMA's. The GNMA certificates gave their owners a proportion of an income generated by pool of mortgages. The certificates' payments were guaranteed by the Government National Mortgage Association, part of the Department of Housing and Urban Development, a fact that made the GNMA-based futures an attractive contract.
4 In 1978, 5 years after organized options trading began, options were traded in 8 other SEC-regulated exchanges.
5 Sadly, John Shad passed away in July 1994 so interviews with him for this research were not possible. The material in this chapter includes interviews with several high-ranking SEC staff members who took part in the discussions between the SEC and the CFTC, as well Phillip Johnson himself and other CFTC staff members.
6 Many of the examples that Miller uses are taken from Over the Counter (OTC) derivatives markets, markets that followed a different historical path from the ones described in this paper. Since Miller's argument is paraphrased in general terms, however, it represents the 'regulators-chase-markets' approach.

References

Arditti, F. (1996) *Derivatives: A Comprehensive Resource for Options, Futures, Interest Rate Swaps and Mortgage Securities*. Boston: Harvard Business School Press.
Ayres, I. and J. Braithwaite (1992) *Responsive regulation: transcending the deregulation debate*. New York: Oxford University Press.
Bank for International Settlements (2006) *Semi-annual OTC derivatives statistics at end-June 2006*.
Barnes, B. (1983) 'Social life as bootstrapped induction.' *Sociology* 17(4): 524–45.
Barnes, B., D. Bloor and J. Henry (1996) *Scientific knowledge: a sociological analysis*. London: Athlone.
Beunza, D. and D. Stark (2004) 'Tools of the trade: the socio-technology of arbitrage in a Wall Street trading room.' *Industrial and Corporate Change* 13(2): 369–400.
Black, J. (2001) 'Decentring regulation: understanding the role of regulation and self regulation in a 'post-regulatory' world.' *Current Legal Problems* 54: 103–146.
Black, J. (2002) 'Critical reflections on regulation.' *CARR Discussion Paper* no. 4, London: CARR, London School of Economics.
Board of Trade of City of Chicago v. SEC., 677 F.2d 1137 (7th Cir. 1982).
Bowker, G. and S. Leigh Star (1999) *Sorting things out: classification and its consequences*. Cambridge (Massachusetts): MIT Press.
Callon, M., C. Méadel and V. Rabeharisoa (2002) 'The economy of qualities.' *Economy and Society* 31(2): 194–217.
Callon, M. and F. Muniesa (2005). 'Economic markets as calculative collective devices.' *Organization Studies* 26(8): 1229–1250.
Chance, D. M. (1995) *An introduction to derivatives*. London: Harcourt Brace College Publishers.
Clark, G. (1978) 'Genealogy and genetics of 'contract of sale of a commodity for future delivery' in the commodity exchange act.' *Emory Law Journal* 27: 1175–1176.
Cronon, W. (1991) *Nature's metropolis: Chicago and the great west*. London: W.W. Norton & Company.

Fabian, A. (1990) *Card sharps, dream books and bucket shops: gambling in nineteenth-century America*. Ithaca: Cornell University Press.
Ferris, W. G. (1988) *The grain traders: the story of the Chicago board of trade*. East Lansing: Michigan State University Press.
Granovetter, M. (1985) 'Economic action and social structure: the problem of embeddedness.' *American Journal of Sociology* 91(3): 481–510.
Hills, R. (1975) Letter by Roderick Hills, chairman, SEC to the CFTC concerning the approval given to CBOT to trade futures on GNMA certificates.
Hutchins, E. (1995) *Cognition in the wild*. Cambridge (Massachusetts): The MIT Press.
Johnson, P. (1976) 'Commodity futures trading act.' *Vanderbilt Law Review* 29(1): 1–30.
Kolb, R. W. (1997a) *The financial futures primer*. Oxford: Blackwell.
Kolb, R. W. (1997b) *The options primer*. London: Blackwell.
Leyshon, A. and N. Thrift (1996) 'Financial exclusion and the shifting boundaries of the financial system.' *Environment and Planning A* 28(7): 1150–1156.
Lyotard, J.-F. (1984) *The postmodern condition: a report on knowledge*. Manchester: Manchester University Press.
MacKenzie, D. (2004) 'The big, bad wolf and the rational market: portfolio insurance, the 1987 crash and the performativity of economics.' *Economy and Society* 33(3): 303–334.
MacKenzie, D. (2006) *An engine, not a camera: how financial models shape markets*. Cambridge (Massachusetts): the MIT Press.
MacKenzie, D. and Y. Millo (2003). 'Negotiating a market, performing theory: the historical sociology of a financial derivatives exchange.' *American Journal of Sociology* 109(1): 107–145.
Markham, J. W. (1987) *The history of commodity futures trading and its regulation*. New York: Preager.
Melamed, L. (1988) 'Evolution of the international monetary market.' *Cato* 8(2): 393–404.
Miller, M. H. (1986) 'Financial innovation: the last twenty years and the next.' *Journal of Financial and Quantitative Analysis* 21(4): 459–471.
Minsky, M. (1986) *The society of mind*. New York: Touchstone Books.
Shapiro, S. (1984) *Wayward capitalists: target of the securities and exchange commission*. New Haven: Yale University Press.
Stein, J. L. (1986) *The economics of future markets*. Oxford: Basil Blackwell.
Tamarkin, R. (1993) *The Merc: the emergence of a global financial powerhouse*. New York: Harper-Business.
US Congress. (1974) 'Commodity exchange act.' in US Code, Title 7, Chapter 1, Sec.2.
Yamey, B. (1985) 'Scope for future trading and conditions for success.' In B. S. Yamey, R. L. Sandor, and B. Hindley (eds), *How commodity futures markets work*. London: Trade Policy Research Centre.
Zelizer, V. (1989) 'The social meaning of money: 'special monies'.' *American Journal of Sociology* 95(2): 342–377.

Interviews

All interviews were conducted by the author, recorded and transcribed in full. All interviewees' names and details were kept anonymous.

R* – Chicago, February 2000
M* – Washington, DC., March 2001
G* – Washington, DC., April 2001
H* – Washington, DC., April 2001

The Q(u)ALYfying hand: health economics and medicine in the shaping of Swedish markets for subsidized pharmaceuticals

Ebba Sjögren and Claes-Fredrik Helgesson

Introduction

In markets, settling the qualities of an exchanged good and determining who should pay which price for what, are central activities.[1] As it has been well understood by now, not only sellers and buyers are engaged in such activities. Settling qualities also involves entities such as classification tools, standardization bodies, consumer organizations, advertising agencies, and so on. In this chapter, we focus on one instance of such ancillary qualification work in order to develop a better understanding of how classification practices participate in shaping market exchange.

Our interest in classification is related to the 'performativity programme' developed within the social studies of markets (see Callon, 1998; Slater, 2002; Holm, 2003; Helgesson *et al.*, 2004; Kjellberg and Helgesson, 2006; MacKenzie, Muniesa and Liu, 2007). In particular, our interest lies in how theories and tools – from economics or other sources – participate in configuring elements of markets. The performance of markets is observable through the classification or qualification work implied by the establishment of similarities and differences among objects to be exchanged (cf Callon, Méadel and Rabeharisoa, 2002).

Classification work, that is, the work that must be done to qualify goods and agents, generally relies on a diversity of logics. Numerous studies have recently been devoted to analysing and describing these different logics, the devices in which they are materialized (standards, labels, certifications), as well as the actors that conceive of them and certify their implementation (regulators, critiques, analysts). Their assembly, which is an outcome of compromise and hybridisation, has also been the subject of investigation (Thévenot, 2001). Classification work that draws directly on economic theories, however, has attracted limited attention.

The case presented in this chapter is characterized by the presence of many different, competing classification devices, where the one most recently added is directly linked to economics. What is more, this introduction of economic classification devices has been conceived of and enacted by an organization whose principal mission is to assure its implementation. The case therefore provides a choice terrain for studying an ongoing process of economization, in a setting where multiple classification systems are at play.

The organization at the centre of our investigation is the Swedish Pharmaceutical Benefits Board (henceforth referred to by its Swedish acronym as 'the LFN', or 'the Agency'). It has a formal mandate to determine which prescription pharmaceuticals, out of all of the ones approved for use, should be included in the public pharmaceutical benefits scheme. Although the LFN is neither involved in buying nor selling pharmaceuticals, its work nevertheless involves settling the qualities of these goods.

Two general features of the qualification work undertaken by the LFN are worth emphasising. Firstly, *economic* qualification is only one type of qualification amongst many, potentially conflicting, qualifications. Pharmaceuticals have already been qualified in numerous ways and in various settings prior to the LFN's activities. Secondly, the Agency's own requalifications also have many ramifications and different modalities. They intervene in the definition of what a subsidized use of pharmaceuticals is going to be, as well as in determining what patients are to pay for their use of prescription medications. In addition, they establish equivalences and dissimilarities between pharmaceutical products. Thus, the LFN's classifications explicitly aim at determining how physicians use prescription drugs in their practices (that is, at least, the idea), and how markets for pharmaceuticals are delineated.

Economics, and in particular the applied branch of health economics, has been provided a crucial role in the (often commented upon) process of increasing economization in the health arena. This economization has come into being, in large part through the conception and implementation of devices that qualify drugs and health care as economic goods. The contribution of health economics to the process of economizing health care is a relatively new phenomenon. In this empirical case, its role is explicitly laid out because the law specifically instructs the Agency to assess drugs' cost effectiveness when deciding whether or not their use should be subsidized.

As we will explain further, the concept of *cost effectiveness* conveys a straightforward reference to health economics as an important aspect of the legal framing of the organization's activities. This codification of a health economic approach in health care policy has been increasing over the last few years. From modest beginnings some thirty or forty years ago, health economics has, in the last decade and a half, become increasingly entrenched into policy-making about health care. Of particular interest in the chapter will be efforts within the LFN to use calculative tools and metrics taken from health economics, such as 'quality-adjusted life years' (QALY), to achieve comparisons of pharmaceuticals on the basis of their (relative) cost-effectiveness. This follows from Callon and colleagues' argument that the qualification of objects is an integral part of making them calculable (Callon, Méadel and Rabeharisoa, 2002; Callon and Muniesa, 2005).

In promoting an economic modality for qualifying goods that relies on health economics, the Agency has contributed to enacting a space of calculability in which economic calculation tends to overshadow other forms of qualification.

Yet as we will show, these other qualifications are not completely effaced. On the contrary, economic calculation accommodates and makes compromises that leave space for other forms of qualification, with which it must become and remain compatible. Notably, in the aforementioned law, the Agency is also instructed to uphold principals of solidarity and of equity. The work of economization should therefore not be envisaged as a simple attempt to colonize the health care's terrain and its practices. As Zelizer (2005) has clearly demonstrated, market behaviours are enriched by non-market behaviours.

In the first section of the chapter we present different logics of classification that are present in the work of the LFN, with particularly attention to those that are directly borrowed from health economics. The second section sketches out the difficulties that the Agency encountered in establishing a metric that could render economic calculation possible, while at the same time maintaining other metrics and forms of qualifying goods. What was explicitly at stake in these attempts to achieve metrological unification was the construction of a doctrine and of tools for deciding on the subsidization of drugs. In the third section, the question of how economization takes hold is posed in an exploratory manner. Using Annemarie Mol and John Law's conception of multiplicity we show how an economic calculation is forged in the presence of an amalgamation of different modes of calculation. In the conclusion we propose some general reflections that underline the complexity and ambiguity in economization processes. To succeed in achieving economic calculation, economization must preserve some non-economic spaces, without abdicating the force of its own calculative power. In order to succeed, a process of economization always means having some sort of 'dis-economization'.

Three prevalent modes of pharmaceutical qualification

It requires little effort to recognize that a pharmaceutical is, at once, a chemical compound, a treatment, a brand, a tradable good, a cost and a political issue for the government. Medical practices are obvious sites for enacting versions of a drug. And there are many others. In this section we will outline a few crudely defined practices – in bio-medicine, clinical medicine and health economics – for classifying/qualifying pharmaceuticals.

Classifications of pharmaceuticals within bio-medicine

There are several types of medical practices that perform classifications of pharmaceuticals. Bio-medical practices, such as clinical studies, classify pharmaceuticals and attempt to intervene in medical decision-making. Bio-medical groupings often centre on representations of pharmaceuticals' usage and their therapeutic similarities and differences.

The Anatomical Therapeutic Chemical Classification System (henceforth 'the ATC') is a system for classifying drugs which is maintained by the WHO's Collaborating Centre for Drug Statistics Methodology.[2] The ATC categorizes pharmaceuticals according to the organ or system on which they act, as well as on the drugs' therapeutic and chemical characteristics. In all, the classification system has five tiers, stretching from a first tier of anatomical groups down to a fifth level that identifies specific chemical substances.[3]

ATC-based classifications are widely used to standardize and compare measurements of usage patterns and the costs of pharmaceutical groups across countries and regions. The Swedish Medical Products Agency ('the MPA') and its European equivalent (the European Medicines Agency, 'the EMEA') both use adapted versions of the ATC in the product résumés that outline approved usages for pharmaceuticals in Sweden. Although the classification of pharmaceuticals as manifest in the MPA's register of approvals does not exactly mirror the groupings embodied in the ATC exactly, both are comprehensive systems for classifying drugs. There are, in addition, more targeted ways of organising pharmaceuticals according to therapeutic effect.

One kind of therapeutic classification is provided by the clinical guidelines and assessments concerning specific treatment areas that are issued by governmental agencies, professional associations, and international organizations such as the WHO. These systems discriminate between various kinds of drugs (and sometimes also other, non-drug based treatments) used to treat a particular illness, and define these as being recommended or not. This can result in fine mappings of pharmaceuticals, recommended in relation to specific kinds of patients, based on evidence reported from clinical research.

In summary, bio-medicine has various schemes for classifying pharmaceuticals according to both therapeutic characteristics and chemical composition.

Classifications according to clinical practice

Classifications of pharmaceuticals in bio-medicine aim, more or less explicitly, to inform treatment choice decisions in clinical practice. But as Keating and Cambrosio (2003) have convincingly shown, bio-medicine (or scientific medicine) constitutes a form that is as yet emerging and remains a minor part of medical practice. In other words, it seems well established that neither physicians' prescription behaviours nor patients' use of pharmaceuticals completely match representations made in guidelines, product résumés and similar instances of qualifying pharmaceuticals (eg, Berg, 1997; Greer *et al.*, 2002; Lagrelius, 2004). Thus, although both scientific and clinical medicine use therapeutic characteristics for classifying pharmaceuticals, the basis for defining similarity and difference between them can vary substantially. Notably, clinical medicine can readily produce delineations of similarity and difference relying on the singular relationship between a doctor and an *individual* patient. Scientific medicine, though obviously interested in accounting for the effects of a pharmaceutical on patients, commonly configure patient attributes according to statistically significant groups.

The differences between how pharmaceuticals are classified in guidelines and how they are grouped through practice might be – and has, at times, been –

regarded as reflecting an undesirable deviance from scientific medicine. We will not further consider explanations of such deviations but will, rather, point out that the qualification of pharmaceuticals enacted in clinical practice bears some resemblance to principles of reasoning in economics and marketing. When these disciplines grapple with the issue of defining the boundaries of a given market from that of another, or of defining on what grounds two goods can be said to be exchanged on the same (or different) market, a regular recourse for revealing the proper classification is to consider actors' *behaviours*. A sophisticated answer from economics to the question of what defines market boundaries is that a market should ideally be defined on the basis of substitutability *as viewed from the side of demand*. Goods are part of the same market to the extent that buyers regard them as being substitutes (see Scherer and Ross, 1990).[4] The behaviour of market participants is seen as continuously producing (the relevant) classification of similarity and difference. Similarly, we could say that local medical practitioners in close relation with their patients enact clinical classifications/qualifications. Thus, clinical practice can be conceived as performing a 'demand-side' qualification, and hence enacting a classification that differs from the more 'supply-side' classifications provided by scientific medicine.

Health economic techniques for qualifying treatments

The various tools developed for health economic evaluations are typically policy oriented, and are often presented as methods that assist decision-making within health care. One fairly simple technique designed by health economists is to compare the costs of different treatments that are considered as therapeutically identical (Drummond *et al.*, 1997). Several techniques of evaluation and of calculation were proposed by health economics. They might be ranked on a scale according to their function and their degree of generality.

A so-called *cost-minimization analysis* answers the question of what is the least costly treatment for gaining a given effect. This evaluation relies on both the type of effect and the equivalence of effects between the treatments being compared, having already been established, for example through clinical trials. The technique can therefore, at most, draw a simple distinction between pharmaceuticals that are identical in terms of clinical effects as being different based on cost.

Other health economic techniques can be more sophisticated. A *cost-effectiveness analysis*, for instance, compares the cost per unit of effect of a treatment using the same metric. This makes it possible to determine which of the relevant treatments has the lowest cost per defined effect, and is therefore *the* cost-effective treatment. Like cost-minimization analysis, cost-effectiveness analysis can be used to compare different treatments that from a clinical perspective are deemed similar and used for treating the same illness. It can also be used, however, for comparing treatments of different illnesses if the effectiveness of treatments is expressed through the same metric. As illustrated by this non-pharmaceutical example, if the effectiveness of a kidney transplantation and a heart surgery are both expressed in terms of *life-years saved,* they can be both compared using cost-effectiveness analysis (eg, Drummond *et al.*, 1997: 13).

The *quality-adjusted life year* (QALY), a unit of measurement created within health economics pushes the comparability of drugs even further. Coined in the 1970s, but with a genealogy stretching back further, QALY embodies the idea of having a unit of measurement that allows for comparison among very different treatments (Nord 1999). The core idea is to take into consideration the effectiveness of treatment in terms of both *quantity* of life and *quality* of life. A critical step in calculating QALYs is to rank different states of health and illness on a scale of 0 (defined as death) to 1 (defined as perfect health).[5] Having made a ranking of different states of health and illness by translating them into a standardized metric, it becomes possible to compare treatments which are deemed very different in medical terms. Using QALY allows, in principle, for a comparison to be made between treatments, drugs, services provided, regardless of underlying cause of the disease or the strategy followed to derive a therapeutic solution. This serves to broaden the possible scope of (economic) comparison and analysis beyond that afforded by medical practice. The QALY metric has a universal vocation, as it proposes a criterion that permits the comparison between the most diverse (therapeutic) alternatives.

In comparison with other health economic techniques, a cost-effectiveness comparison using QALY enacts a more advanced economization of health practices. QALY-based calculations are not limited to comparisons between treatments targeted to patients having the same illness. A pharmaceutical that has its qualities assessed through a cost-effectiveness analysis using QALY can differ substantially from one assessed in a clinical trial or on clinical use. The QALY metric performs the dual function of a) rendering treatments that are not comparable in clinical practice, comparable such that b) treatments which are different by clinical standards can become equivalent in terms of cost per QALY. The use of QALY provides an economic qualification that seeks to apply no matter what the clinical or bio-medical qualifications are elsewhere. Qualifying drugs using QALYs is intended to transcend how these pharmaceuticals are defined/qualified by firms, researchers or physicians interacting with patients. The qualification of pharmaceuticals produced in this way establishes a metric that renders more specialized qualifications local and specific, without denying their relevance. The scope of comparison provided by the health economic calculations is in principle only limited by the ability to configure a common effect metric with which to compare pharmaceuticals or indeed any other treatment. For this reasons, we can say that QALYs establishes an economic space which constitutes in and of itself a powerful economization device.

Enacting an economic space through the use of QALYs forges some comparability between qualifying practices of lesser scope. Yet, various other modes of qualification can prevail in parallel. This multiplicity poses no demand on coordination as long as different versions of the same pharmaceutical are enacted in different practices. This is no longer true, however, if and when a particular metric seeks to enact its own version across a multitude of practices. It is precisely this challenge of coordinating multiple versions of drugs which is what the LFN faces. As we will now briefly present, this confrontation can be crucial for the work of economization.

The negotiation of an economic qualification and its devices

The LFN is one of several Swedish government initiatives launched in the last 20 years to influence public health care spending. The Agency was established in October 2002 following widely publicized Cabinet decisions in 2001 to exclude Xenical and Viagra from the public pharmaceutical reimbursement system (Junker, 2003).

Prior to its creation, there was no general evaluation of the subsidization status of prescription drugs. After a new product was approved for use in Sweden based on a medical evaluation undertaken by the Medical Product Agency (or by the EMEA, its European equivalent), the product was automatically included in the public benefit (LFN, 2002). The decision of whether or not to subsidize a product was left to the discretion of the attending physician who decided whether to prescribe a product with subsidy, on a case by case basis.[6] Since it was rare for prescription medication to not be subsidized, the creation of the LFN de facto disentangled the decision to prescribe a drug from the decision to subsidize its use. When a product is denied subsidization by the Agency, it can still be prescribed but its full cost must be assumed by the patient.

The LFN is responsible both for evaluating new products being introduced to the Swedish market and for reviewing the subsidization status of the existing pharmaceutical assortment. In its decisions, the LFN can choose to include or exclude a product from the public subsidy. Products might also be included with restrictions, as was the case when the Agency limited subsidy of Xenical to patients with severe obesity.[7]

The LFN's goal to 'contribute to a rational and cost-effective public use of medicinal products' (LFN, 2002: 2) frames the Agency's work as that of comparing benefits and costs of treatments *according to a health economic approach*.[8] It is said, however, that the Agency is not to make its decisions based only on economic calculations. The Agency must also take into account ostensibly 'non-economic' variables. In particular, the LFN is instructed to adhere to three governing principles in its evaluations: (1) *equal human value*, stating that all people have an equal right to life and health; (2) *need solidarity*, meaning that those with greatest need of treatment should have priority over those with lesser need.; and (3) *cost-effectiveness*, imposing that the benefit of treatment must be reasonable in relation to the cost of treatment (New Pharmaceutical Benefits Bill, 2001).[9] The practical interpretation of these principle instructions, however, is left to the LFN, thus the Agency has been given the explicit directive to 'build practice' (New Pharmaceutical Benefits Bill, 2001: 36, 47).

In what follows, we will examine several exemplary cases in order to shed light on the conditions under which this economization work occurs, as well as on the interpretations it requires.

During its first year of operation, the Agency concentrated on evaluating newly introduced products. In October 2003, the LFN began to work on evaluating the full product assortment under subsidy at the time of its creation (LFN, 2003c). The first evaluations concerned two therapeutic areas: migraine and stomach acid-related syndromes (henceforth migraine and stomach-acid) and were undertaken by project groups designated within the Agency.[10] Undertaking these evaluations required a successive mobilization of various resources to forge comparisons between products. The project groups were required to determine exactly what they should be comparing, how, and which conclusions to draw regarding each pharmaceutical's future subsidy.

Delineating which products should be compared

Different ways of classifying/qualifying encountered one another when the LFN began delineating comparable groups of pharmaceuticals. To resolve the clash between different classifications, the Agency sought to establish a 'mediated register' of similarity and difference.

The first step was designating migraine and stomach-acid groups as pilot cases. Both of these groups were created using the ATC (LFN, 2003b: 6; 2003e: 1). The second tier of the ATC – therapeutic subgroups – was chosen to serve as the primary point of departure for the LFN's categorization since '... this level corresponds in most cases to the pharmaceuticals which are treatment alternatives for an illness' (LFN, 2003b: 6). In creating groups of comparable pharmaceuticals, the drugs' similar physical therapeutic impact qualified them as essentially the same. This forged a link between the ATC-codes' classification of pharmaceuticals and the use of the pharmaceuticals in clinical practice.

In the case of migraine, the use of the ATC classification system to delineate a group of products was considered 'straight-forward' (project manager, migraine, interview 2004-02-27). A key reason for this was that the chosen ATC-code delineated a group of products primarily used to treat a single main diagnosis: migraine.[11] The ATC-defined category was therefore similar to the categorization of products made in clinical medical practice. In the case of stomach-acid, however, the classification of products using the ATC was not deemed to reflect medical practice. Specifically, the ATC-based group was insufficiently differentiated and did not reflect that the pharmaceuticals were used to treat different types of illnesses (project manager, stomach-acid, interview 2004-01-28). The discrepancy led to modifications of the ATC-based group.

The ATC code identified as relevant for delineating the stomach-acid group (as described in LFN, 2003e) defines a group of *Drugs for Acid-related disorders*.[12] Simply put: the code forges a link between *all* pharmaceuticals in the group and *all* acid-related disorders. Yet this link was seen as problematic since all acid-related disorders were not treated in the same way. Both clinical practitioners and clinical studies described dissimilar usages of pharmaceuticals for treating different illnesses. The ATC-based definition of similarity and difference between the pharmaceuticals also differed from another classification of these products: their MPA-approved treatment areas.[13] The MPA classification forged other links between drugs and their use in clinical medical practice. The difference can be illustrated using the example of the proton pump inhibitors, a number of chemically similar stomach-acid treating drugs which were described by project group members as widely recognized for 'problematic usage in medical practice' (project member, stomach-acid, interview 2004-03-23).[14]

The previously mentioned level of the ATC classification system makes all proton pump inhibitors the same. The differentiation according to chemical structure and defined treatment dosages which occurs further down in the classification scheme is not visible. In contrast, there are slight differences in the MPA-approved wording of each proton pump inhibitor's treatment areas. This is the case both for chemically different proton pump inhibitors and for chemically identical products. In short, the MPA-approved treatment areas qualify none of the proton pump inhibitors as exactly the same. Since this did not reflect that products were used as substitutes in medical practice – albeit for treating different illnesses – the LFN project group found it necessary to re-arrange both the ATC and the MPA-based classifications.

A re-arrangement was necessary to reduce the differentiation between pharmaceuticals, as defined by the MPA's approved treatment areas, while not completely removing the differentiation of products, as in the case of the ATC category (project manager, stomach-acid, interview 2004-03-14). The LFN's own classification needed to reflect that products were used differently to treat certain dissimilar illnesses, since these differences were anticipated to create disparities in the calculated effectiveness of products (project manager, stomach-acid, interview 2004-06-09). The project group decided upon a 'working categorization' of five types of acid-related diagnoses in discussion with the formally appointed expert group.[15] Costs and effects of product usage were subsequently sought for each of the five diagnoses.

To summarize: in the stomach-acid group of products, representations of medical practice were brought in to temper both the ATC-generated groups and the MPA treatment areas. Establishing a 'mediated register' of similarity and difference was perceived to be necessary for the LFN's credibility among medical practitioners. Medical practice was a target for intervention by the LFN, but the Agency lacked powerful techniques for ensuring compliance with its decisions.[16] The Agency's own qualification system therefore needed to take into account how clinical practitioners, as represented by the formally appointed group of experts, apparently qualified various pharmaceuticals in terms of similarities and differences.

Choosing which use of pharmaceuticals to compare

Creating groups of comparable products, then, was problematic. This was not for a lack of existing classifications tools. The concern was rather that none of the individual classifications worked fully for the LFN. Different versions of pharmaceuticals were brought in as resources to contribute to the making of new qualifications. In particular, a representation of medical practice was used to modify other classifications of pharmaceuticals when delineating groups of comparable products. But representations of this practice were not a coherent resource. While they supplied a means of modifying and stabilizing a categorization of products in the aforementioned case, they could also disrupt the Agency's work of comparing and evaluating drugs. Notably, classifications of pharmaceuticals from medical practice were set aside when they were seen as interfering with the inferred classification of relevant similarity and difference in the Agency's legal instructions.

In the stomach-acid group, where LFN had configured a working classification of five diagnoses, there arose the possibility of diagnosis-based restrictions on subsidization.[17] But such restrictions were considered problematic for several reasons.

Firstly, diagnosis-based restrictions on subsidization were not thought to be effective tools for modifying medical practice (in order to make it more effective). A perceived problem with diagnosis-based restrictions was that they risked being too 'fussy'. Having too many or too detailed restrictions was thought to have the potential of decreasing doctors' compliance (LFN Board chairman, interview 2004-03-24). Yet because medical practice was the target of intervention, LFN had to provide a frame for comparing pharmaceuticals that would make it possible to change this practice.

A second general concern with diagnosis-based restrictions was that they ran counter to the expressed intentions of the legislature that a product-based reimbursement system be maintained (New Pharmaceutical Benefits Bill, 2001). The LFN has the legal right to place diagnosis-based restrictions on a product's subsidization and had already done so in the case of Xenical and a few other drugs. Yet there was a cautious attitude towards foregoing the articulated principle of a product-based subsidization system, precisely because it would be easy to do in most cases. Eventually: 'every product is effective for *some* usage' (project member, migraine, interview 2004-09-28).

The principle of product-based subsidization stated in the law stands in potential conflict with how pharmaceuticals are routinely qualified by (certain levels of) ATC-classification tools, the MPA-approved treatment areas and medical practice. The latter three classifications share a focus on therapeutic effects. A given pharmaceutical can be qualified as having many effects, and therefore multiple costs when used to treat different diagnoses. This gives rise to a range of possibilities regarding a given pharmaceutical's use. In contrast, the idea of a product-based reimbursement system implicitly demands that a drug have only *one* given effect and cost. This means that comparing products in a way which reflected its use in clinical medical practice would frequently lead to conclusions counter to the legislators' wishes.[18]

The law was therefore interpreted as formally excluding certain medical practices from consideration by the LFN. So-called off-label prescription of drugs was one such aspect that was not considered acceptable grounds for subsidy in the LFN's first two subsidization decisions (LFN, 2003f, 2003g). When a pharmaceutical is used 'off-label' it is prescribed for medical conditions for which the drug has not been formally approved by the MPA. There was suspicion, based on accounts from clinical practitioners, that significant off-label prescription was taking place for certain products in the stomach-acid group. This was considered problematic, since off-label prescription was generally described as a possible source of cost inefficiency (LFN director general, interview 2003-11-20). Thus, the example of off-label use illustrates how aspects of medical practice could be disqualified, if they clashed with the Agency's legal instructions.

To reiterate, the two previous examples illustrate that the LFN's difficulties in qualifying drugs was not for lack of existing classification systems. On the contrary, pharmaceuticals were already being performed as similar and different: in ATC-classifications, in their approvals by the MPA, in treatment guidelines, in clinical studies, in representations of clinical practice and in law. Yet none of these individual classifications were deemed fully adequate to work as the classification to be used by the LFN.

Different versions of a pharmaceutical were brought into the LFN as resources for achieving – but also shaping – the Agency's own qualification of the drug. This became further evident in work to determine how to compare the pharmaceuticals *within* the two product groups.

Deciding how to compare products: establishing what kinds of effects and which figures to use when calculating comparisons

An important concern in both project groups was to establish how to make comparisons/qualifications *within* the migraine and stomach-acid groups and more specifically to find a measure of products' effect(s). But what was more precisely an 'effect'? A starting point for discussions in the project groups was an early document issued by the LFN, which stated a preference for using QALY (quality-adjusted life year).

The perceived advantage of QALY was that the metric provided a way to standardize the measure of a product's effects (and its attendant costs) both within and between different therapeutic areas where it might be used. This was thought to allow for greater consistency in the Agency's decision-making. A perceived problem with other effect metrics was their tendency to be closely linked to illness-specific units of measurement. Such measurements were relevant in a specific treatment area, and made it possible to compare products *within* a therapy group, but they made meaningful comparisons *between* therapy areas impossible:

> We want to be able to compare different types of medicines with the same measurement in order to make consistent decisions. Otherwise we have to compare 'a day without stomach-acid symptoms' with 'a day without migraine' or 'one mmHg decrease in blood pressure'. Those are impossible comparisons. Or rather, they are possible but . . . to make a decision you still need a valuation of those states, otherwise it is random. (Health economist, migraine, interview 2004-02-13)

In theory it was uncontroversial to use the QALY as an effect measure. The practical use of QALY, however, soon became problematic in both cases due to perceived difficulties with finding 'good' QALY-measurements.

One complication was that most studies of pharmaceuticals' cost-effectiveness had been done in countries other than Sweden. This was considered to be a potential problem since the cost structure of health care was seen to differ both between countries and between studies (regardless of their geographic location). The project groups did not want to make irrelevant comparisons (between different types of costs) or draw conclusions irrelevant to the Swedish context. There were ways, however, to make foreign studies relevant in a Swedish setting. One way was to replace the values used in calculations with domestic prices for pharmaceuticals and other cost components such as doctors' salaries, the cost of hospital treatment, etc. Another way was to include additional costs in order to broaden the perspective of a study.

So, a lack of *Swedish* studies could be compensated for by using foreign studies as a template and by modifying the actual numbers used in order to calculate appropriate costs per QALY. The qualifications of pharmaceuticals provided by foreign studies were re-qualified by figures from the Swedish market for pharmaceuticals (prices, etc.) and the use of pharmaceuticals in Swedish medical practice (cost of physicians care, etc.).

In the case of migraine, however, there was a lack of clinical studies using QALY measurements. This was judged to be a consequence of the illness itself not being amenable to quantification in QALY terms. One reason for this was that QALY measurements are based on valuing the 'life quality' of different health states. Since migraine is not a 'continuous state of illness', it was difficult to value the quality of life effects of migraine treatments (project member, migraine, interview 2004-03-29). The questionable results of two identified studies which *did* try to compute QALYs were evidence of this difficulty. In one study, the computed QALY value for migraine sufferers was a negative number. This was considered a theoretically thorny issue, since QALY is defined as a value between 1 and 0. It was also deemed a practical problem, since the interpretation of a negative value would be that suffering from migraine was 'worse than being dead' (project member, interview 2004-04-19). Furthermore, since this negative value referred to the temporary situation when the person actually *had* migraine, it was questionable how to compare this QALY-value with QALY measurements in other therapy groups. While the negative value was subsequently supported by results from other studies (albeit using other measurements), it was deemed necessary to find a more robust measure.

The recourse in the case of migraine was to define a 'successful treatment' in accordance with the standard of the International Headache Society (IHS). This was considered a good source, since many pharmaceutical companies had used the organization's definition in their clinical studies of pharmaceuticals. Using this measurement therefore made it possible to compare data from clinical studies of different pharmaceuticals:

There aren't QALYs but there are other effect measurements in the studies, like pain-free at different times . . . And its a special type of pain-free. You have to move from a state of severe or moderate to mild or none. It's a 4-level international scale issued by the International Headache Society . . . and since everyone uses it, you can construct composite measurements afterwards. (Health economist, migraine, interview 2004-09-08)

The classification system used in clinical studies provided an alternative resource for qualifying pharmaceuticals when QALYs could not be put to practical use.

Once again, however, complications arose. One problem was that the International Headache Society standard had changed over time. There was a 'golden standard' at all times, yet not a *common* golden standard (project manager, migraine, interview 2004-06-10). The solution decided on in the project group was to primarily use an older standard when comparing the effect of different products. The effect measure was chosen in part because there was more data available using this measurement. But it was recognized that the measurement did not explicitly encompass a broader number of concerns such as frequency of relapse, side effects and so on.

A second complication when comparing products' effects was that few clinical studies involved direct, so-called head-to-head, comparisons between different pharmaceuticals. Many studies compared a single pharmaceutical compound with a placebo, or with the first patented product within its chemical class. Studies also differed with regard to the selection of patients and the length of time studied. As a consequence, each clinical study provided a *partial* qualification of *certain* drugs in the migraine group. The difficulty in creating a *complete* comparison of *all* products was attributed, in part, to pharmaceutical companies' lack of interest in having their products become the same as other pharmaceuticals. According to one migraine project member:

> The LFN is interested in comparing all the different therapeutic alternatives for treating migraine. But this is not necessarily the interest of the pharmaceutical companies. They don't want their product to be like everyone else's. For them it is valuable to be differentiated and the studies are arguably set up to show a product's specific advantages, such as quick response or sustainable effect. (Pharmacist, migraine, interview 2004-06-10)

The LFN's choice of an effect measure did not resolve these underlying concerns, which refer to more general metrological problems mentioned above. The choice of an effect measure was a necessary step to enable *any* comparison within the delineated group. The Agency resolved the clash of multiple versions by recourse to an external source rather than an Agency-mediated version.

More figures are needed: relating the chosen effect measure to forms of product usage

Another situation, where a particular version of drugs was privileged over another, arose when it came to comparing effect by the milligram or by dose.

This became an issue in the stomach-acid group when the project members identified a review article (Hellström and Vitols, 2003) claiming that the effect per mg (where 'effect' in this case was defined as level of inhibition of gastric acid secretion) of the various stomach-acid medicines was identical, barring one product. The pharmaceuticals, however, were prescribed and sold in tablets of varying strength. The article therefore offered (yet another) delineation of relevant similarity and difference between the pharmaceuticals.

> Deciding whether to use weight or dose as a basis for comparing effect raised the question about how to define a 'dose'. There were many possible sources to draw on. One possible 'dose' was the recommended dose defined by the MPA when approving the product for sale in Sweden. Another 'dose' could be the DDD[19] issued by the World Health Organization (WHO). Clinical trials could be the source of yet other definitions of dose. And all these three (or more) doses could be different than the dosage typically prescribed in Swedish clinical practice. Which dose was the right one to use when comparing costs and effects?

The goal articulated within the stomach-acid group was to use the dosage which most closely represented actual usage in clinical practice (project manager, stomach-acid, interview 2004-06-09). Since this dosage was what was being paid for through the public reimbursement system, it was considered better than more 'theoretical' measurements:

> DDDs are made by going through the literature and finding what the normal dose is for the main diagnosis for an adult. [. . .] [The measurement] was developed to be able to measure pharmaceutical sales with something more clinically relevant than the number of boxes sold. But one might call it a theoretical measure that has been negotiated. So sometimes the defined daily dose works well . . . and for others it is more difficult. For pain relief, the recommended dose might be 2–3 tablets 3–4 times a day. And then looking at how much is really used, there are variations between countries and regions. So what we want is the actual cost in clinical practice but we don't have that data. So it would be easier if it were mg compared to mg, or defined doses if they are correct. The problem is that the doctors may have a completely different idea [from the MPA's]. (Pharmacologist, stomach-acid, interview 2004-06-09 and 2004-09-28)

There were no readily available measurement(s) for 'real' product dosage. The discussion about which of the sources of dosage definitions to use, however, was put on hold when questions were raised regarding the legal status of the MPA's approved doses. While there had been limited concern with modifying the products' MPA-approved treatment areas, as had been done when defining a mediated registry of comparable products in the stomach-acid group, there was less certainty concerning the possibility of redefining the approved doses. The matter was taken out of the project group and the LFN's in-house lawyers were given the task to determine whether the Agency was legally required to use the MPA's dosage definition. Their conclusion was that this was indeed the case. Hence, the MPA-approved doses were used to specify the comparable dosage for each pharmaceutical in the stomach-acid group. As in the case of off-label prescription, the actual medical practice was not the relevant source of the LFN's qualification of pharmaceuticals.

To sum up, then, the question of defining effect measurements which was theoretically resolved using QALY was reopened when QALY measurements were not readily available in these two cases. Defining an alternative effect measure required the mobilization of resources, notably clinical studies of various kinds, where other effect measurements were supplied. As with defining the product groups for comparison, however, it became necessary to confront alternative qualifications of pharmaceuticals and their usage provided by legal documents, other governmental agencies, scientific articles and medical practice. In the case of dosages, the conflict between versions was resolved when the classifications articulated by the MPA were imposed for legal reasons.

How to determine a reasonable cost of pharmaceutical treatment: reflecting on calculating values

The previous examples show how LFN devised new versions of pharmaceuticals, 'disqualified' certain ways of grouping them and resolved conflicts by privileging classifications systems and by establishing tinkered compromises. But, having brought into being a way of articulating the cost-effectiveness of pharmaceuticals, the LFN's employees reflected on the need to modify the conclusions being drawn on the basis of these calculations. Just as we signalled earlier, the economization work demanded by the Agency included broader concerns than just computing and comparing costs and effects. 'Economization' also meant reflecting on issues such as the importance of maintaining competition among firms; a calculation of the costs and advantages of diversity; and taking into account intellectual property rights. To perform economic markets, then, meant going over and above the implementation of QALY as a device. What was required of the Agency was that it internalize in the design of tools and devices of evaluation, elements that would permit it to promote a process of economization while still considering ostensibly non-economic qualities of the drugs being evaluated. This broadening of purpose is precisely what is implied by the decision criterion of 'reasonable cost' (which, as a reminder, must equally enact the notion of equity and solidarity).

Deciding on an effect measure did not resolve the crucial question of what constituted a 'reasonable' cost of product usage. A comparison of the cost per chosen effect metric provided an order of *relative*, not absolute, cost-effectiveness. Another problem was that the relative effect measures were seen to create 'too precisely' defined categories of cost-efficient use. This was not coherent with the 'sliding scale' of cost-effectiveness in medical practice. To define a precise boundary for effective usage and then use this boundary as a decision-rule for including or excluding a product from the public pharmaceutical benefits scheme was not desirable:

> There is no measurement were at 100 you're ok and at 98 you're not. There are no clear limits. [. . .] When looking at cost-effectiveness you have a patient with a cost of

1 SEK and then a progressively increasing cost. You don't have one group with a common cost of 100 SEK for each QALY and another where the cost is 10,000 SEK and it is easy to define. (Pharmacologist, stomach-acid, interview 2005-05-25)

So, the effort made by the LFN to define 'good' – representative, accurate, common – measurements still did not solve crucial matters regarding the *absolute* and *precise* value of a pharmaceutical. A recurring opinion was that the Agency's calculations of cost-effectiveness should not be used to identify the (most) cost-effective product and remove subsidy for all products but this one within a given therapy area (LFN director general, interview 2003-10-24; project manager, stomach-acid, interview 2003-10-09). Product diversity was perceived to be necessary for reasons such as allowing doctors a variety of treatment choices, fostering competitive pressure on products' prices and giving economic incentives for further research. The calculative tools used by the LFN to create comparable registers of effects and costs were not themselves a source of 'reasonable' solutions:

> Theoretically, even the smallest difference in price for the same effect of treatment means an infinite cost per QALY. But that is not reasonable, to exclude everything else but one . . . So the question remains: what is an acceptable cost for diversity? (Health economist, stomach-acid, interview 2005-06-01)

The question of what constituted a 'reasonable cost of diversity' became a practical concern when discussing the comparison between branded (patented) products and generic products (for which patents have expired) in the stomach-acid group. Here, the theoretically posited advantage of competition on price formation was one argument for not comparing branded and generic pharmaceuticals too closely. In addition to limiting therapeutic choice, it would be detrimental to future medical research in the field if only the cheapest product(s) were left in a group (Health economist, stomach-acid, interview 2004-12-17). Yet competition was also an argument for why branded products *should* be compared with each other and with generic products. The use of common metrics for comparing pharmaceuticals was supposed to standardize the products and support an informed choice of effective treatments. Pharmaceutical companies had a choice whether to develop and patent products after similar products had come to market:

> To have a patent does not mean a complete lack of competition. It only says no one else can produce and sell a specific substance [. . .] [and] therapeutic competition between substances is very important. Companies developing me-too products know that other products are ahead of them [. . .]. So on the one hand you want competition but also incentives for further research. (Health economist, stomach-acid, interview 2005-06-01)

Qualifying branded and generic products as the same or different had profound implications for the LFN's conclusions regarding products' continued subsidization. For example, since the effect of all but one of the proton pump inhibitors in the stomach-acid group had been deemed to be similar (as there was no adequately convincing evidence that they were different), the differences in price between certain branded and generic pharmaceuticals suggested that most of the former products be excluded from the pharmaceutical benefits scheme.

The migraine group, where all the products were still under patent, faced a somewhat different question: how to compare products when it was known that the patent for one pharmaceutical was due to expire in a few years. Patent expirations were expected to lead to a significant fall in product price. This was relevant, since one of the drug's doses was twice the cost per tablet as the competing products. In the future, this price could be expected to fall and if the future price was used to evaluate the product it might remain subsidized. One argument for not considering future prices was that the future was uncertain. Only observable, current prices and products should be considered when performing evaluations. A further argument for not using future or historical prices when drawing cost-effectiveness conclusions was that pricing was market-based and therefore subject to further change following patent expirations. Since price was thought to be a critical factor for determining cost-effectiveness, it was always necessary to use actual prices (Project manager, migraine, interview 2004-06-10; Health economist, migraine, interview 2004-06-07).

In the end, the then-current prices of migraine products were compared, and one dosage of the market leading product was denied further subsidy (LFN, 2005). In the stomach-acid group, a direct comparison of patented and non-patented pharmaceuticals ultimately supported decisions to remove subsidy for a number of the branded drugs (LFN, 2006). Products to be removed were defined on the basis of a price corridor. Products which had been deemed to have 'the same' treatment effect could not be priced at more than 25 per cent of the cheapest pharmaceutical. The tolerance of seeming cost-inefficiency (paying more for the same thing) was justified in part with reference to the smaller variations in effect that were not captured by the common effect measure. Additional arguments related to the aforementioned matters of competitive pricing and adequate research incentives.

Advancing a process of health care economization by redistributing agencies

The Agency's work described in this chapter has translated into the implementation of an ensemble of qualification and calculative devices that seek to take into account various sources of medical, ethical and legal classifications of drugs, while at the same time constructing a calculative space that can advance a process of health care economization. The case of the LFN has exemplified how this work depends on making a compound calculative space by coordinating existing classification devices. Step by step, we have seen how the qualification of pharmaceuticals by the LFN takes into account their clinical characterization. In some cases, the Agency's qualification work reduced the multiplicity of recommendations for the same treatment, or introduced a metric for identifying and comparing costs and effects. It took into account central categories for practitioners such as dosage, and in a more general manner, internalized institutional elements usually considered relevant to politics or ethics within algorithms of valuation.

To address the matter of which manner of coordination is achieved in a detailed and convincing manner would require that we take a sufficiently large step back into history in order to give details on the evolution of the decision criteria used, and the qualification practices of different actors in health care. The next section will be limited to a few preliminary considerations that highlight the (potential) effects of the Agency's work on the calculative capacities of these actors, notably on the configuration of practitioners and patients as buyers of pharmaceuticals. We argue that the LFN configures both practitioners and patients as 'users', regardless of the qualification of drugs enacted by these actors. The Agency thereby corners them into the supply side of markets-in-the-making. To give a sense of one possible interpretation of these mechanisms, we will use Mol and Law's approach to multiplicity. This approach allows us to nicely capture how a certain autonomy of practitioners and patients can prevail while they at the same time are framed, by economic calculations.

Coordinating multiple versions of pharmaceuticals

A focus on multiplicity in practices of qualification implies a close attention to how *conflicting* versions of objects are coordinated. Mol talks of *incompatible* versions of an object *clashing* when encountering one another in the same practice.[20] As Mol (1999, 2002) and Law (2002a) have stressed, to talk about 'the multiple' is to talk about how what could be termed as different versions of an object are enacted. An object is made to be different things in different practices. The object is not fragmented, yet not unitary.

Mol (2002) identifies two overarching techniques for coordinating multiple versions of an object: *addition* and *calibration*. These notions provide our starting point for discussing the coordination of the multiple versions of pharmaceuticals' qualification. *Addition* is reasonably simple to achieve when different versions of an object *coincide*, for example when different measurement practices both ascribe an object the same quality (say, for instance, two different measurement techniques suggesting the same health-economic value for a pharmaceutical). In such cases, the different versions of the object support one another in becoming a common qualified object. Mol also describes addition of incompatible versions of an object. This activity involves the conflict between versions being dispelled by *privileging* one version over another (Mol, 2002: 63–64).

Calibration is an alternative to adding up different versions of an object. Calibration counters 'the threat of incommensurability [. . .] by establishing common measures [which allow for] the possibility (never friction free) of *translations*' between different versions of an object' (Mol, 2002: 85). This implies reaching an agreement on the means of translation. Once such 'rules' are available, it is possible for different versions to stand in for one another. For example, having a certain result in one measurement could be taken to imply a certain measurement in another (making it unnecessary to actually perform the second measurement).

Our account of LFN's work arguably contains instances of both these techniques for coordination. Yet we have also found other examples of coordination not as precisely outlined within this framework. We can expand on Mol's typology to include additional means through which to coordinate multiple versions of objects.

When following LFN's work, we found few examples where different versions of pharmaceuticals *coincided*. This is perhaps in part a consequence of the fact that it may be easier to identify instances where versions clash and where effort is spent to coordinate them. Coordinating versions of a pharmaceutical that agree is not necessarily a visible achievement. When, as in the case of the headache group, it was 'straightforward' to add up versions of pharmaceuticals into the same group since ATC and medical practice coincided, no further effort was put into coordinating these two versions of the pharmaceuticals.

We have seen instances where coordination was achieved by *privileging,* in the sense of excluding certain versions. Such exclusion, however, was not as complete as suggested by Mol's notion of privileging. We have only seen partial privileging where certain qualities of a version were excluded. There was no instance where a single version of a pharmaceutical was fully privileged over all others.

One clear example of partial privileging was the definition of the dose for comparing drugs' effects and costs. Appropriate dose was a quality of pharmaceuticals as performed in many different practices: in medical practice, by the MPA, in clinical studies and by organizations such as the WHO. In this case, the different versions were coordinated by privileging the MPA's version of pharmaceuticals' doses. One reason for doing so was the perceived legal status of this version. Yet, as we will return to below, the MPA register of similarity and difference was not fully used to delineate comparable groups of drugs. Hence *partial privileging* denotes the case where one quality of one version is privileged, but where the version as a whole is not privileged over other versions.

The most obvious example of *calibration* was the use of the International Headache Society migraine measurement. Different versions of pharmaceuticals performed in different clinical studies were coordinated using a version from elsewhere. Another example was when LFN tackled the lack of domestic studies of products' effects and costs by using known techniques for translating these results into Swedish conditions. Once this had been done by the LFN project group's health economist, it was not considered critical to conduct Swedish studies.

The three preceding techniques for coordination are largely based on Mol's notions of addition and calibration. The following two – negotiation and suppression – are outcomes of the present study, in so much as they outline other observed techniques of coordination.

Coordination through *mediating* versions of pharmaceuticals is best illustrated in the work to create groups of comparable stomach-acid drugs. The quality being mediated here was for which indication the pharmaceuticals should be used. Here the ATC-code and the MPA-approved treatment areas did not add up to create a common register of similarity and difference. The recourse was to use medical practice to craft a 'mediated register' of five diagnoses which performed both similarity (ATC) and difference (MPA) between drugs. This was necessary to ensure acceptance among professional practitioners. This can be seen as an insight that it was necessary for the LFN to perform a version which would make it possible to intervene in medical practice. *Mediating,* then, denotes the case where the resulting quality is the outcome of negotiation among the diverging qualities of the clashing versions.

Another example of coordinating versions through mediating qualities was the discussion concerning the status of the LFN's own cost-effectiveness calculations. Cost-effectiveness was needed as a basis for the Agency's decision, and calculations establishing cost-effectiveness were at work. Yet such calculations were not used to the extent that they created a set of therapeutic markets with only one subsidized pharmaceutical. Competition, it seems, was also to be given room in the qualifications. The notion of cost-effectiveness and the notion of efficiency through competition were made to collaborate by introducing and accepting a cost of diversity as defined by a price corridor. The mediation sought was thus to not let cost-effectiveness calculations fully qualify the pharmaceuticals. In short, differing versions were coordinated by creating a 'composite' of versions of pharmaceuticals (cf Mol, 2002: 71).

Coordination through *suppression*, finally, is akin to both partial privileging and mediating. It is exemplified by the LFN's consideration of off-label prescription of drugs when determining what product usages to compare. Off-label prescription reveals that medical practice finds drugs useful in ways not aligned with their MPA approval. Yet, the classification inferred by off-label use was not included in LFN's qualification. This coordination of versions was not a pure case of privileging the MPA-based classification, since other uses of pharmaceuticals in medical practice were allowed to inform LFN's grouping of comparable stomach-acid drugs.

What more, there is an underlying ambiguity which is contained in the coordinated version. An analogy would be to sit on a suitcase in order to close it, knowing full well that the wrapped gifts inside might be ruined – but not being overly concerned because someone else will be opening them. It is our speculation that suppression is a fairly instable form of coordination – though not necessarily for the LFN. It risks breaking apart in another setting (in the case of off-label use, this might occur in the budgeting process of organizations where off-label prescription of drugs gives rise to costs). What suppression denotes is thus a postponement of the resolution of ambiguity regarding a pharmaceutical's qualities (cf Rappert, 2001), while still achieving present comparability and calculability. The concept of suppression seeks to *explicitly* capture a more tenuous achievement of coordination than that captured by the concept of privileging.

Interfering with economic agents and reframing their agencies through the economic qualification of goods

Mol assists us in understanding the complex coordination of multiple versions of an object when engaging in qualification to enact economic calculation. Our interest in this section is for how 'the Agency', in coordinating between many qualifications of pharmaceuticals, contributes to formatting *agencies* with calculative capacities that can be called economic.

Each version of a pharmaceutical is associated in specific ways with *other* objects/actors. Enacting one version of a pharmaceutical may very likely entail enacting a specific version of an illness, a specific stratification of patients and non-patients and indeed a specific version of efficiency of treatment (Mol, 1999: 82). One version of an object might interfere with other competing versions without reducing them (Mol, 2002: 142–144). On this notion of interference see also Haraway (1991), Law (2002b) and for its very first conceptualization in social sciences: Serres (1972).

When looking at the work undertaken to qualify pharmaceuticals, it is clear that it produces interferences in terms of other subjects' agency. Such considerations surface in questions about what scope of calculative agency is and ought to be allocated to physicians, patients, pharmacies and pharmaceutical companies, and so on.

One reason why the issue of agency becomes pertinent is that the LFN is set to intervene in what pharmaceuticals patients use, and hence what physicians prescribe. Yet, agency is also pertinent since the resources LFN draws upon in making its qualifications – such as the ATC-classification, health economic assessment techniques, economics, representations of clinical practice – bring about interfering performances of these subjects' respective agency. Take a calculation of cost-effectiveness, for instance. In its pure form, such a qualification of pharmaceuticals leaves it to the physicians and patients to establish the diagnosis and then to prescribe and use the corresponding qualified cost-effective pharmaceutical. In such a case, much of the calculative capacity is reserved for a calculative centre like the LFN, where metrological networks establishing costs and effects convene to perform the calculations.

In the work described here, however, we encountered a more composite distribution of agencies. The LFN's work aims at not circumventing other subjects' agency too much, yet still intervening in these other agencies. It also entails the LFN constructing its *own* agency through its use of different techniques and tools. As Ashmore, Mulkay and Pinch (1989: 88) also noted in their study of health economics introduction in the Bristish National Health Service, the QALY measure was developed as a way to circumvent a perceived lack of 'normal' markets within health care.[21] Calculating and comparing cost per QALY might therefore be seen as a way to perform a 'societal buyer', since the measurement allows for comparisons between treatments which are not choice alternatives in medical practice. Clearly the work to qualify pharmaceuticals at the LFN involves not only the qualification of goods transacted on the market for pharmaceuticals. This work also entails formatting and distributing the calculative agencies in these markets in the making.

Conclusions

In this chapter, we have looked at some ancillary qualification work which participates in constituting the (so-called/not so) invisible hand of markets through the qualification of goods to be exchanged and a consequent configuration of market actors.

What we have seen, indeed, is a qualifying hand, coordinating the multiple and involving a wide gamut of techniques and principles (including such notions as equal human value, need solidarity and cost-effectiveness). This hand takes part in actively qualifying the goods traded, and by configuring calculating tools and agencies which can further perform the market.

The case presented here suggests the constitution of an economic space which performs actors and objects as *economic* agents and goods through the enactment of tools and devices from the applied branch of health economics. As we have seen, these devices essentially consist of an assembly of instruments and rules which are intended to classify goods. To take up the vocabulary suggested by the 'performativity programme', these devices qualify and render calculable, and therefore make economic evaluation possible. In contrast to analyses done by Mary Hesse (1974), these classification activities are not limited to the universe of mental or conceptual categories. They are, rather better described as devices, mixing discursive elements, categories, algorithms, rules and regulations, and material practices (Bowker and Star, 1999). Although made up of many heterogeneous elements, these devices are market devices because they render, as we have shown, a process of economization.

The economization of ways of doing evaluation requires coordination between multiple qualifications. In this example, the emergent pre-eminence of explicitly economic forms follows from a certain success with crafting a calculative metric that enacts the usual actors in health care as economic agents, by formatting and redistributing their calculative capacities and competencies.

The analysis which we have proposed is a contribution to social studies of processes of economization. This approach shows how market spaces can be built in a way to include goods, and the practices of actors that have previously been situated outside of market exchange. The approach also shows that if this economization succeeds it is because it retains its compatibility with other modalities of qualifying and valuing goods. It reinforces ideas, like those of Zelizer (2005), that insist on the multiplicity of market forms and of their inescapable interweaving with non-market forms. But the analysis also benefits from the social studies of science, notably from Law and Mol's work, to show that this multiplicity, because it is anchored in material devices, is not a linear performance of 'the economy' but an emergent shaping of 'economy'.

Notes

1 The empirical material used in this paper was collected by Ebba Sjögren as part of a study on the work within the LFN (Sjögren, 2006). Primary data was collected through tape-recorded semi-structured interviews with employees within the LFN. All secondary sources are public documents. A previous version of this paper was presented at the session 'On social and consumer sciences shaping market(-ing) practices' at the 4S/EASST Conference in 2004. The authors would like to thank Barbara Czarniawska, Lars Norén and colleagues for comments.
2 A precursor to the current classification system was first developed by Norwegian researchers in the late 1960s and early 1970s. In 1981, the WHO Regional Office for Europe recommended the ATC system for international drug utilisation studies. In connection with this, the WHO Collaborating Centre for Drug Statistics Methodology was established. In 1996, WHO recognized the need to develop use of the ATC/DDD system as an international standard for drug utilisation studies. The Centre was therefore linked directly to WHO Headquarters in Geneva (http://www.whocc.no/atcddd/atcsystem.html; downloaded 2004-09-28).
3 The first level of the ATC code is based on a letter for the anatomical group, eg, 'B' for blood and blood forming organs. The second level is therapeutic subgroup, eg, 'B03' for anti-anemic preparations. Level three is pharmacological subgroup, eg, 'B03A' for iron preparations. The fourth level is chemical subgroup, eg, 'B03AA' for iron, bivalent, oral preparations. Finally the fifth level is the subgroup for chemical substance, eg, 'B03AA07' for ferrous sulphate. Since pharmaceuticals may have several therapeutic uses, the basic principle is that products are classified according to the main therapeutic use of the main active ingredient.
4 A parallel reasoning in marketing is Levitt's classical argument that firms should not view themselves as belonging to industries of this or that specific product or service but see their business from the viewpoint of why customers want to do business with them. Companies operating railroads should, he exemplified, understand themselves as providing transportation services rather than running railroad operations (Levitt, 1960).
5 An illustrative example: being severely depressed might be given a QALY value of 0,6. A one-time treatment which removed this depression and made the individual otherwise perfectly healthy, would have a positive effect of 0,4 QALY (the difference of moving from 0,6 to 1). If this treatment cost €500, the cost per QALY would be the cost of the treatment, divided by the increase in QALY for the patient's remaining life expectancy, hence €500/(0,4 QALY*remaining life years). For a further elaboration of QALYs and how they are assessed, see (Drummond *et al.*, 1997) or indeed the discussion in chapter 5 of Ashmore, Mulkay and Pinch (1989).
6 In addition, there were, and still are guidelines issued to guide the physicians in their choice of treatments. For instance, a pharmaceutical committee in each county council produces regional prescription guidelines, with recommendations about which pharmaceuticals should be prescribed (and subsidized). Yet, national or county council guidelines are not legally binding for the physician.
7 This is defined by a specific clinical measurement (LFN, 2003d).
8 This approach appeared to be an accepted and shared view within the Agency organization, while some members of the Board in later interviews expressed an opinion that there was 'at times too much talk about health economics' (Board member, interview 2004-07-01).
9 The Pharmaceutical Benefits Act of 11 April 2002 (ref. no. SFS, 2002: 160), which governs the LFN's activities, was passsed into law after the submission of the New Pharmaceutical Benefits Bill (ref. no. 2001/02:63) on 13 December 2001.
10 LFN is comprised of two organizational entities: the Bureau and the Board. A project group within the Bureau prepares a presentation memo detailing their evaluation of a pharmaceutical's medical and economic efficiency for the Board. The decision regarding the subsidization status of the product is then made by the Board (LFN, 2003a). Each project group includes two in-house pharmacologists and a health economist, as well as external medical experts within the areas where the products are approved for usage. These experts are formally contracted as

consultants to the project group and lack a veto as to what decision is recommended by the project team (LFN, 2003b).
11 The group of drugs was also used to treat a second, significantly less common diagnosis: Horton's headache, also known as 'Cluster headaches' (LFN, 2005a).
12 As defined by the WHO collaboration centre (http://www.whocc.no/atcddd/; downloaded 2004-09-28).
13 The project members referred both to the MPA's product résumés and to the wording in FASS (FArmaceutiska Specialiteer i Sverige). FASS is an information service provided by The Swedish Association of the Pharmaceutical Industry, the trade association for the pharmaceutical industry in Sweden. Until 1994 the Swedish government (via the MPA) directly approved all texts that were presented in FASS. Following Sweden's entry into the EU, however, the MPA no longer has this role. Instead the MPA issues so-called Summary of Product Characteristics (SPC) which in some cases may include information excluded from FASS. While FASS texts are acknowledged to be written based on approved SPC's, the actual texts are not approved by the MPA (http://www.mpa.se/observanda/obs00/fass.shtml; downloaded 2004-09-28).
14 One perceived problem with proton pump inhibitors was their prescription to patients with less pressing stomach ailments that were not shown in clinical studies to be treatable with these drugs, and/or might be treated by other, non-pharmaceutical means such as dietary modifications.
15 The expert group was appointed early in the study. It is comprised of two medical doctors: one with a research/specialist background, the other with a general practitioner/clinical background. The working categorization was also perceived to be supported by clinical studies and a recent knowledge overview issued by another governmental agency (östman et al., 2000, issued by The Swedish Council on Technology Assessment in Health Care).
16 The exception is when a pharmaceutical is completely removed from the public reimbursement system. When this is done, this total restriction is coded into the pharmacies' product database. Diagnosis-based restrictions, however, can theoretically be circumvented if the prescribing doctor checks the 'with subsidy' box on the prescription form, even for patients who do not fulfil the criteria for subsidization.
17 Diagnosis-based restrictions involve subsidizing a drug for certain treatments but not others, as defined by the patient's diagnosed illness. One example where this was used was in the decision to limit the subsidy of treatment with the drug Xenical to patients with more severe forms of obesity, as defined by a particular measurement of body mass.
18 It should be noted that an additional prerequisite for such a mismatch to occur is that there is a difference between the areas where a pharmaceuticals can be/is used in medical practice, and the areas where the pharmaceutical's usage is deemed cost-effective. If all usage is cost-effective (or ineffective), then there is no visible mismatch between a product-based reimbursement system and a therapeutic-based evaluation of pharmaceuticals effectiveness.
19 DDDs ('defined daily doses') are standardized treatment doses defined by the WHO and linked to the ATC classification system. The official definition of DDD is: 'the assumed average maintenance dose per day for a drug used for its main indication [according to the ATC classification system] in adults'. It is explicitly stated on the WHO collaboration center's homepage that DDD 'is a unit of measurement and does not necessarily reflect the recommended or prescribed daily dose' (http://www.whocc.no/atcddd/atcsystem.html#6; downloaded 2004-09-28).
20 It is perhaps needless to say, but potentially conflicting versions of an object might very well silently co-exist in unrelated practices, although it is questionable whether they in such instances can be said to be versions of *one* object. Such incompatibility between versions is not sustainable in one practice, and much work is done to reconcile and relate versions to one another.
21 Health care is often described by economists as an imperfect market, in part due to difficulties in defining the customer or buyer since both treatment choices and the costs of health care often are carried by third parties ie, doctors and states or private insurance companies, respectively.

References

Ashmore, M., M. Mulkay and T. J. Pinch (1989), *Health and efficiency: A sociology of health economics*. Milton Keynes: Open University Press.
Berg, M. (1997), *Rationalizing medical work: Decision-support techniques and medical practices*. Cambridge (Massachusetts): MIT Press.
Bowker, G. C. and S. L. Star (1999), *Sorting things out: Classification and its consequences*. Cambridge (Massachusetts): MIT Press.
Callon, M. (1998), 'Introduction: The embeddedness of economic markets in economics', in M. Callon (ed.), *The laws of the markets*. Oxford: Blackwell.
Callon, M., C. Méadel and V. Rabeharisoa (2002), 'The economy of qualities', *Economy and Society*, 31(2): 194–217.
Callon, M. and F. Muniesa (2005), 'Economic markets as calculative collective devices', *Organization Studies*, 26(8): 1229–1250.
Drummond, M. F., B. O'Brien, G. L. Stoddart, and G. W. Torrance (1997), *Methods for the economic evaluation of health care programmes*. Oxford: Oxford University Press.
Greer, A. L., J. S. Goodwin, J. L. Freeman and Z. H. Wu (2002), 'Bringing the patient back in: Guidelines, practice variations, and the social context of medical practice', *International Journal of Technological Assessment in Health Care*, 18(4): 747–761.
Haraway, D. (1991), 'Situated knowledges: The science question in feminism and the privilege of partial perspective', in D. Haraway (ed.), *Simians, cyborgs, and women: The reinvention of nature*. London: Free Association Books.
Helgesson, C.-F., H. Kjellberg and A. Liljenberg (eds) (2004), *Den där marknaden: Utbyten, normer och bilder*. Lund: Studentlitteratur.
Hellström, P. M. and S. Vitols (2003), 'All proton pump inhibitors are equally efficacious in standard dosages', *Läkartidningen*, 100(25): 2212–2216.
Hesse, M. 1974. *The structure of scientific inference*. London: Mac Millan.
Holm, P. (2003), 'Which way is up on Callon?', *Sociologisk årbok*, 8(1): 125–156.
Junker, S. (2003), 'Ett läkemedels öde: Dumpning i en politisk soptunna', working paper, *Score Working Papers*, 2003-2.
Keating, P. and A. Cambrosio (2003), *Biomedical platforms: Realigning the normal and the pathological in late-twentieth-century medicine*. Cambridge (Massachusetts): MIT Press.
Kjellberg, H. and C-F. Helgesson (2006), 'Multiple versions of markets: Multiplicity and performativity in market practice', *Industrial Marketing Management*, 35(7): 839–855.
Lagrelius, A.-M. (2004), 'The Trojan Horse: On guidelines, clinical practice and the translation of responsibility', 4S/EASST Conference, Paris (France), 25–28 August.
Law, J. (2002a), *Aircraft stories: Decentering the object in technoscience*. Durham: Duke University Press.
Law, J. (2002b), 'Economics as interference', in P. du Gay and M. Pryke (eds.), *Cultural economy: Cultural analysis and commercial life*. London: Sage.
LFN (the Pharmaceutical Benefits Board) (2002), 'Informationsbroschyr: Ansvarsområden och arbetsuppgifter'. Public information broschure.
LFN (2003a), 'Arbetsordning'. Reference no. 412/2002. Documentation of formal work processes.
LFN (2003b), 'Arbetsplan för den inledande fasen av genomgà6ngen av läkemedelsortimentet'. Reference no. 1023/2003. Documentation of formal work plan for product assortment review.
LFN (2003c) 'LFN provar subvention av 2000 läkemedel'. Issued 2003-10-21. Press release.
LFN (2003d), 'Villkorat bifall Xenical'. Issued 2003-06-04. Decision justification document.
LFN (2003e), 'Företag och läkemedel – genomgången av medel vid syrarelaterad symtom'. Issued 2003-10-23. Documentation of drugs included in therapy group.
LFN (2003f), 'Avslag för Aunativ'. Issued 2003-01-30. Decision justification document.
LFN (2003g), 'Avslag för Robinul'. Issued 2003-01-30. Decision justification document.

LFN (2005), 'Slutrapport: Genomgången av läkemedel mot migrän'. Issued 2005-02-18. Final report for product assortment review of therapy group.
LFN (2006), 'Slutrapport: Genomgången av läkemedel mot sjukdomar orsakade av magsyra'. Issued 2006-01-19. Final report for product assortment review of therapy group.
Levitt, T. (1960), 'Marketing myopia', *Harvard Business Review*, 38(4): 45–56.
MacKenzie, D., F. Muniesa and L. Siu (eds.) (2007), *Do economists make markets? On the performativity of economics*. Princeton: Princeton University Press.
Mol, A. (1999), 'Ontological politics: A word and some questions', in J. Law and J. Hassard (eds.), *Actor network theory and after*. Oxford: Blackwell.
Mol, A. (2002), *The body multiple: Ontology in medical practice*. Durham: Duke University Press.
New Pharmaceutical Benefits Bill (2001), ref. no. 2001/02:63. Submitted 2001-12-13.
Nord, E. (1999), *Cost-value analysis in health care: Making sense out of QALYs*. Cambridge: Cambridge University Press.
östman, J., I. Agenäs, J. Brun, C-E Elwin, L. Engstrand, S. Johansson, G. Lindberg, L-å Maké, A. Norlund, O. Nyrén, R. Seensalu, K. Sjölund, å. Svensson, J. Wallmark and L. Werkö (2000), 'Ont i magen – metoder för diagnos och behandling av dyspepsi'. Stockholm: SBU Yellow Book.
Rappert, B. (2001), 'The distribution and resolution of the ambiguities of technology, or why Bobby can't spray', *Social Studies of Science*, 31(4): 557–591.
Scherer, F. M. and D. Ross (1990), *Industrial market structure and economic performance*. Boston: Houghton Mifflin.
Serres, M. (1972), *L'interférence*. Paris: Editions de Minuit.
Sjögren, E. (2006), *Reasonable drugs: Making decisions with ambiguous knowledge*. Stockholm: EFI.
Slater, D. (2002), 'From calculation to alienation: Disentangling economic abstractions', *Economy and Society*, 31(2): 234–249.
Thévenot, L. (2001), 'Organized complexity: Conventions of coordination and the composition of economic arrangements', *European Journal of Social Theory*, 4(4): 405–425.
Zelizer, V. (2005), *The purchase of intimacy*. Princeton: Princeton University Press.

Price as a market device: cotton trading in Izmir Mercantile Exchange

Koray Caliskan

Introduction

A mysterious certainty dominates our lives in late capitalist modernity: the price. Not a single day passes without learning, making, and taking it.[1] Yet despite prices' widespread presence around us, we do not know much about them. Economists, regardless of the corrective intervention of institutionalists like North and his followers, described markets as price making contexts, and then explained prices as things that are made in markets (North, 1977; Robinson, 1980). Sociologists and anthropologists attempted to shortcut this circularity in a variety of ways, which made visible the social and cultural nature of prices (Robinson, 1980; Zelizer, 1981; Alexander and Alexander, 1991; Zafirovski, 2000; Geismar, 2001; Velthuis, 2003; Zajac and Westphal, 2004; Velthuis, 2005). Inspired by Polanyi's work and frequently drawing on one of his central concepts, ie, 'embeddedness,' researchers argued that prices are culturally constructed amid relations of power in socially and politically embedded markets (White, 1981; Granovetter, 1985; Fligstein, 1996; DiMaggio and Louch, 1998; Dobbin, 2004; Duina, 2004; Lapavitsas, 2004; Uzzi and Lancaster, 2004). One cannot disagree. Currently, however, we are facing a more demanding challenge. We have to understand the material processes where prices are made and the rich world of prices that define the processes of market making.

To give an example, we can show, not with great difficulty, that stock or commodity prices are culturally and socially embedded, constructed or informed. Despite common assumptions, economists do not necessarily challenge this conclusion.[2] One cannot locate a market device that is technological enough to avoid social interaction. Calling prices social or cultural via a form of embeddedness argument, although an important first step to leave the reductionist logic of neoclassical orthodoxy, does not essentially help us locate the rich nature of prices, the multiple forms that they take and the manifold locations where they are produced even in a single local or regional market.

Recently, exciting new research in economic and social anthropology has begun to cross the boundary that embeddedness sociology defined. Instead of locating a world of interaction between the social, the cultural, the political and the economic, and then showing how they are embedded like Venn diagrams, researchers began to focus on markets as socio-technical universes from the vantage point of price making (Callon, 1998; Muniesa, 2000, 2003; Maurer, 2002; Caliskan, 2003, 2007; Chiffoleau and Laporte, 2006; Cochoy, 2004; Grandclément, 2004; Levin, 2004; Barrey, 2006; Beunza, Hardie *et al.*, 2006).[3]

This chapter aims to contribute to the new literature concerning the anthropology of price by focusing on processes and types of price making in a regional cotton market in Turkey, the Izmir Mercantile Exchange (IME), describing how a variety of prices are produced in multiple locations of a single commodity market. The chapter's main argument is that the market prices of cotton at IME can best be seen as entangled into devices produced and deployed by traders to pursue their trading objectives. These devices turn cotton into a calculable and exchangeable entity whose value can be negotiated during various forms of bargaining.[4]

I identify three forms of cotton price at IME: *Rehearsal Price, Transaction Price* and *the Market Price*. These price forms are produced in four temporally and spatially specific places of the market: *the Pit, Post-Pit Trading, Closing Price Committee Meeting* and *Permanent Working Group on Cotton Meetings*. Drawing on an ethnography of the production of market price, the paper argues that prices can best be seen as prosthetic devices deployed to further various trading objectives. As we will see, instead of 'setting the price', traders produce various price forms to prevent or foster exchange. Prices are never set by a mere coming together of supply and demand. They are made, produced, and challenged by a multiplicity of actors in a market process. Some prices are produced to perform exchange for a limited time period, and still some are produced not to be used for exchange at all. Aiming at mapping the geography of prices, the chapter presents an ethnography of cotton trading in Izmir from the vantage point of price making.

A summary of trading activities at IME

The Cotton Trading Pit of IME has historically been one of the important nodes of world cotton trade. Being the first and largest commodity exchange of the Ottoman Empire and then its successor, the Turkish Republic, IME's *Korbey*, as the cotton pit is called in Izmir, hosts the trading of thirty-five percent of lint cotton in the country.[5]

The pit is located in the cotton trading hall of IME. Located in the second floor of the exchange building, the hall is home to small trader offices surrounding the space. The pit, resembling two small amphitheatres standing very closely across from each other, has the capacity to seat approximately one hundred and twenty people. All traders wear an identification card before entering the pit, which has fixed seats for all who have the right to enter. The rest must stay outside of the pit, but not of the market.

The pit has two entrances opening to its center. An IME employee sits at the centre. He is responsible for registering sales and documenting bargaining and exchange. Four circular rows of seats, each becoming higher and longer as one moves towards the outer limit of the pit, help traders, observers and officials, sitting shoulder to shoulder, see and hear each other without difficulty. Every weekday at around 11:30, traders, brokers, spinners, ginners and their representatives begin to enter the exchange building. As they tour around the trading pit, trying to read the market, the trader population reaches one hundred to one hundred and twenty. Strolling around the pit, traders observe their colleagues' bodies and how they act, to locate subtle traces of weakness or strength, self-confidence or insecurity, alarm or tranquility.[6]

Trading opens at 12:20 as an IME employee invites the traders to enter the pit and take their seats. This call takes place as traders walk around the pit or wait in the lobby right outside of the hall. It requires a few calls for all traders to take their place, because being too willing to take one's seat in the pit is a sign of emergency. Traders drag their feet a bit before entering and taking their predetermined seat. Being too eager to demand or supply affects the price so directly that no trader will risk looking like someone with an urgent need to trade.

Ten minutes after opening, pit trading terminates exactly at 12:30. Following an open out-cry system, bid and offer cry-outs frame trading in terms of four dimensions. First they specify the amount of cotton in terms of truck loads. Each truck is expected to carry approximately ten metric tons of ginned cotton; the amount can exceed ten tons, however, depending on the relative size of the truck.[7] Second, the offer locates the quality of cotton by specifying its standard and original location of production such as 'Standard 1', 'Garanti', and 'Bergama'.[8] Third, the offer includes a specific price in Turkish Liras for each kilogram of cotton. Finally, the offer specifies the payment terms such as 'in advance', 'in one week', or 'in two weeks'. The acceptance of the cry-out is indicated by saying 'write'. The word in the pit is a bond enforced not only by rules and regulations of IME but also by peer pressure. It is unlikely that a trader can change his or her mind after accepting the bid.[9]

At 12:30, with the ringing of a bell, trading in the pit terminates. In an interesting contrast to the slowness of traders in entering the pit, they leave it rapidly. In these ten minutes of encounter between demand and supply, individual dyadic prices are made. The end of pit trading is not the end of trading at IME, however. Trading continues after 12:30 until 1:15. For forty-five minutes more, traders walk up and down in the area between the pit and their booths, making comments, jokes, bids and offers as they pass by each other, while constantly holding their cell phones in their palms, connecting them to their clients. After 1:15, trading can be carried out, but rarely is. Prices made after 1:15 are not considered as representative of the day's prices.

After 1:15, the Closing Price Committee, consisting of leading buyers and sellers, exchange brokers and merchants, comes together. Following deliberation and study of all registered transactions in and outside of the pit, the committee writes a price report. This document establishes the closing price of the market and turnover of the day, to be closely watched by other traders around the world.

Rehearsal price of the pit

Taking a closer look at these various price forms and how they are produced in multiple locations of trading requires us to open the black-box of the market as we follow the making of its prices, but, how, where and when to locate the market and the price?

The official publications of IME follow a neo-classical logic: 'The price is made in the immediate universe of the pit that provides traders the necessary platform for demand and supply to come together and resolve into a market price' (IME n.d.). These documents refer to the exchange as an 'institutionalized market place' based on five pillars: the commodity, the seller, the buyer, the legal structure and the organization of the exchange (IME n.d.). 'The objective of mercantile exchanges is to create all the necessary conditions to achieve free competition, in other words, to make the laws of supply and demand work. It is in this way that mercantile exchanges come quite close to being ideal free markets' (IME n.d., 18). It is as a result of this 'almost ideal market setting' that it becomes possible for commodities to be traded at their 'real values' (IME n.d., 18).

Traders agree with the way their organization sees its functions. 'Here is the market,' whispered an experienced exchange broker to my ear, while he and I were sitting in the pit. It was the first day of my field work. Trading had started a few minutes ago, after the exchange officer, with a cordless microphone in his hand, invited the traders to the pit at least three times. I looked around and saw people looking around, yet unlike me, seeing a universe of encounter almost invisible to the naked eye. I have read all the rules and regulations of the exchange and even conducted a few preliminary interviews about the everyday workings of the exchange. To say the least, I was not among the least informed visitors of the cotton hall, yet it took a while for me to realize that traders were actually trading. After an exchange broker cried-out 'write,' I leaned towards my host and asked, 'What happened?' 'I'll explain it to you later,' replied my host.

The ten minutes passed rapidly for me, at a snail's pace for my host. With the ringing of the hall's bell, traders emptied the pit quickly. The sales officer of TARIS (the Unions of Agricultural Co-Operatives for the Sales of Figs, Raisin, Cotton, Olive and Olive Oil), representing the largest seller of the market, was the fastest to leave. He was followed by five other agents some of whom chased the TARIS representative.

I left the pit with my host and began watching him show a potential client the cotton samples he kept in his booth. Another trader came to the booth, entered it and listened to the discussion. I could see others looking at my host, his potential customer, and the other agent who was listening to them. I stepped outside to the then almost empty pit and decided to take a look at the electronic board where the world prices of cotton were projected, just to keep myself busy as I felt out of place in the market, the object of my research.

A waiter interrupted my 'studying' of the world prices. He handed me a cup of tea, sent by another exchange agent. I looked around to spot him, and caught his gaze, accepting my gesture of thanks by gently moving his head up and down. I stood there, right in between the pit and the booths surrounding it, having sips from my cup and trying to register what was going on in the market. It was going to take close to one hundred formal and informal interviews and three months of observation for me to begin to appreciate what 'here is the market' meant for the cotton traders of IME.

'This is the market,' said another exchange agent two months after that first day in the pit. He was the oldest and perhaps one of the most respected trader at IME. He had been active in export markets all of his life until 1987, when Turkey became a net cotton importer for the first time in history. 'Gin owners, speculators, exporters, importers . . . Everyone is here. Buyers and sellers call them, ask what the market is. They say, buy me two trucks of this and that,' he continued, showing me the traders around us with his hand holding a constantly ringing cell phone, set to Mozart's Rondò Alla Turca.

Thinking that he had spent enough time keeping the caller waiting, he apologized and took the call while shielding his lips with his right hand, a common gesture to prevent others from understanding what he says. After a few seconds, he hung up the phone and continued:

> Here, everything depends on trust. Once you say 'write,' it is written on the board. Once it is written, the deal is cut, the market is made. Your word is your bond. You cannot say later that you misunderstood this or that. People would laugh at you. You lose your reputation. You are not taken seriously. The hall is made of one hundred and ten years of trust, institutionalized around this pit.
>
> – But not all trade is carried out in the pit.
>
> – Yes. The pit is only the beginning. It sets the stage. But even before the pit trading starts, things begin to happen in the hall, the market begins to appear. We observe each other before the pit. We want to learn the level of refused cotton.[10] We probe the market by reading other brokers' faces, the way they talk on the phone, they way they approach each other. This doesn't take a long time if you are experienced enough. I have been working here for decades. So it is very easy for me.
>
> – The pit?
>
> – Yes, then, we enter the pit. We make more deals outside of the pit. But it is the pit that makes this possible. You sit and look around, traders start making offers and bids. I sell this, I buy this. Depending on the price, you make your decision and if you are buying, you say, for example, write me a truck.

The everyday performance of trading both in and around the pit is crucial for pricing cotton. On one hand it would be misleading to argue that it is only these performances that structure price levels. On the other hand it would also be problematic to argue that it is the unmediated workings of supply and demand that make the price. Because the levels of supply and demand should be located by various market agents for supply and demand levels to have any effect of the market. 'Market forces' have to be perceived and processed by traders. The making of supply and demand is not independent of traders' perceptions of them, and it is only through institutionalized filters and deliberations that their effects are felt by market agents. It is also through speech acts and conscious and unconscious bodily performances that the invisible hands of markets are located by traders. These performances are central for the everyday working of trading pits.

Another exchange broker explained the working of the pit and its role in bringing together supply and demand of cotton by using analogies and rhetorical questions that depict, in his own words, how the way market forces of supply and demand are mediated in trading floors on the ground.

> The pit makes sure that demand and supply meet each other in a disciplined way. And it is by the pit that the exchange carries out this intermediary role. The supply and demand are made there. So, the pit is an instrument for the exchange. How does a carpenter work? With a saw. How does an exchange make supply and demand? With the pit. So the pit is the tool for making a market. Where is Shakespeare's Hamlet played in Izmir? It is played in theatre. The pit is the theatre of the market.
> – It seems to me that there is more than crying out 'I sell this,' 'I buy this' or 'write.'
> – The pit is a performance place. Traders and brokers are in a situation like that of poker players. Traders know that when they sit in the pit, their facial expressions, the way they talk and the way they don't talk, the time they enter the discussion and when they don't, everything they do and not do are crucial. Imagine that your client calls you and orders you to buy twenty tons of cotton on that day's price. You know that you have to buy or else the factory will stop. What happens when others also know that? You can't be selling at a price lower than the market price. But you don't know the market price. What if the market price turns out to be lower than the one you took? You can do it once, do it twice, and then you lose your customer. We have to catch the market price and if possible make it. We'll do everything to make the price. We'll look like we don't want cotton, we'll pretend that we're not interested; we would probe others and watch what they do. We have to do this as if we are not doing this. Yet however cool you are, your body . . . reveals what is going on inside. This is how we read each other and decide what to do.

Trading performances have their own limits: they are effective ways of bargaining that are used frequently, but their effect depends on one's market position and power in the pit. If a trader over-performs in the pit, without necessary means of supporting his performance, he usually fails to meet the market price. One exchange broker made this mistake of over-performance and made a deal without probing the market effectively. It was the first time he spoke in the pit since I started observing traders in the cotton hall. Another broker, whose typical market positions were among the largest in IME, explained what happened that day when I met him in his office.

> It is not possible for everyone to make the price at IME. It requires a strong heart. It requires courage. It requires experience. Our job here is to create stability. We are

> responsible to those who trust us. This is the spirit that informs us in the pit. But some people make too many zigzags. There are two different groups in the exchange. The first group just talks in the pit for satisfaction. Does this, does that . . . I mean like a real actor. We all have the same gun, but different amount of bullets. We all know how much ammunition we all have. For example, today one man wanted to buy. Of course we didn't sell. I don't let others make the price. I make it. What happened to this man? He bought the same cotton spot cash, but others bought it on credit. We all know each other. If you follow what is going on in the hall before the pit starts, you can make the price. Not many people can make it. I would say only five to ten people are really good at what they do. Their power relies on their experience and the firms they represent.

The limits of performance in trading and the efficacy of their acts in making prices are related to the performer's market power. Those who observe these performances in the pit interpret them with reference to the performer's market position and the firms he represents. That is why when these 'five to ten people' come to the pit, the whole atmosphere changes. Moreover, when one of them does not come and join the session that day, the pit is even more affected.

According to another exchange broker, one whose absence 'moves things in the pit', observing individual traders is not enough to probe the market. For him, the way individual traders behave and feel that day creates a synergic whole, a specific air, or *hava*, as he calls it in Turkish. To him, traders affect each other and also interact in a rather unconscious way to produce a combined effect that cannot be observed by looking at individual traders only. The market has to be 'smelled'.

> Once you enter the pit, you are all ears and eyes. What one really has to do is to smell the air in the pit to locate the supply and demand of the day. Traders may be talking to you, but at the same time watching what is behind you. Before going to the exchange, I always make a research and study the market. You can't make the price if you don't study it. I make projections, and relying on them I observe traders and smell the air in the pit. If the business is hot, I can read it in advance. I read the market's pulse. In our exchange, traders make many beautiful manoeuvres. For example, if I don't go to the pit, if they don't see me there, they know what it means.

Whether they smell the air, made up of a synergic whole traders co-create; probe the market by carefully registering how others act before and during the pit session; or perform in a way to cloak one's intentions to gain a better bargaining position, traders rely on various forms of bargaining to affect other's perceptions.

Trading performances in the pit have immediate effects, visible only after the session terminates. According to a broker who has had a seat in the pit for more than two decades, 'the pit is nothing compared to what happens afterwards. The pit is the trial run on the market. You try to make it there and then get your deal later. For every deal cut in the pit, there are three deals outside of it.' This estimate was challenged by another trader a few days later:

> The pit is a total show. It is not the market where the prices are made. They are made later. I'd say only ten percent of trade takes place during the ten minutes of the pit

session. Brokers and traders try to fix a price there so that they can make money later. For example they would say 1.60 in the pit, but sell later for 1.50.[11]

If the pit is 'nothing' compared to 'what happens later', and if the pit is only a fraction of later trading, what then makes it the place of the market for traders? One immediate answer is that it is through the temporal and spatial framing of the way supply and demand meet each other that it becomes possible to engage with the market. It is the pit that brings them together and helps buyers and sellers meet each other. Otherwise, the market would be 'everywhere' and could not be effectively engaged. Although partially valid, this answer cannot take into account the fact that the vast majority of trading takes place outside of the pit, both temporally and spatially.

Instead of seeing it as the market's place, a better answer would locate the pit as a design of intervention in the making of the market. It is misleading to assume that there is only one boundary between the market and the non-market. Markets have multiple boundaries even in their immediate universes like that of the IME. In other words, markets have various places with various price forms even in a single geography of trading.

One has to be careful, however, when using geographical analogies to make these different market 'places' visible, for these boundaries are not only spatial but also temporal. The cotton market at IME has multiple locations, strategically separated by temporal and spatial limits.

Traders, when they are in the pit, perform and watch performances to weigh their validity. By and large, the pit is a preparation for the post-pit trading that takes place before 1:15. Working to produce a price in the pit is a performative investment. These pit prices will very soon be referred to in making deals during post-pit trading. By quoting the prices made in the pit, traders discuss strategies with their clients and then readjust them according to the price levels of the day. It prepares the ground for marketing by marketing cotton itself, though in smaller amounts.

It is important to note that many traders use theatrical analogies to describe their everyday experiences in the pit. It is either 'a place that looks like a theater where Shakespeare is played' or just 'a show' that 'real actors' put together. Yet actual transaction prices are made in this 'show'.

This new form of price produced in the pit for post-pit trading presents an interesting puzzle: these prices are made to exchange cotton. They are actual transaction prices. They are also prosthetic prices, however. They are used as devices to affect post-pit trading that witnesses around ninety percent of actual trading at IME. As a result, this interesting price form is both an actual price and not. It is both a prosthetic price and not.

Drawing on traders' analogies, I call this price form *rehearsal price*, for it is caught in the middle of actual performance and non-performance – traders rehearse actual trading by using rehearsal prices. The volume that they trade as they rehearse trading is only a fraction of the trading that takes place after the pit. The price produced during pit trading is a rehearsal price also because it is produced to probe and to make the market. The rationale of its production is not to make a transaction, but to affect the process that will make the post-pit trading price. These rehearsal prices, however, are also transaction prices because it is by taking them that cotton is exchanged. For the price to be rehearsed, it has to be taken by a trader. As soon as one hears the cry-out 'write!' a rehearsal price is produced. In a given session of pit trading, depending on the season and the volume of the market, tens of different rehearsal prices can appear. All of these prices are used as devices that enable traders to strategize their trading moves during the post-pit session.

What happens when no trade takes place during the pit session? This means that no rehearsal price is made. But traders still produce a form of price rehearsal by making bids and offers that are not taken.[12] The absence of rehearsal prices does not indicate that no rehearsal has taken place. A rather explicitly displayed disinterest may actually be indicative of an urgent interest. In the next section we will see how rehearsal prices play a significant role in post-pit trading by discussing an empirical example.

Transaction price of post-pit trading

After the pit session is called off at 12:30, traders leave the pit and either go back to their booths or begin walking in the circular quarter between the pit and their office cubicles. Immediately after the pit, they call their clients to reconsider their trading decisions depending on their ideas about the rehearsal prices. If they are representing buyers, they would do their best to buy cotton in terms better than those that are made during pit trading. Their dilemma is that those who are representing the sellers are motivated by an opposite objective. Sellers try to take a price that is a bit higher than the rehearsed prices in the pit. When they rehearse prices, buyers always try to pull them down, whereas sellers try to make them appear high.

Bargaining in post-pit trading typically takes place with reference to rehearsal prices, either by taking them seriously, or by looking down upon their importance, depending on one's market position. The following instance of bargaining that took place between two exchange brokers, witnessed by at least four other traders and me, presents a case that exemplifies both technologies:

> A: So you say 1.60?
> B: You heard it. You know the cotton.
> A: It is high. You know C. sold it for 1.55 a few minutes ago.
> B: Why don't go buy from him then. But who buys his own cotton, eh?
> A: Ok, ok, 1.60 it is, payment in a week. Shall I call the factory?
> B: Go ahead.

In this round of bargaining, the rehearsal price played a major role in two respects. First, the buyer mentioned it to make the point that the sellers' price is higher than what was taken a few minutes ago in the pit. Indeed, a few minutes ago one truck of Bergama was sold for 1.55. This was a rehearsal price made to be used later. The seller, however, recognized the power of rehearsal price only to a certain extent. B accepted the fact that the bargaining had to be around 1.55, yet he implied that the rehearsal price was made to depress the actual prices that will take place after the pit session. The question 'who buys his own cotton?' was meant to decrease the power of the rehearsal price by rhetorically underlying the fact that the price was made as an investment for later use to structure the possible range of prices in post-pit trading. He suggested that the rehearsal price was 'rehearsed' between two traders who work for different companies but buy and sell for the same yarn producer.

Immediately after the rehearsal price was itself challenged by the seller, the buyer, who already was willing to pay up to 1.625 for the same cotton, made the deal. His client's factory needed cotton. Being very experienced and strong – one of the 'five to ten people who knows how to make the price,' he managed to buy for less than what he had anticipated. The trade was a success. For the seller however, the trade was not a success, if not a big failure. He had to sell immediately, for the ginning factory that owned the cotton needed cash soon, so they ordered him to sell for as high as possible, yet no cheaper than 1.60.

I interviewed both A and B after this round of exchange took place. A, who had successfully bought for less than he expected, let me know the range his client had given him. Immediately before the trade had taken place, during the pit trading, A seemed disinterested. B, a broker representing relatively less powerful clients, had to sell. He did not skilfully cloak his feeling of urgency. He was still a bit upset for having sold the cotton at his lower limit. It was A's power, his performance's strength that put together a well-rehearsed price.

One main difference between pit and post-pit trading is that trading in the pit is an individually performed and publicly observed act. After the pit however, trading can still be observed by others, yet to a limited extent. Traders' individual encounters are scattered. Their place in the market is not fixed as in the pit; they move in it, literally by walking up and down in the space between the pit and the walls of the mercantile exchange building. Crossing the boundary between pit and post-pit trading also makes it possible for buyers and sellers, represented by brokers, to meet each other individually and make individual dyadic prices. They utilize the prices made or rehearsed during the pit session and center their trading and bargaining strategies on these prices.

Another central difference between these two locations of the market concerns the visibility and registration of trading. All trades in the pit are registered as soon as a deal is cut by saying 'write!' This literally means that the trade is registered and the names of the buyer and seller, the quantity of the sale, the price and the payment conditions are written down. All sales are visible in the pit. Because of both the level of visibility and the requirement of pit trading, traders cannot always choose their trading partners, for anyone who says 'write' can take the bid or offer.[13] Yet in post-pit trading, traders have more freedom to choose their trading counterparts. This is crucial because, according to cotton traders no two offers, that have exactly the same amount, price, payment conditions, are the same. The trading records of sellers and buyers always play an important role in making a deal. Traders tend to choose bids or offers made by a relatively more trusted trader. For this reason, traders may choose not to reveal their deals in post-pit trading, where deals are not necessarily visible. Traders may also choose not to reveal their sales for it may let others better know their trading policies and put them in better position in the near future to guess others' moves in the market. As we see, the first boundary of the market, the one located between the pit and the post-pit and demarcated by time (12:30 p.m.) and space (the outer circle of the pit), held together and made possible trading performances that produced the rehearsal price. Once the first boundary is crossed, transaction prices are made during various sessions of bargaining. As these sessions take place, the forces of demand and supply are performed, registered, contested and perceived differently by traders who have diverse market positions, information, orders and consequently, different performances. These technologies of mediation, interpretation, translation and performance structure the effects of supply and demand on the ground. Without these technologies, supply and demand are nothing but ineffective abstractions.

The trading during post-pit session has a huge volume: hundreds of truck loads of cotton are sold and bought on its basis. Indeed, the rehearsal prices, as prosthetic devices, are used extensively during post-pit trading. This second market place hosts the great majority of trading in IME, producing hundreds of transaction prices, some higher and some lower than the rehearsal price.

Making the market price of Turkish cotton

The various rounds of post-pit bargaining, drawing on rehearsal prices and carried out in dyadic form, continue for another forty-five minutes and end as traders begin to leave the cotton hall around 1:00. Just before the trading day ends, however, one crucial market activity remains to be carried out. Members of the Closing Price Committee come together at 1:15 to locate the market price of cotton. It is in this location of the market that the market price of Turkish cotton traded in Izmir is set. Indeed, it is this market price that other cotton traders and market analysts around the world take into account as they carry out their daily routine of trading and research.

Although it is illegal to carry out an unregistered transaction, it is performed frequently, for the hands of the market can indeed be invisible if wanted. But it is not possible to render the market price invisible.

Market price is a price form that is shaped by the deliberation among the members of this committee. Without it, dyadic relations of exchange that take place in a scattered manner in time and space could not be brought together. It is this interception of the market process that makes it possible for the market price to appear. Because it entails a daily routine of deliberation and yet another form of bargaining, it connects market positions to power, usually by mirroring power relations on the market. The committee members have historically consisted of large traders and a few smaller sales brokers who are included to present an image of equality.

The first difficulty consists of linking the rehearsal price of the pit with the transaction price of the post-pit. Market agents know that rehearsal prices are simultaneously prosthetic devices used to shape future bargains *and* transaction prices that are taken to buy or sell cotton. These rehearsal prices are made to appear lower or higher than acceptable levels to be able to trade in desired future prices. The actual, but scattered, prices of the post-pit trading are not rehearsal prices; they are not made as investment to be appropriated for future use. Yet they draw on rehearsal prices and it is only with reference to them that it becomes possible to make the transaction prices. Hence, when the number of rehearsal and actual prices increases, the range within which they oscillate gets wider. In these situations, it becomes more difficult and strategically important to locate a market price that represents these different trading levels.

The second difficulty of locating the market price arises because post-pit trading provides traders, to a certain extent, with an invisible ground of interaction. They do not have to register their trades. Legally, all trades have to be registered but in practice there are many ways of not registering a deal either immediately or after the deal or even never.

The committee follows a few rules of thumb to establish a range of representative transaction prices and trading levels. First, the committee members remove the highest and the lowest market prices from the list of prices they get from the IME administration, and take the weighed arithmetic average of individual transaction prices that are registered. Second, only registered prices are taken into account as one cannot know for sure the price level of invisible trading. This challenge does not make the Closing Price Committee helpless in filtering out possible tactics of manipulation. For example, when a seller and buyer representing the same company or brokerage house make a registered deal, their trade and price are filtered out from consideration.

The market price is usually set by looking at transaction price levels: rehearsal prices always set a range of bargaining before transaction prices are taken. Yet sometimes, especially when the trading volume increases, it becomes more difficult and contentious to set the market price. In these situations deliberation takes more time and another round of bargaining takes place, affected on a daily basis by the market power and positions of the traders. To give an example, one day in 2003, after one market price announcement, TARIS, the cooperative representing cotton farmers, protested the committee, did not accept its decision and asked the IME Board to include the Coop's member to the committee. It did not take long for the IME to include TARIS in the committee, and since then the committee is regarded as more representative of the market players.

The committee's coming together helps us locate yet another market place in the halls of IME. Now all trading has been carried out, the prices have been rehearsed and then realized during various rounds of transaction. This third location of the market, spatially still located in the cotton hall of IME, yet temporarily located 'outside' of marketing, is the place where *the market price* is produced. It is crucial at this point to make note of the fact that in order for the markets to produce a price, market participants should leave the immediate location of marketing and recreate another one by using social technologies drawing on arbitration and deliberation.

Another market place: Permanent Working Group on Cotton

These three temporal and spatial places of the market, the pit, the post-pit, and Closing Price Committee Meeting are not the only locations where prices in their multiple forms are made in Turkey. Over lunch in an upscale restaurant in Izmir an experienced cotton trader said, 'Tomorrow, we'll determine the supply of this coming cotton season.' Reaching for his beer slowly, he continued, 'Everyone will be at IME tomorrow, the ministry, the cooperative, traders, and cotton research people. You can see the real market there.' Learning the fourth *real* location of the market since I had started my urban field work ten weeks ago, I asked:

What do you mean by determining the supply?
– I studied economics. It is true that supply and demand come together to make the price. This is what takes place at IME. But before it happens, we have to discuss its amount and fix it somehow.
– Before what happens?
– You know. The supply. What you see in the market depends on what you want from it. I cannot accept a declining production figure before the new season starts. If it declines, if I, as a trader, say that it is going to decline, the price will go up, so I'll sell less cotton. So I have to find more capital for turn-over, and make less money. So we do our best to present a higher supply figure.

The following day, after post-pit trading ended and the Closing Price Committee decided on the market price of Aegean cotton and posted it, not all traders left the IME for their offices or warehouses. Some went to IME's historical conference room to join the meeting of the Permanent Working Group on Cotton, a gathering described by the above trader as another 'real market place'. This new market place was comprised of the Ministry of Agriculture bureaucrats, traders, economists, agricultural engineers, a few large landowners and the officials of TARIS, the cotton sales cooperative representing farmers producing more than a quarter of the crop in the country.

Coming back from lunch with a sales broker, I entered the conference hall and sat with a few traders and one ginning factory owner from Söke, whose plain is the second largest cotton growing land in Turkey. A bit worried that I had missed the first ten minutes of the meeting, I leaned towards the ginning factory owner I had interviewed during my rural fieldwork and asked whether I had missed anything. 'Nothing.' he replied, dismissing the importance of these first ten minutes. 'Regular stuff, welcoming, underlining the importance of cotton for the country and using scientific techniques to develop the cotton sector, etc. The real stuff is yet to start.'

Indeed it was. Nazilli Cotton Research Institute's director ended his opening remarks by commenting on the importance of the Committee for the Turkish cotton sector. Moving his eyes from the text he was reading, looking at his audience in a distinctly more serious way, he closed his speech by saying, 'We have to be very careful in estimating the supply levels, for they will affect cotton prices greatly. So we have to discuss the matter very seriously and reach a decision that represents the interests of the cotton sector the best.'

This was not an easy objective. There were three main groups in the meeting, with three diverse sets of motivation prefiguring their approach to cotton supply estimates. Traders, merchants and brokers comprised the first group who had an interest in depressed prices, because lower prices would make it possible for them to trade larger volumes. As a result they would do their best to prevent the caucus from producing an underestimated production level, for a forecast of decreasing supply would push the prices up.

The large landlord and the cooperative representatives had an opposite motivation. Obviously, they would benefit more from increasing prices. Thus they had an incentive to prevent the overestimation of the production level, for guessing a higher supply would depress prices.

The ministerial representatives, however, did not care for the price levels as much as the previous two groups. Their main purpose was to note the cotton supply levels as accurately as possible in order to inform the minister of agriculture so that he could ask for an accurate amount for agricultural subsidies from the annual budget of the prime ministry. A lower estimate would result in a deficit in his budget. A higher estimate would make the ministry look unsuccessful.

It did not take long for these three positions to gain visibility in the meeting. After the cooperative representative presented his production estimates for the 2002 crop, estimating that there would be a considerable decrease in production, traders, merchants and the ginning factory owner sitting next to me simultaneously began to fidget and shift their body weight from side to side in a rather uncomfortable manner, displaying obvious movements of disagreement. A few went even further and voiced their disagreement by making loud noises of discontent and flying their hands over their heads as if trying to get rid of a fly.

Merchants and brokers, however, did not present a figure of their own. Although the research department of the exchange had been working on estimates of some sort, they were understaffed and lacked required funds to carry out a regular survey. There was an ongoing project on monitoring production levels by using satellite remote sensing imagery, yet it was not yet deployed effectively.

After a long and heated deliberation, the caucus reached a consensus that made everyone unhappy, but content. The estimated cotton supply was pinpointed as lower then the previous season. But it was determined to be higher than the cooperative's estimates and lower then most of the individual traders' guesses.

Cotton supply was not merely a function of production but also a matter of everyday market politics. This is why the traders who invited me to this meeting referred to it as another location of the market, for the very processes of price making were also intercepted in meetings like that of Permanent Working Group on Cotton, whose decisions inform trading decision and thus the very making of the price in all its three forms.

The consensual mood disappeared quickly when the next item in the agenda was introduced – the production cost of cotton, making the differences in the way things are seen even more observable. After a rather lengthy presentation on the techniques of estimation and data gathering, the Cotton Research Institute representative finally revealed the Institute's estimate of cotton's production cost: 1.10. This estimate created such an uproar that for a good ten seconds nothing but chaos ruled the meeting hall. A ginning factory owner, whose main occupation was to fund indebted farmers to secure an annual supply of cotton to his enterprises and then sell his cotton at IME through his agent, sitting close to him that day, told me in a quite irritated manner, 'This is a lie. A straight lie! What kind of a cost is this? Even if one gives two liras to the peasant, he would say 'oh I go bust.' It is their nature. It is a lie. The cost is not more than 0.40. I myself am a farmer. I know it.'

Both his and others' anger somewhat calmed down as the speaker stepped down from the podium and the meeting's attention turned toward the cooperative's representative. His estimates dragged the institute's figure down, yet still not enough for the merchants, I thought observing the uneasiness of their attendance to the speaker's presentation. The large landlord's estimate of 0.60 pulled the production cost estimate even lower, injecting into the meeting a more peaceful ambiance.

The cost of production was important for the making of prices yet in an indirect manner compared to the role of supply estimates. A high cost estimate would fuel farmer and cooperative grievances as it would make historically low cotton prices look even worse. In addition, a higher cost estimate would also contribute to a negative public image of brokers, merchants and traders. Finally, from the government's side however, a higher cost estimate would corner them, giving the opposition parties ammunition to criticize them for not extending enough support to the farmers.

The institute's calculations of the cost of production treated farmers as workers with a forty hour work week, enjoying national and weekend holidays and earning a minimum wage. That is, the institute calculated all costs by attaching monetary values according to the standards the Ministry of Labor and Social Security set for all workers. Yet the mercantile opposition was fierce enough both to silence the institute director and to force the caucus not to consider the institute's estimate, taking it out from the arithmetic average calculated by adding the landlord's, the cooperatives and the exchange's estimates and then dividing them by three. An arithmetical formula helped the three parties reach a consensus.

The cost of production estimate, like that of the supply, was again 'determined', as the ginning factory owner told me over the lunch, in a new place of the market, where the forces of supply are negotiated and the cost of production is calculated within a context informed by various interests crossing class, status and scientific boundaries. Furthermore, the Ministry of Agriculture's representatives remained silent, thus preferring the registry of lower estimates. They were aware of their limited power in economic decisions because of the stand-by agreements the government had made with the International Monetary Fund. They also knew that they would be criticized harshly if a high, yet more accurate, cost estimate was published.

Meetings such as that of the Permanent Working Group on Cotton are peculiar locations of the market that are rarely considered to be market places. It is in these meetings, however, that the very building blocks of markets – supply and demand – begin to take shape. The coming together of supply and demand is probed, prefigured and even produced as estimates by a caucus representing all market actors. The making of rehearsal prices, transaction prices and market prices is directly affected by this last location of the market. That is why the meeting itself should be seen as a market activity as central as trading itself, thus making the Permanent Working Group on Cotton meeting a new market place where various prices are made.

Conclusion

Exchanging of cotton takes place in the various locations of the market. The institutionalized universe of the market is demarcated by multiple boundaries. Pit trading, the point of entry to the study of cotton trading in Izmir, was framed in temporal and geographical limits, bringing traders together for ten minutes between 12:20 and 12:30.

It is in this temporal and spatial location that 'the theatre of the market' takes place. Market players located in that theatre produce *rehearsal prices*, a heterodox form of price caught in the middle of indicative and transaction prices. It is created to exchange cotton, yet it is created to exchange only a very limited quantity of the commodity, making it a rehearsal for the actual volume of trade that has yet to be reached during post-pit trading. The pit price is a market device deployed and produced by merchants to strengthen their bargaining positions as they make actual transaction prices. The rehearsal price is a device because its making is a simultaneous investment for post-pit trading, yet it is an actual transaction price too, for the actual cotton is exchanged by its acceptance. This process of rehearsing the price during pit trading draws on various trading performances and represents the effects of perceived levels of the demand and supply of cotton.

Once this first boundary of the market is crossed, by leaving the physical location of the pit at 12:30 sharp and by entering the second space-time location of the market, the post-pit, traders begin to use these rehearsal prices to negotiate actual transaction prices. Post-pit trading, where traders are not brought together as closely as in the pit, produces actual transaction prices. Both traders and their prices are scattered, however, in this second location of the market.

Hundreds of registered and unregistered prices are made in this most vibrant location of the market. More arresting still, this is not the place where *the market price* emerges.

In the end of post-pit trading, the *market price* appears in a categorically different setting – in the meeting of the Closing Price Committee. Following a heated process of bargaining and haggling, the committee makes a decision on the Izmir cotton market price. As discussed earlier, the market price is born through process of heated bargaining and discussion in the midst of which an arithmetical formula is used (weighed average). This has to be stressed, market price is not set by the mere coming together of demand and supply as the neoclassical price theory suggests, but instead it is produced in a political process of deliberation. If we would like to gain a better understanding of markets and prices it is crucial that we study such processes.

Demand and supply also play their role, yet again in a surprising setting. Before their effects were perceived by the traders, supply and demand effects are negotiated in committees specifically formed for this task.[14] The actual demand and supply figures of any market are known after the market is made. As the market is made, one cannot know them for sure. Thus, it would be misleading to deduce the price from the levels of supply and demand, for prices in their multiple forms are made *before* these levels are known. In meetings such as those convened by Permanent Working Group on Cotton, the perceptions of 'what the market will be' are discussed and negotiated, and figures such as supply volume or costs of production are literally produced, contributing to the process whereby prices are made are turned to market devices. Regardless of what the actual cost of production and supply will be, the effect of their estimation is a product of a deliberate market process. In fact, the actual figures of supply and cost will be known, yet only after the cotton is consumed and thus disappears.

That is why it is appropriate to see prices as prosthetic forms produced, deployed, resisted, and at times, abused by traders. Seeing the market price as a summary of a market activity is misleading, for every summary reflects the vantage point of its writer. Markets, as 'theaters of exchange', draw on many stories informed by a diverse set of constraints and interests. So do prices. In Izmir, market prices are produced in three main forms in four different market places. Studying the market from the vantage point of the price, then, requires us to look at the very production of process of prices as market devices. Future research on the anthropology of prices as market devices has a great potential to provide us tools to forcefully address this pressing need.

Such an ethnographical attendance to price production also helps us approach markets as socio-technical contexts whose working can be studied and critically questioned in a novel way. Furthermore, making visible the very processes in which various price forms are produced can help those who are affected by these prices be more active in participating in the making of prices. Because, as we have seen in the discussion of the making of three prices forms at IME, markets are intervened and maintained constantly. This is their condition of possibility, not an exceptional state. If this is the case, *laissez-faire* acquires a new meaning, for letting them but not others produce the price, directly affects the livelihood of those who make and consume the very commodity, whose price is produced amid relations of power.

Notes

1 This article draws on field work I carried out for a total of eight months in 2001 and 2003 in Izmir, Turkey. The research was funded by American Research Institute in Turkey and Wenner-Gren Foundation for Anthropological Research. I would like to thank Michel Callon, Yuval Millo, Tim Mitchell, Fabian Muniesa, Julia Elyachar, Hayri Özmeriç and Amy Quark for their careful reading, extensive comments and suggestions.
2 For a review of how economists see the cultural and social aspects of prices and markets see Bakshi and Chen (1996). For a review of price theories in economics see Brems (1991).
3 For an exciting set of new work in the anthropology of the market that came out recently see Bestor (2001), Mitchell (2002), Preda (2002), Maurer (2003), Miyazaki (2003), Knorr Cetina and Bruegger (2004), MacKenzie (2004), Riles (2004), Yükseker (2004), Callon and Muniesa (2005), Elyachar (2005), Lépinay and Hertz (2004), Millo, Muniesa *et al.* (2005), Ong and Collier (2005), Roitman (2005), and Zaloom (2006).
4 For a more comprehensive discussion of how prices are made in global, regional and local market contexts and a theoretical account of their interaction see Caliskan (2005).
5 For the history of the exchange see Yetkin and Serçe (1998).
6 For ethnographies of trader performances in other markets see Hertz (1998), Lépinay (2003), Beunza and Stark (2004), Levin (2004), Elyachar (2005), Knorr Cetina and Preda (2005), and Zaloom (2006).
7 If the offer is well more than a few trucks, it is specified in terms of metric tones.
8 For more information regarding Turkish Cotton Standards see Gencer, Özmeriç *et al.* (1999).
9 One can stretch a bid a bit, however, if the accepted offer turns out to be worse than the market price that would be set later in the trading day. In these situations, payment terms can be relaxed a bit in an informal manner.
10 Refused cotton is the commodity whose quality is contested. Buyers can refuse to accept the cotton sent to them if they are not sure about the quality until an arbitrator of IME solves the problem.
11 When I carried my field work in 2002, Turkey was using Turkish Lira. In 2005 the government introduced the New Turkish Lira (YTL) erasing six zeros from the TL. The prices I use in the paper are converted to YTL.
12 It would be somewhat inaccurate to say 'nothing happened in the pit today,' because even if nobody makes a bid or offer during pit session, a very infrequent situation, it still means something valuable for traders.
13 It is possible, however, to make a bid or offer to a specific market agent by directly spelling out his name, but this is a rather rare occurrence in the pit. I'd like to thank Hayri Özmeriç, a trader from IME, for correcting me on this point.
14 For an analysis how the perception of supply and demand contributes to the making of prices and exchange volumes see Odirici and Corrado (2004).

References

Alexander, J. and P. Alexander (1991), 'What Is in a Fair Price? Price Setting and Trading Partnership in Javanese Markets', *Man*, 26(3): 493–512.
Bakshi, G. S. and Z. Chen (1996), 'The Spirit of Capitalism and Stock-Market Prices', *American Economic Review*, 86(1): 133–157.

Barrey, S. (2006), 'Formation et Calcul des Prix: Le Travail de Tarification dans la Grande Distribution', *Sociologie du Travail*, 46(2): 142–158.
Bestor, T. C. (2001), 'Supply-Side Sushi: Commodity, Market, and the Global City', *American Anthropologist*, 103(1): 76–95.
Beunza, D., I. Hardie and D. MacKenzie (2006), 'A Price Is a Social Thing: Towards a Material Sociology of Arbitrage', *Organization Studies*, 27(5): 721–745.
Beunza, D. and D. Stark (2004), 'Tools of the Trade: The Socio-Technology of Arbitrage in a Wall Street Trading Room', *Industrial and Corporate Change*, 13(2): 369–401.
Brems, H. (1991), 'Price Theory: A Stylized History', *History of Political Economy*, 23(4): 675–686.
Caliskan, K. (2003), 'The Price of the Market', Paper presented at the 'Development after Development' Conference, New York University.
Caliskan, K. (2005), 'Making a Global Commodity: The Production of Markets and Cotton in Egypt, Turkey, and the United States', PhD thesis, New York University.
Caliskan, K. (2007), 'Neo-liberal, Piyasa Nasil Isler? Pamuk, Ikdar Ve Ticaret Siyaseti,' *Toplum ve Bilim*, 108: 52–81.
Callon, M., (ed.) (1998), *The Laws of the Markets*, London: Blackwell.
Callon, M. and F. Muniesa (2005), 'Economic Markets as Calculative Collective Devices', *Organization Studies*, 26(8): 1229–1250.
Chiffoleau, Y. and C. Laporte (2006), 'Price Formation: the Case of the Burgundy Wine Market', *Revue Française de Sociologie* 47(5): 157–182.
Cochoy, F. (ed.) (2004), *La Captation des Publics: C'est pour Mieux te Séduire, mon Client. . . .*', Toulouse: Presses Universitaires du Mirail.
DiMaggio, P. and H. Louch (1998), 'Socially Embedded Consumer Transactions: For What Kinds of Purchases Do People Most Often Use Networks', *American Sociological Review*, 63(5): 619–637.
Dobbin, F. (2004), 'The Sociological View of the Economy', in F. Dobbin (ed.), *The Sociology of the Economy*. New York: Russell Sage.
Duina, F. (2004), 'Regional Market Building as a Social Process: An Analysis of Cognitive Strategies in Nafta, the European Union and Mercosur', *Economy and Society*, 33(3): 359–389.
Elyachar, J. (2005), *Markets of Dispossession: Ngos, Economic Development, and the State in Cairo*, Durham: Duke University Press.
Fligstein, N. (1996), 'Markets as Politics: A Political-Cultural Approach to Market Institutions', *American Sociological Review*, 61(4): 656–673.
Geismar, H. (2001), 'What's in a Price? An Ethnography of Tribal Art at Auction', *Journal of Material Culture*, 6(1): 25–47.
Gencer, O., H. Özmeriç, et al. (1999), 'An Evaluation of the Cotton Standards and Grading System in Turkey and Recommendations for Improvement', Ankara.
Grandclément, C. (2004), 'Bundles of Prices: Marketing and Pricing in French Supermarkets', Paper presented at the 4S-EASST Annual meeting, 2004, Paris.
Granovetter, M. (1985), 'Economic Action and Social Structure: The Problem of Embeddedness', *American Journal of Sociology*, 91(3): 481–510.
Hertz, E. (1998), *The Trading Crowd: An Ethnography of the Shanghai Stock Market*, New York: Cambridge University Press.
IME (n.d.), 'Ticaret Borsalari Ve Izmir Ticaret Borsası'. Izmir: Izmir Ticaret Borsası.
Knorr Cetina, K. and A. Preda (2005), *The Sociology of Financial Markets*, Oxford: Oxford University Press.
Knorr Cetina, K. and U. Bruegger (2004), 'Global Microstructures: The Interaction Practices of Financial Markets', in F. Dobbin (ed.), *The Sociology of the Economy*. New York: Russell Sage.
Lapavitsas, C. (2004), 'Commodities and Gifts: Why Commodities Represent More Than Market Relations', *Science and society*, 68(1): 33–56.
Lépinay, V. (2003), 'Les Formules du Marché. Ethno-économie d'une Innovation Financière: Les Produits à Capital Garanti', PhD thesis, Ecole des Mines de Paris.
Lépinay, V. and E. Hertz (2004), 'Deception and Its Preconditions: Issues Raised by Financial Markets', in C. Gerschlager (ed.), *Deception in Markets: An Economic Analysis*. New York: Palgrave Macmillan.

Levin, P. (2004), 'Engendering Markets: Technology and Institutional Change in Financial Futures Trading', PhD thesis, Northwestern University.
MacKenzie, D. (2004), 'The Big, Bad Wolf and the Rational Market: Portfolio Insurance, the 1987 Crash and the Performativity of Economics', *Economy and Society*, 33(3): 303–334.
Maurer, B. (2002), 'Repressed Futures: Financial Derivatives' Theological Unconscious', *Economy and Society*, 31(1): 15–36.
Maurer, B. (2003), 'Uncanny Exchanges: The Possibilities and Failures of 'Making Change' with Alternative Monetary Forms', *Environment and planning D, Society & Space*, 21(3): 317–340.
Millo, Y., F. Muniesa, N. S. Panourgias and S. V. Scott (2005), 'Organised Detachment: Clearing-house Mechanisms in Financial Markets', *Information and Organization*, 15(3): 229–246.
Mitchell, T. (2002), *Rule of Experts: Egypt, Techno-Politics, Modernity*, Berkeley: University of California Press.
Miyazaki, H. (2003), 'The Temporalities of the Markets', *American Anthropologist*, 105(2): 255–265.
Muniesa, F. (2000), 'Performing Prices: The Case of Price Discovery Automation in the Financial Markets', in H. Kalthoff, R. Rottenburg and H. J. Wagener (eds), *Economy and Society Yearbook 16. Facts and Figures: Economic Representations and Practices*. Marburg: Metropolis.
Muniesa, F. (2003), 'Des Marchés comme Algorithmes: Sociologie de la Cotation Electronique à la Bourse de Paris'. PhD thesis, Ecole des Mines de Paris.
North, D. (1977), 'Markets and Other Allocation Systems in History: The Challenge of Karl Polanyi', *Journal of European Economic History*, 6(3): 703–716.
Odirici, V. and R. Corrado (2004), 'Between Supply and Demand: Intermediaries, Social Networks and the Construction of Quality in the Italian Wine Industry.' *Journal of Management and Governance*, 8(2):149–171.
Ong, A. and S. J. Collier (2005), *Global Assemblages: Technology, Politics, and Ethics as Anthropological Problems*. Malden, MA: Blackwell Publishing.
Preda, A. (2002), 'Financial Knowledge, Documents, and the Structures of Financial Activities', *Journal of Contemporary Ethnography*, 31(2): 207–239.
Riles, A. (2004), 'Property as Legal Knowledge: Means and Ends', *The Journal of the Royal Anthropological Institute*, 10(4): 775–795.
Robinson, J. (1980), *Collected Economic Papers*, Cambridge (Massachusetts): MIT Press.
Roitman, J. L. (2005), *Fiscal Disobedience: An Anthropology of Economic Regulation in Central Africa*, Princeton: Princeton University Press.
Uzzi, B. and R. Lancaster (2004), 'Embeddedness and Price Formation in the Corporate Law Market', *American Sociological Review*, 69(3): 319–344.
Velthuis, O. (2003), 'Symbolic Meanings of Prices: Constructing the Value of Contemporary Art in Amsterdam and New York Galleries', *Theory and Society*, 32(2): 181–215.
Velthuis, O. (2005), *Talking Prices: Symbolic Meanings of Prices on the Market for Contemporary Art*, Princeton: Princeton University Press.
White, H. (1981), 'Where Do Markets Come From?', *American Journal of Sociology*, 87(3): 517–547.
Yetkin, S. and E. Serçe (1998), 'Kuruluştan Günümüze Izmir Ticaret Borsası Tarihi', Izmir: Iletişimevi.
Yükseker, D. (2004), 'Trust and Gender in a Transnational Market: The Public Culture of Laleli, Istanbul', *Public Culture*, 16(1): 47–65.
Zafirovski, M. Z. (2000), 'An Alternative Sociological Perspective on Economic Value: Price Formation as a Social Process', *International Journal of Politics, Culture, and Society*, 14(2): 265–295.
Zajac, E. J. and J. D. Westphal (2004), 'The Social Construction of Market Value: Institutionalization and Learning Perspectives on Stock Market Reactions', *American Sociological Review*, 69(3): 433–457.
Zaloom, C. (2006), *Out of the Pits: Traders and Technology from Chicago to London*, Chicago: University of Chicago Press.
Zelizer, V. A. (1981), 'The Price and Value of Children: The Case of Children's Insurance', *American Journal of Sociology*, 86(5): 1036–1056.

Parasitic formulae: the case of capital guarantee products

Vincent-Antonin Lépinay

Introduction

This chapter[1] discusses parasitism as an economic action of interesting properties. Financial derivatives help us to understand what lies behind a supposedly dramatic turn in economies, their increasing 'abstraction' and distance to real economies (Carrier and Miller, 1998). Finance (Poovey, 2003) has long been stigmatized for having been transformed from the real to the abstract, and for parasiting the sound workings of traditional production factors in its efforts to lure investors into easy money (Hertz, 1998). This chapter challenges this view by focusing on the conditions of success or failure in a recent type of a derivative contract known as 'Capital Guarantee Products'. The chapter describes how a financial product that was designed to be a parasite failed to live up to the expectations of its makers. As the chapter will show, the derivation of value 'at a distance' failed, partly because formulaic products are not more abstract or more versatile than their industrial counterparts but, instead, because being a parasite entails a very specific adjustment to the surrounding economies that this product-formula did not achieve.

To begin to understand how derivation works, it is necessary to observe the process of building of goods that it entails. Since the mobility and versatility of financial capital is at stake, it has been necessary to go and observe the winding circulation of one of these formula products in order to grasp the general economy of derivation.[2] In this case, building a parasitic good failed because the dual requirement of living 'off' the economy and 'inside' the economy conflicted: two different temporalities were at play that could not be resolved. Living 'off the economy' entailed fast reactions to the outstanding securities markets' price changes and called for a cautious proximity to these markets. Living 'inside the economy', and, more precisely, inside the bank involved different demands: surviving in an organization such as a bank ruled out the versatility needed for a parasite acting at a distance on outstanding chunks of economies.

The chapter proceeds as follows. The notion of economic parasitism is illustrated through two notions that help demonstrate the specificity of Capital

Guarantee Products: a) economic derivation and b) economic definition. After a preliminary description of the Capital Guarantee Product, the chapter depicts the front office set up and its relation to these formula-products; it then describes the puzzle of preservation and the difficulties raised by their globalized blueprint. As a parasite of definitional economies, a formula-product does have different properties from the 'organisms' underlying it, but it is embedded in concrete processes of valuation, preservation and maintenance. Finally, the chapter ends by telling the story of the slow transformation of the derivational economy into a definitional one.

Economic parasites, derivation and definition

An introductory detour through two different classes of economic goods will serve to grasp the notion of parasitism. The mechanism of parasitic financial formulae is of great interest because they circulate in an asymmetric milieu that protects them from being fully accountable and because they display interesting features when operating in markets. Bundling goods and services is their modus operandi. For the purposes of this chapter, two types of bundles need to be distinguished.

The first kind of bundle is not specific to formula products, but is shared by all goods and services as bundles of properties or qualities. A car is red, has ABS breaks and a turbo engine. These qualities can usually be chosen in a wide range of colours and styles, but most of the elements making up the final good are designed and engineered with a view of being part of this good. They have a fate, built into their design and this fate or downstream use makes them ill-designed for other productive associations. For example, the turbo engine cannot be moved easily to another site, or it would require some major investment to detach it from its initial bundle and integrate it into another bundle. This is the fate of most industrial components. The final good – be it an industrial good meant to be part of another cycle of bundling, or a consumer good meant to disappear – gives value to the components. Without cars, no value could be attributed to rear view mirrors.

Yet, there is another sort of bundling, one that turns final goods – goods never meant to be components of new cycles of production – into meta-goods. The formula (fig.1) operates to achieve what the industrial process of putting together and fusing intermediary components used to do in the first case of bundling. This second type of bundling recycles goods and services that were meant to have an entirely different fate. Consider a service such as the travel package, the travel services that now offer combinations of flights, hotels, car rental and insurances.[3] Each of these elements was not initially devised to complement the other or to feature in packages that take care of the whole Easter break travel puzzle (finding a cheap flight, an even cheaper hotel and a car without spending hours on this search). These travel formulae compete with other solutions that do not belong to the same format of economy. If the flight, hotel and other services had all been developed with the same travel objective, then they would produce a service from integrated parts, and not derive them from unrelated lines of activities.

This second form of bundling belongs to parasitic economic activities, that manipulate goods already available and subvert their initial project (Serres, 1980). Pursuing a non-critical epistemology, Serres came up with the metaphor of the parasite as a model for describing the complex interference that occurs in and across sciences (Serres, 1972). In Serres' language, interference and parasite are not critical terms.[4] They seek to capture the process by which sciences operate and advance, processes that combine and mix together domains, and continuously subvert the search for an origin based on a referential epistemology. Strongly opposing what he calls the regressive method, Serres delineates a 'structural path' to the history of sciences. This structuralist approach shares very little with Lévi-Strauss' brand of structuralism: both are interested in the circulation of goods – women, theories, etc. – and in the formal dimensions of these circulation networks. Serres, however, focuses on the recombinant properties of these networks, not on their general underlying patterns. From his point of view, Lévi-Strauss sides more with regressive methods that try to excavate the ultimate mechanism at work behind observable configurations. In contrast, Serres' notions of interference, parasite and translation endow the actors with more strategic abilities and the capacity to understand, manipulate and graft onto the local properties of a network. That is exactly what parasites do when they enter an organism; the metabolisms of the parasite and the host are compatible and the parasite takes advantage of the by-products of this combination. Yet, in so doing, it does not leave the organism it feeds upon unchanged. It has effects in return, feedback contributions that need to be stabilized to a certain extent so that both the host organism and the parasite hang on in this dance.[5]

The second form of bundling does not focus on the exercise of definition that usually comes with the first form of bundling – that is, of assigning properties to a good and designing this good's combination with other goods into a stable arrangement. Instead it derives a new good or service from previously unrelated goods and services, never meant to meet each other and become part of a distinct economic entity. Derivation is to definition what interference is to reference: it benefits from an already existing good; it inherits rather than produces. Being a parasite is a constant adjustment for the organism grafted onto. Overstressing the difference between definitional economies and derivational ones, however, has its limit too, since, for example, the production processes entailed in the first form of bundling also requires its forms of inheritance and derivation. The threshold between these two forms of economic activities comes down to the control over production factors. As far as it can, definition limits the uncertainty over these factors; it closes the list of events that are likely to interfere with the undertaking. Derivation, on the contrary, allows a passage to uncertainty: it accommodates and curbs, facilitates and channels the flexibility around its host.

The World-wide Secured Exposure 8 Year EMTN on Global Indices S&P 500, Nikkei 225, Eurostoxx 50

- 100% Capital Guarantee At Maturity
- 120% Participation in the Quarterly Average Rise of the Portfolio
- 120% Participation in the Best Performing index in Case of Portfolio Underperformance
- In Euro with Exchange Rate Guarantee

The 'Double Chance' Note – How Does It Work?
Thanks to the double chance mechanism, this note offers two chances to make a return on the global equity market. Indeed, contrary to a classic capital-protected investment, should the final value of the portfolio be below its initial value, the Note will offer a second chance and pay the highest positive performance of the individual indices comprising the portfolio.

Redemption at maturity

The first chance
On the launch date, the value of the portfolio is set at 100.
Every three months following the Start Date (each being a fixing date), the performance of the portfolio is calculated as a percentage of its initial value.
The Final Value of the portfolio will be the arithmetic average of the 32 levels recorded on each Fixing Date.
If the Final Value of the Portfolio is greater than or equal to its initial value, the investor receives 100% of his investment amount plus 120% of the Portfolio performance as calculated above.

The second chance
If the Final Value of the Basket is less than its initial value, the investor receives 100% of the nominal amount plus 120% of the average performance of the best performing index in the portfolio.

Maturity date   February 25, 2008
Underlying   Equally weighted basket composed of the following indices:
                     - DJ EUROSTOXX 50 (STX)
                     - S&P 500 (SP)
                     - NIKKEI 225 (NIX)

Issue Price — 100% nominal Amount
Reoffer Price — 95% of Nominal Amount
Capital Guarantee — 100% of Nominal Amount at Maturity
Redemption at Maturity — Maturity, the holder will receive the greater of the following:
- Nominal x 100%
- Nominal x (100% +120% x [Max(BKT(m) − 1;0)])

with

$$BKT_m = \frac{1}{32}\sum_{t=1}^{32} BKT_t$$

$$BKT_t = \left[\frac{1}{3} \times \frac{SP_t}{SP_i}\right] + \left[\frac{1}{3} \times \frac{STX_t}{STX_i}\right] + \left[\frac{1}{3} \times \frac{NIX_t}{NIX_i}\right]$$

where t means the 32 quarterly fixing dates taken over the life of the Note. SP_t, STX_t, NIX_t is the Closing Price of the fixing date 't' of the relevant index. SP_i, STX_i, NIX_i is the Closing Price on Start Date of the relevant index.
$BKT(i)$ is the Closing Value of the equally weighted basket on Start Date.
Double Chance   If $BKT(m) < BKT(i)$, the Note pays

$$Nominal \times \left(100\% + 120\% \times MAx\left[\frac{SP_m}{SP_i} - 1; \frac{STX_m}{STX_i} - 1; \frac{NIX_m}{NIX_i} - 1; 0\right]\right)$$

with

$$SP_m = \frac{1}{32}\sum_{t=1}^{32} SP_t \;;$$

$$STX_m = \frac{1}{32}\sum_{t=1}^{32} STX_t \;;$$

$$NIX_m = \frac{1}{32}\sum_{t=1}^{32} NIX_t$$

Figure 1: *Term Sheet of a fictional product that resembles the Capital Guarantee Products traded at $Bank (similar structure, illustrative specific values and indices).*

The fact that uncertainty is a resource in financial markets helps to explain why these markets are among the privileged sites of derivation. They have two features that lend themselves so easily to complex formulaic derivation. First, these markets are born out of definitional projects. They are highly standardized: to be granted access to an exchange, a financial security must first become one of these formatted contracts, under the supervision of the exchange authority. It is not the moment of uncertainty but, on the contrary, a purification of the economy into a transferable property right or the possession of a company's debt. This purification is the ultimate exercise of an economic definition: it carves an economic entity and attaches it to regulatory rules. This precise carving out of a stable economic good, however, only lays the ground for exercising uncertainty. Listed securities lend themselves to derivation under this guise, being uncertain in mercantile value but certain under any other considerations, precisely because the initial formatting is a free resource for a parasitic formula-product that does not need to generate this standardization. It is the coming together of definition and derivation that locates the economic specificity of the parasitic formula. If it were only about a precise definition of wealth that an investor was going to get ten years from now – just as when a cautious and timid investor buys the Treasury Bills of a financially conservative State – there would be no space for derivation.[6] Conversely, if an investor wanted to take a position on worldwide economic uncertainty, it would be an impossible task to accomplish from the dispersion of the underlying host.

Financial formulae are oscillating between definition and stabilization of their object on the one hand, and hyperbolic derivation on the other hand. Trying to capitalize on a smart recombination of existing financial products, $Bank does not have control over the underlying hosts. The very design of the formula prevents any simple stabilization, as then the bank would face the risk of killing it. The strategy of $Bank was clearly to graft its activity on an already standardized world and thus benefit from the investments that were made previously and turned these indices and stocks easy to observe and to play with. Similar to a parasite that feeds on an animal whose metabolism provides for the regulation of temperature, the formula hopped onto an economic machine that was invented and maintained elsewhere: the bank only needed to understand the outcomes of this machine, and the variety of scenarios that it could produce. Observing these outcomes was not so easy as it might appear at first sight. All sorts of problems could hinder the smooth grafting of a formula on a set of unrelated indices.

Where should finance be observed?

At first sight, the product under consideration seems very different from existing species in the economy. Indeed, it is a life-size experiment, where the integration of national financial markets is tested on a daily basis. It tries to accomplish the motto of all proponents of the global financial market since the beginning of the 1980s: unifying the different parts of the world economy and creating a system of financial securities reflecting all the pieces of this integrated puzzle. It is somewhat similar to what Donald MacKenzie and Yuval Millo (2003) tracked down when they studied the CBOE and the institution of futures valuation through the Black & Scholes formula. Millo (2003), though, adopts a different approach in focusing primarily on the financial exchange and its actors' interests. The standardization of index futures raises a series of problems that the clearing-houses have had to solve. They had done so through a valuation formula that settles the issue and redistributes the interests. Some groups ended up better off while others lost room to manoeuvre in the institutionalization of an activity that, until then, had been mostly made of secret know-how.

This chapter approaches the creation of the Capital Guarantee Product from a different perspective; it focuses on the creation of a similar product in a very different environment. A bank is the vantage point for the story because there is no organised exchange for this class of products. They are still exchanged over-the-counter (OTC), beyond the purview of market authorities, or beyond the arms-length authority of the regulatory bodies. This location of the products – circulating between banks and next to the exchanges in which standardized goods are traded – makes it a particularly good candidate for observing parasitic economies at work. OTC markets have risen in the past twenty years. Although their volume must be read with great accuracy and a cold mind, it is huge, accounting for several times the volume of the American economy.[7] The parasite has grown big compared to its host.

Banks, as such, are not new in the recent landscape of the social sciences, but they have, first and foremost, been submitted to sociological analysis through their most visible side: the front office, the site of fast and big money (Godechot, 2001, 2007), of fancy careers (Hasselström, 2003), of rugged or genius traders (Beunza and Stark, 2004) and of complex socio-technical devices linking traders to the outside market world (Knorr Cetina and Bruegger, 2002c). Yet, another side of the bank has come under little scrutiny from social scientists, the back and middle offices. Although they are not so glamorous and thrilling, the middle and back office are as important as the front office in the felicitous achievements of deals. The fact that they have been overlooked in recent social studies of finance may stem from their seemingly low potential to challenge current economic sociology. At first sight, they appear not to provide little more than access to another puzzling case for organizational sociology. The front office, to the contrary, shines with all the expectations raised by an exotic and hectic world.

Yet, this way of dividing the bank is not fruitful if one's aim is to grasp what is specific about financial institutions. The organization may seem poor when it is stripped of its linkage to the front office and of the constraints specific to the dealing of financial contracts. The front stage is exciting, full of astounding accounts that disregard the structuring backstage. Making deals without the scaffolding of the middle and back office may be thrilling but it leaves unanswered the bulk of the problem: how can an allegedly global financial market work amidst partitioned financial institutions? The speed that is observed on trading floors reinforces the myth of an information sphere detached from the other flows of goods and services still attached to the materiality of face-to-face exchange. Nevertheless, finance is still as much a business of accuracy, of bean counters double checking, as it is an exercise of expert engineering and fast reaction to price changes.

Following the formula product offers an alternative to this dichotomy. As its name clearly hints, it is both formula and product. As a formula, it belongs to the world of fast deals achieved on financial markets that are fairly well integrated. It can be changed and amended and it retains fluidity and variation. As a product, it needs to be maintained and processes of maintenance do not have the same fluidity as formulae. They are embedded into slower material frames. They cannot be recast quickly because products belong to the world of economic definition. Hence, Capital Guarantee Product is a unique case study of a parasitic activity that runs across the bank. It offers a cross section where previously only sections were available.

Birth of a parasite: the front office story

In the middle of the 1990s, $Bank decided to launch a new class of products aimed at a broad array of clients. Dubbed 'correlation products', these had already been tested by the large international bank UBS (Union des Banques Suisses), but the experiment had been a failure. Instead of capitalizing on the innovation, UBS had been drained of a consistent flow of money. $Bank launched a series of new studies to assess the feasibility of the product and soon issued its first contract. The principle of correlation products was simple: the return depended on a formula linking several outstanding securities. The more correlated the components of this formula, the more difficult it was for the bank to hedge and make money on it. Conversely, a highly uncorrelated set of securities made it easy for the bank to hedge and was also synonymous with a bad return for the client. Therefore, correlation of the set elements was crucial in deciding the money that $Bank would have to pay, or would make. The formula assigning the pay off would usually assume the form documented in this chapter.

The number of underlying financial securities (national debts, interest rates, major world-wide companies stocks, national stock markets indices) could vary significantly. Starting from five, it could go up to as many as 20 in some cases. In addition to this variability in the number of the formula components, it was also very flexible in the range of individual component that could contribute to making up the pay off. The client had their say in the design of the product. Given that the issuer bets on the un-correlation of the components and the fact that it will pay only the performance of the worst performing security (or index), the margin of intervention left to the client's discretion was not large, but it did acquire the flavour that customized financial products have. This product realized another trade off beyond the one it achieved within the pool of underlying securities (the correlation). In mitigating the formula (the worst performance) with an insurance (the guarantee) the investment gained increased appeal.

The projected outcome of this financial product is a middle point species, located between the insurance (capital guarantee) and the investment (return linked to the performance of patches of real economy). It plays upon the appeal of both the insurance and the investment, and it is purposively meant to attract business companies that want to hedge their economic activities against downturn (an insurance indexed on real economy data), as well as wealthy individual investors looking for the thrill of the security investment, with the safety net provided with by the guarantee. In addition to a combining two existing types of products, the CGP draws a link that can be customized to suit the needs of either corporations or wealthy individuals.

Combining indices, stocks and currencies from different national markets was not new when $Bank launched the product. Portfolio managers, hedge funds, and even some services for individual investors were already crossing the boundaries between national economies and combining securities exchanged in remote financial places. That said, the real innovation came from the transformation of a service (just like the ones provided by portfolio managers and hedge funds) into a continuously negotiable, transferable security. This was not N services provided simultaneously – as when a wealthy investor asks his fund manager to buy Coca-Cola and Telefónica stocks to balance the risk of his portfolio – but a single service covering the places of each component. Just as securitization was a way to turn into a (sometimes) continuously tradable entity what had been previously a set of completely heterogeneous industrial elements, the Capital Guarantee Product transformed the dispersion of local financial exchanges and their respective activities (brokers, traders, trading rules, dividend payment rules) into a continuously tradable service provided by one bank.

Hedging the new product

Beginning with the continuous growth of the equity market, worldwide, until the collapse of spring 2001, a set of circumstances made the CGP project appealing and attracted investors. Yet, the principle of a worldwide financial instrument started to raise difficulties very early on. Bridging the gaps of distant exchanges was theoretically feasible; the financial integration heralded by the heroes of derivatives – Merton Miller (1986, 1991, 1997) being the most outspoken of these – seemed to be around the corner. But managing these products was far less straightforward. The continuity in trading, long searched by $Bank, proved to be far more demanding to implement. The reason for these hiccups in the management of the new class came from the hedging method adopted. The details of this method highlight both the shrewdness of the approach and its shortcomings.

The guarantee of the formula dictates a very specific mode of investment. On the clients' side, once the money is off to the bank, there is little to do other than hope that the strategy turns out to be successful. For $Bank, things only begin to move when it receives the money. The bank is tied to the guarantee and has to engage in dynamic trading to make sure that the money will grow. It cannot simply keep it in a vault. This dynamic trading entails daily care of the portfolio, investing the money in rising stocks, pulling it out of declining sectors. Several financial places must be browsed every trading day to hedge the formula products portfolio. With the success of its new business, however, it soon became difficult for $Bank to hedge product by product, on each different financial exchange. This proved inefficient, particularly because different products' components could, theoretically, mutually offset their risks and turn the aggregation of individual hedging useless and costly.

Instead of thinking in terms of product, it became clear that the unit to be hedged had to be the portfolios themselves. By aggregating thousands of products with each a different term, basket of underlying assets and sensitivity to market changes, the portfolio revealed new characteristics. There was an obvious time gain achieved through this technique: each exchange was visited only once during the trading day and all the relevant components of the products (risk and return) were handled as one big open position. The script, as expressed by the chief financial engineer of the desk, was as follows: if the portfolio contained 100 products, each with slightly specific characteristics (so that it would not be 100 times product Y) then all of the positions created by these products were aggregated and a measure of risk was computed. Out of this computation would come the net risk position of the portfolio. To hedge these risks, the trader would then buy futures[8] of the underlying components (futures on an index, on a stock . . .) with a view to hedge the portfolio as a whole rather than client contract by client contract. If the formula contained national economic indices, then the trader would buy listed futures of these indices in order to balance the risk that each index might go down. The same mechanism would work for stocks of big corporation for which listed futures were available.

According to the market analysis done in $Bank, the formula accepted by the clients could be hedged without the issuer ($Bank) taking any risks.[9] The engineers boasted about their thorough assessment of the risks involved and cast the analysis in opposition to the failure of UBS.[10] This script, as sleek and transparent as it was, was not familiar with the temporalities of the market and the poor integration of the exchanges. The ordeal of the traders in charge of hedging them was of a different kind from what the engineers had anticipated.

In the engineers' idealized scenario, computation, risks and hedging were only words, and did not take into account the practical conditions of trading. This product was drawing on a world of finance that had not yet been realized. The traders had to tackle hundreds of small difficulties to make this description come true and yet they would not even come close to fulfilling this script. Consider the hedging of Asian securities entering the formula. When the French market opens at 9am, it is the end of the trading day in Japan; Japanese brokers work for only a couple more hours and then, after closing, are less likely to pick up the phone. The hedging must be completed very quickly, that is, before the

US market opens and during the time when the French market is still absorbing the shocks of the last deals completed on the Asian markets. The incomplete overlap of the exchange timetables is not specific to this product, but it contributes to its riskiness due to the fact that the product can be 'recalled' during the French market trading window. If the hedging strategy suggests buying (or selling) on Asian indices while their exchanges are closed, the risk is entirely on $Bank.

This event is not just a thought experiment. It is actually very likely to occur precisely because the product scheme is based on the correlation. The hedging of each component (stocks or indices, as in our case) depends on its relative performance vis-à-vis all the others. When the French and Japanese markets are both open, relative performance can be observed and the hedging strategy corrected – but this is possible only during a short window of time. The partial overlap of each exchange's trading hours destabilizes the claims of continuity and integration that the marketing of the product boasted. The traders in charge of the capital guarantee formula ended up spending hours trying to make sense of market changes and to figure out the best move without risking too much. Instead of acting at a distance, manipulating the stocks that they had bought to hedge $Bank's agreement with its clients, they found themselves mostly confused, glued to their screens and unable to surf from one hedge to the other.[11]

The engineers' script first encountered a problem with the dispersion of the product entailed by the hedging requirements. The dispersion was geographical and temporal, running against the grain of the integration imagined by a formula product designed to graft onto several exchanges of the world economy. This is where profit comes from here: the poor integration of existing financial places creates the added value of the correlation formula product. But this is also where, beyond the ideal scripts of engineers, $Bank agreed, in a daring project, to bet on the ability of its operators to bridge the gap opened between the exchanges. Unfortunately, the motion of the formula products was going to be even slower than that of the exchanges. The front office puzzles raised by practical problems largely unaccounted for by engineers' scripts were only a small part of the difficulties met by these types of products. An even more basic imperative attached to financial contracts spanning several years and making space for customization was that of their conservation. $Bank received a reminder that, before and above the subtleties displayed by modern finance, banking means saving and preserving assets. This basic banking activity was challenged by the fact that formula products had to exist simultaneously in the front office – in the fast whirl of market changes – and in the back office, in the slow world of precise confirmations and accurate maintenance.

Slowing down: keeping track of a parasite

When the formula product is followed beyond the trading room, its narrative is being rewritten. The myth of a smooth intellectual exercise is already behind us, now that the difficulties that the traders encountered have been noted. These difficulties almost exclusively involved the price (hedging a price change) and its operators. The causes of these difficulties, however, were also operating on another floor of the bank. The back office officers were not as concerned with the price and its volatile trajectories, but they had to make sure that the products were kept 'in hand'. Their business was to trade on the basis of what they called the 'perimeters' of the portfolios. Put as simply as possible, the perimeter was the very basic and boring activity of counting and checking the characteristics of the products managed by $Bank. The reason that the execution of these tasks was not as trivial as it might seem comes from the time span of these products' lives and the variety of their characteristics.

Kept in portfolios for up to ten years, CGPs usually underwent several changes over these long periods. One of the first and most acute consequences was that no single trader would remain in charge of a single product over its entire life cycle. Three, four or five traders had already been responsible for the products I analysed. The turnover in trading rooms was high, but it did not compare to that of the back office. Faced with allegedly boring and scarcely rewarding tasks, these officers would not remain in charge of any portfolio for very long. This was a real problem for $Bank, but no successful financial incentives had been put in place to remedy this constant drain. In both the front and back offices, there was no human continuity; on the contrary, while individuals would turn over products would stay.

This was particularly harmful for the bank because of the way formula products were designed. During the negotiation preceding the deal, clients could discuss the underlying components of the contract with the engineers and the trader. Telefónica or France Télécom, IBM or Microsoft; but once the product was launched, several market events could force the partners to meet again in order to redesign the product. France Télécom goes bankrupt: which stock should be substituted? Unexpected events could occur in the markets that would lead to a new or a modified contract.[12] Once again, the fact that these products were written under different regulations through their underlying made things more complicated. The perimeter was not so trivial, simply because it involved the preservation of the product, one of the fundamental functions of banking.

Preserving the product essentially meant preserving the latest and most accurate version of the contract, the one that was shared by the bank and its client. The changes occurring during the life of the product needed to be checked on both sides to ensure that the bank was not taking care of a product that was out-of-date on the client's side. Each change entailed a series of confirmations between the bank and the client. Sometimes, it could take several rounds to settle a disagreement. Each time, the previous version had to be amended and modified. But this waltz involving the bank and the client, actually displayed a fragmentation within the bank. The bank was not represented by one person only. It was divided into (1) the trader who was kept informed of every product change and (2) the back office manager who supervised exchanges with the client (the chief financial officers of corporations or other banks' back offices). Given the huge turnover in both positions, the product itself had to have the last word, because individuals were too volatile.

Sharing this information was not a problem in theory, but the rhythms of the front and the back office were so at odds with each other that it made the circulation of these documents chaotic. The front office was constantly trying to speed up the deals. Sometimes, a product change was vouched for by a trader without even making sure that the back office manager would agree to it. Oral agreements that were enough on the front end were banned in the back. The remedy to these conflicting cultures and practices assumed the form of a folder containing every version of the contract, from the initial deal with its pre-confirmation to the latest changes. This folder also held all of the email and fax exchanges between the parties (client, trader, back office manager). The back office manager kept a second version of the folder, identical to the first, only placed three floors above.

Finally, there was a third version that could seldom be viewed by the back office manager. This threefold architecture was meant to protect the living archives of $Bank transactions. These differences in approach splitting the front and back office were notorious, and to contain them a procedure had been loosely agreed upon to implement the changes in the folders. When a change was in order with the client's approval, the trader would issue a 'ticket' ordering a change in the back office database and the back office manager would confirm to the client and to the trader when the product was 'reconciled'[13] in both databases. But the folders offered a solution that was not fully satisfactory. First, they had to be physically located somewhere in the bank. The traders wanted them right above their trading stations or within reach of their assistants' desk. They were piled up in cardboard boxes on a shelf, above the computers. The traders and their assistants would pick up a box, check the contract by removing the folder from the box, and rush back to their telephone or computer screen. Taking care was not a notorious quality of the traders. And their casual dealing with the folders reached the point where they actually lost one.

The lost folder episode was remembered as a trauma by the back office manager, whose job put him directly in charge of maintaining the living archives. This lost folder helped trigger a change in the organization of the archives for deal conservation. For the product in question the procedure had not been followed and the two versions kept in the back office were completely unrelated to the one running when the loss occurred. Of course, the folders were not the only traces of these deals: they were also written in databases, in both front and back offices. There again, $Bank's division of tasks was also way to cope with incompatible cultures and to safeguard of the deals against hazardous events hitting $Bank. But the serious discrepancy between the hectic traders and the careful and cautious back office managers was marked in database management principles. In the front office the database was treated flexibly and could be modified by several different operators, tracked by their Lotus email code. It was decentralized but limited to the front operators. The back office's practices embodied the exact opposite of this liberal principle. Only the back office manager could ask the supervisor of the database to implement a change, and it had to be kept in written form in some other folders populating the bank. Faced with such a gap, the traders had become used to bypassing the agreed-upon procedure and lived with their database and the folder as the sole evidence of the product.

The discovery of the loss came through an unexpected reconciliation with the client. Upon having to pay a yearly amount of money, the bank discovered that the client expected an entirely different sum. The product-written-in-the-database did not match the product-held-by-the-client. After trying, in vain, to locate the lost folder, the trader and the back office manager realized that the two other folder-versions of the deal were of no use given the disconnection between the front and back office bases. The solution came from collaboration with the client who sent all the changes implemented on the deal since its inception. The shame and embarrassment that seized the desk spurred a new policy initiative to combine the liberal government asked for by the traders and the restricted access required by the conservation imperative of banks.

The initial solution adopted by $Bank entailed building a safe, far from the hectic rhythms of the front office and its unsafe surfaces, an unsafeness embodied in the moving folder, in order to protect deals while being able to follow the succeeding changes. Left alone on this shaky surface, products could easily lose their unity. The bank could hedge the 'wrong' deal and lose significant amounts of money.[14] But the solution provided by the safe did not suit these deals since it froze the contracts instead of opening them up to market changes. The safe was reassuring to the back office manager because it stabilized once and for all what had been agreed upon. Ultimately though, the gains came from the tamed instability, not from a contract's perpetual preservation.[15] Unstable derivation was the only way to gain with these products. Yet the amounts of money invested were so important that accuracy inevitably became a major constant concern. The solution that was eventually devised to sooth this tension was a piece of software that might allow for both protection (the safe) and dispersion (respecting the multifaceted nature of the product). The software did not replace the databases already running in the front and back office. It was placed on top of them, feeding on existing sources with a series of warnings triggered as soon as a product did not feature the same characteristics in the two databases. The novelty of the software came from its digital archives. Instead of keeping faxes, print out of emails, photocopies of confirmation and tickets, it was decided that every relevant piece of material pertaining to the deal would be available in the database, and attached to the software. The software's structure resembled any current email software, with a core – the product identity card, so to speak, instead of the message body of an email – and attached to it all the materials modifying or clarifying the deal.

At the beginning of the software's conception, full and open access was desirable to most traders and, although more reluctantly, by the back office manager. More posted information outclassed the back office's culture of cautious restriction. This liberal stance met its limit when the traders and their assistants realized that opening the software to salespersons would give the latter access to precious information that the traders wanted to keep proprietary. Sharing information with back office operators was not deemed problematic, because the back office was traditionally restricted to secondary tasks. Sharing this same information with salesmen, however, raised another problem, as they, as well as the traders and the engineers, were simultaneously in touch with the clients. The negotiability of the product's characteristics could be taken too far by salesmen who would often try to compromise excessively with clients to make a deal.

The new software was jeopardizing the management of priorities and, more importantly, the distribution of the desk's profit. Fundamentally, the properties of the formula product requested special treatment, against the grain and the routines of this bank. This treatment was tearing apart the old organization, while finance was proving that it had a body, fragile and made of a very tenuous fabric. Even though the formula tried to build upon an existing and stabilized world of securities and to only generate enough uncertainty to distance itself from less appealing forms of investment, this small uncertainty was enough to turn derivational activities into full fledged industrial concerns. Time was a crucial element in this slow transformation: it was that through which return was achieved, but it was also that which called for attentive care.

Protecting the capital

The successes encountered by the products devised by a once small team were such that it was no longer possible to carry out the deals on a client-to-client basis; the craftsmanship of the early age was irremediably gone and it had to be substituted by industrial processing. The choice of a system coupling information management and pricing was quite strategic: first, a large amount of money would be spent to build what was expected to be 'solid and enduring'. Second, it would involve not only the front office (trading and selling activities) but also the middle and back offices. The research group that was set to choose the form of this new system wanted to solve many problems faced by banks all at once; the front-back gap came first on this agenda as it was the source of most defaults and discontentment from the clients. Related to this security problem, the cost of managing each of the deals manually was becoming so significant that it nearly balanced out the profits made through the commercial margins. The market for these kinds of integrated systems was still in its infancy and using a provider for this very specific and evolving need was considered cumbersome. It would also have amounted to helping a software company build what some of the bank's managers considered as the latest weapon for fighting off future competition. This solution would have been available to another bank and the investment would be worthless.

$Bank therefore decided to go for an 'in house' system, which it called OPTIMA. OPTIMA was supposed to provide $Bank with all the functionality of a pricing software able to work for any kind of complex product but, in addition to that, it also provided middle and back office software fed by the front office pricing software.[16] This integrated software was a novelty. Concern for the growing costs of back office processing was being resolved at the same time as the security of the deals was increased through the integrated system. The economic rationale for such a big commitment kept being put forth by the manager, even a couple of years after the system's implementation and the recognition of the flaws in this gigantic and presumptuous project.

Another rationale, put forth by different persons (mostly top management in and above the trading rooms), insisted on another dimension of this project. $Bank wanted to let its clients and competitors know the magnitude of the skills it could claim. An in-house system, driven by this new class of products and bridging the gap of the processing centres of a market department was also supposed to be convincing to clients. It was expected that security issues ($Bank not losing data, not mis-pricing the products and hence not running the risk of going bankrupt) and a conspicuous display of investment in a new domain of the market would attract clients. This second rationale, although slightly different from the first one, also belongs to what could be called an economic argument. They both focused on the same bottom line, the return on such a massive investment.

Yet a different story was also being told and this other narrative pointed to a different 'economy' where the bottom line was not only the return on the investment but the more general definition of the company and of the product for which it had created a market. In this second story, told in more private venues (and sometimes bluntly denied by the managers), capital was not only meant to yield a two digit return and to produce rapid flows of money. It was primarily the fragile and fungible work conditions that had to be taken care of, for fear that this business unit could be removed from the company. In solidly bridging the front and back offices through an information system that had no equivalent anywhere else, the managers who made this decision strongly attached 'complex derivatives' activity to the rest of the company. It became very difficult to imagine that this department of the bank could be detached from the company and sold to another bank. For the managers who had launched this activity at the end of the 1980s, the fear of a merger or of being sold as a service – and attached to another bank willing to complement its gamut of services – faded as this system was finally put to work. Such worries were probably excessive when the project was carried out at the beginning of the 1990s, but they turned out to be justified – retrospectively – when one of the trading rooms (commodities and emerging countries debt) of $Bank was sold because it didn't fit with the bank's new strategy.[17] This particular trading room had never been very prestigious, and it had been run through a standard price-setting procedure and an information system that was compatible with any other financial institution's. It was not embedded in such a way as to make its removal either impossible or too pricy for the acquirer.

After the strategic definitional move achieved through the integrated information system, a competitor willing to buy this very lucrative business would need to get rid of all of his previous systems (pricing software + back office software + accounting software) in order to adopt the one running the business, and they would also need to buy the right to develop OPTIMA on other products because it was proprietary. Alternatively, they would have to detach the business from the spinal structure that held it together and attempt to switch to another system. In both cases, the cost of such translations would be very high, and was expected to keep corporate raiders at a distance. Management also expected that the specificity of these products would hamper efforts to transport them to another environment; the products and the system had been designed in such a way as to not be easily detachable from one another. It came as a bundle but, with the incorporation of back office facilities, it ended up being much more than a package. Actually, management struggled against moves towards a packaged commodification of its activities, doing its utmost to attach it through as many channels to make its substitutability unlikely. The contrast between the software system and the parasitic principles of Capital Guarantee Products could not have been greater. CGPs thrived on the instability of their own formula and their ability to graft, circulate and switch easily from one market to the other. They were not meant to lend themselves to this kind of major investment.

Parasites facing the symmetry

Other financial institutions were monitoring the accounting operations of $Bank and of its activities on the stock market, either to launch a raid on it or more simply to acquire some of its equities or debt. The more conspicuous its success, the more refined the investigations of investors willing to buy shares of $Bank. But this increasing intrusion into more detailed characteristics of the business was also made possible by the parallel move of regulatory bodies that forced a set of new disclosure rules on the company and a new frame to publicize the results of yearly activity. The private activity that $Bank had carried out so far was jeopardized by this pressing request for transparency all the way down. The former way of running the business was gone, and the representation of capital that came with it fell apart gradually. Private capital and the unity of the firm were slowly being challenged by the call for transparency of regulatory authorities and pressing shareholders.

The reluctance to let the company, and more specifically the derivative activity, be commodified – like the services they were selling to more and more clients had been – was also triggered by another set of circumstances also connected to its success. $Bank was making a lot of money because it was also taking risks that other banks could not take. It was feeding on ill-chartered and poorly understood fields of finance: correlation products were exactly that breed of risky services that other banks failed to provide. Due to its sophisticated techniques of pricing, the portfolio of Capital Guarantee Products could not be valued in the same way as the other assets and liabilities in the bank. This made the whole activity rather secretive from the vantage points of the shareholders of $Bank since the greatest source of return was also the least transparent. In practice the whole portfolio of products was off the balance sheet. As such it did not stand on an equal footing with the rest of the bank. Other derivative products could be valued because they had a longer history, and the authorities regulating the financial markets had come to an agreement on the risks that they entailed as well as on the metrics that needed to be applied to assess the value of a bank's assets.

Soon, success raised a significant problem. The provision rules set by the Basle Committee and enforced by the Commission des Marchés Financiers (CMF) in France made it mandatory to withdraw a part of the bank's assets (actually liabilities due at term) from market activities. It was the old precautionary principle prevalent in banks that made them not only intermediaries between cash providers and cash seekers but also sites of conservation. In case of a market downturn, it was expected that this liquidity would be used to pay back the investors and to cover the liability of $Bank. The more risky the trades and the markets $Bank was involved in, the greater the amount of money they were supposed to set aside as a provision. In a way, their success could never be complete because it was always accompanied by an additional constraint and it set a limit to the company's right to deploy refined strategies. Once again, the formulae had to be slowed down and removed from the locus of risk and return.

Calculating the burden of this success (the amount of liquidity to set aside) was derived after a measure ('Value-at-Risk' or VaR) that set the risk exposure entailed by the various degrees of liquidity of the global financial commitment. $Bank had a special risk exposure and hence it could ask for a customized Value-at-Risk that took into consideration the exposure's specific structure. This 'homemade' measure allowed $Bank to adapt the metric of risk to the likelihood of market downturn it really faced.[18] It didn't necessarily mean to alleviate the burden of the provision, but it ensured a better fit between the risks and the provision. $Bank applied for the right to develop its own risk metric when it realized that its very lucrative activity was slowly burdening it with costs through the provision requirements. The application was granted by the CMF, providing a thorough reorganization and what was termed a rationalization of the deals' processing system. The rationale for granting $Bank its own risk metric was the recognition that it had developed a financial specialization that was genuinely one-of-a-kind and that called for a unique set of tools to measure the risk exposure. But this uniqueness had yet to find a common ground with the expectations of shareholders.

As a 'publicly traded company' with a property shared between many isolated investors, $Bank had to allow a public eye into the company's business. Rationalization entailed a clearer circulation of information between the front and back office, the uniqueness of the volatility measures, and a greater transparency. In a nutshell, the operators had to comply with a blue print (seventy pages of technical conditions to be met before $Bank would be allowed to devise its own risk metric) that had effects, right down to risk assessment of the deal.

The managers of the trading room did not receive the pressure for more transparency cheerfully. Instead, they experienced it as a threat to the 'intimacy' of their work. They wanted to keep off the regulatory body's supervision and remain at a distance from the investors' gaze.

The obvious lack of accountability expressed itself on the client's side. The French body in charge of protecting banks' clients had warned $Bank about lack of clarity in their commercial prospectus: the description of the formula, the return and the guarantee had not been made explicit in the first versions of the Capital Guarantee Products. As it was still un-chartered territory, it was decided that when a financial product would assume the form of a formula combining existing outstanding securities, it would be flagged as a 'formula product' in order to raise client's awareness of the risk entailed. All of these clarifications cast tremendous light on an activity that was thriving in the grey zone of regulation.

Integrating the complex derivatives business was obviously not meant to put at risk the competitiveness of the company, and the managers did not attempt to extract more profit from the company through the adoption of this particular technology. The solid but complex tying of their activity to the rest of the company did not take place on the same level as the 'return on property' focused on by the principal-agent theory: it was a different plane occupied by salaried people who had built an emotional tie to the activity and it was not meant to run against the short term efficiency of the activity itself and its contribution to $Bank. Instead, it was usually mentioned that the two would work together. Caring for the very peculiar form of capital they had built was not primarily intended to increase its return but to slow down the process of its commoditization. Investors were looking for a more liquid company, for an investment in which they would not get stuck, and from which they would be able to withdraw as soon as they perceived the slightest signal of weakness. The attempt to transform a parasitic enterprise by anchoring it into the company would represent a drawback for investors, if they sought not only the liquidity of the securities (equities and bonds) but also the liquidity of the company as such (land, buildings, salaried skilful workers).

Nominal liquidity does not require real liquidity, but the latter adds a crucial property to the securities that the former does not offer. In cases of real liquidity, the holder of a security – or of a sufficiently great number of securities – can convert a property directly into real property. One can actually transform social (shared) capital into real capital, one can end up actually owning 'for real' what the company is made up of. This continuity between holding property rights and owning what they stand for is a new feature of this real liquidity called for by the investors. This added feature can be valued but it certainly has a cost. If investors were to become accustomed to the idea of companies as merely interchangeable pieces that can be built up and taken down easily, the resistance of the parasitic business managers would probably scale down the market value of the company. The reason for this stems from the lessened compatibility of the company as an element of a portfolio. The ideal of real liquidity takes the following form: a company flexible enough to allow real time composition and decomposition of its capital according to economic sector trends. This is the exact replication of the principle of Capital Guarantee Products' parasitic formula.

To achieve such a scenario, investors need companies with departments and units built like separable segments. To be viable, the locus of attachment between these basic elements and the whole must be as standard as possible so that any piece might substitute any another. Accounting requirements enforced by the national and supranational bodies (Commission Bancaire and ISDA[19]) contribute to building these sorts of companies. They impose strong criteria on the disclosure rules such that only standard kinds of economic activity can pass these tests. Translation into these accounting categories frames the possibility of economic activity. Departing strongly from this background, the strategy of our team of managers was to seek to preserve a sphere of intimacy, away from the scrutinizing eye of investors, should these even take the form of an independent body like the ISDA. Since they could not pursue this strategy openly, however, and would have run the risk of putting into question the socialized character of $Bank' capital, they borrowed a side track. Investors did not supervise managers' choices with detailed scrutiny. It is important to note that this choice, although advertised as crucial by the managers themselves, was not associated with a conservative strategy when it was implemented. At that time, real liquidity was probably too explicitly linked to the rogue raiders of the 1980s, so much so that this apparently innocuous choice went through and shaped the investors asset in the long term.

Conclusion

The notion of parasitism developed by Michel Serres offers an alternative to an approach of the economy that would focus exclusively on the exchange and the production. Exchange entails a reciprocity against which parasitic goods fight. Being parasites, they must be silent to survive and maintaining the silence proved to be the a major limitation to Capital Guarantee Products principles. As the amount of money invested and the stake for investors grew, regulatory agencies started to threaten an activity that previously had been conducted out of sight. The call for more accountable practices that followed the growth of the formula product's eye-catching success was a way of forcing a symmetry that shed too much light on the parasite. Harrison White (1981, 2002) has long shown that the notions of control and uncertainty are crucial to understand markets but he has also over-emphasized the boundaries that markets and companies trace in order to protect their activities. As a result, his focus on existing production markets has been excessive, yet insufficient on innovations that constantly make these boundaries shift and drift. Even looking beyond innovations, it is questionable that starting out with production helps understand the genealogy of markets. Parasitism may be the condition of the economy, such that production markets are only a fraction of what is at play there. Understanding the system and the rules of parasitism is thus more important than giving a still picture of reified markets. It may then be the case, as numerous anthropological studies suggest (Descola, 2005), that theft and capture are also relevant objects of study (more than exchange and production, for instance) for grasping what is specific to the economy.

Even if formula products such as Capital Guarantee Products are not about theft, they are designed asymmetrically. The outstanding securities from which the product's price is derived are themselves stabilized enough so that $Bank does not have to control its upstream market. A number of institutions take care of that stability and $Bank benefits from this upstream standardization. But who suffers and who gains advantage? Parasites are often beneficial to existing production markets. The literature on standards in economics identifies a series of technologies that were made compatible in order to become standardized and enter into several lines of production (Katz and Shapiro, 1994). Interference is built-in the notion of compatibility so that the norm becomes crossings and crossbreedings of lines of goods and processes rather than stability of markets.

The extraordinary growth of all kinds of derivative-based businesses has spurred an equally extraordinary literature disputing the pros ad cons of derivatives markets (MacKenzie, 2006). At stake are the accounting rules that one should adopt to assess the impact of these goods and markets. As they cross existing markets and hybridize existing processes, parasitic goods disrupt the normative ground upon which their worth is based and call for a political discussion on whether or not and under which conditions we want to live in the wake of their rhythms.

Notes

1 Michel Callon, Julia Elyachar, Kim Fortun, Doug Holmes, Georges Marcus, Fabian Muniesa and Yuval Millo have been very kind to discuss some of the points developed in this chapter.
2 I spent 7 months in the trading room of '$Bank'. This bank, among the leading actors in the area of complex financial products business at the end of the 1990s, is kept anonymous here due to the nature the material I was allowed to use and the depth of access I was given. Subsequently, I was hired as a middle office manager in the bank, stayed there for six months and then moved for two months to the back office. Prior to this stay in the bank itself I studied mathematical finance at Université Paris 7 ('Jussieu') and was enrolled in a MA in stochastic processes applied to financial mathematics. See Lépinay (2003) for an extended version of the fieldwork access issues and the question of finance pedagogy.
3 I am grateful to Franck Cochoy for having pointed out to me the economic importance of these travel packages. Cochoy has been interested in the packaging and its lack of treatment by economists and sociologists alike. See Cochoy (2002).
4 Serres is not widely read by Anglo-American social scientists: see Brown (2002) for an exception. For another reading of some of Serres' most fruitful concepts see also Bowker (2005). Serres (1980) hints at the broader reach of his analysis, particularly at the insights that they offer for a non-foundational economics.
5 Guesnerie and Rochet (1993) offer a sophisticated demonstration of the possible destabilizing effects of an older parasitic financial product, listed futures. Traded alongside the underlying

6. securities, futures can actually operate contrary to the high expectations raised by its engineering in the 1970s: not complete the markets time-wise, but instead introduce 'another' market competing and interfering with the spot market.
6. The USA used to be a good example for financial conservativeness. This is no longer the case. The politics of deregulation is a clear acknowledgement of the superiority of derivations over definitions. The State used to be a fixed point in the Economy on which investors could lean and rely; it has become an actor like any other, trying to exploit markets when they are available, only to sneak away from them before they enter downturns.
7. Most of these OTC deals are swaps or similar products. The 'nominal' value on which the flow of interests is based is usually not exchanged, it indicates what these interests flow have become.
8. Futures are derivatives following a much simpler scheme. Their value is attached to a single stock or index, so that when the underlying moves up or down, the future follows a simple reaction function.
9. It is the risk-neutral world version of these products.
10. UBS had sold correlation products without understanding the risks incurred by this strategy. The component that the Swiss bank had written in its contract were too tightly correlated, as the story would be told in $Bank.
11. Karin Knorr Cetina and Urs Bruegger (2002a, 2002b) have studied with great rigour the emotions that traders experience when they manage to *screw* the market or, conversely, when they fail at making their way into it. The phenomenology that they bring to bear on these issues is most welcome but it emphasizes the informational dimension of finance and does not consider the composition of goods – whether definitional or derivational – as they map these feelings. Their interest for global currency traders could be rephrased if they were to make space for the very peculiar good that is being traded.
12. There were also changes that had no effect on the contract per se, but which called for a new implementation of the contract-in-$Bank database.
13. This was the word (*'réconcilier'* in French) to describe the procedure used when the database of the front and the back office wanted to check the identity of their deals.
14. During the fieldwork, the reconciliation was launched bankwide in order for $Bank to obtain from the French regulatory body the right to create – and circulate – its own VaR ('Value-at-Risk', a risk assessment method taking into account the exposure of banks various financial engagement and setting the amount of capital protected from the market). $Bank appealed to the Commission Bancaire to be granted an in-house VaR because these types of deals needed a customized measure of risk. During these reconciliation procedures, a couple of mismatches were discovered; among them, a deal written 'upside down' by the trader and equally hedged upside down. The term of the deal, was, thankfully, very short term, $Bank was short of 500 000 francs (roughly 80 000 euros) because of this erroneous writing.
15. On a similar puzzle of how adequately to preserve of biodiversity, but in the case of crop fields of Turkey, see the work of Zuhre Aksoy (2004). The seeds can not be separated from their environment – made up of the expert farmers and the soil – and perpetuated *ex situ*. Only the cycles of seasons warrant their reproduction.
16. The person who invented OPTIMA devised a functional computer language that could express any financial product, as long as it respected the basic features of Finance.
17. One must remember that the golden age of the raiders (eg, Michael Milken) and the memories of their deeds were still very vivid in the financial communities. The time was not so long ago that companies started to be literally put to pieces and sold as bits of economic activities or even as capital (land, buildings, etc) through the infamous 'leverage buyout' method.
18. The VaR was developed with a view to covering risks with very definite properties; as soon as the bank could recognize that it faced different patterns of risk, it could prefer to switch to another metrics.
19. The International Swap and Derivative Association (ISDA) is a bankers' coalition aiming at setting standards for derivative activities. Their role in turning off balance sheet products into measurable and respectable services is important. See Flanagan (2001) for an overview of their organization.

References

Aksoy, Z. (2005), 'The conservation of crop genetic diversity in Turkey: An analysis of the linkages between local, national and international levels', PhD Thesis, University of Massachusetts Amherst.
Beunza, D., and D. Stark (2004), 'Tools of the trade: The socio-technology of arbitrage in a Wall Street trading room', *Industrial and Corporate Change* 13(2): 369–400.
Bowker, G. (2005), *Memory practices in the sciences*. Cambridge (Massachusetts): MIT Press.
Brown, S. D. (2002), 'Michel Serres: Science, translation and the logic of the parasite', *Theory, Culture & Society* 19(3): 1–27.
Carrier, J. G., and D. Miller (1998), *Virtualism: A new political economy*. Oxford: Berg.
Cochoy, F. (2002), *Une sociologie du packaging ou l'âne de Buridan face au marché*, Paris: PUF.
Descola, P. (2005), *Par-delà nature et culture*, Paris: Gallimard.
Flanagan, S. M. (2001), 'The rise of a trade association: Group interactions within the International Swaps and Derivatives Association' *Harvard Negotiation Law Review* 6: 211–264.
Guesnerie, R. and J.-C. Rochet (1993), '(De)stabilizing speculation on futures markets: An alternative view point', *European Economic Review* 37(5): 1043–1063.
Godechot, O. (2001), *Les traders: Essai de sociologie des marchés financiers*, Paris: La Découverte.
Godechot O. (2007), *Working rich: Salaires, bonus et appropriation du profit dans l'industrie financière*, Paris: La Découverte.
Hasselström, A. (2003), 'On and off the trading floor', PhD Thesis, Stockholm University.
Hertz, E. (1998), *The trading crowd: An ethnography of the Shanghai stock market*, Cambridge: Cambridge University Press.
Katz, M., and C. Shapiro (1994), 'System competition and network effects', *Journal of Economic Perspectives* 8(2): 93–115.
Knorr Cetina, K., and U. Bruegger (2002a), 'Inhabiting technology: The global lifeform of financial markets', *Current Sociology* 50(3): 389–405.
Knorr Cetina, K., and U. Bruegger (2002b), 'Global microstructures: The virtual societies of financial markets', *American Journal of Sociology* 107(4): 905–950.
Knorr Cetina, K., and U. Bruegger (2002c), 'Traders engagement with markets: A postsocial relationship', *Theory, Culture & Society* 19(5/6): 161–185.
Lépinay, V.-A. (2003), 'Les formules du marché: Ethno-économie d'une innovation financière – Le cas des Produits a Capital Garanti', PhD Thesis, Ecole des Mines de Paris.
MacKenzie, D. (2006), *An engine, not a camera: How financial models shape markets*, Cambridge (Massachusetts): MIT Press.
MacKenzie, D., and Y. Millo (2003), 'Constructing a market, performing theory: The historical sociology of a financial derivatives exchange.' *American Journal of Sociology*, 109(1): 107–145.
Miller, M. H. (1986) 'Financial innovation: The last twenty years and the next', *Journal of Financial and Quantitative Analysis* 21(4): 459–471.
Miller, M. H. (1991), *Financial innovations and market volatility*, Oxford: Blackwell.
Miller, M. H. (1997), *Merton Miller on derivatives*, New York: Wiley.
Millo, Y. (2003), 'Where do financial markets come from? Historical sociology of financial derivatives markets', PhD Thesis, University of Edinburgh.
Poovey, M. (2003), *The financial system in nineteenth-century Britain*, New York: Oxford University Press.
Serres, M. (1972), *L'interférence*, Paris: Editions de Minuit.
Serres, M. (1980), *Le parasite*, Paris: Flammarion.
White, H. C. (1981), 'Where do markets come from?', *American Journal of Sociology* 87(3): 517–547.
White, H. C. (2002), *Markets from networks: Socioeconomic models of production*, Princeton: Princeton University Press.

Scorecards as devices for consumer credit: the case of Fair, Isaac & Company Incorporated

Martha Poon

Introduction

The object of interest in this research is called a 'scorecard' in the consumer lending industry, a calculating tool for selecting and managing consumers of credit.[1] The technology's name is an historical affectation, since early commercial scorecards were literally a simple sheet of cardboard on which was printed a statistically based point distribution to be added up by the lender. Designed from an odds-based prediction of risk, early scorecards served as an aid to establishing whether credit should be granted to a prospective applicant according to the person's responses to a series of set questions. Today there is no card as 'scorecards' are embedded in sophisticated software packages and computer interfaces that co-ordinate between back-stage statisticians, electronic data warehouses, risk managers and front-stage marketing campaigns. Beyond the disappearance of the card, how the insides of the scorecard are constituted has also undergone significant transformations since the first scorecards were developed in the late 1950s, because the architecture of the algorithm or statistical model depends on the raw materials that have been used for its assembly. Without providing a full mathematical description of the scorecard, this chapter will nevertheless show that it is crucial to look closely at scorecard production if its significance as a 'market device' is to be understood, since differences in scorecard design and implementation can significantly change how the technology constitutes markets through risk calculation.

Most academic writings refer to a 1941 report by David Durand (c1941), published through the National Bureau of Economic Research as the first known application of statistical methods to the problem of selecting credit applicants, but it is unclear how influential this work was on any systems that might have emerged in practice. What is certain is that quantified credit application screening, while far from widespread, were initiated independently in a number of retail, mail order, and financial credit services reportedly starting as early as the 1940s (Lawrence and Solomon, 2002: 44). As with other historical movements of statistics, techniques for treating the credit application problem probabilisti-

© 2007 The Author. Editorial organisation © 2007 The Editorial Board of the Sociological Review. Published by Blackwell Publishing Ltd, 9600 Garsington Road, Oxford OX4 2DQ, UK and 350 Main Street, Malden, MA 02148, USA

cally can be seen developing in the hands of practitioners working on the ground with a domain experience, as opposed to being developed and diffused by academic or professional statisticians. Spiegel's, the mail order giant based out of Chicago, to give one example, is reported to have had manual scoring in place in the 1950s, designed by a gentleman named Henry Wells. The Wells system involved teams of women working with boxes of punch cards and 42 pound Fridan calculators.[2] Yet the current credit scoring technology, as it is known today, did not simply evolve out of a repetitious natural process of local discovery. As I will argue, the fact that credit scoring practices were absorbed in a somewhat common form in the USA can be largely attributed to the perseverant commercial efforts of a firm called Fair, Isaac & Company Incorporated[3] (Fair, Isaac), to move its tools throughout the consumer credit industry.

By focusing on the history of the 'scorecard' as a 'market device', this chapter will demonstrate how statistical methods, credit data and banking practices have been mutually adjusted and articulated in the USA to produce several concatenating market forms. In this view, the governance and economic effects of contemporary consumer credit are not the result of a singular calculative revolution but are, rather, largely predicated on the cumulative success of a number of scorecard-centred calculative arrangements. More importantly, it will be shown that while all of these devices arguably issue from the basic 'scorecard', the effects they generate on how consumer credit markets operate has been quite different depending on how they translate the immediate conditions under which risk quantification is being elaborated. Since the three devices discussed in this chapter – application scorecards, pre-screening scorecards, and bureau score(card)s – have been engineered and implemented by groups of experts working in specific locations, in particular at Fair, Isaac, I have sought out and magnified this firm into a locus of study. The company's first credit scoring product was the custom application scorecard, and their most well known product – the FICO® credit bureau score – is currently the standard metric in circulation for evaluating consumers in the U.S. market for consumer credit.[4] To focus on Fair, Isaac then, is not only a means to unpacking a theoretical point about the varieties of calculative effects that credit analytics models can have on markets, but it is simultaneously an exploration of the consolidated configurations that fuse the market for consumer analytics with markets for consumer credit together; it is an exploration of some of the actual apparatuses that most strongly shape the conditions of contemporary US consumer credit consumption.

Credit scoring in the social scientific literature

Contemporary practices of credit scoring have already come to the attention of social scientific authors concerned with the rise of risk management in consumer finance. From the point of view of science and technology studies however, none of this work takes scorecard technology as its object of investigation *per se*, preferring to focus on the more general theme – the transition towards quantification practices. To demonstrate this point, it is worth reviewing three examples. In response to rational choice theories Alya Guseva and Akos Rona-Tas (Guseva and Rona-Tas, 2001) have argued that scoring is a form of rationalization rendered possible only under the appropriate institutional conditions. They compare the USA, the oldest credit card market, and Russia, a nascent market where little data on consumers exists, in order to describe how credit card markets (a subset of consumer credit markets) work differently depending on whether institutions that house and make consumer data available are in existence. Drawing on classic concepts in economic sociology, they propose that in Russia, credit cards are distributed on the basis of subjective evaluations, on social networks and on 'trust' (ie, demonstrable friendships, kinship ties and employment), while in the USA, a mature market, institutions such as credit bureaus make calculative credit scoring practices feasible. The authors deploy Knight's theory of uncertainty to conclude that in the absence of data collecting and data distributing institutions, credit markets must run under conditions of uncertainty, while in the presence of the right institutions uncertainty is transformed. This permits the rise of data driven risk management techniques.

Andrew Leyshon and Nigel Thrift (Leyshon and Thrift, 1999) have also taken note of the enhanced role of business information derived from large-scale consumer data repositories, in retail banking. They have argued that such 'databases herald the arrival of a new form of governmentality based on new practices of knowledge' (Leyshon and Thrift, 1999: 453) encoded into software, and therefore rarely studied. According to these authors a 'quantitative revolution' in retail banking is allowing lenders to overcome the problem of 'information asymmetry' when dealing with prospective borrowers. As formulated in economic theory, information asymmetry occurs because borrowers ostensibly know more about their potential to repay a loan and it is in their own interests to reserve this information from the lender. Leyshon and Thrift's claim is that under conditions of asymmetry, credit scoring is an attractive option since digital data analysis can replace a dependence on information coming directly from individuals. What a reorientation towards scoring does is to 'enable strategists within firms to visualize the complexity of market segmentation' (Leyshon and Thrift, 1999: 440) from which they can construct types of identities through data processing. The title of the piece alludes to the cautionary attitude of the authors: the analysis of 'Lists' through specialized software is said to make their contents 'come alive' in such a way that sovereign individuals are supplanted by the governing power of neo-liberalizing software and electronically managed data.

Most recently, Donncha Marron (Marron, 2007) has discussed credit scoring in the USA as an emerging technocratic form of expertise that allows lenders to treat borrowers at the level of populations. Marron contrasts the inherent instability of risk measurement systems, which must be continuously refreshed to maintain their predictive power, against a proliferation of scoring systems that is multiplying the types of risks at play in consumer credit management. For Marron, there is a searing contradiction between a) the epistemology of risk management systems – he refers to them as being in a 'permanent process of failure' because by definition statistical calculations are imperfect at the level of individuals – and b) what he calls 'credit risk colonization' – the ongoing process of situating the consumer within an increasingly complex spectrum of risk segmentations within the marketplace. With the rise of scoring, the credit industry is observed to have moved 'from strategies of hierarchized avoidance by lenders to ones of polysemous engagement, from the treatment of risk as a cost to its deployment as a profitable opportunity' (Marron, 2007: 105). If the article, in large part, gives the reader pause to wonder why such flawed techniques continue to prevail in the lending industry, the author points to the role of the state in sanctioning these methods, suggesting that there is a kind of elective affinity between credit scoring and a Keynesian rationality of economic governance that reached its height in the 1970's.[5]

The pieces reviewed above all seek to decipher the effects that automated quantification practices writ large have produced on the consumer credit industry, reconfiguring banking and lending practices. Using scoring as a synecdoche for a larger movement towards risk management, each article captures an aspect of the profound transformations that digital mediation has induced on consumer finance as well as on the governance of consumers as subjects living within these markets. While the driving force attributed to the emergence of risk management techniques differs – the presence of institutions (Guseva and Rona-Tas), the impetus to overcome information asymmetry (Leyshon and Thrift), a compatibility of scoring methods with Keynesian rationality (Marron) are each invoked – what these authors do have in common is that they portray quantification as a kind of momentum sweeping across the consumer finance sector. A turn to scoring by economic sociologists seeks to capture what might be called a paradigmatic shift towards risk management in consumer finance that has accompanied consumer credit's dramatic evolution over the last half century from an adjunct of retail into a booming free standing industry with circulating products (for example, the unsecured monoline revolving credit card[6]) all its own (Lewis, 1992; Manning, 2001). Yet although the current sociological work acknowledges the crucial role of calculation in performing this shift towards risk, so far there has been no concerted inquiry into the details of constructing scoring algorithms, their implementation into practice or the specific effects of their multiple materializations through time.

In an era that arguably is overwhelmed by economic discourses, calculation might well seem to be tumbling forward, relentlessly spreading like brushfire now that the laborious collection and digitization of consumer data is securely in place. From a distance, scores can appear to be amorphously produced through the intuitive application of abstract, uniform and neutral mathematical methods to databases that have appeared out of a global information revolution. As historians and philosophers of statistics have aptly shown, however, each time statistical practices have been introduced to a problem in a substantive domain, expertise, networks of associations, technical objects and even new interpretations of probability must be formed to accommodate this extension

(Desrosières, 2000; Gigerenzer *et al.*, 1989; Hacking, 1975; Porter, 1988). If statistical theories change as they travel, and if the places they go must be rebuilt and rearranged to fit to accommodate them in practice, then it is from the details of this mutual refitting that novel calculative effects must emerge. In light of this, the details of how scoring systems are made, how they connect, co-ordinate, and interact, and most of all, how they evolve, should matter in how they have reformatted and reassembled the consumer credit industry through risk calculation. The research being presented here, therefore, draws upon the works cited above, but it also departs from them in several key ways. First and foremost, instead of treating data analysis as a set of delocalized methods or a generalized expertise, it will explore the consequences of treating credit scoring pragmatically as a set of concrete devices. Like Morgan's Drosophila flies (Kohler, 1994), Edison's light bulb (Hughes, 1983), or McLean's shipping container (Levinson, 2006), credit scoring technology has also had a trajectory of innovation through implementation, modification, and dissemination.

Manufacturing custom application scorecards (1958–c1974)[7]

The company's humble beginnings in San Rafael, California are an intimate part of company lore. In 1956, having extricated themselves from the military and academic worlds, William R. Fair and Earl J. Isaac founded Fair, Isaac & Company Inc. in an apartment building with an estimated twenty four hundred dollars in capital. Smart guys and operations researchers by trade, they offered themselves as 'problem solvers' for hire, putting up for sale 'custom solutions' through the application of operations research techniques to civilian problems. It is important to note that their conception of a 'solution' was not a free floating 'idea' or even a 'method'. It was a material system, concretely embedded in paper, then in hardware, and later still with mass computerization, in software, to provide a business with ongoing information that might reduce the guesswork involved in making everyday decisions. Bill Fair, in particular, is remembered as having a strong aversion for what he referred to as 'blue suit consultation' because he felt that this did not deliver a clear value to the client. The pair remained adamant that the company's business was not to 'navel gaze and write papers' whose usefulness was untested and whose contents might never be realized. Until well into the 1990's an emphasis on 'tangible deliverables' fully installed and implemented was an important company hallmark. In addition to cards for scoring, things that would become considered as tangible deliverables included 'an automated packaged application processing software' or 'an estimate on a probability that somebody will repay based upon the information known on his credit report' (Senior executive A).[8]

The company's first contact with credit cards appears to have come in the form of an invitation from Conrad Hilton to design, program and install a complete billing system for the newly invented *Carte Blanche* being distributed to the Hilton hotel chain's many guests. As the informally recorded story goes, when Earl Isaac arrived at the job, he 'opened a closet and found a pile of mail sacks full of payments that no one knew what to do with' (Internal history).[9] It was not until later, when the company took on its first employee, Earl Follet, that they began concerted work on the problem of customer selection in consumer credit. For their first initiative, letters explaining the concept were sent to fifty of the nation's top consumer credit lenders, a range of both banks and finance companies. In an oft repeated story, only one, American Investment, a finance company based out of St. Louis, Louisiana bothered to respond. By 1958, Fair, Isaac had installed the world's first commercially produced credit scorecards, one developed for the company's population of customers in the city of St. Louis area and another for the rest of Louisiana State. By 1960, they had developed a comprehensive system for use in the company's 800 operations nationwide. Although they would continue to dabble in other kinds of projects for another decade, from the late 1960's onwards, Fair, Isaac would eventually turn away from the general sale of operations research solutions towards the specific problem of application screening in consumer finance.

As the story goes, because the first Fair, Isaac credit scoring systems were to be deployed in small towns in rural America at the point of sale, they had to be simple enough to be understood by people with no knowledge of statistics and no access to calculators. The choice of statistical method as well as the card format for presenting the results in a tangibly deliverable and useful form to end-users, were both worked out 'in the field'. As scoring was to be done manually by retail clerks addition *in situ* was possible but multiplication proved more problematic. One third-generation Fair, Isaac analyst (who joined the company in the early 1980s) recounted the history as it was handed down to him as follows: 'the form of the model had to be simple enough that somebody could just ask a question, look up something, write down a single number, write down the question, look up something, write down another number, at the end of which, draw a line and add it up' (Senior R&D analyst). '[I]t is kind of ironic isn't it', he marvelled, 'that the most sophisticated credit decisions these days are easily made based on a model form that started from a small finance company in the South' (Ibid.). The original system was carefully designed so that the answers provided by the credit applicant to a set of questions (in person or on an application form) could be classified in the table printed on the card and the associated point values added up to produce the 'credit score' – a calculation of the empirically assessed odds that a person with a particular combination of characteristics, compared against the known outcomes of a lender's population of clients, would default on a loan.

The basic Fair, Isaac product was an 'application scorecard', a printed card that served as a calculating tool for quantitatively evaluating and selecting applicants for credit above whatever risk threshold (ie, cutoff score) was fixed by management. Assuming that what happened in the past was indicative of what would occur in the future – insofar as the past was captured within the confines of a lender's administrative files – scorecards gave lenders an easy-to-use black box for numerically summarizing the recorded behaviour of previous borrowers in their portfolio in support of rapid, forward-looking decision-making. According to statistical theory and confirmed by Fair, Isaac's empirical tests, the predictive utility of a scoring model was deemed to be intimately bound to the parameters of the data set from which it is modelled. This means that scorecard development was dependent on the availability of data of adequate quality, and the resulting scorecard's predictive utility was considered limited to the specific population and credit product represented in that data. In more sophisticated terms, since 'the model for x could not be used for y' the initial product for sale was a custom-made statistical model of a particular finance or mail order company that rendered visible the past performance of the extant customer base.[10] Early scorecards mechanically replicated the choices that had been previously made by a lender, but refined this replication by sorting the population into statistically salient groups which were now assigned different odds of repayment as a scalar quantity. Using the tool, the operation could either maintain volume while decreasing the rate of default, or could increase production while keeping default rates the same as they had known them before. The modest 'lift' offered (in industry speak) was therefore relative to the texture of the existing operation.

The implementation of scoring and the shift towards quantified risk-based management has demanded significant organizational changes (Sardas, 1993) – for example, disciplining lending operations to invest in the forms (Thévenot, 1984) required for routine, systematic, and later, electronic data keeping. As late as the mid-1970s however, this did not as yet exist in finance companies, and Fair, Isaac worked with paper-based records. Early scorecard production was a labour-intensive endeavour involving the transportation of human expertise and material resources out into the field and then all the way back across the country to the 'centre of calculation' (Latour, 1987) in San Rafael. Data collection trips involved travelling to suburban strip malls to collect samples of ledger cards and other information tucked in the hefty files of finance companies, the main type of client early on. As one retired executive vice-president describes it, '[I]n those days, every shopping centre had a loan office, and you'd go in and get an instalment loan [. . .]. They kept everything on little cards, all handwritten' (Senior executive C). System construction was limited to the physical availability to access consistent paper records from which to draw a statistically adequate sample. The key scientific and organizational figure in the early process of production was called 'the analyst'. It was their job to figure out, on the ground, how best to constitute a sample of cases that could be used to build a statistical model that would adequately discriminate between the performance of both 'good' and 'bad' borrowers.

The analyst was responsible for making numerous strategic decisions that would affect how sampling was to be achieved out of variegated and imperfect conditions. A few examples can serve to illustrate. Case selection was achieved by an imperfect method of sampling, usually by selecting a couple of offices deemed representative by management of the overall operations of the finance firm. Within these offices, each file selected had to have a lengthy enough history from which to extract two 'snapshots' of data. These snapshots were used to establish a statistical relationship between factors assessed at the point of application (first snapshot) and subsequent outcome (second snapshot). From the point of origination, the interval length adequate for declaring a file definitively 'good' (as opposed to 'still good' or 'not yet bad') was therefore of critical consideration, since its status might change if the second snapshot was taken a few months later. What this means is that the very distinction between 'good' and 'bad' was flexible. That a case was considered grievous depended on how 'bad' behaviour was defined (ie, one missed payment, two missed payments in 12 months, not paying at all for three months . . .) and policies on what was considered an account in default varied between firms. And then there was the basic question of sample size – determining just how many files, from how narrow and recent a time period in a firm's history were necessary to build a representative model. While the credit analytics industry has a standardized ways of approaching these design questions today, the minute details of design were all once open issues that required active solution seeking. Analysts in the process of inventing scorecard calculation constantly faced questions about 'where to draw the line so that we got the most robust credit prediction possible' (Bureau scoring vice-president).

It is striking that in conversations with the first generation of analysts, the most memorable part of early scorecard projects is sample collection with little or no mention of the sanitized 'smart' work usually associated with statistical analysis. Far from the idealized image of the ivory tower, doing scientific work at Fair, Isaac could involve fairly intensive manual labour. Even a freshly graduated star PhD student of Robert Oliver[11] coming out of Berkeley's IEOR program could not escape the mundane task of hauling boxes of data out of dusty storage rooms, some of which could be located in some 'pretty unsavoury places'. In a small company, when something had to get done, everyone was expected to lend a hand and to help out. It was not uncommon for spouses to travel with analysts (and in at least one case a son) to aid in the grunt work of collecting the data that kept the company going. Once in the field, selected files were laboriously photographed by hand, page by page. 'When we got a project, the idea was, you'd go out and you'd have microfilm cameras' (Senior executive C). The film was shipped all the way back to the central office in California where it was developed and printed out on long rolls of paper that had to be hand torn and re-stapled to resemble the original files. Incidents of accidentally destroyed records, illegible copies, incomplete documentation, broken cameras, inaccessible records and even neckties caught in microfiche machines, all added to the challenge of assembling a workable sample, and converting it into a digitized information infrastructure.

Once transported, the reassembled credit application information had to be coded into usable data. As Bill Fair himself would find fit to record years later, 'Data entry was demanding and tedious in the extreme. [. . .] Getting a deck of cards ready for a run was a matter of weeks of work, counting the time it took to encode it before keypunching could begin' (Informal memoir). This was a two-stage process performed by housewives working at piece rates of a few cents per sample application out of their homes. The meticulous work of 'the homecoders' was the backbone of the scorecard since it was their job to interpret the writing on the ledger cards and reliably convert it into the standardized numerical codes demanded by the analytic process. Codes were transferred to paper, reviewed for accuracy by a woman assigned as a 'checker', and subsequently transferred to punch cards so that the data could be read by machine. As one of the women who headed coding described it, a punch card machine is 'like a typewriter, you put your IBM cards in – they're about five by seven – and you have to sort them. If we punched a certain digit that would mean [occupation]: housewife' (Senior coder A).

Because of its repetitive and mechanical nature, coding was considered a mundane task in the company. Yet upon scrutiny it is clear that the work that was done involved its own form of skilled decision-making that was far from obvious. A former coder made clear to me that '[t]here was some interpretation on all of this. You couldn't just copy it. That was the hard part, coding it. [. . .] They didn't just say he's been three times thirty days late in nice English' (Senior coder B). Another drew attention to the fact that, 'We had to read these logs of payments and every company didn't do the same thing, and we'd get so confused' (Senior coder C).

The rise of large-scale digital data repositories has certainly advanced the cause of credit scoring, but their absence did not by any means deter early Fair, Isaac from building scoring systems. In spite of formidable logistical challenges, the choice of credit scoring as the company's main business was a pragmatic one. A retired executive vice-president stated that the company focused on scorecards having 'looked around in their business and figured out that credit scoring was something that could be packaged as a solution [and] sold over and over again' (Senior executive A). When asked what the major steps to the success of the company were, another former executive replied that 'one is the innovating of a product, the other is kind of rolling it out into an industry' (Senior executive C). His key point was that 'there was a very routine nature in how we developed these [systems]' (Ibid.). In the early days, 'a big part of projects was actually getting the data into the model. . . . 80 per cent of the task was that a lot of what was coming [to us was] on paper and had to go through data processing and so on' (Ibid.) Data processing involved figuring out its contents, stabilizing relevant codes, computerizing selected fields, and sifting through to find variables suitable for scoring models. A shared 'mindset' among company members, associated with operations research, 'of having a problem and trying to reduce it to a framework of a model in which you can then, basically, replicate the solution, with different kinds of inputs' (Ibid.) is said to have been important to innovating scoring as a refined process out of the melee of papers and analytic choices. '[T]rying to standardize how we developed the scorecards [. . .], that's where the innovation came in' (Ibid.). This is how Fair, Isaac transformed a fragile, location-based practice of custom statistical modelling into a commercially viable process of scorecard manufacture.

The engineer's penchant for standardization towards the constitution of a 'mass production' product, however, should not overshadow the fact that each project continued to be a delicate custom job. Orchestrating client-specific calculations depended on each firm's internal organizational structure, the quality and content of the data kept, and the co-operation of credit managers and other key personalities. Analysis began from scratch in that it started with a fresh data collection, cleaning and classing[12] and was limited to the information that could be gleaned given how the application forms were designed and how the records had been kept. At an approximate development cost of $32,000,[13] the final algorithm was considered non-transferable and relevant to only a specific client-lender's business; and fortunately so for the conservation of Fair, Isaac's business proposition. Even if common factors repeated themselves, the score weights associated with them and the segmentation into multiple scorecards serving sub-populations[14] was specific to the firm from which the sample was drawn. It is important to note that the specificity of scorecard to population meant that there was no single calculation of a person's odds of default, since the measure of this changed depending on the previous performance of the population against which an applicant's data was being run. The score of an applicant's risk which appeared only ephemerally at the moment of application, was the risk faced by a particular lending firm based on their previous experiences. In other words, risk was not stabilized in the person and did not travel around with them, but it was attached to the multiple calculative models cropping up across the credit industry.

From application data to credit bureau data (1980–c1985)

At the end of the 1970s, crucial developments in the US credit analytic market caused Fair, Isaac to shift away from a market for custom scorecards towards a market for credit bureau based products. In the USA the credit bureaus are data gathering organizations that have traditionally serviced the numerous small banks, finance companies and savings and loan associations scattering across the country by providing subscribers with access to first negative, and then positive repayment information on borrowers, as well as on bankruptcies, judgments, voter registration, and credit account histories across a number of industries. From a smattering of regional 'mom and pop' operations, the bureaus have grown historically through a process of consolidation over the last century. At the end of the 1970s there were only five major operations remaining with somewhat regional coverage: CBI, Chilton, Pinger, Trans-Union and TRW. By the end of the 1980s these had been reduced to the three umbrella operations with near national coverage, known today as Trans-Union, Equifax and Experian.[15] From the point of view of people working in consumer analytics, the bureau business is 'intellectually nowhere near as interesting a business as Fair, Isaac's!' (Senior executive A). The original business model of the bureaus did not involve analytics as there was no analysis for sale. Traditionally they had received the data from lenders, dug it up from public sources – ie, newspapers, public notices, court proceedings, and even by soliciting neighbourhood gossip (Black, 1961) – and then aggregated and distributed it, sometimes by simply giving information to inquiries made by phone. They did all of this without considering the statistical meanings that might be made of its contents.

In the late 1970s, the Fair, Isaac team came to appreciate that the rich public record data compiled in American credit bureau reports might be utilized to develop an alternative kind of scoring system to the ones they had painstakingly been producing from internal data. Former head of sales, O.D. Nelson, is commonly given credit for importing the idea of building scorecards exclusively off bureau data, having been inspired by a client contact at First National Bank of Kansas (Informal history). Based on a conceptualization of this client's suggestions, the first product-using bureau data alone was named 'PreScore'. Original PreScore did not disrupt Fair, Isaac's tried and true process of production. Just as with the application scorecard, it was a custom product processed through data entry and their proprietary statistical analysis programs, only the outcomes was a scorecard that allowed a lender to produce a score and to make decisions with only knowledge of an individual's commercially available bureau data. Interestingly, what this idea did overturn was one of the company's strongest sales points. For some time Fair, Isaac had been pushing its systems on the grounds that these might allow lenders to avoid the costs incurred by purchasing credit reports. They had encouraged this by designing scorecards so that it was possible in some cases to meet a critical numeric threshold before the information furnished by the credit report became a necessary contribution to statistical discrimination (Viewpoints, 1980 4:4, 3).[16] At an expensive two to three dollars a report, 'This was major savings. Sometimes it paid for our development' (Senior analyst A). It is not surprising, then, that the bureaus regarded Fair, Isaac as distinctly unfriendly.

At the advent of PreScore, bureau data was already familiar to Fair, Isaac because the files collected for the custom application scorecards had included information from 'credit reports' lenders had purchased and whose contents had generally been taken into consideration. Although they had had no direct contact with the credit bureaus, Fair, Isaac had worked attentively with the consumer credit reports purchased by lenders. For years, they had been including characteristics drawn from these reports into custom scorecards, although they had strictly limited its quantity because of the costs incurred by having the coders enter superfluous data. The five simple variables that Fair, Isaac had been drawing from the bureau reports were: time in file (age of the record at the bureau), number of satisfactory ratings, number of inquiries, number of 'minor derogatories' and number of 'major derogatories'. So to begin the development of the PreScore product the coders were asked to significantly increase their efforts. One former coder remembers that during this period 'We got into doing specifics on credit reports where we copied the tradeline information' (Senior coder D). 'I went line by line,' she vividly recalls. Now, for each and every tradeline, that is, bank loan, mortgage, or credit card on file, they coded things such as the date opened, the maximum line, the current balance, and the delinquencies, such that eventually, the women 'had interpretations for how to interpret each bureau: thick books' (Senior coder D). Expanding amount of bureau data under consideration made hundreds of new variables possible. Assisted by the coders, the analyst responsible for designing the first PreScore products says he 'was able to [analyse] things like the tradeline with the highest use of the line, for example. So if on one tradeline you use 90 per cent [VISA], but on the other you use 95 per cent [MasterCard], is this predictive? [. . .] We'd never tested that before!' (Senior analyst A).

The rise of credit cards had expanded Fair, Isaac's business from the less prestigious and credit oriented finance companies, mail order firms or retail credit operations, towards the credit conservative banks. So the primary use of custom PreScore, as the name implies, was to pre-screen a bank's existing population in order to launch an unsolicited, promotional credit card offering.[17] The practice of pre-screening for bank cards using bureau data was not new at this time. In the 1980s there was a 'very large industry of going out there and just mailing millions and millions of credit card offers' (Senior analyst B). But the way pre-screening was being carried out was based on exclusionary 'knock-out' rules that were extremely rigid and restrictive. An R&D analyst described the process in a 1986 newsletter article. Banks, he wrote, would submit a 'long list of absolute requirements, and if any one of the conditions is not met, the prospect [was] eliminated form consideration' (Viewpoints, 1986 10:3, 1). In other words, '[t]he way that rules work is that binary rules are very exclusionary. You chop off big parts of the population [. . .]' (Senior analyst B). The analyst concluded that '[a]lthough credit criteria do a good job of rejecting undesirable prospects, they also reject many good candidates' (Viewpoints, 1986 10:3, 1). As with application scores, by weighting characteristics in the file PreScore shifted the way people were selected away from a simple yes or no, towards a linear gradation of classes constructed around empirically assessed odds-predictions which lenders could – sliding up and down the scale at will – parse out and treat differently. This means they could do more than focus on deciding who to reject. Now, they could experiment with and adjust how they were going to accept.

Relying exclusively on bureau data meant that the lender did not need to wait for applications to trickle in and get sorted to identify prospective borrowers one by one. To begin building 'a market' they could access their existing clientele's bureau information and filter this information through a custom made PreScore scorecard, effectively collapsing the credit screening process into a genuine marketing function. If the file scored above the risk threshold the campaign was aiming for (and this could be sliced in multiple ways), the person could swiftly be mailed an offer for the credit product being promoted. Unlike rules which rigidly reproduced decision making through rejection, PreScore proved that it was an effective calculative device for imagining an elastic credit market whose 'performance' or 'enactment' was placed within the grasp of lenders. Instead of waiting patiently for individuals to identify themselves into potential customers and to express a desire for credit, this system rapidly placed the possibility of credit cards into the hands of individuals whose likelihood of default on their repayment obligations could be calculated in advance as low enough be acceptable to the lender. At first these offers occurred within the intimacy of a banking relationship, but soon, as the bureaus started generating lists and the finance industry warmed up to the tool, pre-scoring opened up the possibility of offering credit in the absence of a previous banking or lending contact. Thus, the scores from bureau data impelled lenders to 'consider this whole new population which they don't know anything about' (Senior analyst B). In a dramatic reconfiguration of agencies it was now lenders and not borrowers who initiated the economic transaction surrounding consumer credit; it was now lenders not borrowers who expressed desire, initiated calculation, and could be said to hold an active advantage based on information.

PreScore was not without its own implementation issues. Lenders with a national reach who resorted to many bureaus to accommodate regional differences in their data holdings were required to purchase multiple PreScore cards. This was not an attractive proposition where the scorecard was the basic unit that was priced – as it made sense to do in a custom driven business model. The R&D analyst assigned to the project attempted to build a PreScore system that could accommodate data from any of the bureaus. This proved to be impossible because he soon found that '[t]he characteristics were not the same across the bureaus and the contents of some of the fields did not correspond' (Senior analyst A). That is to say, the ways the bureaus kept the data resulted in fundamental incommensurabilities (Espeland and Carruthers, 1991). It was during this period that Fair, Isaac abandoned – but not without a struggle – their long held ideal that each statistical system needed to be a custom job in order to be a quality system. Again at the behest of clients, they agreed to produce a 'generic' PreScore product, based on a generic sample of bureau data, one corresponding to each of the bureaus' data sets. Instead of making custom scorecards using the bureau data found in the files of their clients lenders, Fair, Isaac approached the bureaus for a representative sample of data which they received already digitized and stored on magnetic tapes. The generic scorecards, now embedded in software, were programmed directly into the bureaus' infrastructure which pulled and processed the relevant data in batches for the lists of prospective customers submitted at the lenders request.

Multiple users scoring bureau files off a generic scorecard linked to a particular bureau was more than a new data source or a new product – it introduced the company to a veritably new way of doing analytics business. The 'product' was no longer 'the scorecard'. Now, it was the use of a scorecard implemented at the bureau. '[F]or Fair, Isaac it was a breakthrough and a business model because we didn't have to incur the labour of every custom project' (Senior executive C). That is, they neither had to master the idiosyncratic qualities of locally constructed data sources for each new contract, nor worry about data entry or data cleaning. Moreover, they were now in a position to offer an empirical system to lending outfits that were too young or disorganized to have statistically significant data of their own, or too small to afford a custom model.

The slippage away from the cherished philosophical principles held by the founders out of both scientific and business convictions, was therefore threefold. First, customization lost its fundamental importance. Second, scorecards gained the potential to be transferable. And finally, and most importantly, risk – although still attached to the model and the dataset – was detached from firm-specific customer populations; in the absence of any individual initiative, it could be called up and materialized by lenders, at will. Stated sanguinely, the product's overall effect was to start making 'credit available to people who probably did not have the nerve to walk into a bank and ask for a credit card' (Senior analyst A). More polemically, it might be said that the device began putting the option of credit cards in the way of people who could not have had, until then, any use, desire or preference for them. In other words, it subverted their role as service requesting customers, and positioned them to act as product selecting consumers.

The FICO® bureau scores and the circulation of consumer credit risk (c1986–1991)

The rise of 'bureau scores' pushed the concept of building scorecards out of bureau data to a whole new level. To produce true bureau scores, a complexly segmented scorecard operates inside the bureau and the analytic products sold are neither scorecards made from static application forms, nor the use of a scorecard to produce risk estimates corresponding to compiled lists of selected individuals. Instead, what circulate with commercial value are the discrete *scores* emanating from the generic model. Scores can be calculated for all bureau files fitting the criteria demanded by the model (known as 'scoreable files'). In developing consumer credit markets the bureau model of risk assessment is theoretically considered to be the most economically desirable, because it ostensibly promotes open competition between lenders by providing uniform access to a set of information on a large number of consumers. But in attempting to start an idealized version of such a system from the ground up, as if to replicate US market conditions, what is often overlooked is the idiosyncratic way in which the American bureau system has come into being, and some of the particular effects of how the score product and the market for scores has been configured by Fair, Isaac. Somewhat ironically, Fair, Isaac did not pioneer the bureau scores as they were not the first third party provider of analytics to begin working directly with the bureaus. But by business fiat they created an epistemological machine much bigger than just putting scorecards into bureaus: they created the illustrious FICO® scores.

A business model of selling scores instead of scorecards may have meant generating continuous streams of revenue on a usage-based rather than fixed-price custom product, but unlike custom systems it provided a very limited number of opportunities – five later reduced to three, to be exact – to set up productive systems. So in addition to rethinking the bureau data (yet again) and engineering an intricate multi-scorecard system capable of fitting national level data, Fair, Isaac also had to leverage decades of accumulated social capital in the service of exploiting competitive tensions between the bureaus. Thus client demand for a Fair, Isaac offering is said to have become of the utmost importance leading to a 'snowball effect'. Having provided custom scorecards to nearly every lender of any importance in the country, and having singlehandedly created the market for consumer credit analytics in the absence of competition for the better part of twenty years, Fair, Isaac had become a recognized branding that lenders associated with sound expert products of high quality. Since the bureau's clients were also Fair, Isaac's clients, 'the boys' purportedly 'went to the CitiBanks and the AMEXes and Chases of the world and sold them on the idea of scoring the bureau data' (Informal history). These customers, in turn, went to the credit bureaus and said 'You will code this in, of course, won't you?' and the bureaus really didn't have a lot of choice' (Vice-president A). As it is pithily told today, '[O]nce some of the largest lenders started buying theses scores, then the bureaus would supply the scores [or] they would say well, you don't have the FICO score so we can't do business with you' (Ibid.). When TRW infamously attempted to back out of contract negotiations at the last minute, presumably to favour the promotion of an in-house product, it was client threats to abandon them as a provider that forced them back to the table.

In 1991, Fair, Isaac consolidated joint ventures to maintain a scorecard within each of the three remaining bureaus. The official product name for the generic bureau score was different at each of the bureaus because they are technically and scientifically different calculations of risk. The underlying model was tailored to the specificity of each bureau's data and the scores were distributed from distinct production partnerships. Nevertheless, any score produced by a Fair, Isaac algorithm at a credit bureau, including the many industry specific scores that have subsequently been developed,[18] has come to be known in industry speak as a 'FICO score'. This is more than a symbolic elision. It is the effect of several fortuitously converging processes of 'product qualification' (Callon, Méadel and Rabeharisoa, 2002), qualifications that actually generate the important analytic properties of these scores which distinguish them from other calculations. First, the FICO® scores hinge on a contractual situation, on keeping what is known as the 'tri-bureau solution' intact. Until very recently, Fair, Isaac was the only fourth party provider with access to all three bureaus.[19] As Fair, Isaac discovered, maintaining this delicate situation has meant implementing the technology at each bureau without disrupting the competitive structure within the existing bureau market. The vice-president in charge of negotiating with the bureaus admitted that, 'We didn't really set out in the start to do that when we got started, but once we got involved it became clear that was what we should do. And it worked' (Senior executive C). Fair, Isaac developed a strategy called 'the centre of the pasture'. The idea has been to never favour any bureau over the others and to invest in keeping the playing field even. Thus, 'the typical way to proceed when we had an innovation involve bureau data was we worked just as hard as we could to get one bureau to be the guinea pig. We'd say well we can offer you a lead in the market place if this stuff works' (Vice-president A). Once a new development was made with one bureau, an equivalent would be offered to the other bureaus as well, smoothing out and equalizing the field.

The second element at play in the unification of the FICO® is the result of a process of re-branding and marketing. In the face of all this bullying by its clients, the bureaus had an understandably reluctant attitude towards this parasitic new-fangled score product. It was Fair, Isaac that 'had to sell the scores to the end users. Frankly if we didn't do it the bureaus were never going to do it for us. So, we went out, and really sold it' (Bureau score analyst). Once the scorecards were designed, the work was only beginning. Just as with application scorecards, the introduction of a new risk management tool in the form of scores involved reconfiguring user institutions from the inside out. Personnel at the financial institutions as well as at the bureaus had to be trained to accommodate and integrate bureau scores in practice. '[S]o there were road trips with [the bureau] sales people around the country. At different stops we'd go from city to city around the country in partnership [with a given bureau]' (Bureau score analyst). In light of Fair, Isaac's omnipresence behind what were all clearly 'their' scores, even if manufactured at separate bureaus, it was only good business sense for them to start re-appropriating them under a common brand name. The final and most effective force of product unification results from a feature of product design. Ensuring maximum competition between the bureaus has meant minimizing switching costs for score users. Fair, Isaac used identical segmentations in all three algorithms and 'scale[d] the scores in such a way that the same number was associated with the same risk level no mater which bureau was used. And that turned out to be a big idea' (Bureau scoring vice-president). A big idea because this rendered the scores sold from the three different bureaus, all on log-odds scales of 850, into virtually interchangeable pieces of information from the point of view of the end user.

The effects of free floating bureau scores on the consumer credit market have been manifold. Because the data at the bureaus are constantly being renewed, bureau scores are ongoing, responsive measures that are frequently recalculated. They have been put to many more uses than just application and simple pre-screening, inserting themselves into mortgage origination, portfolio management (ie, adjusting line limits, assigning accounts to collections strategies), experimental design (ie, testing credit product strategies on statistically identical groups), and perhaps most importantly, risk based pricing (ie, making credit products with different promotional terms and interest rates for different market segments). In addition, they have given rise to a whole new category of financial services companies and banks that offer credit products to consumers through co-branding strategies while they themselves maintain no retail fronts (ie, MBNA prior to its merger with Bank of America, Capital One, or GE Capital etc.). In an information-based, expert-driven industry of lending, the equivalence of a person to a commensurate credit product has to be statistically calculated. With the diminishment of personal banking relationships and the quasi-disappearance of application forms for credit cards, to access basic credit in the USA, therefore, an individual must have a commercial score rank, otherwise their value is no longer institutionally visible or 'evaluable' to lenders. It is in this way that the structure of the market for commercially available consumer scores simultaneously constitutes the population of 'credit consumers' and consolidates a market for consumer credit as a fluid transactional space; it transforms a patchwork of markets for consumer credit into 'the market' which can be differentially segmented and competed for.

A more subtle point, perhaps, is how the FICO® standard has acted to objectify risk. Freely circulating bureau scores have exploded consumer choice by offering multiple financial institutions the possibility of simultaneously viewing the consumer market and the individual consumers in that market in exactly the same way. From a pragmatic point of view, they therefore act on the 'same' market, a co-ordination effect that has intensified direct competition, amplified production, and encouraged the manufacture of mass credit offerings. Although Fair, Isaac was unable to create a set of genuine statistical standards (ie, by merging the datasets into a single national population), the *de facto* standard that results from the achievement of a unique market position has proved every bit as robust in its effectiveness to travel and act as a universal metric. At the level of the aggregate, the common scale effaces the differences imposed by statistical theory given the dissimilarities in the datasets and the data retrieval mechanisms underlying each supplier. If custom application scorecards made risk relative to the previous choices of multiple lending agencies; if generic pre-screening generated risk at the level of bureau data; then diffusing tri-bureau scores have dissolved it from any firm association with calculative apparatuses. In circulating everywhere, in appearing as the same kind of number, in being perpetually recalculated, consumer credit risk calculation is no longer anchored in particular moments or in specific places. As such, the synchronic variations in the three bureau scores for each person appear to be errors in measuring some intransigent underlying quality, and their diachronic variation becomes solely attributable to changes in consumer behaviour (even if this is thought to be affected by macro-forces). It is through the FICO® that credit risk in the USA can take on the ontological firmness of being a calculable personal property, rather than being a relative value, constituted and affixed to the person *through* calculation.

Conclusion: multiple scorecard configurations, multiple market forms

This chapter has sought to anchor credit scoring within the material history of the scorecard in order to draw current understandings of the rise of risk calculation in consumer finance back to its humble beginnings. It has argued that a full grasp of the practice of credit scoring means moving beyond, on the one hand, the presumption of a static textbook theoretical understanding of quantitative methods for decision-making in finance, and on the other a separate account of a passive set of conditions (ie, the constitution of mass databases[20]) conducive to the application of these theory. As work in the anthropology of calculability has shown, it takes material and social effort to produce spatial practices appropriate to calculation (Callon and Muniesa, 2005). This means moving towards an analysis of credit scoring as the result of a process of economic production that has been able to achieve an articulation between theory and circumstances, between statistical practices and data, by constantly rearranging the world through active perseverance. While not all of the innumerable tools available to contemporary consumer credit risk managers stem from the Fair, Isaac scorecard, nonetheless the company is an important locus of investigation for tracing the practical innovation, differentiation and expansion of credit scoring technologies. Custom scorecards originally manufactured from a single commercial locus and diffusing outwards in multiple arrangements – this picture offers reasons to move beyond treating risk management as a uniform, abstract movement.

This is not to deny the genuine proliferation of scoring that is occurring from multiple loci today. Credit risk managers and marketers are quick to point out that the FICO® is only one part of the complex machinery of interconnected calculative tools they work with (ie, internal custom scoring systems interact with commercial scores). Against the constant introduction of new analytic apparatuses, the FICO® is slowly sinking into the background. It is discussed more for the cumulative costs it incurs than for its conceptual novelty, as competitive forces from banks, the bureaus and other analytic outfits with an economic stake actively seek to overflow the FICO frame and undermine it. 'Let's face it', said one young global strategic analyst at CitiBank when asked for his opinion on whether the FICO® was indeed an unsurpassable calculation of consumer risk.

> Up until now, it hasn't been the nine hundred pound gorilla. It's been the ninety thousand pound gorilla, because for the longest time it was the only place to go. And that momentum's really, really carried through. [. . .] When you look at the FICO score, it really hasn't changed very much from the initial concepts. It's because it's something that works and you don't really want to change it or innovate too much, because frankly, bankers hate change. I know it sounds stupid, but this tends to be the reason why. Now having said that, there *is* a burgeoning market for tools and stuff like that, so you'll see a lot of companies trying to really start up, build analytic tools. [. . .] If you're large enough like CitiBank, and you have well trained staff, you really don't need this. You don't need any of these tools. You can probably build it yourself. (CitiBank global strategic analyst)

This statement is striking for its contrast with the arduous and limited nature of early scorecard production and the tremendous work required to garner the co-operation of a reluctant lending industry. It requires that we pose questions about the gradual emergence of conditions that have made the mass dispersion of some forms of calculative agency – but not all – possible. Seen as a whole, Fair, Isaac's trajectory recapitulates the movement from an emergent to a consolidated techno-economic network (Callon, 2002). Michel Callon has employed these terms to describe how economic theory, scientific research, and the functioning of markets converge. In the new economics of science following Arrow and Nelson, the output of research, scientific knowledge, is equated to 'information' defined as being a public good. Callon remarks however, that for information to be a public good it must have acquired certain qualities. It must also be non-rival (able to be used simultaneously by multiple actors), non-appropriable (costly to own) and universal (widely generalisable). Yet as his work has shown, 'The Holy Grails of modern economics – nonrivalry, nonappropriability, and universality – are not given but rather obtained at the price of costly investments' (Callon, 2002: 292). Drawing on laboratory studies, the origins of science and technology studies, he argues that since scientific innovation begins locally, scientifically produced information can only become a public good once material investments in the durable metrological networks that allow its replication and dispersion have been made. Callon therefore concludes that 'If non-rivalry, non-appropriability, and universality exist, they are not to be found in emerging science but in what Kuhn termed normal science or in what I prefer to call consolidated configurations' (Callon, 2002: 292).

If technical networks are congealing around similar risk management practices in the consumer credit industry, then this is in no small part due to Fair, Isaac's early dedication to delivering tangible commercial tools and to their active work within client organizations to make them amenable to these manufactured analytic goods. Yet this outward replication has not proceeded with uniform results. Following a simplified trajectory of products – from application scorecards, to prescreening scorecards, to tri-bureau scores[21] – demonstrates how at each moment a 'single' method of calculation (if narrowly conceived), can have a strikingly varied impact on the constitution of risk depending on the moment in which it is networked outwards and established as a technological device. When these distinct scorecard configurations are placed side by side it is evident that the socio-economic effects of concern to social scientists – such as the responsibility placed on consumer choice for debt, the intensification of (monoline) credit cards through aggressive marketing practices, and the personalization of risk – are not inherent properties of risk calculation but are differentially generated and vary according to particular scorecard configurations emerging from activity in the parallel market for analytics.

It can be concluded therefore, that the robustness of scores as objectified/objectifying measures is not the product of a general shift towards quantified risk management. Rather, as I have sought to show, it is 'performed' by a specific assembly of scorecard algorithms acting as consumer credit market devices. This effect is also a cumulative one in that the concrete scoring edifice or consolidated configuration which has emerged in the USA is arguably a direct result of articulating layers of Fair, Isaac activity together, culminating in the circulation of tri-bureau scores – pieces of circulating, non-rival information brought into being 'in the wild' (Callon, 2007). Although not directly issued from professional economists, these avidly circulating risk scores nevertheless do curiously resemble the fluid, scientifically produced, economic information for assessing market quality hypothesized by economists of science in support of economic theories. In all but one way: although serving their function as a market device the scores are appropriated, because their means of production continues to belong to Fair, Isaac.

Notes

1 Acknowledgements are extended to Steven Epstein for his attentive assistance in the preparation of this chapter. They are also due to the participants of Sub-theme 40: *Markets for technologies, technologies for markets* at the 22nd EGOS Colloquium (July 6–8 2006, Bergen, Norway), as well as to C.F. Helgesson, Janet Roitman, Akos Rona-Tas and the editors for their thoughtful comments on previous versions of this text. This material is based upon work supported by the National Science Foundation under Grant No. 0451139.
2 I am assuming that the vivid reference to Fridan calculators by the interviewee was to the ST-W or STW-10 model mechanical calculators, whose weight is infamous, although by the 1960s the first electronic Fridan models were already available.
3 The company changed its name from Fair, Isaac & Co. Inc. to the Fair Isaac Corporation in 2003. I conserve the original name to emphasize the historical nature of the research. While other methods and firms might be resorted to for analytic solutions, Fair, Isaac has dominated the US marketplace for credit analytics since its inception in 1956 until at least the early 2000s. According to the company website (consulted in 2004), Fair, Isaac had made the *Forbes* list of Top 200 US Small Companies 10 times in the previous 11 years. It placed 19th on the Business 2.0 ranking of the 100 fastest growing technology companies in 2003; it was named one of the Top 200 IT companies globally for 2002 by *BusinessWeek*; and until recently all of the top *10 Fortune 500* companies are said to have relied on Fair Isaac technology (http://www.fairisaac.com/Fairisaac/Company/Profile/).
4 Unlike most other countries where credit scoring is the backstage business of banks, card companies and finance houses, the FICO® is a score that has been brought into the American limelight. Home buyers and consumer groups 'discovered' the scores and agitated to bring them to public attention. This is how the 'FICO score' has rapidly become a household word in the USA, whose recognition has been bolstered by the recent real estate and mortgage refinancing boom following the historically low interest rates set by the Federal Reserve in 2001. A way to release scores to consumers was devised, incidentally, in the same year. This product's evolution is largely responsible for growing the company from an estimated 50 million USD in 1991, to over 250 million USD in 1999.
5 According to Marron (2007), Keynesianism explains why legislators accepted scoring in the Equal Credit Opportunity Act (ECOA, 1974) as a means to 'eliminating 'subjective' discrimination and helping to bring about an enhanced mass consumer credit market that would discriminate only on merit'. It is perhaps helpful to note that the ECOA of Oct. 28, 1974, Pub. L. 93–495, 88 Stat. 1521 pertained only to traditional methods of credit decision-making. It was amended a year and a half later to include the clauses that refer to 'empirically derived credit systems' derived through statistical analysis (Mar. 23, 1976, Pub. Law 94–239, 90 Stat. 251). One could argue that placing scientific systems under the control of the law is a sign, not of their outright acceptance as objective and dispassionate systems, but of a profound recognition on the part of lawmakers that these systems could be as guilty of illegal discrimination as traditional methods of applicant selection if not subject to legal definition and control. In this view, regulatory intervention on the part of the state did not seek to sanction empirical methods as non-discriminatory so much as it actively contributed to the establishment and justification of their status as such.
6 An 'unsecured monoline revolving credit card' is a consumer credit instrument for which no collateral is given by the user (unsecured). It is extended in the absence of a bank account or other retail relationship by a company specializing in a specific type of financial business (monoline),

and it automatically renews the amount of credit available up to a fixed amount as the debt is paid down each month (revolving).

7 The dates in brackets loosely correspond to the period of development or consolidation of each type of scorecard technology. Custom application scorecards remain a viable business proposition, although their importance within the overall market for analytics has been greatly decreased by the rise of other analytic products (i.e. bureau scores) and do-it-yourself statistical software applications.

8 The chapter draws directly from fourteen open-ended interviews conducted by the author with (primarily) former Fair, Isaac employees from a number of positions in the production process. Many of these individuals worked with the company their entire careers. Conversations to collect oral histories ranging from an hour and a half to two hours each, and were carried out between June 2004 and October 2006. Three interviews represented here are with former senior executive, five with former vice-presidents, four with former senior analysts, one with a former bureau score sales manager, one meeting with four former data entry personnel, and one with a current member of CitiBank's global strategic analytics group. For the sake of simplicity I have indicated a position that differentiates a speakers' approximate generation within the company hierarchy.

9 The chapter further relies on a number of unpublished internal histories that have circulated informally among employees.

10 A firm that had multiple products and/or regional operations would have had to have purchased more than one independently developed scorecard.

11 Robert Oliver, now an emeritus professor at Berkeley's Department of Industrial Engineering and Operation's Research (IEOR), was a long time friend and confidant of Bill Fair's. The 'Oliver Connection' provided the company with many lifetime employees who would mature to become the company executive in the 1990s.

12 Analysts went through a series of steps to segment variables into 'fine classes', but since these were often much too numerous to be useful, they then regrouped them into the 'coarse classes' that would constitute the options to appear on the scorecard. This kind of classification work and its political consequences (see also the footnote below on segmentation) has been extensively discussed in the science and technology literature, most notably by Geof Bowker and Leigh Star (2000).

13 Sales figures for a custom application scorecard renamed ACCRUE90, in 1990, were $44,000 for the first scorecard with a diminishing scale for each subsequent scorecard. The flat price in 1976 is reported to have been a $32,000 (Former vice-president, Personal communication).

14 Segmentation, a process of breaking data down into sub-populations that are scored on separate cards, is an important part of score system design. In this case the scorecards are not independent, unlike scorecards for different credit products, where an individual might be scored on each and every one depending on whether they are purchasing say, a home loan or an auto loan. In segmentation multiple cards are part of a single model that divides a single population into major sections. Each individual is only eligible to be scored on one of the scorecards, depending on their place in the model.

15 The Credit Bureau is now Equifax, Chilton was bought by TRW, Pinger was bought by Equifax and TRW was renamed Experian. There are other major data gathering operations in business that compile consumer credit histories and provide other marketing services (such as preparing direct solicitation mailing lists), but by strict definition a bureau sells actual credit histories and is subject to the Fair Credit Reporting Act (FCRA) 15 U.S.C § 1581 et seq.

16 'Viewpoints' was a company news letter for clients started by Mary Pellegrino in 1976. It continues to be published by the company (since renamed ViewPoints), but is now solely a vehicle for marketing rather than an informational and community building tool.

17 The first system was installed was for First National Bank of Kansas using Pinger bureau data. As an informal written internal Fair, Isaac history records, 'The success of this project can best be evidenced in the fact that First National Bank of Kansas City went from the third largest bankcard company in Kansas City to the first with just two promotional campaigns' (Internal history).

18 It is important to note that while all scores derived from Fair, Isaac models might be casually referred to as 'FICO scores', only some of these are considered equivalents in practice. For instance, the distinction between each of the industry specific scores and the basic risk score is maintained in the eyes of users, who recognize that the risks constituted by each type of score are used for different purposes. The public has only been exposed to the basic generic bureau score for the prediction of default.

19 At the end of 2006, the bureaus themselves came out with their own joint venture product through a fourth-party company they established to manage the partnership called VantageScore Solutions, LLC. The VantageScoreSM product is built on a scale of 501–990 and is sold separately by all three bureaus, but is calculated from a single shared model developed from pooled data. It is the pressure created by the ascendancy of the FICO® and the pricing pressure it creates that is said to have made this unlikely coalition feasible.

20 The databases have not remained static in response to scoring. The sheer volume of the data has increased as credit use and credit providers have increased, new kinds of data and databases have been generated (ie, transactional data from credit cards), and the contents of the data have been altered in response to uniformity and standardization imposed by data sharing protocols.

References

Black, H. (1961), *Buy Now, Pay Later*. New York: William Morrow and Company.
Bowker, G.C. and S.L. Star. (2000), *Sorting Things Out: Classification and Its Consequences*. Cambridge MA: The MIT Press.
Callon, M. (2002), 'From science as an economic activity to the socioeconomics of scientific research', in P. Mirowski and E.M. Sent (eds), *Science Bought and Sold: Essays on the Economics of Science*. Chicago: University of Chicago Press.
Callon, M. (2007), 'What does it mean to say that economics is performative?', in D. MacKenzie, F. Muniesa and L. Siu (eds), *Do Economists Make Markets? On the Performativity of Economics*. Princeton: Princeton University Press.
Callon, M., C. Méadel, and V. Rabeharisoa (2002), 'The economy of qualities', *Economy and Society*, 31(2):194–217.
Callon, M. and F. Muniesa (2005), 'Economic markets as calculative collective devices', *Organization Studies*, 26(8):1229–1250.
Desrosières, A. (2000), *La politique des grandes nombres*. Paris: La Découverte.
Durand, D. (c1941), *Risk Elements in Consumer Instalment Financing*. New York: National Bureau of Economic Research.
Espeland, W.N. and B.G. Carruthers (1991), 'Accounting for rationality: double-entry bookkeping and the rhetoric of economic rationality', *The American Journal of Sociology*, 97(1):31–69.
Gigerenzer, G., Z. Swijtink, T. Porter, L. Daston, J. Beatty, and L. Krüger (1989), *The Empire of Chance: How Probability Changed Science and Everyday Life*. New York: Cambridge University Press.
Guseva, A. and A. Rona-Tas (2001), 'Uncertainty, risk and trust: Russian and American credit card markets compared', *American Sociological Review*, 66(5):623–646.
Hacking, I. (1975), *The Emergence of Probability*. London: Cambridge University Press.
Hughes, T.P. (1983), *Networks of Power: Electrification in Western Society, 1880–1930*. Baltimore: The Johns Hopkins University Press.
Kohler, R. (1994), *Lord of the Fly: Drosophila Genetics and Experimental Life*. Chicago: University of Chicago Press.
Latour, B. (1987), *Science in Action: How to Follow Scientists and Engineers Through Society*. Cambridge MA: Harvard University Press.
Lawrence, D. and A. Solomon (2002), *Managing a Consumer Lending Business*. Solomon Lawrence Partners.

Levinson, M. (2006), *The Box: How the Shipping Container Made the World Smaller and the World Economy Bigger*. Princeton: Princeton University Press.

Lewis, E. (1992), *An Introduction to Credit Scoring* (2nd edition). San Rafael: Fair, Isaac and Co.

Leyshon, A. and N. Thrift (1999), 'Lists come alive: electronic systems of knowledge and the rise of credit-scoring in retail banking', *Economy and Society*, 28(3):434–466.

Manning, R. (2001), *Credit Card Nation: The Consequences of America's Addiction to Credit*. New York: Basic Books.

Marron, D. (2007), '"Lending by numbers": credit scoring and the constitution of risk within American consumer credit', *Economy and Society*, 36(1):103–133.

Porter, T. (1988), *The Rise of Statistical Thinking: 1820–1900*. Princeton: Princeton University Press.

Sardas, J.-C. (1993), *Dynamiques de l'acteur et de l'organisation: A partir d'une recherche intervention sur la gestion du risque bancaire*, PhD Thesis, Ecole Nationale Supérieure des Mines de Paris.

Thévenot, L. (1984), 'Rules and implements: investment in forms', *Social Science Information* 23(1):1–45.

Notes on contributors

Sandrine Barrey completed in 2004 a PhD in sociology on the commercial work in the mass retail sector at the CERTOP (Université de Toulouse II). This work explored the skills, activities and devices deployed by retailers when they try to connect supply and demand. After a one-year post-doctoral experience at INRA (Institut National de la Recherche Agronomique), she is now an assistant professor at the Université de Toulouse II. Her current interests relate to the processes of commercialization, standardization and products' qualification in the agro-food industry.

Daniel Beunza is assistant professor at Columbia Business School and external faculty member at the Center on Organizational Innovation of Columbia University. His research interests include economic sociology, science and technology studies, and in particular the social studies of finance. His research has appeared in *Industrial and Corporate Change*, *Socio-Economic Review*, as well as in several edited volumes. His article with David Stark, 'Tools of the Trade: the Socio-Technology of Arbitrage in a Wall Street Trading Room' (*Industrial and Corporate Change*, 2004), won the 2005 Outstanding Paper Award of the Communications and Information Technology division of the American Sociological Association.

Koray Caliskan is assistant professor of politics at Boğaziçi University, Istanbul. His doctoral dissertation drew on two years of field work in three cotton growing villages in Egypt and Turkey and four merchant cities: Izmir, Alexandria, Memphis (Tennessee), and New York City. Becoming among the first ethnographies of a contemporary global commodity market, the project passed the doctoral defense at New York University with distinction, and received the best dissertation award in social sciences from the Middle East Studies Association in 2005. Currently, Caliskan is pursuing field work on the ways in which different global markets relate to each other. His latest article 'How does a Neoliberal Market Work? Cotton, Power and Price' appeared in *Toplum ve Bilim*, No 107.

Michel Callon is professor at the Ecole des Mines de Paris, and a researcher at the Centre de Sociologie de l'Innovation. Together with Bruno Latour and John

Law he was one of the early developers of actor-network theory. He works on the anthropology of markets and the study of technical democracy, and is completing research on French patients' organizations with Vololona Rabeharisoa. His recent books include *Le pouvoir des malades* (Presse de l'Ecole des Mines de Paris, 1999, with V. Rabeharisoa) and *Agir dans un monde incertain* (Seuil, 2001, with P. Lascoumes and Y. Barthe). In 2002, the Society for Social Studies of Science awarded him the Bernal Prize.

Franck Cochoy is a professor at the Université de Toulouse II and member of the CERTOP. His work in the sociology of markets focuses on the different mediations that frame the relation between supply and demand, such as packaging, marketing and standardization. He is the author of *Une histoire du marketing* (La Découverte, 1999) and *Une sociologie du packaging ou l'âne de Buridan face au marché* (Presses Universitaires de France, 2002), and the editor of *La captation des publics* (Presses Universitaires du Mirail, 2004).

Raghu Garud is Alvin H. Clemens Professor of Management and Organization and the research director of the Farrell Center for Corporate Innovation and Entrepreneurship, Pennsylvania State University. Raghu Garud's research currently explores the emergence of novelty. Specifically, he is interested in understanding how new ideas emerge, are valued, and become commercialized. He has written extensively on these topics, offering concepts such as path creation, technology entrepreneurship and bricolage as a collective process. Raghu Garud is currently working on narratives as the generative force for the emergence of novelty within a system of meaning that shapes and is shaped by entrepreneurial foresight. His most recent article in *Organization Science* explores how organizations can transform even as they perform. He is a co-editor of a special issue of *Organization Studies* on institutional entrepreneurship. He is currently associate editor of *Management Science* and co-editor of *Organization Studies*.

Claes-Fredrik Helgesson is a research leader at Stockholm Center for Organizational Research (Score) and associate professor at the Stockholm School of Economics. At Score he is involved in developing the research theme of the organising of markets. His own research tends to centre on the intertwining of science, technology and economic organising (including markets). In one project, 'Market and Evidence', he is currently studying the practices of large multi-centre clinical trials and particularly the intertwined epistemic and inter-organisational facets of their coordination. In collaboration with Hans Kjellberg, he is involved in a research project on how marketing theories and tools participate in shaping markets and its actors.

Petter Holm is a professor in fisheries management at the University of Tromsø. His published work on the sociology of science, markets and fisheries include 'The Dynamics of Institutionalization: Transformation Processes in Norwegian Fisheries' (*Administrative Science Quarterly*, 1995), 'Crossing the Border: On the Relationship Between Science and Fishermen's Knowledge in a Resource Management Context' (*MAST*, 2003), 'Creating Alternative Natures: Coastal Cod as Fact and Artefact' (with S. A. Rånes and B. Hersoug in D. Symes ed., *Northern Waters: Management Issues and Practice*, Oxford, Fishing News Books, 1998) and the edited volume *Community, State and Market on the North Atlantic Rim: Challenges to Modernity in the Fisheries* (with R. Apostle, G. Barrett, S. Jentoft, L. Mazany, B. McCay, K. Mikalsen, 1998, Toronto University Press). He is also the author of 'Which Way is Up on Callon?' (in D. MacKenzie, F. Muniesa and L. Siu eds, *Do Economists Make Markets?*, Princeton University Press, 2007).

Hans Kjellberg is associate professor at the Department of Marketing and Strategy at the Stockholm School of Economics. His research focuses on economic organizing from a practical constructivist perspective. Together with C.-F. Helgesson, he is currently studying mundane market practices and how marketing theories and tools participate in shaping markets and its actors. Recent publications include 'Multiple Versions of Markets: Multiplicity and Performativity in Market Practice' (*Industrial Marketing Management*, 2006) and 'On the Nature of Markets and their Practices' (*Marketing Theory*, 2007). Together with Claes-Fredrik Helgesson and Anders Liljenberg he has edited *Den där marknaden* (Studentlitteratur, Lund, 2004), a volume that was awarded Marketing Book-of-the-Year by the national Swedish Marketing Association.

Vincent-Antonin Lépinay is assistant professor at MIT (Program in Science, Technology and Society). He was trained as an economist and an anthropologist at the Ecole Normale Supérieure and at the Centre de Sociologie de l'Innovation (Ecole des Mines de Paris). His doctoral work focused on an ethnographic, multi-sited study of complex financial products. He currently works on banking technologies in the life sciences, with a special emphasis on stem cell banking.

Javier Lezaun received a PhD in Science and Technology Studies from Cornell University with a dissertation on the transatlantic politics of genetically modified organisms. He is currently a visiting assistant professor of law and science at Amherst College (Department of Law, Jurisprudence and Social Thought), and a research associate of the Centre for Analysis of Risk and Regulation, London School of Economics and Political Science. His research focuses on the political sociology of the life sciences and on experimentation in the policy and social sciences. His work has recently appeared in *Social Studies of Science*, *Public Understanding of Science*, *Science and Public Policy*, and the *Journal of European Integration*.

Alexandre Mallard is a sociologist at the social sciences research laboratory at France Telecom R&D. He is the head of a research team involved in the study of professional uses of ICTs (Information and Communication Technologies). He has published on the uses of telephony and the internet in small and medium size firms and on the role of technology in market practices in various contexts. Alexandre Mallard is also an associate member of the Centre de Sociologie de l'Innovation (Ecole des Mines de Paris).

Notes on contributors

Yuval Millo is a lecturer in the Department of Accounting at the London School of Economics and Political Science. Having background in the sociology of science and economic sociology, Yuval Millo applies qualitative approaches combined with social networks analysis in the study of financial risk management and corporate governance. Among his latest publications are 'Negotiating a Market, Performing Theory: The Historical Sociology of a Financial Derivatives Exchange' (*American Journal of Sociology*, 2003, with Donald MacKenzie), 'From Risks to Second-order Dangers in Financial Markets: Unintended Consequences of Risk Management Systems' (*New Political Economy*, 2005, with Boris Holzer), and 'Regulatory Experiments: Genetically Modified Crops and Financial Derivatives on Trial' (*Science and Public Policy*, 2006, with J. Lezaun).

Fabian Muniesa is a researcher at the Centre de Sociologie de l'Innovation, within the Ecole des Mines de Paris. His work primarily aims at analysing the role of technical instruments in the shaping of markets and at contributing to an empirical, pragmatist approach to the study of calculation. He is the author of several articles and book chapters on the social studies of finance. His main research topics in this area are trading technologies and the automation of financial markets. He is also the co-editor (with D. MacKenzie and L. Siu) of *Do Economists Make Markets? On the Performativity of Economics* (Princeton University Press, 2007). His current research interests include economic experiments, public management and the sociology of architecture.

Kåre Nolde Nielsen is currently finalizing his doctoral work at the Institute for Social Science and Marketing at the Norwegian College of Fisheries Science in Tromsø, Norway. He holds a master degree in international fisheries management and a bachelor's degree in biology. His doctoral research project, which can be located academically within STS (Science and Technology Studies), is a study of the boundary formations and boundary transgressions concerning science and politics within the development of modern fisheries management systems.

Martha Poon is completing doctoral work in science studies and economic sociology at the Department of Sociology in UCSD (University of California, San Diego). Her research traces the history of commercial credit scoring technology in the USA (1950s-present), and the effects of statistical risk management tools in transforming consumer credit into a product-centered industry with links to high finance. Through a Bourse Chateaubriand Fellowship, she has recently been a visiting student at the Centre de Sociologie de l'Innovation, Ecole des Mines de Paris.

Alex Preda is reader in sociology at the University of Edinburgh. He is the author of *AIDS, Rhetoric, and Medical Knowledge* (Cambridge University Press, 2005) and the co-editor of *The Sociology of Financial Markets* (Oxford University Press, 2005, with K. Knorr Cetina), among others. His current research concerns non-professional traders in electronic financial markets.

Ebba Sjögren is a researcher at Stockholm Centre for Organizational Research (Score) and the Department of Management and Organization at the Stockholm School of Economics. Her recently completed dissertation concerns the decision-making practices of a Swedish governmental authority (The Pharmaceutical Benefits Board) tasked with deciding which pharmaceuticals' usage should be subsidized by the state. In this study, one theoretical interest was to understand how this authority seeks to ascribe pharmaceuticals attributes of, among other things, cost-effectiveness by coordinating multiple versions of pharmaceuticals originating from diverse practices such a clinical studies, medical practice and health economic calculations.

Index

60 millions de consommateurs 152, 157, 161, 166, 167, 170

Abbott, A. 43
Abelson, Abel 22, 27–9
abstraction 4–5
actor-network theory 2–3, 174, 197–8
addition 232, 233
Advisory Committee on Fisheries Management 177, 178
Agar, M. 133
agencement 2–3, 10; economic 3–4
agency: and economic qualification 235–6; networked 212
agricultural products, forward contracts 199, 201, 202
Aldridge, A. 154–5
Amazon.com 14–15, 22; estimates of value 25–6; financial controversy over 24–32
analysts (*see also* financial Chartism) 13–15, 17–18, 40–1; as-critics 13–14, 20–1, 34; as forecasters 15–16, 17–18; as frame-makers 27, 33–4, 35; as imitators 16–17, 18, 19, 24, 52; as information processors 15–16, 18, 19–20, 24, 34, 49–51; and uncertainty 13–14, 18–21, 33–4, 35
Anatomical Therapeutic Chemical Classification System (ATC) 217–18, 222
Arnason, R. 176
Ashmore, M. 235
Ayers, I. 211

Babson, Roger Ward 49–50, 51, 52, 53, 54, 56, 59
Babson Reports 50
Babson Statistical Organization 49, 51
Bachelier, L. 58
banks 267; back and middle offices 267, 272–5; front-back gap 273, 275, 276
Barron's 27
Baudrillard, J. 153
Bayesian models, and economic calculation 19–20, 29
Benner, S. 53–4
Beunza, D. 40
Beverton, R.J.H. 180
bio-medicine, classification of pharmaceuticals within 217–18
Black, J. 211
Blodget, Henry 16, 22, 23, 33; and Barron's 27–9; debate with Cohen 24–7; debate with Suria 23, 29–32
Bloor, M. 142
Bogart, L. 146
Bostock, R. 134–5
Boucicaut, Aristide 93
Bourdieu, P. 153
Bowker, G. 197
Braithwaite, J. 211
brands 98–9
Brenner, L. 18
bucket shops 48, 52, 200
bundling, of goods and services 262–3

calculation 287, 301–2; of value 19–21, 24–32, 33, 41, 229–31
calculative devices 75–7, 85, 87–8

calculative frames 14–15, 26–7, 28, 30, 33, 78–81; frame abandonment 31–2, 35; frame-making 27, 33–4; framing controversies 29–30, 34–5; and mediation of value 22–3, 28, 29, 34–5
calculative space 6, 75–7, 110, 216
calibration 232, 233
Callon, M. 19, 44–5, 87, 109, 155, 197, 198, 301–2
capital guarantee products 9, 261, 268–81
Carrefour 98, 100, 104, 119–20
cash-settlement 200, 208, 209
Casino 104
categorical discount 14, 21
categorization (see also classification) 21, 26, 40
category management 104
Chartism see financial chartism
Chicago Board of Trade 199, 201, 202, 205–6
Chicago Board Options Exchange 206
Chicago Mercantile Exchange 202, 203, 204
Christy, Francis 175–6, 182
classification 160, 215, 236; new categories 14, 21; of pharmaceuticals 8–9, 217–19, 222–3
clinical practice, classification of pharmaceuticals within 218–19, 223, 227
closure mechanisms 17
Coase, R. 85
Cochoy, F. 3
Cohen, Jonathan 24–7
commodities futures markets 199–201; financial products 203–4; regulation of 202–7, 209–10
Commodity Exchange Authority 202
Commodity Futures Trading Commission 203–4, 205, 206, 208
comparative testing 157–67, 168–9
competition, and price formation 229, 230
consumer-citizens 123
consumer credit, scorecards 9–10, 284–5, 289–90, 297–300, 301–2
consumer panels 101, 102

consumer press 152, 154–5; performance tests published in 155–6, 158–9, 164–6; relationship with manufacturers 166–7
consumer tests see performance testing
consumers: engagement with goods 155, 163; information for 153–4, 158, 159; making choices 156, 165–6, 169; and political issues 123–4
contact-men 77, 79–80, 81
correlation products 268–9, 271
cost effectiveness, in health economics 216, 219–20, 235
cost-minimization analysis 219
cotton: market prices 242–4, 245, 251–3, 257; Permanent Working Group 253–6, 257; production costs 255–6; rehearsal price 248–9, 249–50, 252, 256; transaction price 248–51, 256
Cowles, A. 15, 54
credit bureaux: circulation of credit risks 297–300; use of data from 293–7
credit cards, screening for 295
credit scoring 9–10, 285–8; early technology 288–93; use of data from credit bureaux 293–7
currency markets 201–2
customers (see also consumers), capture of 97–8
cycles 53–4

de la Pradelle, M. 125–6
definition 263, 266
Deleuze, G. 2
deliverability of assets 200–1, 208; index-based contracts and 207, 208–10
de-marketization 86
derivation 263, 26
derivative contracts 196, 199, 210, 261; index-based 196–7, 207, 210–11, 212; standardization of 199–200
device 2, 10
distributor brands 98–9
distributor panels 101, 102
Dow, Charles 51, 53
drugs, prescription see pharmaceuticals
Durand, D. 284
Durkheim, E. 61
Duval, M. 125

Index

economic agencies 88–9
economic exchange 67, 73, 87, 109, 244
economic orders 85–6, 87
economic sociology 1, 10, 109
economic theory, fish quotas and 176, 182
economization of health 216–17, 219–31, 236
Elliott, A.B. 50
embeddedness 241
EMEA (European Medicines Agency) 218
Euromarché 100
expert knowledge 41, 43–6, 60–1; adoption of 45; authority of 43–4; discourses of 44; double bind of 46, 47, 57; of financial chartism 42–3, 47–57; New York Stock Exchange and 49–51; production and use of 41, 45–6, 47, 52–3, 55–7, 60–1

Fady, A. 100
Fair, Isaac and Company Inc., credit scoring 285, 288–93, 301; circulation of credit risk 297–300; use of credit bureaux data 293–7
fair trade 123
financial chartism 6, 42, 47, 61; as expert knowledge 42–3, 47–53; invention of tradition 53–5; production and use of 52–3; as theory of market 57–60; users 55–7
financial derivatives (*see also* capital guarantee products; derivative products) 8, 261
fish quotas 174; economists and 175–6, 192; market for 8, 173–4, 177, 183, 185, 188
fisheries 175; Individual Transferable Quotas 175–7, 182–4, 189, 190, 192; Norwegian 175–80, 181–2, 184–92; Virtual Population Analysis 180–1
Fishermen's Association (Norway) 187, 191
focus groups (*see also* opinions) 7, 130, 143–4, 147–8; moderation of 132–5, 140–2, 143, 147; problem of influence 138–43; reflexivity of subjects 136–8; rhetorical persuasion 141; settings for 144; silence in 142; use of one-way mirror 144–7
food retail 66–7; wholesale-retail transactions 67, 68–74, 85
forecasting 15–16, 17–18, 42; early technology 53–4, 55–7; prophesizing the past 58–9, 61
formula products 261, 262, 266, 268, 271
Foucault, M. 142–3
France: price theory 58; Royer Act 97
France-Glaces Findus, merchandising 94–6, 103–4
frozen food market 94–5
futures contracts 199–201; regulation of market 201–7, 211; standardization of 267

gambling, trading commodities as 200, 205, 208, 209
Gann, W. 60
Garfinkel, H. 138
Garud, R. 40
Goebert, B. 142, 146
goods catalogues 73, 77, 80, 88
Grandclément, C. 3
Granovetter, M. 198
Greenbaum, T.L. 134, 139, 145, 149
grid, for display 95
Guattari, F. 2
Guseva, A. 286

Hacking, I. 44
Hakon deal 65, 67, 69, 70, 72, 84; as calculative device 75–7, 85, 87–8; as de-marketization 86; membership rewards 74–7
Hakonbolaget 67, 68–9, 84–9; as purchasing centre 70–4
health economics 216, 231–6; techniques for qualifying treatments 219–21
Hecht, G. 3
hedging products 269–71
Holt, S.J. 180
Hong, H. 17
Hutchins, E. 212

ICA-retailers 84
Iceland, Individual Transferable Quotas 176, 183

Index

imitation, analysts and 16–17, 18, 19, 24, 32, 52
index-based derivatives 196–7, 210–11, 212; delivering assets 207, 208–10
Individual Transferable Quotas (ITQs) 175–6; in fisheries 175–7, 182–4, 192
Individual Vessel Quotas (IVQs) 182, 185–7
information, as a public good 302
information asymmetry, credit scoring and 286
information processing, by analysts 15–16, 18, 19–20, 24, 29, 32, 34, 35, 49–51
Institut Français du Merchandising 100
Institut National de la Consommation) 167
interference 263
International Council for the Exploration of the Seas (ICES) 178
International Federation of Technical Analysts 42
International Monetary Market 202
Internet commerce (*see also* Amazon.com) 24, 31–2
IRI-Secodip 101, 102, 104
isegoria 140, 141
ITQs *see* Individual Transferable Quotas
IVQs *see* Individual Vessel Quotas
Izmir Mercantile Exchange 9; Closing Price Committee 243, 251–3, 257; cotton trading 242–53

Johnson, Philip 208, 209
Joint Norwegian-Russian Fishery Commission 178–9, 190

Karger, T. 134
Kendall, P. 135, 137
Knight, F. 13
Krueger, R.A. 134, 142

Lancaster, K.J. 154, 162
Langer, J. 144, 146
Latour, B. 109
Leigh Star, S. 197
Lenoir, M. 58
Lévi-Strauss, C. 263

Lévy, G. 105
Leyshon, A. 211, 286
LFN (Swedish Pharmaceutical Benefits Board) 216, 221–2, 235; qualification of new drugs 222–32
Lofoten fisheries 178–80, 181–2

MacDonald, J. 133
MacKenzie, D. 3, 44, 267
manufacturers: action at a distance 93, 94–5, 98, 103; merchandising 93–6, 102–5, 106; relationship with consumer press 166–7; relationship with retailers 99, 104–5, 123
Mare Liberum 179
market, theory of 57–60
market boundaries 219, 248, 251, 256, 280; fish quotas 188
market devices 2, 3, 4–10
marketing 86–7, 130
Marron, D. 286
Martin, D. 106
mass distribution 96–7, 100
Masson, J.-E. 100
Matthíasson, T. 176
measurement 9, 26; fish stocks 179–81; of risk 270, 278–9
mediation, coordination through 234
Medical Products Agency (Sweden) 218
Melamed, Leo 202
merchandising 6, 92–3, 105; in France 92–3; manual of 100; manufacturers and 93–6, 102–5, 106; market for 100–3; retailers and 95, 96–100, 102, 105–6
Merton, R.K. 135, 137, 148
Miller, D. 125
Miller, M. 210, 269
Millo, Y. 44, 267
Minsky, M. 212
moderators (of focus groups) 132–5, 147–8; diplomacy of 140–2; disciplining of subjects 136–8; as interviewers 135; and invisible observers 145–7; personality of 135; and quality control 140–2; skills of 134, 140, 141
Mol, A. 232, 235
Moody, John 50, 51

Index

Moody Manual Company 50
Morrison, D.E. 133, 138, 145, 149
Muniesa, F. 198
Myers, G. 138, 142

National Quotation Bureau 50
NEAFC (Northeast Arctic Fisheries Commission) 179
Nelson, S.A. 51, 53
New York Stock Exchange 52; and expert knowledge, 49–51
New Zealand, Individual Transferable Quotas 176, 183
Nielsen company 101, 102, 104
'no name' products 98
normal line 50
normal zone 60
Northeast Arctic Fisheries Commission 179
Norway fisheries 177–80, 181–2, 187, 189; individual quotas 191; Individual Transferable Quotas 176, 183, 184, 189, 192; Individual Vessel Quotas 185–7; Structural Quotas 188, 191, 192

Oliver, Robert 291
'Olympic fishing' 183
opinions, of focus groups 130, 131, 132, 139, 142, 147–8; idiosyncratic 139; non-direction 137–8; problem of influence 139–40
Optifroid 103
over-the-counter markets 267

packaging 120
panel survey institutes 101–3, 104–5, 106
parasitism 9, 261, 262–6, 280–1
Parmentier, Antoine-Augustin 115
parrhesia 140, 142–3
performance: in markets 245–7, 248; in supermarkets 106
performance testing 7, 152–3, 155–6, 168–9; of telecommunications goods and services 157–60, 164–7 (criteria for tests 162–4; selection of goods 160–2)

performativity 33, 44, 61, 176, 193; classification and 215; of expert knowledge 46
Permanent Working Group on Cotton 253–6, 257
pharmaceuticals 8–9; coordination of multiple versions 232–4; cost-effectiveness of 225–7, 229–30, 234; qualification of 216, 217–21 (negotiation of 221–31)
point-of-sale promotions 95
Points de Vente 92, 102, 105
Polanyi, K. 113, 241
Potter, J. 141
Preda, A. 3
prescription 154–6
PreScore 294–5, 296
price data 47–9, 54, 56, 58–9; compilation of 56, 57; interpretation of 56, 57
prices 9, 241; competition and 229, 230; movements of 42, 47, 58–60; of Turkish cotton 242–57
privileging 233
product qualification 155–6, 197–8; financial futures 203–4, 205, 208–10
product safety 162–3
professional associations, technical analysts 42, 43
property rights, fish quotas as 175–6, 185, 189
Puchta, C. 141
purchasing centres (*see also* Hakon deal) 6, 70, 72–3, 96; new agencies within 78–81; regional 96–7

QALY (quality-adjusted life year) 220; to compare drugs 225–7, 235
qualification (*see also* product qualification) 5, 8–9, 216; coordination of multiple versions 232–4; economic 216–17, 235–6; of pharmaceuticals 216, 217–31, 235–6
quantification 285–6, 287
Que choisir 152, 155, 157, 161, 166, 167, 170

Rao, H. 17, 19
regulation, of futures markets 202–7, 210–12
representation 162, 167, 168
retail universes 122
retailers (*see also* food retail): and brand proliferation 99; merchandising 95, 96–100, 102, 105–6; power over manufacturers 99–100; relationship with manufacturers 99, 104–5, 123; relationship with wholesalers 70–7, 85
Richard D. Wyckoff Analytical Staff Inc. 51
risk management, and consumer credit 286–7, 290, 297–300, 301, 302
risk measurement 270, 278–9
Rona-Tas, A. 286
Royer Act (France) 97
Rozwadowski, H.M. 180
Russia, credit cards in 286

sabotage of focus groups 136
Sagoff, M. 149
salesmen 81, 82; in Hakon deal 72–3, 81–2; travelling 66
Savage, L. 19–20
Schaffer, S. 157–8
Scharfstein, D. 16
Schutz, A. 61
securities analysts *see* analysts
Securities and Exchange Commission 202, 203, 204, 205, 206, 208
segmentation 160–1, 293
Selden, George 50–1
self-fulfilling prophecy 46
self-regulation 211
self-service 93, 114–15, 116
Seret, M. 100
Serres, M. 263
Shad, John 208, 209
Shamdasani, P.N. 134
Shapin, S. 157–8
Silver, A. 149
Slater, D. 86
social context, of analysts' interpretation of information 31–2, 35
Spiegel's 285

STAFCO (*Statistiques Françaises de la Consommation*) 101
standardization of price data 47–9
Stein, J. 16
Stewart, D.W. 134
stock ticker 48, 49, 54, 55
Structural Quotas 188, 191, 192
structuralism 263
supermarkets (*see also* merchandising) 97, 111, 115; cycles in 111; interactions with objects 7, 115–17; at night 111, 113, 114; performance management in 106; positioning of products 120; retail universe management 122; signalling in 118–19; supply and demand 113, 114; work of distributors 117–23
suppression, coordination through 234
Suria, Ravi 23, 29–32, 35
survey panels *see* panel survey institutes
Swain, G.E. 50
Sweden: food distribution in late 1940s 66–7; Medical Products Agency 218
Swedish Pharmaceutical Benefits Board (LFN) *see* LFN
Swenson, Hakon 81–2

TAC (Total Allowable Catches) Machine 181, 190–1
technical analysts (*see also* financial chartism) 41, 42; early 49–51
Teiresias 61
telecommunications, performance testing of goods and services 157–67
Test 167
Thrift, N. 211, 286
The Ticker 49, 51
time discontinuity, in supermarkets 113–14
Total Allowable Catches (TAC) 178, 180–1, 183, 190
traceability 124
trading in cotton market 242–51
translation 232–3, 263
trend line 50
Turner, S.P. 43–4

uncertainty 263, 266, 275, 280; for analysts 13–14, 18–21, 33–4

Index

United Nations Convention of the Law of the Sea 178
USA, professional associations of technical analysts 42, 43
usage, as criteria for performance testing 163

value, calculation of 22–3, 28, 29, 34–5, 41
Virtual Population Analysis (VPA) 180–1

Wellhoff, A. 100
Which? 154, 166

White, Harrison 280
wholesalers 66, 67, 68–74, 85
Wilen, J. 176, 192
Wirsäll, Nils-Erik 68–9, 74
'witching hours' 209, 210, 212
Wyckoff, R.D. 49, 50, 51, 52, 53

Zelizer, V. 198, 217
zero-probability events 20
Zola, E. 93
Zuckerman, E. 14, 20–1